HORIZONS WEST

ENTRE

HORIZONS WEST

Directing the Western from John Ford to Clint Eastwood

NEW EDITION

Jim Kitses

 Publishing

In memory of Paddy Whannel

First published in 2004 by the
British Film Institute
21 Stephen Street, London W1T 1LN

The British Film Institute is the UK national agency with
responsibility for encouraging the arts of film and television
and conserving them in the national interest.

Cover image: *The Searchers* (John Ford, 1956), C. V. Whitney Pictures Company
Cover design: Ketchup
Set by Fakenham Photosetting Limited, Fakenham, Norfolk
Printed in the UK by The Cromwell Press, Trowbridge, Wiltshire

British Library Cataloguing-in-Publication Data
A catalogue record for this book is available from the British Library

ISBN 1–84457–050–9 (pbk)
ISBN 1–84457–019–3 (hbk)

Previous page: *My Darling Clementine*: the classical Western *par excellence*

Contents

Acknowledgments

I am grateful to Edward Buscombe, Andrew Lockett, Jonathan Tilston and Rob White for their support on behalf of the British Film Institute during various stages of production. My gratitude as well to Sophia Contento and Tom Foley for their expert technical assistance. The Autry Museum of Western Heritage housed the project briefly, for which I am indebted to Kevin Mulroy, Director of Research. Special thanks to Ed Buscombe for staying the course throughout, and for his valuable advice and helpful comments.

I owe a special debt of gratitude to Alan Lovell for the constancy of his interest, the lucidity of his ideas, and the gift of his good friendship. Gregg Rickman was kind enough to help with stills, and to share his responses to early drafts. I am grateful to Scott Simmon and Noel King for their interest and assistance with the bibliography. Warm thanks to Joseph McBride for his sharing of research and especially scripts of *My Darling Clementine*. Steve Chack of San Francisco's Naked Eye is always generous with his knowledge and materials. Jody Mahoney helped with printing glitches, for which she has my love.

Portions of the analysis of *My Darling Clementine* and of the Peckinpah chapter first appeared in *The Western Reader* (New York: Limelight Editions, 1998), edited by Jim Kitses and Gregg Rickman. Comments are excerpted from essays that appeared in *Sight and Sound* on *The Hi-Lo Country* ('Racing with the Moon', vol. 9 no. 8, August 1999), *All the Pretty Horses* ('Bloodred Horizons', vol. 11 no. 3, March 2001) and *Open Range* ('Forgiven', vol. 14 no. 1, January 2004). My thanks to Mel Zerman and Nick James for permission to reprint.

I am grateful to the Lilly Library, Indiana University, for awarding me the Helm Fellowship in 1998 to support research at its John Ford Archive. Many thanks to my colleagues over the years at San Francisco State University for making its Cinema Department the congenial and productive place that it is. I am also in debt to all my students whose contributions have taught me so much and sustained my work.

Many of this book's ideas first took shape in debates with comrades in the early film education movement that was nurtured by the BFI's Education Department. I am grateful to them all – they are too numerous to detail but know who they are – and trust they understand my dedication in memory of Paddy Whannel is meant to acknowledge a larger debt to that era and to the polemics and pow-wows that we shared.

Finally, I am grateful to my beloved Paula for her invaluable support and understanding, and to Angela, Jesse, Jasmine and Anastasia for helping to make the trail a happy one.

1
Directing the Western: Practice and Theory

The Western is one of America's grandest inventions. Like jazz and baseball, two other unique pastimes, it represents a distillation of quintessential aspects of national character and sensibility, and has entertained millions of audiences with its intense aesthetic and ideological pleasures. Such original cultural forms and institutions testify to the American genius for the popular, expressed in a creative interplay of collective ritual and individual will, convention and invention, team play and stardom. The frontier between the personal and the social is archetypal and trans-cultural: yet is there a more American drama than of the individual performance played out within and against the checks and balances of the communal?

However, for years the freedom provided by generic narrative, the interplay of the familiar and the different, was ill-understood with reference to cinema: Hollywood movies were formulaic, empty, the enemy of art. Moreover, when French, English and American critics challenged this mid-twentieth-century mind-set, although genres achieved a measure of redemption, it was essentially as a side effect of the emergence of the director as film author. Genres provided a canvas for the creativity of the individual auteur, functioning as a pre-condition for authorship. Out of this clash of notions of dream factory versus visionaries, came the impulse to honour the tale as well as the teller that characterises my approach here.

A study of the Western through the lens of its major directors, a study of its major directors within the framework of the genre: such is the dialectical premise that structures this book. John Ford and Anthony Mann, Budd Boetticher and Sam Peckinpah, Sergio Leone and Clint Eastwood: these film-makers can be seen as constituting a great tradition of the Western genre.

In my view this binocular approach, with an eye on both film-maker and form, is called for precisely because directing the Western as a process is hardly the simple one-way-street application of creative authority by the director that the phrase may suggest. All genres are not created equal: undemocratic as that may sound, the Western does occupy a special place within the American cinema. No other popular film form rivals it in the peak achievements and unsurpassed productivity of its artistic tradition. The genre's unique centrality to the nation's history and ideology has provided the fertile ground to inspire, support and shape – in a sense to direct – the careers of some of America's most accomplished film-makers. Yet the cliché of reviewers that the distinguished

Stagecoach: the challenge of America

film 'transcends' its genre provides evidence of a continuing disrespect for popular forms like the Western. In short, my aim herein is not to put forward its practitioners as the magnificent six, the heroic masters who created art out of a lowly popular formula. I come not to bury America's greatest genre – as so many have over its long history – but to praise it as itself a creative force in the system of its authorship, a dynamic partner especially for those who have returned to the form repeatedly to accomplish their most personal work.

Will we see their like again? The Western has proved unbelievably resilient over a history that stretches back to the very dawn of cinema. Over the years the genre has frequently had its enthusiastic if premature gravediggers. In particular, many opined that a funeral was in order towards the end of the last century. From a peak of popular appeal in the 1950s, when Hollywood production of A-Westerns was at an all-time high and series like *Wagon Train* and *Rawhide* dominated American evening television, the genre had begun to decline in the 1970s, and virtually vanished in the next decade.

Once again, however, the Western confounded expectations with another renaissance, high points of which included the production of Kevin Costner's *Dances with Wolves* (1990) and Eastwood's *Unforgiven* (1992). Both of these were not only commercial and critical successes but also achieved Academy Awards, a rarity for the genre. Even more impressive in some ways was the remarkable deployment of the form in two smaller, independent films: Maggie Greenwald's *The Ballad of Little Jo* (1994) and Jim Jarmusch's *Dead Man* (1996). These enterprising, distinguished efforts – the first a

Post-modernising the genre: *Dances with Wolves*

ground-breaking Western directed by a woman, the second a revisionist vision from a film-maker closer to the experimental film than Hollywood – illuminate the greater openness and diversity that obtain in a multicultural, post-modern era.

A marker in the virtual disappearance of the genre was *Star Wars* (1971), one of the most successful films of all time. George Lucas has been explicit in acknowledging that the Western's absence was a prime motivating force in the creation of his series. In his eyes, the decline of the genre had created a lack, especially for the young audience, of one of the Western's traditional forms, the morality tale. The enormous success of his efforts shows how he filled that gap with a vengeance. A generation of moviegoers emerged for whom the characters, narratives and technologies of science fiction are far more familiar than those of the Western, whose own heroes and behaviours appear quaint if not positively alien, as though from a time capsule if not from outer space. Ironically, in some families at least, an alienating divide opened up between parents who had grown up on cowboy fare and the children they dutifully squired to Lucas's success in an altogether different generic landscape.

Yet in trying to come to grips with the apparent vanishing of America's oldest and heretofore most enduring of genres, some critics – perhaps following Lucas's lead – dissolved differences, suggesting that in fact the science fiction movie is indeed the Western in futurist dress. Still others have deciphered the genre beneath the disguise of the road movie: after all, what is the latter about if not the nomadic and the settled, the challenge of the unknown, the quest for America? Frequently heard, such appropriating claims suggest a need to account for a popularity that almost rivals that of the Western of old for these genres by actually perceiving them as Westerns. These arguments depend on the trick of promoting a key component of the genre – its operation as morality play, its journey structure – to the status of a defining feature of the form.

An earlier era took the reverse tack. Anxious to advance a definition of the genre that had meaningful boundaries, critics were troubled when films appeared to stretch the form, denying, for instance, that films with colonial or modern settings could be Westerns. Hewing to the notion of an ideal type naturally led critics to adopt a prescriptive stance. Most famously, the genre's earliest and most distinguished of theorists, André Bazin and Robert Warshow, both lamented the tendency they saw in 1950s films like *Shane* (1953) and *High Noon* (1952) to justify the genre either by bringing to bear content that lay outside traditional themes or an unnecessary aestheticising.[1]

Those who claim that all of Eastwood's films are essentially Westerns suggest just how far the pendulum has now swung in the opposite direction.[2] On the face of it outrageous, such a claim becomes understandable, given – ironically enough – an equally narrow view of the genre as essentially a vehicle for the exploration and validation of masculinity. As the great majority of Eastwood's films work to construct or subvert a superhero male figure, *ipso facto* all of his films are Westerns. What such a formulation ignores is the classic structure of agreement between film and filmgoers, the institutional nature of genre that includes the audience as part of the system of production. In such a system, genre conventions function as a means both of meeting audience expectations and of organising their experience and comprehension of the film. Relevant here is an essay on the 'nouveaux Western' by Chris Holmlund in her *Impossible Bodies: Femininity and Masculinity at the Movies*. Holmlund enterprisingly groups

Posse (1993), *The Quick and the Dead* (1995), *Desperado* (1995), *Last Man Standing* (1996), and *Escape from L.A.* (1996) as examples of a latter-day 'nouveaux Western' form. The case is principally made on the basis of the heroes, all of whom are seen as referencing Eastwood's Man With No Name persona, and the films' concern with machismo.[3]

Reading these post-modern hybrid action films as Westerns can be illuminating. Obviously, *Posse* and *The Quick and the Dead* are in fact revisionist examples of the genre, *Desperado* is a modern Western and the other films reference aspects of both the traditional and revisionist forms. But *pace* John Carpenter, *Escape from L.A.*'s director, who himself muddies the waters by asserting that all of *his* films are 'really Westerns underneath', the questions remain of how the dominant conventions of these various films position the audience and which genre – if any – provides the most relevant context for their reading.[4]

As with many post-modern films, these 'nouveaux Westerns' depend on a sophisticated generic fusion and interplay. Pronouncing a film like *Last Man Standing* a Western is useful precisely because it highlights how a generic subtext – its source in *A Fistful of Dollars* (1964) – informs and extends the film's dominant noir character. This is arguably also a useful polemical strategy, a kind of generic pigeon-holing in reverse (or rather perverse). This tactic is perhaps even more extreme given the futuristic setting of *Escape from L.A.*. The danger, however, is of obscuring that in structure, action and iconography, it is the noir and science fiction elements that provide a set of conventions and references that shape audience understanding of these films.

But given how post-modern genre fusions hold different sets of conventions in tension and play them off against each other, trying to assert definitive identities can be

John Carpenter's *Escape from L.A.*: a Western 'underneath'?

problematic. Genre boundaries have always been unstable; in post-modern times they have become positively porous. At the same time, bringing to bear genre perspectives can certainly help to highlight which traditions are being drawn on, and aspects of the generic mix. Moreover, it does seem useful to make clear distinctions where we can. In the case of *Posse* and *The Quick and the Dead*, the impact of both depends directly on audience awareness of the genre's traditional white male hero, against whom Mario Van Peebles's African-American and Sharon Stone's feminist protagonists are posed. Given its setting and action, it is difficult to see *Desperado* without an awareness of frontier mythologies: it is clearly post-modern, a pastiche Western. In contrast, it is possible for audiences to view *Last Man Standing* and *Escape from L.A.* with minimal awareness of Western referencing, and consequently little sense of that genre as a supervising source of meaning and value.

British theorist Steve Neale has argued that Hollywood cinema has always had hybrid genres.[5] While certainly true, insisting on the point in the context of post-modern examples characterised by pastiche and recycling represents a conservativism that tends to deny the feverishness and pervasiveness of current practice, as well as its often multicultural energies. The Westerns of a new millennium have clearly displayed this treatment. Thus the big-budget *Wild, Wild West* (1999) frenetically married the genre to both comedy and science fiction, and starred African-American movie and rap star Will Smith alongside Kevin Kline as gunfighters. More conventionally perhaps, *Shanghai Noon* (2000) featured Asian mega-star Jackie Chan following the venerable example of earlier Hollywood comics going West – from Buster Keaton and Laurel and Hardy to Bob Hope and Mel Brooks.

The multicultural perspective of these efforts originated in Costner's breakthrough success *Dances with Wolves*. After a dormant period stretching back over much of the previous decade to Michael Cimino's blockbuster failure, *Heaven's Gate* (1980), this epic tale of a cavalryman taking on Indian identity generated the last post-modern cycle of substantial and interesting Westerns. After Costner, a number of the films that followed – *Geronimo: An American Legend* (1993), *Posse, The Ballad of Little Jo, The Quick and the Dead* – reversed the genre's traditional focus on the white male as the embodiment of America's Manifest Destiny.

Balancing and complementing these was a series of films that shared the agenda of re-imagining and/or downsizing the Western hero: *Unforgiven, Wild Bill* (1995), *Tombstone* (1993), *The Last of the Mohicans* (1992), *Wyatt Earp* (1994), *Dead Man*.[6] This critical approach to the Western hero has also been a feature of later efforts, two of which updated the genre to the modern era by setting the action in the aftermath of World War II: *The Hi-Lo Country* (1998) and *All the Pretty Horses* (2000). The nostalgic heroes of these two ambitious films are born too late and yearn self-consciously for a return to cowboying, which they romanticise as the purest way of life. Both commercial failures, these films dramatise the plight of a heroic form trying to find a commercially workable equilibrium in an era of debunking. They also shed light on the challenge contemporary directors can face in working with the form for the first time.

Max Evans's slim little novel was published, curiously enough, in the same year as Peckinpah's breakthrough film of a similar title, *Ride the High Country* (1962). Much enamoured of Evans's portrait of cowpokes resisting the onslaught of a mechanised, corporate takeover of the West, the director struggled unsuccessfully throughout his career to set up the project. In the event, it was British director Stephen Frears who drew the assignment for *The Hi-Lo Country* from producer Martin Scorsese some forty years after the book first appeared, and long after Peckinpah departed the scene. At first glance an eccentric choice, in fact Frears has made a career out of interrogating America's popular genres, most notably in the screwball comedy *Hero* (1992) and the noir *The Grifters* (1990). A post-modern affair, Frears's Western is fused with both film noir and family melodrama, with Patricia Arquette's adulterous Mona causing its modern-day cowboy heroes to fall out. Following Evans's original, Frears constructs *Hi-Lo*'s protagonist as the anachronistic embodiment of the Old West, a throwback reminiscent of John Ford's martyrs, fighting a futile last stand against the corporate agribusiness for which both his young brother and Arquette's husband work. However, the juvenile overtones of the character's name are all too vividly realised in Woody Harrelson's half-cracked Billy Boy, a casting decision and performance that tilt the film away from its tragic potential towards absurdist comedy.

Billy Bob Thornton takes a more reverent approach in his adaptation of *All the Pretty Horses*, Cormac McCarthy's acclaimed neo-Western novel tracing the coming of age of its young Texas cowboys who journey to Mexico after World War II in a doomed attempt to live and work like 'ole time waddies'. As in McCarthy's work generally, the film constructs the US/Mexico border as the classic frontier between the modern world and the Old West, youth and manhood, the civilised and the savage. Authentic life in America is no longer possible: having lost both family and family ranch, a disillusioned John Grady (Matt Damon) heads south of the border with his buddy, Lacey Rawlins (Henry Thomas). Reaching the paradise of Mexico, where they live out their dream breaking mustangs, and where John Grady is drawn into a forbidden affair with the ranch-owner's daughter, Alejandra (Penelope Cruz), the boys lose it all when they are arrested and imprisoned. In a scene that achieves the tragic dimensions of the book, John Grady is reduced to a stark barbarism in a knife-fight in the prison's dining hall, Thornton staging a bloody ritual witnessed by an audience of silent convicts. But in general the film fails to capture the bleak perspective – the death of innocence – hinted at in the ironic naiveté of its title.

Judged by some as the Shakespeare of the West, McCarthy gives creative voice to today's revisionist historical studies wherein the frontier is seen as embodying conquest, savagery and exploitation. A Southerner before he was a Westerner, McCarthy grew up in Tennessee, where his first four books, all classic Southern gothic novels, are set. His Westerns are really Southwesterns, laced with a dark fatalism and grotesque incidents. McCarthy is less about redemption and transcendence, more about failure and survival. Peckinpah, of course, was wont to talk of the mystical communion between the hunter and the deer, and to evoke Robert Ardrey's theories of man's savage nature as a gloss on his ultra-violent movies. With its born-too-late characters and trajectory towards Mexico and the savage, *All the Pretty Horses* would have been red meat for Peckinpah.[7]

Without Frears's transatlantic detachment, would *The Hi-Lo Country*'s wacky white-trash hero have achieved tragic stature? Without Thornton's slavish approach to

McCarthy, would *All the Pretty Horses* have realised the dark potential of its material? Hypothetical speculation aside, perhaps nothing marks the Western's changed situation more vividly than the passing of the old order, the gallant tradition of Western specialists that this study examines. Yet a serious loyalty to the genre in keeping with that tradition appears to survive in at least one transitional figure, Kevin Costner, who flirts with following Eastwood's example as a Western director-star. Earlier a film-maker like Ford, seeking safe ground after too much freedom had resulted in commercial failure, would head for the bread-and-butter Western. Times have changed, but after severe setbacks in the new mythic formats of *Waterworld* (1995) and *The Postman* (1997), Costner has done the same, albeit following an artistic rather than box-office logic. In fact, Costner takes risks with an unfashionable genre, gambling that a post-modern audience can rise to a film that despite its sophistication is unabashedly romantic, and against revisionist norms.

By far the most impressive Western since *Unforgiven*, if only a modest success commercially, *Open Range* (2003) is a staunch neo-classic affair in post-modern dress. Costner raids the Western's history for tried-and-true material, recalling the 'already said' on a Leone-like scale. To establish Robert Duvall's Boss Spearman as the film's icon of mature masculinity, Costner recycles the image from the credits of Anthony Mann's *Man of the West* (1958), a statue-like Duvall, like Gary Cooper before him, sitting astride his horse in a horizon-gazing pose. Other shots echo Ford, framing Boss against the sky: one stunning dawn image outlines his silhouette in gold. Out-Fording Ford (and his *Searchers* [1956]), Costner has a bitter Boss defer to Costner's Charlie for some words at the graveside, refusing to talk to God – 'that Son-of-a-Bitch' – for allowing the murder of a good-hearted cowboy. There is a squirrelly old geezer evocative of Leone, a bit of Hawksian spatial strategy with the heroes invading the jail to wait for corrupt lawmen, a Butch-and-Sundance moment, in which the two sheepishly share their real names – Charles Travis Postlewait and Bluebonnet Spearman – before they face superior numbers, and elegiac Peckinpah grace notes when Costner shifts into slow motion to memorialise his heroes' march into action.

But in many ways, both small and large, *Open Range* is *Unforgiven*'s heir, sharing the same producer, David Valdes, locations in Canada's Alberta as a stand-in for the frontier, and the character construct of the hero as tortured murderer, here embodied in Costner's Charlie Wait. In Western writer Lauren Paine's *The Open Range Men* (Thorndyke, ME: Thorndyke Press, 1990), Charlie is an ordinary range hand who must rise to the occasion of violent combat in the perilous last days of open or 'free grazing'. But in their radical surgery on the original, Costner and writer/executive producer Craig Storper provide a back story or prequel to Eastwood's film, reversing its action, dramatising the conversion of an earlier middle-aged Will Munny type to the settled life that is abandoned in *Unforgiven*. As with the ageing ex-pig-farmer, dark storms and disturbed dreams, the signs of a noir history of gunfighter butchery, haunt Costner's Charlie Wait. But here the guilt-ridden lethal cowboy is redeemed as he steps back from the abyss, twice grudgingly forgoing the *coup de grâce*, the head shot that Eastwood's ghoulish hero uses to execute Gene Hackman's wounded Little Bill.

To trump *Unforgiven*'s dark hero and noir storms, Costner retreats even further back in film history to a great classic, Ford's sun-drenched post-World War II masterpiece,

Open Range: homage to the classical Western

My Darling Clementine (1946). After the parallel opening of cowboys working the range, we are introduced to the family group devastated by the loss of its gentlest soul, with the promised violent response held off until the very end, as the heroes are drawn into the community and feelings blossom when a nurse enters the picture. Reworking its narrative of the civilising effect of Tombstone and Cathy Downs's Clementine on Henry Fonda's Wyatt Earp, *Open Range* echoes the distinction Ford's film makes between justice and revenge insisted on in the final action of the gunfight at the OK Corral. But the borrowings even extend to key details, as in the coda each film offers of the couples bidding farewell on the outskirts of town with a play on names – Clementine and Postlewait – as they part.

It is Eastwood versus Ford, the noir Western versus the transcendent, *Open Range* successfully juggling film noir's bleak determinism and a life-affirming redemption. The legacy of a murderous frontier is vivid in Charlie's struggle to vomit up the undigested violence of his past. But although his damaged hero has to return to violence in classic genre fashion, he is not alone. A virulent anti-populism is always possible in the Western, as we know from the cowardly citizens of *High Noon*, the contempt for amateurs in Hawks and the token commoner assistants who accompany Eastwood's superheroes. While *Open Range* does not preach or 'empower', it does provide pleasure in the crucial support its ordinary citizens give Boss and Charlie in the protracted and bloody final battle.

Costner gives a disciplined performance as a solitary, tortured man tentatively entering the open range of language and feelings as he responds to Annette Bening's gracious and intelligent frontier heroine. Not unlike the legend's diseased Doc Holliday in his efforts to regurgitate the poison of his past, Costner's tired pragmatist has lost faith, the line blurred between justifiable bloodshed and take-no-prisoners slaughter. But in contrast to the genre's countless heroines who beg the hero to avoid violent tests, Bening's lucid Sue can make the distinction, and is consequently instrumental in Charlie's rebirth and their successful union. Costner thus updates and corrects *My Darling Clementine* and Earp's departure from his lady fair that Darryl Zanuck had forced on Ford, a last-minute narrative turn-about that has haunted and divided the film's scholarship. The decorous parting kiss on the cheek that Fonda had bestowed on Clem is replaced here with a full-bodied passionate clinch.

The Western is not the dominant form that it was, but it is America's defining myth and remains a vital tradition available to film-makers despite the facile pronouncements of its 'demise', the habit of reckless journalism and even academic studies (see, for instance, Michael Coyne's *The Crowded Prairie*). Indicative of its reach and achievement, *Open Range* provides a distinguished bookend to both *Unforgiven* and *Clementine*. In doing so, it also suggests a new level of sophistication in the post-modern era, a creative intertextuality that testifies to the continuing relevance and dynamic potential of the genre, be it at the hands of seasoned veterans or of newcomers to the form.

Of course, the Western was never an exclusive club belonging to its more prolific practitioners. The glory that was the Western was constituted precisely in its democratic status as a medium of mass culture, a common language embodied in a stream of products that included the vast repertoire of B-movies that operated far below the selection of A-movies that are our main focus here. Moreover, at the comparatively prestigious level of the Hollywood main feature, for every John Ford or Anthony Mann or Sam Peckinpah, film-makers who repeatedly returned to the Western and produced their most personal work within it, there have been numerous directors who turned to the genre infrequently, as projects occasionally presented themselves, nevertheless eventually delivering an often sizeable body of indispensable films: Howard Hawks and Raoul Walsh, Allan Dwan and William Wellman, Henry Hathaway and Henry King, Fritz Lang and Jacques Tourneur, Sam Fuller and Nicholas Ray, Don Siegel and Robert Aldrich, Arthur Penn and Robert Altman – the list is extensive.

The centrality of the Western myth, its quintessential American character, the appeal and challenge of articulating its codes, characters and settings, its popularity and commercial viability, the outdoor out-West adventure of its productions – these are the factors that made the genre so attractive to both veterans and newcomers. The list is also long of those who visited the genre rarely but nevertheless produced significant outcomes. Take, for example, the extraordinary cases of George Stevens's *Shane* and Fred Zinnemann's *High Noon*, two of the most famous and influential Westerns. Further examples of singular visits to the form that readily come to mind include Otto Preminger's *River of No Return* (1954), the sole sagebrush turn of both its director and its star, Marilyn Monroe; George Cukor's equally distinctive effort with Sophia Loren, *Heller in Pink Tights* (1960); Martin Ritt's *Hud* (1962); and Douglas Sirk's *Taza, Son of Cochise* (1954).

Of course, the sheer extensiveness of the Western offers a wide range of perspectives for study quite apart from a focus on its key directors, an approach that arguably highlights the film-maker over the genre. Yet the case for an intensive study that concentrates on a limited sample supplied by a diverse group of outstanding specialists in the form, each deploying it to different ends, seems self-evident. Moreover, in writing about the genre in these terms, my goal has been precisely to explore the Western's conventions and their usage, and to contest the notion of the unified and transcendent author.

Nonetheless, the six film-makers that make up this study are all veritable icons of the Western. Each of their names invariably brings the genre to mind, and with it a distinctive vision. At the height of the explosion of film theory in the 1970 and 80s, the practice of auteurist and thematic critics of employing terms such as worldview and vision was criticised for ignoring the ideology and industrial conditions that militate against personal expression in the mainstream cinema. Yet in surveying the work of these film-makers, it is difficult to escape the conclusion that each found in the genre a canvas to which they could return time and again, and within which they could create a unique world and, yes, a personal vision.

In my view to suggest such is not to subscribe uncritically to a pure theory of great directors. None of these film-makers stands alone, not even the imperious Ford. Despite the misleading popular notion of auteur cinema as supremely a director's art, the evidence of creative collaborations, of a shared or multiple authorship, of apprenticeships, mentorships and partnerships is everywhere in the American cinema, and in the works studied here. Moreover, as I have argued, the Western can be seen as an active creative agent:

> Rather than an empty vehicle breathed into by the filmmaker, the genre is a vital structure through which flow a myriad of themes and concepts. As such the form can provide filmmakers with a range of possible connections and the space in which to experiment, to shape and define the kind of effects and meanings they are working towards. We must be prepared to entertain the idea that auteurs grow, and that genre can help to crystallize preoccupations and contribute actively to development ... Bazin came to praise both Boetticher and Mann for returning to what he felt to be the essence of the genre in their small revenge movies. But in my view the reverse is true: these two men, together with Sam Peckinpah, can be said to have found *their* essence within the Western.[8]

Taking Ford, Leone and Eastwood also into consideration only strengthens the argument that the genre has a special value for those film-makers who return to the form. Indeed, to erase it from the filmographies of Mann and Boetticher, Peckinpah and Leone would be to drastically downsize their achievement.

From time to time, the claim is made that studies such as my analysis of Anthony Mann do him a disservice in neglecting the early low-budget noir and the later grand epics. Perhaps predictably, such poses often give way to further study by these writers also of the Westerns.[9] In fact, Mann without the Western is unthinkable, a minor figure despite the enterprising small crime movies and the huge imperial productions, a career with a vacuum at its centre. With Boetticher and Leone, the case is even stronger: to remove the Western is to devastate the body of work. In Boetticher's case, we are left with his idiosyncratic bullfighting dramas and the excellent *The Rise and Fall of Legs Diamond* (1960). Although these films stand on their own, they also evidence the richness that is gained through genre and authorial study – which is to say they undeniably grow in stature and interest once seen through the lens of the director's Western cycle. With Leone the case is self-evident: his maiden effort, the peplum *Colossus of Rhodes* (1960), and his broken monument, the gangster epic *Once Upon a Time in America* (1984), are the solitary bookends that would remain minus the five extraordinary Westerns that fall between.

For some critics, Peckinpah is He-Who-Must-Be-Admired – the director as great artist who brought respect to the lowly Western by transcending it in the face of philistine studio interference. This Great Man myth positions Peckinpah ideally as a test case of the genre theory advanced here. Do the director's non-Westerns achieve a commensurate stature and force? Although a Peckinpah film is never entirely without quality and interest, a dispassionate study of his career exposes the extent to which his remarkable Westerns largely make up his distinguished contribution, and of how sorely he missed the conventions and traditions of the genre in his uneven efforts outside it.

With Ford, the grand master of the genre, and Eastwood, its last master, the situation is still more complex. In each case, the body of work is much larger, the film-maker less dependent or contained by the form. Yet in both the special place of the genre as a source of personal meaning is especially strong, overpoweringly so in Ford's magisterial string of post-war Westerns, and undeniable in Eastwood's double duty as Western star and director. For both, the genre made a crucial contribution in shaping the identity and thematic core of their body of work.

This study originated in the 1960s when sustained work on the American cinema was just being launched, and auteur theory was establishing itself as a serious method for understanding Hollywood cinema. Latter-day critics have speculated on why early genre studies focused on the Western. Was there a masculine bias involved? This quarrelsome suggestion rather recalls Pauline Kael's pernicious notion that what lay beneath England's *Movie* magazine analyses of Howard Hawks's work was adolescent passion and

Olive Carey, Vera Miles and John Qualen in *The Searchers*: genre as a semiotic field

fantasies.[10] But there should be no mystery about why the Western demanded attention. By the middle of the 1960s it was obvious to any critic not blinded by notions of popular culture's inferiority that the Western was Hollywood's richest tradition, producing a unique, distinctively American body of work that was the envy of other national cinemas.

However, most critics of the time *were* blinded by the wars that had erupted in the 1950s over high and low culture. Dominant views of the period pitted popular music against classical (teachers asking working-class pupils why they listened to the Beatles instead of Beethoven!), and saw Hollywood movies in monolithic terms as exploitive entertainments, in contrast to the art cinema then emerging of Kurosawa and Bergman, Fellini and Antonioni. Genre – and most prominently the Western – offered a persuasive vehicle for combating dismissals of the popular. Recent accounts of genre theory err in positioning the sort of auteur criticism practised in *Movie* as being the principal inspiring force in the rise of genre studies. In fact, it was the period's prejudicial views of Hollywood that first led scholars and teachers of the period to seize on genre as a valuable tool in the classroom and in critical argument.[11]

THE WILDERNESS	CIVILISATION
The Individual	**The Community**
freedom	restriction
honour	institutions
self-knowledge	illusion
integrity	compromise
self-interest	social responsibility
solipsism	democracy
Nature	**Culture**
purity	corruption
experience	knowledge
empiricism	legalism
pragmatism	idealism
brutalisation	refinement
savagery	humanity
The West	**The East**
America	Europe
the frontier	America
equality	class
agrarianism	industrialism
tradition	change
the past	the future

Nevertheless, it is fair to suggest that in common with Colin McArthur's later study of the gangster film, *Underworld, USA* (London: Thames and Hudson, 1970), *Horizons West* was partly reacting to the challenge posed by auteurism at this embryonic stage of film studies. While usefully offering a systematic approach in a period dominated by an elitist criticism of personal taste, auteurism presented problems. There was no pressure on critics to distinguish the contributions of the author from other mediating factors. Accounts of individual films could make claims for a director's personal creativity rather than explicate the inflecting of pre-existing conventions of genre and narrative structure. Arguing for the Western as a common language within which individual films were framed was thus a strategy that was employed early on to take account of genre as a system of signification, to assert the director as existing within a semiotic field – although such terms and theory were then only just emerging.

Another reason for seizing on the Western was its comparative stability – as opposed to the more amorphous melodrama, film noir and comedy – which was helpful in the defining of codes and conventions. Against this, as numerous theorists have since argued, the Western's sharper boundaries meant that in some ways it was less useful as a prototype of Hollywood's genre system. Indeed, arguments have now been made that genres are differentiated branches of the same narrative system rather than the discrete traditions isolated studies suggest, and that genre may be closer to an industrial process rather than a system of fixed forms.[12]

But even in these early accounts of the Western, the openness of the genre was stressed, that ultimately only a pluralist vision could account for the diversity of forms. In taking an inventory of this diversity, I found it useful to try to define the thematic and ideological structure that so many of the films have in common, and that makes its range of viewpoints possible. The result of that research was a structuralist grid focused around the frontier's dialectical play of forces embodied in the master binary opposition of the wilderness and civilisation.[13]

Although some critics were to suggest that such oppositions were germane to other Hollywood forms as well, if anything the point only underlined the centrality of both the genre and its frontier mythology to the American cinema.[14]

The cornerstone of the Western, this scaffold of meanings grounds the genre in issues of American identity at both individual and national levels. Focused by Henry Nash Smith's seminal study, *Virgin Land*, these oppositions capture the profound ambivalence that dominates America's history and character. Was the West a Garden threatened by a corrupt and emasculating East? Or was it a Desert, a savage land needful of civilising and uplift? Filtered through the classic plots, stereotypes and conflicts of the genre, this dialectical scheme positions the Western hero between the nomadic and the settled, the savage and the cultured, the masculine and feminine. This interplay of ideas accounts for the charged racial and sexual dynamics of the genre, wherein the Indian and the woman can be constructed principally as archetypal agents that define the hero's direction.

This shifting ideological play illuminates the genre's basic function, its enquiry into the roots and circumstances of American character. In his biography of the greatest star of the period, Gary Wills posits that millions of immigrants in mid-century were asking 'What is an American?', and that Hollywood's answer often took the form of

Western star John Wayne, its most popular performer. But, of course, the Western myth also provided, in Richard Slotkin's phrase, 'one of the central tropes of American ideology' with 'westward expansion as a metaphor for America's rapid rise to industrial world power'.[15]

Numerous critics have pointed out that this frontier perspective of ideological oppositions by no means applies universally to the genre, to earlier, pre-classical Westerns, for instance, or more extreme revisionist works. Thus post-modern theorist Jim Collins has suggested the grid may be most applicable to Westerns that draw on its traditional myth. Ironically, the earliest criticisms of this account of the genre faulted it for advancing American history as the bedrock of the Western, its *sine qua non*. It was even pointed out that two of the book's case studies – Mann and Boetticher – largely ignored or de-emphasised historical themes and action, as if this discredited the analysis.[16] In fact, the grid must be seen not as a prescriptive taxonomy but rather an exploration of the frontier mythology that defines the world of the genre. Where does the emblematic nature of the Western's vocabulary, its iconic characters, situations and images, come from if not from America's past? Defining the furniture of the genre is not the same as suggesting how film-makers must arrange it, or what they will choose to stress. Indeed, a basic utility of this frontier taxonomy, even as the genre takes new directions, is that viewing the individual film against its matrix can help to illuminate where it falls in relation to genre traditions. In an era of neo-Westerns and a post-modernising of the genre, bringing such classical parameters to bear can demarcate the fault lines in hybrid works, and help us to understand how the fusion works.

My basic premise is that at its core the Western marries historical and archetypal elements in a fruitful mix that allows different film-makers a wide latitude of creative play. Where Ford and Peckinpah generate an epic historical canvas, Mann, Boetticher and Eastwood explore archetypal and existential aspects of the frontier experience. The inclusion of the Italian Leone highlights how this approach can also be illuminating for those who appropriate the genre to their own mythology, national ethos and authorial system. Leone clearly demystified and dismantled it, but the traditional form also provided him with an education and, ironically, with a stimulus in his subversive project.

The structural analysis of authors has come in for its share of criticism over the years. In the revised edition of his influential *Signs and Meaning in the Cinema*, Peter Wollen addressed the problem of attribution of authorship to a unified originating source by arguing the necessity of distinguishing between the actual director, John Ford, and the structural analysis of themes and stylistic properties, the authorial or author-name 'John Ford' that the critic constructs in reading the films.[17] Underlying the distinction was an awareness of the critique flowing from the theoretical work of Roland Barthes and Michel Foucault suggesting variously that the author is dead, a fiction, a creature of the text rather than a creator of the text. Wollen proposes a halfway point whereby the author is both determining and determined, a creative agent consciously developing themes and formal strategies, and simultaneously an effect or product of pre-existing linguistic forces in and surrounding the text – as in genre and narrative conventions, industrial practices and social contexts.

A structural analysis centred on the formal and internal character of the film within the framework of genre begins to address this issue by exploring the meaning-laden conventions available to the film-maker. Ideally, further attention must also focus on the immediate social and industrial context of the work. In fact, the great bulk of film criticism suffers from a far too general evocation of social contexts. Suggesting, for instance, that the civil rights movement or feminism play into an increasing awareness of minorities in late Ford does not take us very far in our understanding of 'John Ford'. On the other hand, where a specific contextual case has been argued – as in Richard Slotkin's reading of Ford's *Rio Grande* (1950) as a parable concerning American intervention in Korea – the objection has been of a too directly causal relationship.[18]

Yet arguments are made that precisely more studies of such contexts are needed to arrive at a detailed understanding of how Hollywood inflects its system of genres. The implication is that the industry develops cycles of popular film in a continuous process of reading and answering audience needs and trends, and that at any given moment genre has less to do with a prototype, which in any case is the construction of critics, than with market forces. Carried to an extreme, such theory asserts that there are no genres, only genre films, no Western, only westerns.

In this context, a film-maker like Samuel Fuller comes to mind, whose largely uncontested control of his work allowed him the freedom to adapt genres to his idiosyncratic vision. The results – as in his Westerns *I Shot Jesse James* (1949), *Run of the Arrow* (1957) and *Forty Guns* (1957) – were unique, although the adventurous approach may well have contributed to the relative modesty of his success. The point, however, is that invoking a traditional model can focus the nature and extent of difference, and foster appreciation of the work.

Such extreme privileging of difference to the neglect of the cornerstone commonality tends to discredit the experience of genre as a foundation or matrix for populist ritual, the basis of its power and appeal, and to stress the art over the popular. Earlier studies in genre are critiqued for erecting such a model, however provisional and open-ended, against which the individual film could be analysed, a top-down approach. Yet the value of such models as a foundation even for later studies that critique them is undeniable. In any case, given the complete absence of any sustained investigation of genre, addressing issues arising from the form as a whole – as, for instance, Robert Warshow did, invaluably – was obviously a logical place to begin.[19]

Another objection often raised to early genre studies has been their tendency to generalise accounts of the individual genre from a limited sample, too often the same films and authors. Neale has suggested that the practice has 'canonised' particular films and produced a 'distorted picture of Hollywood's practices and Hollywood's output'.[20] Rather than a dispassionate analysis of all the generic products of a particular studio or era, the norm has been the study of films indicative of critical preference and evaluative bias.

Horizons West is guilty of such an approach. Colouring the attempt to be systematic in the analysis is a belief in the value of the poetry and ritual inscribed in the work of the film-makers studied here. I have termed these directors specialists in the Western. In fact, although the Western is the cornerstone for the edifice all of these film-makers erect in their careers, each is very different in their approach, scope and productivity. In some cases – as with Leone and Eastwood – only a handful of Westerns were actually produced.

The same is true for Boetticher if we exclude minor works before the Ranown cycle. Yet other, more prolific film-makers of often more prominent Westerns, such as John Sturges (*Bad Day at Black Rock* [1954], *The Magnificent Seven* [1960]) and Delmar Daves (*Broken Arrow* [1950], *3:10 to Yuma* [1957]) are not included here. Such a decision reflects the belief that not all the work of those directors who favoured the genre is equally distinctive and distinguished. My goal has not been to provide a comprehensive account of the genre's veterans, but to explore how the genre has functioned as a creative canvas for those directors who achieved a body of work at the highest level. In this, it is fair to say that I have wanted to challenge and contextualise auteurism rather than abandon it.

Other frontiers: Mario Van Peebles as Jesse in *Posse*

It is not surprising that authorship was attacked and discredited within the academy just as it became institutionalised as both an industrial marketing strategy and an accepted critical practice. Equally ironic has been the increasing attention given to the Western in contemporary theory even as the genre has largely vanished from the screen. Indeed, the irony becomes particularly marked if one bears in mind the contempt the Western suffered from critics and educators of the time when it was actually at its most productive as a dynamic source of popular works that touched the very pinnacle of cinema's expressive potential.

As new approaches to the Western have been taken in recent years, cultural and formalist studies of the cinema have been thrown on the defensive. Other frontiers – between insiders and outsiders, between white males and Others – have increasingly come into focus. New Western historians have argued for a frontier whose meaning lies less in transcendence than in violence: the bleached skull in the desert has emerged as the apt icon for this bleak vision. With the cumulative impact of identity politics, affirmative action, feminism and queer politics, ideological studies of gender and race have become pervasive within the academy. In the past, university film departments were often approached with requests from other departments to offer a film-related curricular offering. The premise, customary in the academy, was that different departments had the knowledge and expertise appropriate to their province, and therefore were enjoined to safeguard the integrity of the discipline. Such a practice now seems quaint in the face of the current situation, where discipline boundaries have blurred and film offerings emanate from every corner of the academy. A significant force in this development has been the increasing focus in areas such as cultural, women's and ethnic studies on the issues of representation, stereotyping and attitude/value formation.

Such ideological perspectives have even penetrated the traditional bastions of belles-lettres, the humanities and English departments, as is evidenced by book-length studies of the Western that have emerged in recent years. Enterprising scholarly works, such as Jane Tompkins's *West of Everything: The Inner Life of Westerns* and Lee Clark Mitchell's *Westerns: Making the Man in Fiction and Film,* have in common the single-minded reduction of the genre to its discourse on masculinity. Tompkins argues that the Western genre usurped the primacy of Victorian domestic melodrama, replacing a female culture of intimacy with masculine conventions hostile to language. Yet it is revealing that Tompkins completely ignores Ford but for an extended discussion of his treatment of *horses*! As the account of that director included here will demonstrate, the Western in fact subsumed the melodrama as one of its central forms and can be inflected as positioning women at its very centre. Tompkins professes to have an ambivalent love for the Western, but her antipathy is suggested by her slighting dismissal of *My Darling Clementine,* one of the most literate of Westerns, for its portrayal of the travelling player who declaims *Hamlet* as a drunk who welshes on his hotel bill. Moreover, her tactic of employing quotations from Shere Hite's *Women and Love: A Cultural Revolution in Progress* (New York: Knopf, 1987) of women who suffer a lack of communication with their men suggests an ideological agenda. Tompkins puts these forward as evidence that the 'Western's hatred of language ... has codified and sanctioned the way several generations of men have behaved verbally toward women in American society'.[21]

Mitchell usefully brings to bear an analysis of Western literature as a background to his discussion, but he too makes the sweeping suggestion that the genre above all is con-cerned with 'making the man'. For Mitchell, all aspects of the genre – its epic themes of nationhood and identity, its stress on honour and law, its focus on freedom and rebirth, the issues of violence and justice – all are subsidiary to the master theme, the construc-tion of masculinity. Like Tompkins, he is also inclined to relate genre directly to a period's milieu and social concerns. Thus, to contextualise his discussion of the preva-lence of the theme of growing up in 1950s films (which he sees as central to *Shane*, *Hondo* [1953] and *High Noon*), Mitchell invokes Dr Benjamin Spock's *Book of Baby and Child Care* (New York: Duell, Sloan and Pearce, 1946). According to Mitchell, Spock pro-vides ambivalent advice about the issues of freedom and boundaries that families faced in post-war America; the popular success of 1950s Westerns is the result of their own conflicted engagement with the concerns that Spock addressed. As with Tompkins, the stretch of such formulations may be useful if nothing else as a challenge to look differ-ently at the genre.[22]

This focus on the Western from a gendered perspective has been animated in par-ticular by the impact in film analysis of what may succinctly be described as body theory. Thus Linda Williams has employed the lens of 'bodily excess' to focus on similarities in the treatment of women in horror, melodrama and pornography.[23] Both Tompkins and Mitchell fasten on the body as intimately related to landscape in terms of manhood. For Tompkins, landscape replaces the woman whom the Western has 'cast out', and the hero courts, conquers and lies down with the land, embracing it, suggesting his desire 'to become a phallic butte, immovable and sere'.[24]

More conventionally, Mitchell sees landscape as defining the male in terms of heroic attributes and mastery, the body 'at one with the terrain yet able to rise above it'. He notes the frequent scenes of bodily violation in 1960s films as evidence of the failure of the previous decade's commitment to education, and notes the prevalence of 'convales-cence narratives'. Perhaps because they complicate his thesis, Mitchell ignores the fact that some of the most spectacular physical violence suffered by the Western hero actu-ally takes place in Anthony Mann films from the 1950s. However, he does refer to Mann in disputing Neale's argument that the sadistic beatings often suffered by the Mann hero are homoerotic signals of sexual repression that have the effect of punishing the erotic potential of the male body. Mitchell argues that the male is repeatedly presented in the Western as a desirable sexual object, but that the ritualistic battering the hero suffers is 'the masculinising process' that confirms his manhood.[25]

Where these critics agree is in seeing the Western's conventions, in Neale's phrase, as functioning 'precisely to privilege, examine and celebrate the body of the male'. Neale reproduces my structural analysis of frontier oppositions and argues that they articu-late the space between Law and the Other, the natural landscape and the community, with the body of the hero at its centre, the focus in the Western's drama 'as the object par excellence of its spectacle'.[26] As with Mitchell, Neale argues that the body is an eroti-cised figure enacting an Oedipal struggle with the Father that is evident in the homoerotic tensions in the Westerns of Mann, Peckinpah and Hawks. Given the enor-mous diversity within the Western – and the countless films where the male body is hardly central or celebrated – such a blanket generalisation referencing the Western as the supreme spectacle of masculinity seems indefensibly extreme.

Identifying the hero as occupying the centre of a heroic form is unexceptional. Indeed, although he is rarely credited, Robert Warshow was there first: 'Men with guns. Guns as physical objects, and the postures associated with their use, form the visual and emotional center.'[27] This is not, however, the same as saying that masculinity in fact *is* the genre's spectacle, and that the Western exists above all else to celebrate the male body. Indeed, if we allow ourselves to emerge from theoretical argument for a moment, we see a very different picture. Unless we are jaded, we must recognise that first and foremost the Western is historical fable, a saga as well as a drama, and that it provides a fascinating and never-ending series of diverse spectacles and rituals: the pioneer community's odyssey and putting down of roots, its gunfights and poker games, dances and funerals; journeys of stagecoach and rider, cattle and cavalry; the land and its awesome vistas that incorporate the picturesque and the sublime; scenes of galvanising action and adventure, as in the robberies and pursuits, cattle drives and buffalo stampedes, Indian wars and cavalry rescues. In my view, to focus single-mindedly on manhood as the principal content, the heart and soul of the genre, is to impoverish it.

Above all, it is Mann's work – a film-maker whose neurotic hero and tone are hardly typical – that has provided the impetus for this kind of reading. Neale's study is indebted to Paul Willemen's essay, 'Anthony Mann: Looking at the Male'. Hostile to thematic analysis, Willemen posits that Mann's films are essentially formalist spectacles within which the male hero is consistently positioned as a site of visual pleasure, refining Laura Mulvey's seminal study that defined the cinema's apparatus as systematically objectify-

Facing mortality: Joel McCrea and Randolph Scott in *Ride the High Country*

ing the female for the male (audience) as the bearer of the look. Willemen argues that the guilt of a patriarchal genre at such pleasure renders the look of the man anxious, and provokes the violence inflicted on and by the hero, the signs of a repressed and 'fundamentally homosexual voyeurism'.[28]

I will return to Willemen's argument in considering Mann, but I invoke it here to illustrate how psychoanalysis and ideological readings have sought to marginalise traditional approaches. A cultural perspective that provides purchase on the popular cinema as ritual can be rudely dismissed as failing to take account of how genres function as vehicles for or challenges to mainstream ideology. To see genre films as collective cultural communications and forms of myth and poetry is said also to ignore their status as commodity items, the role of the film industry and the complexity of audience formations. But, of course, to neglect formal and aesthetic values can be seen as equally reductive. Indeed, formal analysis is essential to achieve an understanding of how convention and stereotype can be transformed into meaningful rituals. Obviously, both formal and ideological perspectives are necessary, albeit hopefully without doctrinaire application.[29]

Popular cinema is an industrial product driven and marketed in terms of genre and the star system that unquestionably functions in ideological terms. But genres prevail because they create dramatic and archetypal situations peopled by diverse human character types enacted by stars who have achieved the status of legitimate fantasy figures. Ageing and mortality represent perhaps the most profound of life's stages that we all face, one that the Western has often addressed. Examples come readily to mind: John Wayne wiping away a tear as he accepts a gold watch ('Lest we forget') in *She Wore a Yellow Ribbon* (1949); more recently, Clint Eastwood's geezer struggling to mount a horse in *Unforgiven*. Another example appears at the end of Peckinpah's *Ride the High Country*. Randolph Scott has spent the long ride up into the mountains trying to persuade his old sidekick Joel McCrea to abscond with the gold they are transporting. Have they not earned it after many long years of dispatching the bad guys? But McCrea is adamant: 'All I want is to enter my house justified.' Coming across more bad guys at the end bent on the rape and pillage of America's future in the person of the fair Mariette Hartley, the two old men are reunited for one last gunfight.

As they march in the shade of autumnal trees into a hail of bullets, we see in their stalwart demeanour that the quick draw is less important than virtue, maturity, wisdom. Peckinpah, of course, is famous for his obsession with the codes and rites of manhood, and certain of his films can indeed be read in terms of a homoerotic subtext. Nor is it possible here to overlook the importance of the male body, the erect and flinty stature of the heroes as they stride into the final battle. Certainly, the impact of the bullets register – even though Peckinpah was yet to employ their bloody entry of his later films – on the body of McCrea. Bidding farewell to his friend, the old man takes one last look at the mountains and dies.

Such images and denouements lend themselves to ideological and psychoanalytic readings. Laura Mulvey has made an insightful distinction between Western heroes whose Oedipal progress culminates in a settled state and those, as with *The Man Who Shot Liberty Valance*'s (1962) Tom Doniphon, who remain isolated and thus can be seen as embodying a masculine narcissism.[30] Applying this argument to Peckinpah's nostalgic Westerns, Steve Neale has suggested that 'the threat of castration is figured in the wounds and injuries suffered by Joel McCrea'.[31] These readings are relevant for a character as righteous and threatened as McCrea's. Yet they should not obscure the film's philosophical and moral thrust, or how its elegiac tone transcends its masculine conventions to cross over in its appeal. Peckinpah's framing and detailing suggest that above all McCrea marches not toward a final affirmation of masculine ego but to his final judgment, that the male body is less a sexual object than the corporeal vessel for the human spirit, and that what the film celebrates is not a spectacle of masculinity but the challenge we all face to fight the good fight, to rise above our failures and live a life of meaning.

The recasting of the frontier as a border between the powerful and the dispossessed, men and women, whites and peoples of colour has unearthed other meanings for the form. Correcting an ideologically innocent criticism of the past, a strong consensus fuelled by feminism and psychoanalysis now finds the genre guilty of bad faith. From this perspective, the feminine in the genre exists to validate masculinity as the dominant norm. Encounters with the Indian, regardless of whether the latter is seen as savage or noble, ultimately function only to secure white identity.

But the case against the Western does not stop at sexism and racism. The national myth rehearses a foundational violence necessary to the frontier's resolution of problems, a promise of rebirth and redemption through conquest. The result of the frontier myth, historian Richard Slotkin has argued, is a 'gunfighter nation' that has grown by destroying the Other, that demonises adversaries and authorises a regenerative violence. As in the attack on Saddam Hussein's Iraq, the process allows a righteous America to see itself as virtuous even as it initiates an invasive violence.[32]

Such a critical perspective is essential in an era and world where America remains the uncontested superpower. The habit of other nations' leaders to critique American foreign policy as driven by cowboy attitudes testifies to the persistence with which this dominant icon of America colours perceptions and behaviour. Moreover, especially given today's multicultural perspectives, we would be remiss in discussing the Western without recognising its compromised nature, its masculinist fantasy that can marginalise women and describe a Manifest Destiny that authorises the elimination of America's native peoples.

Such ideological readings of the Western, currently predominant, can inevitably be narrow, ignoring other values and appeals. The problem is that ideology and aesthetics are inextricably bound up. Popular culture elevates the spirits of its audiences but also massages them by often reinforcing shallow and damaging images and views. For decades, race and gender were overlooked as critics celebrated film as art and entertainment. The pendulum has swung back with a vengeance: much criticism, scholarship and commentary now speaks with one voice. The danger is the cultivation of a mindset that isolates itself from the cinema audience, where 'the masses' are seen as victims of a culture irredeemably corrupted by its regressive pleasures. The thrust of ideological and psychoanalytic analyses can be to suggest a sick culture, a cinema of symptoms, toxic elements and pathologies.

In such a critical climate, the Western's positivist and progressive associations can be overlooked, its affective power and aesthetic achievement slighted. Yet one reason we go to the movies is because we seek more poetry, joy and transcendence in our lives. As composer Richard Rodgers, source of hundreds of popular songs, shows and movies, once put it: 'People have a need for melody, just as they need food or personal contact.'[33] Taking account of such transactions is in fact essential if we are to understand the power of popular cinema and the influential role it plays in so many different guises in an image-saturated post-modern society. In any case, however circumscribed by its ideological formations, the Western remains a distinguished and productive artistic form, a uniquely American tradition. We would be all the poorer if we were to fail to recognise and respond to its formal richness and humanist function.

Horizons West is informed by and records a changing relationship with the Western that dates back to my earliest memories of the movies. For the son of Greek immigrants growing up during World War II in a small New England factory town, the genre and films like Ford's *My Darling Clementine* were a source of great pleasure and a rich fantasy life. Yet it was in reversing the direction of my ancestors' voyage, in journeying to Europe and England to pursue graduate study in literature, that paradoxically I made my own discovery of America, the cinema and an identity as teacher and scholar. Defending popular culture, Hollywood and the Western in the 1960s was a radical act, a social and political priority; *Horizons West* developed as a critical and educational project within that context.

In expanding the book, I have had a number of goals. Above all, my prime objective was to try to provide a greater accessibility to the genre and films, and to the critical and theoretical issues that they raise. I have always regretted that the limitations of the original project had made a study of Ford impractical. In now including his work, I feel that a large debt born of the benefits of four decades of teaching his films has finally been addressed. Adding Leone and Eastwood also has allowed the study to realise the logic of its potential as a survey of the genre's major practitioners. In picking up the project again, while I have brought recent representational and psychoanalytic perspectives to bear in the new studies, I have not attempted to rewrite earlier chapters. Rather, where needed I have expanded and reconfigured the original analysis to address relevant material in recent critical literature, as with the studies of Mann and Peckinpah.

Needless to say, films do not have fixed meanings, and much depends on the context, ideology and objectives of the viewer. One purpose of these prefatory comments has been to sketch the viewpoint from which I have tried to read the films described in this book. Although seismic changes have occurred in culture and society in the interim, I have still found it necessary to defend the immediate experience of these films from ideological positions that tend to read them too narrowly for social and political import, from an emphasis on wherein they fail rather than succeed. The more things change, the more they remain the same. For me, study of the Western has provided a critical journey of discovery and delight; I hope to communicate something of this to the reader.

Notes

1. Robert Warshow, 'Movie Chronicle: The Westerner', in *The Immediate Experience* (New York: Doubleday, 1962), pp. 96–103; Bazin, André, 'The Evolution of the Western', in Hugh Gray (ed.), *What is Cinema?* (Berkeley: University of California Press, 1971), pp. 140–8.

2. Shari Roberts, 'Western Meets Eastwood', in Steve Cohan and Ina Rae Hark (eds), *The Road Movie Book* (London and New York: Routledge, 1997), pp. 45–57. Roberts argues that after his work with Leone, Eastwood's films 'all fall within or allude to the Western genre'. A film like *Honkytonk Man* is linked to the genre 'partly through the presence of Eastwood himself', and also in its 'Western articulation of the American dream'.

3. Chris Holmlund, *Impossible Bodies: Femininity and Masculinity at the Movies* (London and New York: Routledge, 2002), pp. 53–67.

4. Ibid., p. 63.

5. Steve Neale, *Genre and Hollywood* (London and New York: Routledge, 2000), pp. 249–51.

6. See Jim Kitses, 'Introduction: Postmodernism and the Western', in Jim Kitses and Gregg Rickman (eds), *The Western Reader* (New York: Limelight Editions, 1998), pp. 15–31, for further discussion of this cycle.

7. As in the 'Playboy Interview: Sam Peckinpah', *Playboy* vol. 19 no. 8 (August 1972), pp. 65–74, Peckinpah often referred to ideas from Ardrey's writings such as *The Territorial Imperative* and *African Genesis*. Stephen Prince discusses Ardrey's influence on the director extensively in his *Savage Cinema: Sam Peckinpah and the Rise of Ultraviolent Movies* (Austin: University of Texas Press, 1998), pp. 103–13.

8. Jim Kitses, *Horizons West* (London: Thames and Hudson/BFI, 1969), pp. 26–7. 'The model we must hold before us is of a varied and flexible structure, a thematically fertile and ambiguous world of historical material shot through with archetypal elements which are themselves ever in flux.' 'Authorship and Genre: Notes on the Western' has been reprinted in Jack Nachbar, (ed.), *Focus on the Western* (Englewood Cliffs, NJ: Prentice-Hall, 1974), pp. 64–72; Robert Lyons, (ed.), *My Darling Clementine* (New Brunswick, NJ: Rutgers University Press, 1984); Kitses and Rickman (eds), *The Western Reader*.

9. See, for instance, Paul Willemen, 'Anthony Mann: Looking at the Male', *Framework* nos. 15/16/17 (Summer 1981), also anthologised in Kitses and Rickman (eds), *The Western Reader*, pp. 209–12.

10. Pauline Kael, *I Lost it at the Movies* (Boston: Little, Brown and Company/Bantam, 1969), p. 96.

11. Stuart Hall and Paddy Whannel's *The Popular Arts* (London: Hutchinson, 1964) laid the foundation for much of the earliest cinema studies work in genre as well as other approaches. See, for instance, the dedication as well as pp. 64–5 and 72 in Peter Wollen's *Singin' in the Rain* (London: BFI, 1992), and the acknowledgments in editor E. Ann Kaplan's introduction to her expanded edition of *Women in Film Noir* (London: BFI, 1998, rev. edn), p. 2, along with the Introduction to Kitses and Rickman (eds), *The Western Reader*, pp. 21, 23–4.

12. Neale, *Genre and Hollywood*, pp. 207–20; Rick Altman, *Film/Genre* (London: BFI, 1999), pp. 54–68.

13. The binary grid was developed in reaction to Henry Nash Smith's *Virgin Land: The American West as Symbol and Myth* (Cambridge, MA: Harvard University Press, 1950) and Peter Wollen's chapter on auteur theory in *Signs and Meaning in the Cinema* (London: Secker and Warburg/BFI, 1969).

14. Robert B. Ray, *A Certain Tendency of the Hollywood Cinema 1930–80* (Princeton, NJ: Princeton University Press, 1985), pp. 73–4.

15. Garry Wills, *John Wayne's America: The Politics of Celebrity* (New York: Touchstone/Simon & Schuster, 1997), p. 14; Richard Slotkin, 'Violence', in Edward Buscombe (ed.), *The BFI Guide to the Western* (London: Andre Deutsch/BFI, 1988), p. 233.

16. Jim Collins, *Architectures of Excess: Cultural Life in The Information Age* (New York: Routledge, 1995), pp. 127–31. See also Robin Wood, '*Duel in the Sun*', in Ian Cameron and Douglas Pye (eds), *The Book of Westerns* (New York: Continuum, 1996), pp. 189–95 for discussion of films that elude classification in terms of the frontier. For an early critique, see Edward Buscombe, 'The Idea of Genre in the American Cinema', *Screen* vol. 11 no. 2 (1970), pp. 33–45.

17. Wollen, *Signs and Meaning in the Cinema* (rev. edn., 1972).

18. Richard Slotkin, *Gunfighter Nation: The Myth of the Frontier in Twentieth-Century America* (New York: Atheneum, 1992), pp. 353–65.

19. Warshow, *The Immediate Experience*, pp. 89–106.

20. Neale, *Genre and Hollywood*, p. 52.

21. Jane Tompkins, *West of Everything: The Inner Life of Westerns* (New York: Oxford University Press, 1992), pp. 47–67.

22. Lee Clark Mitchell, *Westerns: Making the Man in Fiction and Film* (Chicago: University of Chicago Press, 1996), pp. 204–6.

23. Linda Williams, 'Film Bodies: Gender, Genre and Excess', *Film Quarterly* vol. 44 no. 4 (Summer 1991), pp. 2–13.

24. Tompkins, *West of Everything*, pp. 80–5.

25. Mitchell, *Westerns*, pp. 175–87.

26. Steve Neale, *Genre* (London: BFI, 1980), pp. 56–62.

27. Warshow, *Immediate Experience*, p. 89.

28. Willemen, 'Anthony Mann,' p. 211; Laura Mulvey, *Visual and Other Pleasures* (Bloomington: Indiana University Press, 1989), pp. 14–26.

29. Ritual is discussed in John G. Cawelti, *The Six-Gun Mystique* (Bowling Green, OH: Bowling Green University Popular Press, 1970), pp. 26–35; Thomas Schatz, *Hollywood Genres: Formulas, Filmmaking, and the Studio System* (New York: Random House, 1981), pp. 29–41; Neale, *Genre and Hollywood*, pp. 207–30; Altman, *Film/Genre*, pp. 21–9.

30. Laura Mulvey, 'Afterthoughts on "Visual Pleasure and Narrative" inspired by King Vidor's *Duel in the Sun* (1946), in Mulvey, *Visual and Other Pleasures*, pp. 29–38.

31. Steve Neale, 'Masculinity as Spectacle: Reflections on Men and Mainstream Cinema', in Steve Cohan and Ina Rae Hark (eds), *Screening the Male: Exploring Masculinities in Hollywood Cinema* (London: Routledge, 1993), pp. 9–20.

32. Richard Slotkin, *Regeneration through Violence: The Mythology of the American Frontier, 1600–1860* (Middletown, CT: Wesleyan University Press, 1973).
33. John Lahr, 'Walking Alone', *The New Yorker* (1 July 2002), p. 82.

2

John Ford: Founding Father

Keeping the peace is no whit less important.

'My name is John Ford. I am a maker of Westerns.' In a highly public, politically charged debate in 1950 in which he spoke against the establishment of a loyalty oath (and hence a blacklist) in the Directors Guild, Ford had stood and thus introduced himself. From *Stagecoach*, his first sound Western in 1939, to his last film, *7 Women* in 1966, John Ford made fourteen Westerns. Was Ford a Western specialist? Certainly, this was true of that particular moment in his career. Ford had been highly active in the genre after World War II, and was then working on the last film of what would come to be called his cavalry trilogy, *Rio Grande*, with the small and highly personal *Wagon Master* (1950) on the horizon. But by delivering the latter two films the director was also manoeuvring to gain support for a long-standing project, the contemporary, Ireland-based comedy, *The Quiet Man*, which he was finally to direct in 1952. Moreover, no one in a Directors Guild audience would have been unaware of the irony of the esteemed director of the prestigious, pre-war Academy Award-winning works, *The Informer* (1935), *The Grapes of Wrath* (1940) and *How Green Was My Valley* (1941), at so introducing himself. Was this false modesty? It was certainly in keeping with the gruff style of the man, and may well have been a tactic aimed at puncturing the pompous Cecil B. DeMille, one of Hollywood's heaviest hitters, who was leading the charge toward a loyalty oath.[1]

Either way, the introduction was reductive. Over his long career stretching from his earliest efforts in the silent era –*Straight Shooting* (1917) is a rare surviving work from that period – Ford directed some 160 films, including two-reelers, shorts and features, of which perhaps a third, approximately fifty-five, were Westerns. Beginning in 1939, we can count fourteen films in the genre plus the Civil War episode of *How the West Was Won* out of a total of thirty-five features, plus numerous shorts, TV programmes and documentaries. Of course, significance is not defined by numerical counts. Nevertheless, the Western's prominence in Ford's filmography points to the genre's place as the cornerstone of his work, although critics of the period did not recognise it as such. Given the condescending attitudes in post-World War II America towards popular culture in general and the Western – the era's most favoured entertainment – in particular, it was inevitable that understanding of Ford's work was poor, his stature contested.

The Man Who Shot Liberty Valance: Vera Miles as Hallie, the waitress who births a nation

Ford's career first peaked in the mid-1930s, some twenty years after he had followed his brother Francis, by then an established director, to Hollywood in search of work. Writing in the then-definitive *The Rise of the American Film*, Lewis Jacobs saw 'a new social viewpoint' in Ford that promised more 'serious artistic efforts' like *The Informer* (1935). But apart from *The Grapes of Wrath*, released a few years later, Ford disappointed. Writing in 1957, nearly two decades after Jacobs, in *The Liveliest Art*, Arthur Knight had faint praise for a 'still active' veteran whose style combined 'the visual continuity of silent editing technique with a perfect instinct for just how much each shot should tell'.[2] But tell of what? Such comments testify to the general unavailability of critical methods in the mainstream American film scholarship of that era. Dominated by personal taste and a sociological bent, most criticism of popular cinema was not open to the proposition that a Hollywood director's work could add up to a totality of theme, vision or personal meaning.

During those lean years, Ford found a champion in England's Lindsay Anderson. Advocating a socially engaged criticism, a discussion of cinema grounded in political issues, Anderson was one of the driving forces behind Free Cinema, the documentary movement committed to recording the strengths and qualities of everyday life in Britain. In Ford, Anderson saw a vision that clearly resonated with this aim, a poetic celebration of common virtues and human feeling:

> To those who accuse *She Wore a Yellow Ribbon* of sentimentality there is no answer, for the distinction between true sympathy and mawkish weakness is one that we have to

Visiting the grave: John Wayne with Joanne Dru in *She Wore a Yellow Ribbon*

make for ourselves. It is rash, though, to avert one's eyes on principle from a scene in which an elderly man sits quietly before his wife's grave and talks to her . . .[3]

Anderson's writings single-handedly kept Ford's critical reputation alive and reversed traditional judgments on his career, rejecting as 'showy' the use in *The Informer* and *The Long Voyage Home* of expressionist techniques 'of heavy-contrast lighting, studied grouping and deliberate non-realism'.[4]

In both France and Britain, adherents of the *politique des auteurs* largely neglected Ford, already prominent for his success as a director of literary adaptations, and focused on Alfred Hitchcock, Howard Hawks and Nicholas Ray as test cases for critical combat. However, in America, Andrew Sarris – always eloquent when it came to Ford – would position him high in his pantheon in his influential application of auteur theory to American film history:

> John Ford is the American cinema's Field Marshal in charge of retreats and last stands. In the work of no other director is the pastness of experience so vivid, and the force of tradition so compelling. No other American director has ranged so far across the landscape of the American past, the worlds of Lincoln, Lee, Twain, O'Neill, the three great wars, the Western and Trans-Atlantic migrations, the horseless Indians of the Mohawk Valley and the Sioux and Comanche cavalries of the West, the Irish and Spanish incursions, and the delicately balanced politics of the polyglot cities and border states.[5]

A key step in the refinement of auteurism followed when British critic Peter Wollen provided a structuralist foundation that treated films as myths embodying repeated motifs with systematic oppositions – antinomies – embedded in the narrative. Advancing the body of his work as a test case, Wollen's argument effectively positioned Ford as a central figure in an evolving critical practice:

> A number of Ford films are built around the theme of the quest for the Promised Land, an American re-enactment of the biblical exodus, the journey through the desert to the land of milk and honey, the new Jerusalem. This theme is built on the combination of two pairs: wilderness versus garden and nomad versus settler; the first pair precedes the second in time. Thus in *Wagon Master*, the settlers cross the desert in search of their future home ... But, during Ford's career the situation of home is reversed in time. In *Cheyenne Autumn* the Indians journey in search of the home they once had in the past.[6]

Now recognised as a giant of the cinema, Ford is America's greatest director. Yet as ideological perspectives have become dominant, Ford, like the Western itself, has been attacked on the grounds of regressive images of gender and race. Such critiques carry weight but can be simplistic. It is regrettable that compared to a parallel figure like Hitchcock, Ford is now hardly prominent in the greater cultural picture. Yet it is foolish to deny the vast influence his work has exerted, its reach, depth and complexity.

By any standard, Ford is an exemplary auteur. As Jean Mitry, one of his earliest critics, pointed out, Ford and his characters repeatedly rise to the occasion of a surrounding threat, the pressure against which they test their mettle.[7] The stagecoach in Indian country, the isolated fort, the mission behind the lines, settlers on the frontier, communities on the cusp of change – these are the raw materials of Ford's subject. As Olive Carey's matriarch in *The Searchers* puts it apropos the new America, 'we just be Texicans . . . way out on a limb'. In American history, Ford gravitated to tests and crises in which he saw a national character being formed, archetypal situations that provided the foundation for a romantic, heroic America.

Fundamental to Ford's depiction of these situations was the belief in the need for strong leaders. Finding and developing John Wayne would be a crucial step for Ford, who would turn to Wayne repeatedly to dramatise the challenge posed by authority, and to give voice to his values and ideology. Yet if Ford's films celebrate strong masculine leadership, it is invariably grounded in the social. One reason Ford found the genre so accommodating was the classic frontier's historical moment, poised between individualism and the community. The freedoms of a new world were tempered by the demands of the old, for law, culture, progress. The typical Ford hero acted not for himself but for larger causes – duty, honour, loyalty.

Above all, there was the family, the ties that bind, the basic unit that sustained the individual and was the foundation of the community. Criticism of Ford has often made the feminist charge that his men are actors in history, autonomous agents of action, while his women occupy traditional roles defined in relation to the male. The classic comparison has been with Hawks, who is preferred for his independent-minded heroines – insolent Lauren Bacall of *The Big Sleep* (1946), *His Girl Friday*'s (1940) fast-talking Rosalind Russell, unsettling Angie Dickinson in *Rio Bravo* – who challenge and threaten the jaundiced Hawks hero. What such a view obscures is that the illusion of autonomy flaunted by Hawks's women is less a sign of maturity than an imitation of the male, the highest form of flattery. Hawks's characters exist in pre-social or tribal situations dominated by the male group. Women are defined in relation to its style and values; in all of Hawks is there a single scene of childbirth?

Of course such scenes are commonplace in Ford, as in both of his films from 1939, *Stagecoach* and *Drums Along the Mohawk*. Men may act in history but it is through women and the family that they are connected to the human chain of life. Ford is clearly interested in the actual lived domestic life of the family. In films both within and outside the genre, from *Drums Along the Mohawk*, *Grapes of Wrath* and *How Green Was My Valley* to *Fort Apache* (1948), *Rio Grande* and *Wings of Eagles* (1956), there is a consistent detailing of the bonds and rituals, the conflicts and defeats, that mark the family at different stages. The ideal of the family in its purest form is that of the O'Rourkes in *Fort Apache*, the union of Ward Bond's clan head and Irene Rich's Mrs O'Rourke, the mother of the fort. As appropriate to a project prophetic of a new nation, however, Ford's work also returns often to the young couple starting out, as in *Drums Along the Mohawk* and the courting couples of the cavalry films, as well as in *My Darling Clementine*'s poetic pairing-off.

Ironically, however, Ford's films also constitute a gallery of men without women, a title handily provided by the director's 1930 drama of men trapped in a submarine. Even these heroes are consistently defined in relation to women, and especially in their absence. A lack of the feminine marks *Fort Apache*'s Colonel Thursday, the rigid martinet who destroys his command. Unfeeling with his daughter, out of step with the extended family of the fort society, the character never refers to his absent wife. In *She*

Wore a Yellow Ribbon, the bond of partnership is idealised as stretching beyond the grave, to which the ageing Brittles, on the verge of retirement, makes daily visits to report to his long-dead wife. Another absent wife and a broken family provide the back story in *Rio Grande*, again accounting for a lonely, damaged hero. A battle-scarred prisoner of the desert, the love of whose life had chosen the wrong man, *The Searchers*' Ethan is raised to tragic proportions, as is Tom Doniphon, who loses Vera Miles's Hallie in *Liberty Valance*. Significantly, in both of these key works the aggressive individualism of its ultra-masculine heroes is seen less as principled strength than as an impoverishing independence.

Asked what had drawn him to *Liberty Valance*, Ford had replied after a pause: 'It was a good story . . . two people . . . simple people in a kitchen.'[8] How interesting that Ford should recall the film in that way. *Liberty Valance* is dominated by its historic struggle of charismatic actors in an epic theatre, but Ford remembers its foot soldiers and groundlings. Doniphon is cut from the same cloth as Earp and Brittles, leaders of authority and guarantors of order, but it is Hallie, the waitress who will become the senator's lady, who is at the film's centre. Behind the epic events and political drama played out in the state assembly are the kitchen and its goings-on that drive those events. The heroic actions of the white male heroes are set off against the daily grind of the meek, as they learn their ABCs and the bill of rights. The frontier school constructed by Ford for Hallie and her classmates is a multicultural mix of reluctant cowboys, proud Swedish immigrants, the eager Mexican-American offspring of Andy Devine's prodigious Link Appleyard, the black Pompey and Hallie herself. Ford celebrates the grassroots pioneers learning to read, the humble immigrants, the ex-slave, the cowboys and dog-faced ex-soldiers.

The end of *The Searchers*: impoverishing independence

Celebrating the formation of a socially regulated community, the films foreground the crucial formative acts of mavericks, underdogs, outsiders – driven heroes. Ironically, Ford's films are sometimes discussed as if they represent a mainstream America, prisoners of a blinkered patriotism and romantic chauvinism. In fact, inspired by his own immigrant roots, Ford's perspective is invariably critical of higher authority and the chain of command. In all the films, heroes typically are at odds with Washington or West Point, the struggle suggesting a perennial disrespect from above for the lower orders or local authorities.[9] Ford had grown up with the sense of cultural dislocation many ethnicities experienced in a new polyglot nation. The Irish were frequently stereotyped as cartoon figures sustained by brawling and alcohol, an image that Ford himself, together with his characters, both variously reinforced and challenged. The Irish, it was said, loved their talk, literature and culture. These had been Ford's salvation growing up in Maine, the first generation American son and thirteenth and last child of an Irish immigrant saloon-keeper, John O'Feeney; the luminous poetry of his films would be the outcome. Reflecting his own upbringing, the cornerstone of the world of the films was their powerful sense of family, the nourishing roots of the clan, the importance of home, the pain of exclusion.

Nothing if not a popular artist, Ford's great success testifies to how well he connected with his audience. During the quarter-century spanned by his Westerns, he produced a body of work that represents one of America's great treasures. Its scars, distortions and omissions, so visible from the perspective of a new millennium's multiculturalism, are, of course, reflective of marks on the face of America itself. Intolerant and racist attitudes in the 1940s and 50s comprised a virtually hegemonic ideology concerning race. The guilt that runs through American history inevitably infects the genre. The facts of history, the dispossession by force of ancestral lands belonging to Native Americans, had been suppressed. Few schoolbooks of the period told of how the massacre by the Powhatan Nation in Jamestown in 1622 had allowed colonists to turn on the Indians who had greeted them and taught them about new crops and methods of agriculture. Forced to watch as their hunting grounds were ruined and ancient way of life destroyed, Powhatan warriors had finally staged an uprising, slaughtering 357 settlers and taking twenty captives. As Edward Waterhouse, secretary of the Virginia Company, wrote of that pivotal moment:

> Our hands which before were tied with gentlenesse and faire usage are now set at liberty by the treacherous violence of the Savages ... So that we, who hitherto have had possession of no more ground than their waste, and our purchase at a valuable consideration to their own contentment gained; may now by right of Warre, and laws of Nations, invade the Country, and destroy them who sought to destroy us ... Now their cleared ground in all their villages (which are situate in the fruitfullest places of the land) shall be inhabited by us, whereas heretofore the grubbing of woods was the greatest labour.[10]

It is understandable that the Western is held so accountable for its racial politics. Displacing the historical events, the genre's narratives are often marked by bad faith and guilty symptoms. Characters of a single dimension – marauders or victims, savage or noble – Native Americans cannot be recognised in the Western. Unable to be seen for

themselves, vanishing into myth, Indians provide encounters with the savage that validate the white world, repeating history by serving to justify the status quo. Ford is no
more exempt from this double bind than anyone. Indeed, Ford was guiltier than most
in lifting the material to epic and heroic levels, an aesthetic that had its problems. Resisting the genre's masculine bias, his innate respect for the feminine had insisted on women
– from Dallas to Hallie – as heroic partners at the drama's centre, their leadership in the
personal sphere underlying and shaping the political. However, the needs of the mythic
aesthetic trapped Ford in an ambiguous vision of the Indian too often as antagonist
located outside and hostile to the emerging nation.

Dispossessed of their identity and land, America's indigenous peoples were doomed
to see the original process re-enacted repeatedly in the movies. But if the genre's depiction of history amounted to a 'racist discourse', it is true that attempts by Ford and others
to come to grips with that racism, however compromised, also contribute to that discourse.[11] Ford's underdog mentality gave him a complex, often sympathetic attitude
towards the Indians' plight. All the films are ultimately seen from the white point of view,
of course, and Ford was nearly seventy when revisionist attitudes towards race began to
become more prevalent in the 1960s. Yet despite being bound by the period's ideology
and conventions, Ford's Indians nevertheless escape a fixed meaning. If in some of the
films – *Stagecoach* and *Drums Along the Mohawk*, *Rio Grande* and *Two Rode Together*
(1961) – the Indian fulfils a mythic function as a savage force, it is also true that in *Fort
Apache*, *Yellow Ribbon* and *The Searchers* the representation was more complex, the point
of view less external. Inevitably, an awareness of the nation's sins sometimes forged more
nuanced deployments of the characters. Ford knew that he had dealt with the Indian
differently in different narrative contexts; he often remarked that he had been on 'both
sides' of the issue. Despite the inviting notion of a great white father insensitive to the
rights of women and racist in his minority representations, Ford was actually closer to
the ideal of a man for all seasons, all types and characters.

A contrarian, Ford has never been an easy read. As countless studies have pointed out,
his work is pervasively marked by paradox and perversity. Wherever one looks – at personality and politics, style and themes, overall career and individual films – a straight
line is never discernible. Indeed, one can argue that the great power of his work stems
directly from his struggle to resolve ultimately irreconcilable conflicts.

His main theme was the birth of America, the establishing of nationhood, the shining City on the Hill; yet he is also the poet of America's decline, the melancholy
chronicler of defeat and loss. Peter Bogdanovich suggested a key motif – 'the glory in
defeat' – that Ford acknowledged fitted his work.[12] He was a liberal conservative, a union
man and populist, but also an enthusiastic militarist – Rear Admiral Ford. The master
of the Western, America's greatest genre, he was honoured for it only late in his career,
and never with an Oscar. The ideals of family and community were overarching preoccupations in his work; yet in many ways he was a loner, and a failure as a family man.[13]
Seen as one who hated actors, he had a cadre of loyal stars, character actors and extras
who awaited his every production.

Temperamentally a professional Irishman, Ford relished contradiction and whimsy.
In the dramatic construction of character, of course, contradiction is a great humanis-

ing force. The secret weapons of screenwriters and directors, contradiction and paradox as aspects of behaviour fascinate us; we see our own weakness, the inability to live logically. *The Searchers'* dark hero, the obsessed Ethan, is the ultimate example of Ford's alienated and self-destructive characters, his black sheep who act to preserve a community they themselves cannot join. Essentially, this is the ultimate plight of the genre's tragic hero as defined by Robert Warshow, the Westerner facing the closing of the frontier whose actions contribute to a social order that will render his special skills anachronistic.[14] Unquestionably, this historical framework is one reason the genre provided Ford with such meaningful material.

The legacy of Ford's Catholicism, a Christian subtext often seems to inform the action, as with the sacrifice and implicit martyrdom of these characters. Of course, many artists have recognised the uplifting dramatic potential of the debased character. The whore with the heart of gold is a tired cliché, but given the requisite conviction and invention can achieve sublime heights. Irene Dunne in John Stahl's *Back Street* (1932) lectures her young neighbour about the foolishness of accepting a married lover, only to visibly melt when the doorbell rings and her own paramour enters. We may also recall Jane Fonda's call girl, quietly humming 'Amazing Grace' in a private moment in Alan Pakula's *Klute* (1971).

Ford's own contribution to this gallery is Claire Trevor's Dallas in *Stagecoach*. The harlot ostracised by frontier society, she is redeemed for her sweet surrogate motherhood, nursing the babe born in – and emblematic of – a new America. Paradoxes abound: Dallas's whore and John Wayne's Ringo, the escaped convict, make up one of Ford's prototype couples, iconic representations of early American nationhood. Yet the film ends with a typically perverse coda, as the true heads of the American family are gleefully allowed to escape to Mexico, where they will be spared civilisation's dubious benefits. Still another spin on the fallen woman type in Ford is Natalie Wood's Debbie in *The Searchers*, the hostage wife of the Comanche Scar who initially refuses rescue – 'these are my people'. A compelling construct, the character so damaged or driven – or so assimilated and loyal – as to embrace their exile has been reworked in a whole generation of major American films such as *Taxi Driver* (1976), *The Deer Hunter* (1978) and *Hard Core* (1979), one measure of *The Searchers'* influence.[15]

The consistency of Ford's vision is remarkable. From *Stagecoach* in 1939, the beginning of Ford's most accomplished work, to *7 Women*, his last film in 1966, the line of descent is direct. A kind of distaff Western, *7 Women* is the story of a group of women missionaries in China holed up in a compound and menaced by Mongol bandits. Paralleling the degraded Dallas, we have Ann Bancroft's atheist doctor who prostitutes herself with a monstrous Mongol chieftain in order to barter the freedom of the mission's members. Here again we have a newborn, emblematic of the continuity of the community that has no place for its saviour.

The embattled community, the need for strong leadership and sacrifice, the promise of new life – these themes echo throughout Ford, but found an especially supportive fit in the conventions of the Western. Their centrality in his work in the genre can be suggested in groupings that abstract some of the relevant elements of the films. Structurally, as this outline makes clear, the films are balanced between journey and community-based narratives, as one might expect of a director so torn between opposing visions. Fundamental in Ford's articulation of the genre was the traditional Western, the historical Western, the redemptive Western, the drama of the community's survival, the rescue of civilisation. Ford's paradigm is the base narrative that enacts a threatened community incapable of eliminating the conflict. A heroic figure will resolve

Films	Setting/Action	Imperilled Community	Sacrifices
Stagecoach (1939)	journey West/ revenge	stagecoach travellers, the baby/new America	Hatfield
Drums along the Mohawk (1939)	War of Independence/birth of union	the couple, family, new nation	General Herkimer, Mrs McKlennan, Joe Boleo, first baby
My Darling Clementine (1946)	civilising of Tombstone/revenge	family, new community	James and Virgil, Doc, Chihuahua
Fort Apache (1948)	Indian wars/cavalry massacre	the family, army	the regiment, Thursday
3 Godfathers (1948)	journey/rescue of new life	the baby	mother, the Kid, Pedro
She Wore a Yellow Ribbon (1949)	Indian wars/peace secured	the military, families, the Comanche	
Wagon Master (1950)	journey West	pioneer community	
Rio Grande (1950)	Indian wars/the family restored	family, children	Corporal Bell's wife
The Searchers (1956)	journey/rescue/ revenge	the captive Debbie, the family	Martha, Aaron, Lucy, Brad, Look, Ethan
Horse Soldiers (1959)	journey/Civil War mission	the Union	Lukey, Colonel Miles, rebel charge
Sergeant Rutledge (1960)	trial and vindication	cavalry, its black soldiers	Moffat
Two Rode Together (1961)	journey/rescue of captives	the family	Mrs McCandless, Running Wolf
The Man Who Shot Liberty Valance (1962)	coming of law and statehood	the nation	Tom Doniphon, Liberty Valance
How the West Was Won (1962)	Civil War/coming of age/Grant's rescue	the nation	rebel deserter
Cheyenne Autumn (1964)	journey/vindication	the Cheyenne nation	Red Shirt, Dull Knife

the issue typically through violence, perhaps beyond the law. A woman may unite
romantically with the hero, or possibly another character; others will die. The action is
twofold: disposing of the threat to the social system and ensuring its continuity in perpetuating the family.

Certain patterns can be teased out. The earlier films benefit from simplicity of structure, as in the journey films – *Stagecoach*, *3 Godfathers* and *Wagon Master*. The films
based in the community – *Drums Along the Mohawk*, *Clementine* and the cavalry trilogy – all reflect Ford's passion to document life on the frontier and to celebrate the birth
of a nation. The personal drive and affirmative energies of this period can be seen to
culminate in a second unofficial trilogy enfolded within the cavalry films, a quasi-Cal-
vary trilogy made up of *The Fugitive* (1947), which incorporates elements of Western
narrative and iconography, plus *3 Godfathers* and *Wagon Master*. Here Ford explicitly
married the frontier and Christian myth, his characters pilgrims suffering tests in a biblical wilderness: Fonda's incarnation of Graham Greene's fugitive priest; the godfathers
– surrogate parents to a baby Jesus; the holy train of Mormon immigrants. In all of the
earlier films, barring the darkly stained *Fort Apache*, community ideals trump individual and masculine values; revenge is a footnote to the social.

The Searchers is clearly the turning point, a bridging work whose power arises precisely from its pitched battle between the values of the wilderness and the community,
between Ethan's savagery and the demands of family and law. Of the films that remain,
Liberty Valance alone matches the extraordinary force of the *Searchers*, another titanic
conflict played out between a charismatic leader and the social. In these two outstand-

The Fugitive (above) and *3 Godfathers* (opposite): Argosy Productions, personal projects,
Calvary films

ing works, it is now the individual who is embattled, Ford insisting that the bedrock American values of independence and self-reliance as embodied in the Wayne heroes can become isolating, self-destructive and inhumane. In late Ford it is the protagonist rather than supporting figures such as Hatfield, Doc Holliday or the Abilene Kid who must be sacrificed for the survival of the community. Ford's last film, *7 Women*, confirms the pattern, Anne Bancroft's doctor a final martyr.

Given his advancing age and an America increasingly divided, it is inevitable that Ford's work changed and darkened. As Robin Wood has argued, it is difficult not to correlate a lesser achievement in much of late Ford with a decline in the films' values and conviction.[16] As in the cases of *The Searchers'* Marty and *Liberty Valance's* Ranse, voices that speak for the community are increasingly on the defensive and often shrill. Paralleling the loss of authority in Ford's feminised males, women characters are also a less dynamic presence, a decline especially discernible in *The Horse Soldiers*, *Sergeant Rutledge*, *Two Rode Together* and *Cheyenne Autumn*. The settled world becomes an increasingly ambivalent factor, divided in *The Horse Soldiers*, indicted in *Sergeant Rutledge*, corrupted in *Two Rode Together* and *Cheyenne Autumn*. Ford's touch in dealing with the increasingly central racial issue in these later, lesser films, betrays uncertainty. *The Horse Soldiers* explores and yet avoids the Civil War; as if in compensation, the narratives of *Sergeant Rutledge* and *Cheyenne Autumn* both confront race directly, but in a schizoid style of melodramatic pitch and hysterical comedy. In all of these films, the protagonists are in conflict with their communities, most sharply in *Two Rode Together*. A vivid indicator of Ford's attempts to stay abreast of a changing society, James Stewart's hero begins by cynically exploiting families trying to reunite with their captive children, and ends by going off with a survivor despised for her marriage to an Indian.

No American film-maker has approached Ford's function and achievement as a filmic historian. His nationalist narratives are works of the historical imagination, evidencing a constant tension and interplay between the past and present, the present and the future, between reality and memory. Above all, Ford's personal frontier was the blurred boundary between history and myth, narrative and melodrama. With sharp insight, Andrew Sarris once pinned down Ford's visual style as having 'evolved almost miraculously into a double vision of an event in all its immediacy and also in its ultimate memory-image on the horizon of history'.[17]

But double vision in the director encompasses far more than *mise en scène*, extending as it does to the typically ambivalent focus on character, the simultaneous regard for opposing values and the turning back that often comes at the end. For all Ford's Christianity, his household deity was Janus, the two-faced Roman god of gates and doorways who simultaneously looks in opposite directions, inside and out, forward and back, left and right, high and low, to the centre and the margins. If Ford can be critiqued as often having had it both ways, the breadth of his vision nevertheless relates to and illuminates the foundation for his work's conception of character and its dramatic action. It is the absence of perspective, the inability to recognise virtue in others (and the Other) that afflicts so many of his characters, and that is invariably corrected. *Stagecoach*'s Lucy Mallory is an exemplary figure: the myopia of class that diminishes her even as she looks down on others must be unlearned. Original sin in Ford is the readiness of benighted souls to cast the first stone at the saintly, the downtrodden and the pure of heart – however impure in behaviour. It is after all from the ranks of sinners, holy fools and timid souls that Ford recruits so many of the suffering and sacrificial figures so critical to his work's restorative spirit: Dallas and Doc Boone, Chihuahua and Thorndyke, Debbie and

The Iron Horse: Ford directs a defining moment in America's history

Look, Joe Boleo and Mose Harper, Peacock and Peabody, the godfathers and the top sergeants, not to mention Rutledge's black troopers and the Mormons, or the Comanche and the Cheyenne.

Ford's gaze strives for omniscience, in the roundness, but is fundamentally populist, patriarchal, democratic. Accused with some justification of his own blindness and prejudice, Ford was consistently scathing of prisoners of hypocrisy, intolerance and discrimination. Above all, it was the inability to *see* that the films critiqued, characters who could only look through screens and distortions darkly, unevenly or partially, seeing only the flags, as it were. Although an eye-patched and bespectacled Ford was sensitive enough from early on to optical problems, the key theme of vision and blindness in his work goes far beyond the physical to ethical and ultimately spiritual sight. Whether individual heroes or whole communities, whether tragically as with a Colonel Thursday, or comically as with the population of *Wagon Master*'s frontier, Ford's people suffer from a tunnel vision narrowly focused on their own goals, loyalties and ideologies. Such an insensitivity to others must be healed in a fledgling nation composed of competing interests, ethnicities and races. It is because of the primacy of this issue for Ford that the Civil War is such a key reference in his films, the ultimate signifier of the failure to achieve diversity in the nation's history.

The inevitable conflict between the objective and subjective in any art was immeasurably sharpened in Ford's work, given his historical subjects. Robert Frost talks of the ideal in one of his greatest poems, 'Two Tramps in Mudtime', of vocation and avocation merging 'as my two eyes make one in sight' – a model that bears directly on Ford's attempts to marry history and myth. Ford's attempts often fail, the films struggling to balance the demands of the historical material against his use of it, the story of the past and his story.

Liberty Valance, one of his last Westerns, foregrounded the problem famously. There the myth of the triumph of legal authority over the West's anarchy and violence is both exploded and reaffirmed: 'When the legend becomes fact, print the legend.' Ironically, to point the moral the film does the reverse. What is the moral? Ford suggests that the nobility of America's heritage is specious, that Manifest Destiny involved cold-blooded murder. Violence in Ford is rarely retributive as in Mann and Eastwood, payback for personal injury or social trauma. Ford violence is transformative, ritual enactments of the bloodshed that made the formation of America possible. In *Liberty Valance*, Ford insists that national progress involved not only violence but its suppression as well, mythic fabrications to maintain the community's high traditions and ethical image.

This is a self-conscious Ford, looking deeply at himself as well, providing a second look at the myths he played a key role in constructing. Here again, the richness of Ford is in his ability to see things in the round. Given the film-maker's career and *Liberty Valance*'s place in it, it is an extraordinary turn of mind. But despite this correcting second image, distilling America's murderous past into this single allegorical act obscures as much as it illuminates. In some respects, the film still turns a blind eye, its duality a kind of duplicity, the violence of Doniphon's killing of Valance standing in for much darker stains, the slaughter of the native peoples.

The first of the cavalry trilogy, *Fort Apache* addressed the same dialectic directly with even more problematic results. A Custer story, the film exposes the glory-seeker that official history disguises. Leading the Seventh Cavalry in a suicidal charge, Henry

She Wore a Yellow Ribbon: vision as ethical and spiritual sight

Fonda's Colonel Thursday recklessly destroys the fort's idealised community. Yet shockingly, the film doubles back on itself, ending with its heroic survivors explicitly endorsing the myth of a noble sacrifice – 'No man died more valiantly.' Ford himself sees no contradiction in a false martyr – the system and tradition must be upheld: 'The country needs heroes.'[18]

It is to the director's credit that at a relatively early moment – anticipating the pro-Indian Westerns of the 1950s – *Fort Apache* depicts Cochise positively, portraying the massacre as forced by Thursday's vainglory. Reinforcing the genre's overall ideological project, however, the film again suppresses the complexity of American history. Custer's objective in going to the Dakotas was to help put down the Indian uprising that had been prompted by an invasion of their reservation after the discovery of gold.[19] What was governmental expansion and imperialist policy is displaced in the film's action onto flawed individuals. It is in large measure the ideological gap created by this distorting allegorical economy that fractures the film's ending.

Fort Apache and *Liberty Valance* are not unique in their about-face resolutions to the action, attempts by Ford to serve two masters, guilty knowledge breaking through if only symptomatically. For all their classical virtues of order and balance, Ford's movies often end surprisingly, sometimes illogically, with a twist or wrinkle or reverse, in an attempt to tweak, resolve or transcend the problems they explore. The three earliest Westerns – *Stagecoach*, *Drums Along the Mohawk* and *Clementine* – all end almost mischievously, inviting a double take. In a darker key, *How Green Was My Valley*, one of Ford's favourites and arguably his most personal film, describes the destruction of community and family, and culminates in the death of its patriarch. But in its closing moment, the film pirouettes to escape the bleakness – 'Men like my father cannot die' – and returns to images of the Welsh mining village's bright past, Ford's triumph of memory. *Grapes of Wrath* describes a similar pattern, the dispossessed Okie family coming apart as it heads West, but ending with Tom Joad's spiritual rebirth and then Ma's speech: 'We keepa' comin' ... we're the people.'

The dualities and doubling back, the double images and duplicities testify to Ford's Homeric struggle both to dramatise the birth of his nation and deliver its vision, to balance the ideal and the real. Inevitably, Ford was an ambivalent dreamer of Frederick Turner's vision of the ideal pioneer community, the bright future of American democracy, equality and justice, forged on the anvil of the frontier. As time went on, as both he and the society aged, losing the early innocence and faith, his historical mirror blurred and darkened. Yet it is reductive to imply a simple process of progressive disillusionment; troubling issues had roiled his work as early as 1948's *Fort Apache*. Moreover, Ford is always binocular, incorporating a double personality and, at times, double-talk too. America may have lacked a truly epic past of honour and glory: here as elsewhere, however, Ford was on both sides of the issue. He tried to serve the needs of the American imagination both in providing a bright romantic vision as well as to debunk it, to intoxicate the audience with dreams of a lost heroic frontier and to sober them with its violence and savagery. Ford's struggle is larger than himself, speaking – as so much in Ford does – of uniquely American challenges and mind-sets. That Ford inevitably fails at times in this balancing act provides a final paradox: the dualities and flaws are intrinsic to his distinguished achievement as the greatest and most American of American film-makers.

Ford is not simply a major author. Like D. W. Griffith, whom he often named as an early influence, Ford helped to shape the language of the cinema. In particular, his distinguished efforts within the Western, from its earliest days through to the form's high point of

The Horse Soldiers: Ford's work helped crystallise the contours of the genre

achievement in mid-century, position him as its principal architect, one whose contribution was crucial in establishing and crystallising genre themes, structures and iconography.

It is in Ford's Westerns that his allegiance to contradictory perspectives and dichotomous realities found their most powerful and creative expression. In the dynamic conventions of the genre, Ford found an ideal framework for inscribing the opposing forces at play in the American experience and psyche. Above all, he was concerned with the formation of America's character and nationhood. Seizing on the narrative structure of the Western, he described and celebrated the journey as the cornerstone of America's origins. The competing images of the garden and wilderness, the settled and nomadic, that Henry Nash Smith first outlined in his seminal *Virgin Land*, dominate the films.[20] Ford's central subject became the experience of being uprooted and of searching for roots, of leaving home and coming home, of exile and return. Ford tapped into deep feelings, foundational in the American identity.

Ford spoke to an America itself in psychic transit, poised on a quest for personal and national meaning. He never dramatised the journey of his parents and their generation, leaving the old country for the new. Elia Kazan, a great admirer of Ford's who had inherited the racial drama, *Pinky* (1949), when Ford had difficulties with the material and fell ill, virtually alone among American directors has attempted the epic of emigration in his *magnum opus, America, America* (1963). But the fact that many of Ford's enactments fell largely within the traditional historical window of the Western, between the end of the Civil War and the closing of the frontier in 1890, in no way obscured their emotional truth resonant of the immigrant experience for the huge audience the Western enjoyed in mid-century America.

Ford's allegiance to the experience of his own family was obviously reflected in the Irish projects and stories and in the recurring characters, notably the top sergeants in the Westerns. But, of course, the scripts might also include a Swede or a Frenchman, a Pole or German or Dutchman. Such minor characters were handy reminders of the European exodus that underlay the films' action, and, indeed, the lives of many in the audience. Moreover, the structure and action of Ford's Westerns that so often focused on alienated characters, on cultural dislocation and the search for roots also spoke eloquently to new Americans. Both explicitly and implicitly, Ford's was an ethnic frontier.

At the core of the films were the structure and motifs of melodrama, the community seen invariably as the endangered family, the action often calling for sacrifice. Jane Tompkins has argued that the Western's sexual politics is of a threatened masculine genre that struggles to cast out everything feminine. In her terms, the Western was a reaction to the feminised American culture of the 19th century, supplanting its Victorian sentimental women's literature and its interior dynamic with violent action, shifting the stress from the domestic and spiritual to the public and physical.[21] Such an argument is patently inapplicable to Ford. Toiling in the early days of the emerging narrative form in the 1910s, the director worked with the plot structures of the time, which reflected a mixed parentage. Redemptive stories of hero and villain, staples of Victorian melodrama, combined with adventure and action motifs associated with the West, drawing on the penny dreadfuls of pulp literature and Wild West shows. *Straight Shooting*, one of the few available Ford silents, shows the pattern, with good-bad hero Harry Carey weeping over the family victimised by his villainous big rancher employers.

With *The Iron Horse* (1924), Ford's first major success, the director escalated the pattern into the epic structure that would recur in much of his work, the family melodrama of the son searching for his father's killer played out against the quest for nationhood. A film of arresting parts rather than an organic whole, a studio film in many ways, *The Iron Horse* is remarkable for its historical panorama. Showing an epic ambition, the film surrounds its core of the heroic saga of the construction of the railroad with sketches of westering pioneers, cattle drives, Indian attacks, land rushes, buffalo hunters and the pony express. Ford appears fascinated with slices of history, both august and humble, as in the tableau of Lincoln's signing of legislation and the cameos of Buffalo Bill and Wild Bill Hickok, balanced with colourful incidents involving the various ethnic groups – Italian, Irish and Chinese – who are building the railroad. Seen as a successor to James Cruz's *The Covered Wagon* (1923), the film is more visibly marked by the influence of Griffith in its spectacular birth-of-a-nation canvas, parallel cutting, crowd movements and Victorian heroines.

Infinitely more successful in orchestrating the domestic and the historical is Ford's earliest triumph, *Pilgrimage* (1933). An affecting maternal melodrama, the film describes a feminine incarnation of the rigid sensibility Ford would explore in *Fort Apache*'s protagonist. Possessively refusing to allow her son to marry the girl he loves, Hannah Jessop (Henrietta Crosman) engineers his draft into the army and World War I, in which he dies. If her redemption (rescuing a youth in Paris in a mirror image of her son's situation) is too pat, it is executed with great brio and feeling. The whole project, and especially the Grand March of the war's Gold Star Mothers before a grateful French officialdom, is vivid evidence of Ford's early commitment to honouring ordinary women for extraordinary, historic sacrifices.

Pilgrimage's Gold Star Mothers: Henrietta Crosman, right, and Lucille Laverne

Within the Western, Ford was able to develop and refine his project of dramatising history at both domestic and national levels. The odd exception, as in *3 Godfathers*, with its Christian saga's primacy, only confirms the general principle whereby the historical rules. The revenge motif was of little interest to Ford. In *Stagecoach*, although it is prominent as a premise, the revenge is enacted in a brief epilogue to the journey. In *My Darling Clementine*, the action awaits official sanction, and is deferred until the end. Although choreographed with enormous creativity, the violent climax is still overshadowed by the church dance and dedication, the film's luminous celebration of community.

'The only thing I ever had was an eye for composition,' Ford once declared.[22] His genius as a film-maker was his unerring instinct for iconic designs and emblematic rituals, the horizon shots and words spoken over a grave that allowed him to humanise history and monumentalise the mundane. The gun and the gunfight were obligatory, part of the genre's furniture, but were by no means the preferred sign and privileged rite.

The most obvious contrast is, of course, with Anthony Mann. His Westerns show an undeniable interest in different moments in the frontier's progress but the primal duty of revenging deep wounds is always the dominant theme. His is archetypal theatre, rather than historical drama. Boetticher's films also provide an illuminating contrast. Completely outside history, his small films enact existential closet dramas. The vanishing frontier, the construct that shaped America's understanding of herself for a century, provided Ford with the setting and heroes for his enormous contribution. Excavating the genre and developing the themes that preoccupied him, Ford was able to express his vision and faith in a clutch of crowning achievements. In the process, Ford, the great populariser, helped to consolidate the main contours of the traditional genre.

The appeal of the Western was obvious for Ford, allowing regular personal re-enactments of the genre's journey that was also one of the reasons for the form's great popularity: the escape into the wilderness away from routine, from wife and family, from studio and Hollywood. In this, as in the manifold contradictions and deep ambivalence that drove and enriched his films, Ford was an eloquent representative of his era, its society and culture. As the post-modern that he himself foreshadowed with his own interrogations has become the dominant cultural milieu, Ford has been marginalised. In an age of irony and revisionism, his films may seem curious to some audiences, museum studies. If so, education is called for, as the director, whose films so often display a strong didactic commitment, would surely agree.

John Ford is the grand patriarch of the classic Hollywood cinema. One of the creators of the Western genre, America's national epic and its richest tradition of popular film, Ford is a monumental figure in the 20th century's art and culture. Undervalued by some in his own era as a calendar artist, his work has been reclaimed over the years, a body of films that set standards of depth, subtlety and substance for the narrative film. Ford's work in the Western will never fade: it resonates with too much meaning for the American character.

Stagecoach (1939)

André Bazin, the great French theorist, had hailed *Stagecoach* as the ultimate classical Western, as symmetrical and balanced as a wheel, each spoke of which satisfies a different dimension – history, society, psychology, iconography.[23] It is an insight that is

A community emerges

difficult to dispute. The genre had been a B-movie form during the 1930s, and Ford had not assayed a Western since 1924's *The Iron Horse* and *3 Bad Men*, two years later. Attacking the genre anew in the sound era, Ford produced a film that crystallised and fixed its language in bold relief: Western archetypes, the epic journey in vast landscape, the chase and final confrontation.

Another measure of the film's equilibrium was its insistence on balancing the individual heroics of John Wayne's Ringo with the trials of the coach's other travellers. This democratic articulation of the characters and their journey defined the genre's role as national epic, and the encounter with the frontier as the process by which the American character is formed. *Stagecoach* is a foundational work in Ford and in the genre. Although it may not match his later films in depth or complexity, the film nevertheless achieves a pure expression of Ford's – and America's – traditional ideology. Suffering their test in the wilderness, most of the characters in their various ways achieve redemption and transformation. The promise of America perennially held out to its immigrants is reaffirmed – rebirth, regeneration, reinvention of the self, new life.

A neat conceit, Bazin's wheel also underlines the centrality of the stagecoach as the film's organising narrative device. *Stagecoach* is arguably American cinema's most functional title. A summary of the film's action structured around the journey comfortably breaks into five separate chapters of approximately equal length:

Prologue: Scouts report to the cavalry: Geronimo and the Apache are on the warpath. In the distance the stage crosses the prairie.

I: The stage arrives in Tonto. The group travelling on to Lordsburg takes shape. Two aristocratic types – Mrs Mallory, a cavalry officer's wife, and Hatfield, a gambler and 'fallen' gentleman – are joined by commoners: a prostitute, Dallas; Doc Boone, a drunk doctor; and Peacock, a liquor salesman. As the stage departs, a late addition is Tonto's banker, Gatewood, a pillar of the society who is robbing his own bank.

II: The journey to Dry Fork. En route, Ringo, an escaped convict, joins the group. At Dry Fork, the passengers discover that no further cavalry escort is available. A vote taken is nearly unanimous for continuing. At lunch, Mrs Mallory and the other upper-class types snub Dallas.

III: Travel to Apache Wells. Avoiding the Apache, the coach takes an icy route through the mountains. At Apache Wells, Mrs Mallory gives birth, attended by Doc Boone and Dallas. Ringo proposes to Dallas.

IV. Travel to Lordsburg. Indians attack the stage. Peacock is wounded and his injuries are worked on by Doc Boone; Hatfield dies as the cavalry arrive.

V. Arrival in Lordsburg. Gatewood is arrested. Dallas reluctantly discloses her past, letting Ringo walk her home to the bordello district. Ringo kills the Plummer boys.

Coda: Curley, the US marshal who has ridden shotgun, and Buck, the coach's driver, free the couple so that they can escape to Mexico.

The construction of Dudley Nichols's screenplay stresses the class differences between the characters from the outset. First introduced – as if by divine right – is Lucy Mallory (Louise Platt), the Southern lady en route to her cavalry officer husband. Her highborn status is immediately visible in her imperious manner with the driver, Buck (Andy Devine). Proceeding along the boardwalk, she is greeted by a cavalry couple, from whom she learns that her husband has been posted to Dry Fork. Turning to enter the hotel, she is given pause by an evidently familiar figure exiting, Hatfield (John Carradine), 'a notorious gambler' who served under Mallory's father in the Confederate Army, and who will offer her his protection. There is a haughty, theatrical air about the character – much like Lucy's – that Ford underlines by framing him in the hotel window, posing with cape and cane, while she and the others discuss him.

One passenger who is not introduced at this point is a nondescript little man (played by Donald Meek, the ultimate example of type casting), whose ironically unsuitable name – Peacock – no one can remember. Also ironic, given his demeanour, is his occupation of 'whiskey drummer', as he is termed by Doc Boone (Thomas Mitchell), the town drunk with whom he will inevitably be joined at the hip. Also referred to but nowhere in sight is the escaped convict, the Ringo Kid, who may be bound to Lordsburg to exact revenge on the Plummer boys. The marshal, Curley (George Bancroft), decides he will ride shotgun.

The scene shifts from the sheriff's office to the bank, where Gatewood (Berton Churchill), a pompous banker with a steely stare, accepts delivery of the payroll brought by the stage and lectures the agents – 'What's good for business is good for the country.' Like both Hatfield and Ringo, Gatewood will be a last-minute addition to the group.

The implied theme of class warfare being planted here now flowers with the introduction of Dallas (Claire Trevor), town whore, who is being run out of Tonto by the Law and Order League, a militant group of hatchet-faced women. As the procession passes, Doc Boone is being evicted by his landlady and joins Dallas, elegantly squiring her down Tonto's main street. Cadging a last drink at the saloon, he gleefully makes the acquaintance of the hapless liquor salesman. Thus the order in which the characters are introduced descends from the aristocratic and privileged – Lucy Mallory, Hatfield and Gatewood – to the disreputable and/or powerless – Dallas, Doc Boone, Peacock and Ringo.

The most famous of all Westerns, *Stagecoach* for most people invariably brings to mind the spectacular prolonged pursuit of the coach across the salt flats by the attacking Apache that culminates in the classic last-minute rescue by the cavalry. Ingeniously, Ford balances the hyperbole of that scene with the economy of his presentation of Ringo's long-awaited gunfight with the Plummer brothers in the film's penultimate scene. Taking the opposite approach from the attack on the coach – where we see every Indian bite the dust – Ford builds suspense as the adversaries advance towards each other, but cuts away as Ringo dives to the ground and gunfire breaks out. This subtler method is equally powerful for some. The hero of Walker Percy's novel, *The Moviegoer*, finds his real life less memorable than various movie scenes: 'What I remember is the time John Wayne killed three men with a carbine as he was falling to the dusty street in *Stagecoach*, and the kitten found Orson Welles in the doorway in *The Third Man*.'[24]

Ford gives the Indian attack and the shoot-out special weight because they punctuate two important narrative strands. The journey through hostile terrain and the menace of Indian attack provide the film's frame, while the vengeance that drives John Wayne's Ringo is a key dramatic component that also affects both Dallas and the marshal. Foregrounded at the very outset of the film and referred to throughout, these themes, together with *Stagecoach*'s rigorous organisation around the journey, suggest a film of a physical nature, dominated by exterior action. Yet the moving stage can also be seen as a theatre stage. The conflict between characters inside the coach, along with the crucial action in the close settings of the way stations, actually gives the film the character of closet drama rather than traditional Western fare. In his account of the film's production history, Edward Buscombe has reported that to avoid the low-class image of the Western, the film in part was marketed as a melodrama with an emphasis on elements that would appeal to a female audience.[25] Given the dramatic contours of the film, such a strategy hardly amounted to false advertising. Absent the two culminating action scenes, and there would be nothing at all in the way of the genre's conventional confrontations or violence.

In some respects, it is Ford's extraordinary skill in evoking the physical challenge of the landscape that compensates. *Stagecoach* was the first film in which Ford employed Monument Valley as a key location. His awed response to it, the extraordinary imagination of his choice of set-ups and the breathtaking images that result bear witness to the mastery of a veteran of the silent era. One sequence in particular stands out. The stage is rolling on after picking up Ringo. As the passengers talk, all manner of divisions begin to surface. Gatewood is impressed that they have taken aboard 'the notorious Ringo Kid', but a boyish Wayne seems discomfited – Ringo is simply a childhood nickname. Moments later, the Civil War erupts: Doc Boone had attended Ringo's brother after being discharged from the Union Army in 'the War of the Rebellion'. Hatfield interrupts – 'You mean the War for the Southern Confederacy, sir.'

The tensions escalate as Hatfield demands that Doc Boone extinguish his cigar, which is making Mrs Mallory feel nauseous. Boone apologises, but Hatfield lectures him on the duties of a gentleman. Boone rebuts him by distinguishing between manners and ethics: a recent patient of his had been shot by a gentleman – 'in the back'. These two little vignettes are separated by a brief but magnificent shot of the stage with its team of six horses labouring up a grade in the foreground, the valley's wide open spaces extending to the horizon beyond, broken only by the three huge buttes that balance the image in its middle ground. After the second exchange, we cut again to the exterior point of view, slowly panning from an extreme high angle as the tiny stage crosses the valley floor far below, dwarfed by the immensity of the terrain and its enormous geological formations. The nuances of this landscape are remarkable: freedom, danger, the eternal, the monumental. The special weight Ford gives these images is suggested by their positioning, as the journey's first leg to Dry Fork is completed.

It could be argued that in juxtaposing the imposing landscape and the discord within the stage, Ford stresses the petty concerns of the travellers. In fact, the magnitude of the environment works to ennoble these pioneers. The expansive scale, overwhelming contours and ageless character of this landscape evoke the awesome challenges and tests of the frontier experience. The action of *Stagecoach* has less to do with attacks or revenge than with the achievement of a community forged in the encounter with a primitive world. In the face of elemental tests, a transcendent America emerges beyond the differences of class, manners, morality, geography and history that bespeaks a common humanity. Ford's vision is democratising and egalitarian, indeed even rabble-rousing – it is the misfits and losers who are the soul of the new nation.

Populist to its core, the film withholds sympathy from Gatewood, the corrupt capitalist, and grudgingly extends it to Mallory, the wilting Southerner for whom childbirth appears an affliction, a weak sister compared to Dallas. On parting in Lordsburg, stretcher-bound, she acknowledges the harlot's helping hand but is unable to bridge the social gulf. There is honour enough for all the others. Testifying to the implicit Christian logic that underlies the action, redemption is the order of the day. Hatfield's nobility, elitist and anachronistic, has nevertheless contributed to the survival of the emerging new community. Doc Boone delivers Mallory's baby – the future – and also repays Peacock for all the booze by attending to his injury. Ever cast as the victim, the latter has the distinction of being wounded in the Indian attack. But he also has asserted himself earlier, authoritatively shushing the others after the baby's birth, and has the grace to ask Dallas to visit if she is ever in Kansas.

The antagonists are only schematically defined. Ford employs the Indian as a mythical narrative element, the challenge of the wilderness, rather than as a developed historical force. At the same time, the film insists on the Apaches' savagery; Hatfield, ever gallant, lays his cloak over a dead woman at the burnt-out ferry station. It is also Hatfield who is about to dispatch Mallory when the battle seems lost, the idea – better dead

'Haven't I any right to live?'

than wed to an Indian – one that will recur with Ford. In keeping with the film's strategy of arresting entrances, the Indians are introduced with a dramatic camera pan up from the stage on the canyon floor to their massed presence on the rim above, another of the film's memorable shots that immediately defines their command over the vast terrain they inhabit.

Such minimal but effective detailing is also afforded to Plummer's character. Like Hatfield, who also draws fateful cards, Plummer is doomed with the dead-man's hand when we meet him. Agitated at the prospect of facing Ringo, he is abusive towards his woman when she tries to stop him. Loyal nevertheless, she drops a rifle down to him from the saloon's balcony at the last minute. Such vivid visual touches sketch a relationship with characteristic economy and add to the film's gallery of diverse alliances and behaviours, ranging from Gatewood's haughty bullying and Hatfield's elegant gallantry to Ringo's instinctive good manners.

Although an ensemble film, a collectivist heroic drama, it is clearly Ringo and Dallas who are at the centre of *Stagecoach*. After a decade of leading roles largely in sixty-minute B-Westerns, Wayne's career was decisively upgraded with the role of Ringo. The film itself seems to mark the significance of Wayne's participation with its famous introduction, the camera dollying in to a close shot of the cowboy, his rifle a-twirl. Wayne's performance, quietly understated, persuades us of the character's innocence, and balances nicely against the histrionics and hyperbole of Gatewood, Hatfield, Doc Boone and Buck. Wayne's huge success in later years inevitably colours the film for viewers, retroactively throwing more focus on his role. But certainly, Trevor was the established star at the time (she received $20,000 to Wayne's $3,700), and enjoyed top billing.[26] Latter-day credits – as in the Simon & Schuster *Classic Film Scripts* series – are more likely to list her below Wayne.

But more than Ringo, it is Dallas who is the heart of *Stagecoach*, occupying a position at the centre of both its emotional life and symbolic reach. In her role as midwife to Mallory, she delivers the baby and shields it during the Indian attack. She holds the miracle of a new America, the promise of the future. A Christian soldier, she repeatedly turns the other cheek, repaying the slights of Mallory's superior WASP behaviour with caring and love. The film seems essentially structured around her Calvary. In contrast to the commanding introduction of Ringo, her own entrance, a forced march down Tonto's main street, is prolonged and humiliating. If alleviated for us somewhat by the humour of Doc Boone's intervention, it is no laughing matter for Dallas, whose poignant question hangs in the air: 'Haven't I any right to live?'

It is certainly Dallas whom the film positions as the crux of its politics. A key scene in terms of the egalitarian logic of the film's action is the vote by the passengers as to whether the stage should continue. Completely downtrodden, Dallas's instinct is to locate protectively on the edges of the group, eyes downcast. There is a brief insert of her leaning idly against a hitching post, bemused, as the argument swirls about her. She is accustomed to being ignored, and is visibly shocked by Ringo's courteous prompting of Curley to ask for her vote after the cavalry wife's. Moments later, Ringo will seat Dallas opposite her at the table, triggering an exchange of long looks. Mallory's gaze is ice cold, Dallas looks resigned. Seconds later, she is humiliated again, as Hatfield, Mallory and Gatewood move ('It's cooler by the window'), while Doc Boone and station manager Billy Pickett (a non-speaking role for Francis Ford, the director's brother) watch knowingly.

The growing regard between the couple, together with Ringo's ignorance of her past, puts Dallas in an impossible situation. His innocence and honourable intentions, her desperate yearning and shame, place her in a cruel double bind. Her abject hope that she can avoid the truth coming out is defeated when Indian war signals on the horizon prevent Ringo's escape. They will have to run both the Apache gauntlet of the attack on the stage as well as personal tests in Lordsburg.

The attention paid to Ringo's shoot-out with the Plummers in most accounts of the film seems out of proportion compared to Dallas's own confrontation. Balancing her painful parade out of Tonto at the outset of the film is her even more anguished private journey at the film's end. With the unsuspecting Ringo at her side, she must return to the noir-lit world of her past. Ringo's revenge evens the accounts for a dead father and brother, but Dallas's ordeal is the more harrowing. *Stagecoach* enacts biblical prophecy, humbling those who would exalt themselves, exalting the humble. From this perspective, Dallas can be seen as the very soul of the film. She emerges cleansed: she has been 'a great lady', 'an angel in the jungle', to quote Hatfield's descriptions of Lucy Mallory.

Ford has said that Ernest Haycox's story reminded him of Guy de Maupassant's 'Boule de suif', in which travellers during the Franco-Prussian War who found themselves behind enemy lines are allowed to continue only after a prostitute in the group obliges a Prussian officer's lust.[27] Although direct links between the two stories are few, both exhibit a critique of class focused in de Maupassant by the hypocrisy and ingratitude of the aristocratic travellers toward Boule de suif (bowl of suet or ball of fat, to reflect her evidently Rubenesque proportions), despite benefiting from her sacrifice.

Whether indebted or not, Ford's film is unquestionably in keeping spiritually with the original. The notion that Ringo's revenge represents the plot's main strand and that Dallas is a secondary character – the orthodox interpretation – seems unduly masculinist. In fact, the salvation of Dallas is the narrative's most prominent focus, sustaining a largely abstract structure of threatened conflicts and promised violence that is unrealised until the final sequences.

Richard Slotkin has argued that *Stagecoach* is basically a reworking of 1930s B-Western conventions rather than an epic, since there is no progress, the society of Lordsburg essentially a mirror image of Tonto's, corrupt and hypocritical.[28] This is debatable. The design of the film posits the stagecoach as an America on the move, its purgatorial trek nothing if not epic, and the society that emerges the nucleus of an ideal future. Tonto is essentially defined in terms of a moralising East, a bigoted and judgmental Europe left behind. For all its limitations, Lordsburg belongs to a more open frontier world, where problems are externalised and resolved. Buscombe has pointed out that in terms of real geography, the journey described in the film is in a northeasterly direction.[29] But in terms of the Western myth, the journey is distinctly westward, the encounter with the frontier redemptive and ennobling – the transformational Western experience *par excellence* as defined by the positivist ideology of American Manifest Destiny.

Drums Along the Mohawk (1939)

Following *Stagecoach* with *Young Mr Lincoln* (1939) and *Drums Along the Mohawk*, Ford completed three great films in the single year of 1939. A remarkable populist trilogy, all three films focus on the rise of the commoner and the underdog, a dynamic that the post-Depression audience could certainly appreciate. American history lessons all, they incarnate a basic Fordian strategy, a dual vision of the past that inscribes the present and looks to the future. With *Stagecoach*, Ford had captured a new nation, still hurting from the Civil War, rising to the challenge of new tests. In *Young Mr Lincoln*, Ford fastens on the early life of The Great Emancipator, the gawky stripling lawyer who provides the prototype for the American man of the people, the populist hero that is fundamental to American individualist ideology, and to Ford himself. As the influential *Cahiers du Cinéma* study of the film points out, Ford's portrait of the overbearing leader (*Cahiers* actually finds him 'monstrous') seems to conjoin his power to sexual repression, his tragic loss of Ann Rutledge and embrace of the Law.[30] The film's famous last shot has the lonely figure steadily walking uphill as lightning crackles overhead.

With *Drums Along the Mohawk*, Ford continues his project of domesticating the West, albeit an early, colonial frontier. 'It's a pretty flag, isn't it?' observes Claudette Colbert's Lana at the end of Ford's first colour film. Given that the film is a tribute to women, to their endurance and grit and vitality, it is apt that the film's graphics and colourful images evoke a quilt as opposed to *Stagecoach*'s wheel. Both films construct imperilled communities with last stands and last-minute rescues, but the scale and style are very different. The contrast between the closed black-and-white world of *Stagecoach* and the vivid epic vision of *Drums Along the Mohawk* does not work in the latter's favour. With its homely needlepoint inter-titles, its brightly coloured early America and its resolutely pretty American Rose heroine, *Drums Along the Mohawk* has been seen as much the weakest of Ford's output in 1939. For some, the mix of dark drama and cartoonish humour is too much, as is a range of acting styles that extends from realist to Keystone Cops, and a heroine (Colbert typically seen as miscast) too protected by make-up in the midst of battle.

This seems hardly fair given that the whole film sports an immaculate cosmetics. Like storybook illustrations, its images consistently present pleasing colour, balance and movement despite often disquieting content, as when the couple stands before their burnt-out home. Clearly flexing his muscles with Technicolor, Ford produces the kind of 'Hollywood gloss' that has customarily been seen as an essentially decorative poetics. Negative judgments are all the more understandable, however, given that this picture-perfect romanticism also serves an epic patriotism. That a Ford sensitive to the new expressive possibilities of chromatic film should end his first departure from black and white with a focus on the red, white and blue of America's new flag (and Lana's costume) is perhaps to be expected. Much less predictable, however, is the film's opening shot, a close-up on Lana's radiant wedding bouquet, a symbol of the new family that will be the foundation for the new nation.

Thus *Drums Along the Mohawk* begins where *Stagecoach* had left off, with the formation of the couple. How often do action or adventure films centre their action or adventure on a married couple? Given the focus he had established with *Stagecoach*, it comes as no surprise that Ford here gives Colbert's Lana an equal place alongside Henry Fonda's Gil. Indeed, like Dallas, Lana is the very centre of the film, which records her progress from Eastern privilege to pioneer community, from immature maiden to seasoned wife and mother. 'I'm no frontier-woman!' sobs a shattered Lana, demoralised by her stormy introduction to a new life. But in a film that is as much melodrama as it is

The climax of a matriarchal Western

Western – 'Lana's Story' – our heroine does indeed metamorphose into a pioneer mother, a frontier citizen who shares absolute parity with husband Gil in courage, duty and sacrifice.

The film's insistently symmetrical narrative structure and Ford's immaculate detailing testify to the couple's partnership. The film's first campaign features Gil marching off to defend the Mohawk Valley against the British, with Lana desolately searching for him after the exhausted colonists return. The film's last sequence is a mirror image, with a uniformed Lana defending the fort against the invading forces, and Gil now searching for her in the aftermath. They are the ideal couple, a perfect match in their courage and passion.

Ford has been regularly taken to task for his puritanical view of women, his prudish inability to see them in sexual terms. Ford is certainly not Hawks, who clearly revelled in the erotic byplay of his characters. But perhaps because of the generally decorous air, moments sometimes occur that carry a quiet erotic force. I am thinking here of Gil and Lana's honeymoon night, which they spend at an inn presided over by a tubby innkeeper who is both nosey and hard of hearing, a fatally embarrassing blend. He is quick to spot them: 'Honeymooners – you got it written all over you.' Genially, he blows their cover to the only other guest, a dark, caped character, John Carradine's villainous Caldwell, who is clearly less interested in their union than in their politics. Projecting, the busybody landlord is quick to understand the iconography of his eye-patch: 'I bet he lost it trying to see something wasn't any of his business.'

As they stand at the bottom of the shadowy staircase up which the brooding Caldwell has just disappeared, Gil is solicitous. Have the stranger's speculations that Indians may be banding with the British upset her? A solemn Lana corrects him: it is not Indians she is thinking about – rather, it is whether he loves her as much as she him. She moves closer to him as she speaks, her tone intense with passion. Then she turns to climb to a landing, from which she looks back before proceeding upward to their room. No highlighting by Ford is necessary: first things first, she is saying, marking this momentous passage in their life.

A rare Revolutionary War Western, *Drums Along the Mohawk* is thus notable as well for being a matriarchal Western. This should mark the film as interesting by any standards, but for some audiences its décor is too functionally at the service of the American Dream. *Drums Along the Mohawk* is nothing if not the well-made movie, embodying in some ways an even more perfect classicism than *Stagecoach*. Was destiny ever so manifest? The marriage ceremony that opens the film leads inevitably to the national birthday at its close, one perfect union the foundation for another. These pilgrims of the earliest frontier lead God-given, God-driven lives, members of the 'American Party', whose belief in their Maker, their mission and themselves makes them invincible.

The Fordian Christian subtext is pretty much text here, in a film that is both a quasi-documentary on colonial life and a portrait of America's Chosen People defending their Eden from satanic forces. Immaculately crafted, the *mise en scène* features heavens and climes that accord with the action, a narrative cycle of bright moments and dark despair, of sun and rain punctuating ups and downs. Classical antinomies abound: East/West, civilised/savage, life/death, fire-as-hearth/fire-as-destruction.

The genesis of an American Adam and Eve is here etched in generational terms. Eastern aristocrats metamorphosing into yeoman farmers, the couple enacts the American populist agrarian myth. Their immigrant status is confirmed when they are hired to work as domestics by the widowed Mrs McKlennan, who gives them their second chance after they have been burned out by the Indians. Structurally, the curmudgeonly McKlennan (Oscar-nominated Edna May Oliver) stands behind Lana, bequeathing her not only her home but her feisty pioneer spirit as well. A remarkable character, McKlennan's defining moment comes when Indians invade her home and set it afire. There is a kind of craziness at work in the scene, the widow hectoring the whooping Indians into saving her bed, the remnant of her life with the passionate Barney. Manifest Destiny operating at the most personal level, McKlennan's imperious behaviour is evidence of a character with blind faith in the superiority of her culture, for which the reality of the Indian world – the Other – does not even exist. McKlennan's opposite number, Gil's spiritual forebear, is General Herkimer (Roger Imhof). Although less prominent, the general's role in organising and directing his scruffy army is presented by Ford in a warm portrait of frontier leadership and sacrifice, the old soldier dying from battle wounds.

Ford's habit of heightening the tone of his films at their end, often shifting gears into a memorial reprising of the narrative, or breaking into a prophetic mode, operates here. Ford punctuates the celebration of the colonists after their successful repulsing of the fort's final siege with the raising of the new stars and stripes. As the flag reaches its summit, Ford ends the film with a montage of characters looking up: McKlennan's slave, Daisy; Blue Back, the Christianised Indian; a burly blacksmith; and finally Lana and Gil, who has the film's last line: 'There's a heap of work to do.' The low-angle shots and the formal poses, the pacing and music, all work to petrify and memorialise these characters – they are America's pioneers. At the same time, the stress on the birth of the new nation and the challenges that lie ahead simultaneously projects them as the future as well. Ford is open to the charge of racism here. The suggestion implied by this montage of a narrative summary on the one hand, and a glorious multicultural future on the other, creates a weight that the images themselves cannot carry. One senses Ford's conviction and optimism overriding and distorting both the film's action and the history it is reworking, giving minor and minority characters a disproportionate prominence. (It does not help that in a new millennium racial harmony remains a dream.)

In general, the Indians in *Drums Along the Mohawk* are portrayed as either murderous savages, moving like wraiths through the forest, or comical vandals, as in the attack on the widow's home. The one friendly Indian, Blue Back, is not as marginal as either the blacksmith, who does not figure at all in the action, or Daisy (Beulah Hall Jones), who hardly speaks. It is Blue Back who raises the alarm when the Indians first attack, and he also dispatches Caldwell, whose eye-patch he sports at the battle's end, evidence of Ford's attempt to give the figure some ideological weight.[31] But Blue Back nevertheless remains essentially a token comical figure who is given monstrous overtones to scare Lana on her arrival. Despite the role being filled by Chief John Big Tree, the greatest of Indian actors, this exploitation makes him as authentic as a character in blackface.

The film's alternating periods of peace and conflict, of hope and despair, are clearly meant to signify the process of 'history'. The film's strategy is to highlight the pioneering sacrifices that made possible the birth of America, the old world giving way to the new. This idea is focused in the film by the deaths of key characters: Mrs McKlennan and General Herkimer, icons of the early pioneer spirit, and Joe Boleo, the old scout who volunteers to sneak through Indian lines. Captured by the Indians, the geezer is wheeled out to be burned alive on his own funeral pyre. Symbolically crucified, Joe (another bit part for brother Francis Ford) is an early model of the holy fool that Ford, like Shakespeare, found useful as a means of democratising his heroic narratives. A truer reprise of the narrative would have required appearances by these more significant players, but Ford was obviously restricted in casting this coda to survivors, however marginal.

In a typical twist that demonstrates the visual character of his sensibility, Ford seized on an iconic solution to a narrative problem. But although Daisy's image recalls the widow McKlennan, however indirectly, it is a stretch to suggest that the blacksmith and Blue Back stand in for General Herkimer and the colonial army. The result is a void, a tear in the well-made fabric, a disconnection between our experience and the crucial final images. Yet the aplomb and conviction of Ford's orchestration suggests that the director can live with any perceived duplicities, and that he subscribes to the ultimate truth of his statement. Ford's populist faith is all: as in *Stagecoach*, he insists it is history's humble, the normally overlooked minor players, who were early America's salt of the earth.

My Darling Clementine (1946)

The stuff of history, legend and perhaps a dozen movies, the gunfight at the OK Corral (as the 1957 John Sturges production with Burt Lancaster and Kirk Douglas was titled) first appeared in two 1930s films both entitled *Frontier Marshal*. That it continues to command attention is evidenced in the 1990s by the competing efforts of Kevin Costner's *Wyatt Earp* and Lawrence Kasdan's *Tombstone*, both sprawling three-hour post-modern affairs.

A modest ninety-seven minutes, Ford's film is the absolute jewel of the cycle, one of the masterpieces of classical American film. Its title tells all. While purporting to rework one of the more violent confrontations of the Wild West's storied bad men, *My Darling Clementine* constructs a loving hymn to the values of civilisation. All the narrative's basic elements are present – the violent frontier town of Tombstone, the Earp brothers led by Wyatt, former marshal of Dodge City, dissolute Doc Holliday, the villainous Clanton gang and the OK Corral showdown. But as in both *Stagecoach* and *Drums Along the Mohawk*, and true to his way of seeing throughout his long career, Ford is less interested in violent action than in its aftermath – in 'keeping the peace'. *Clementine* opens as a revenge Western, but Ford was to enter this terrain sparingly. His single major entry is, of course, *The Searchers*, where the motif provides the poisonous fuel that drives Wayne's unbalanced Ethan throughout. In *Clementine* as in *Stagecoach*, the progress towards vengeance is less a drive than a leisurely circuit of indirection, the audience primed for action only to have gratification postponed.

Screenwriter Winston Miller referred to this delay as 'flaws in the construction. Earp stays in town to get his brother's killer and we vamp for about sixty pages with what we hope are interesting scenes.'[32] For most audiences, however, this suggestion of filler material is far from their experience. With its unfolding strategy of beguiling pauses, digressions and diversions, *Clementine* takes us into a distinctive world that stubbornly insists on its own integrity. Whether we realise it consciously or not, the narrative's *longueurs* in fact represent priorities fundamental to the film's vision. However, not least of the accomplishments of this singular movie is the synthesis it achieves between a sharp clarity on the one hand, and a rich ambiguity on the other. Dismissed as horse opera by some reviewers of the period, *Clementine* also failed to find favour with critics like Robert Warshow. Lamenting the self-consciousness he detected in the post-World War II Western, Warshow accused Ford of indulging a soft stylistic excess.[33] But over the years, the charm and depth of the film, as well as its intriguing balance of ostensibly irreconcilable elements, has engaged successive generations of critics and audiences.

The pronounced tilt of the film away from its violent premise is part of its intriguing appeal. It is all of a piece with the distinctive look and tantalising pace, the strong sense of a world being filtered through a personal lens. As usual with Ford, the lines between objective and subjective representation are not that clear. *Clementine* again evidences a documentary impulse, the desire to record faithfully the look and manners of a frontier settlement. One senses both research and a deep love for the period, the images composed with immense care. Interiors draw in the eye with their depth and detail, as in the case of the hotel dining room with its rows of tables covered with gingham, the sun slanting in on the far wall. It is as if the images are making a claim to accuracy – 'This is how it once was,' they seem to say, 'these people once lived and looked like this.'

Yet at the same time, it is impossible to escape the ever-present feeling of being in a world constructed and seen dynamically, of a narrative transformed by style. The more Ford films one knows, the more pronounced becomes this perception of a remarkable melding, of a historical material reverberating with personal themes, characters and touches. Ford's preference for a static camera and for tableau composition are examples of this melding, where the style feeds into the sense of a record, of early photographs. Another recurrent element with this effect is the placing of characters against the sky, the desert, the mountains and the horizon. Images of great depth ground the characters in their surroundings, framing them against adversity and the wilderness, history and eternity.

The opening of *Clementine* is effortless. In brilliant sunshine on open range we see cowboys riding herd. Framed against the sky, they are posed like moving statues, turning as they work the cattle. Although we will not be introduced until the next scene, these are the Earps, and moments later a buckboard approaches bearing the silent Clantons, who eye the herd and make a lowball offer. The brief scene is masterful in establishing a sense of balance and opposition, of bright and dark forces destined to engage. The open valley beyond adds to the drama, contributing to the sense of an archetypal encounter.

Typically, the film insists on introducing the Earps on horseback, as working cowboys, only to ground them for much of the film thereafter. Do the cowboys tame Tombstone, or does Tombstone tame the cowboys? Wyatt will spend much of the film comfortably ensconced in a chair on the hotel porch. Apart from two hell-for-leather chases in open range, the film will stay resolutely within town limits – not much of a horse opera. Similarly, on their visit to the barbershop – the Bon Ton Tonsorial Parlor – the offer of haircuts and baths is righteously rejected: a shave is the only concession our cowboys are prepared to make to civilised protocols. Soon enough, however, Wyatt will be cropped and perfumed like a new bridegroom.

The change is not that surprising. Despite the pose of incorrigible nomads, the Earps have been introduced to us by their youngest member, brother James, a veritable icon of the settled, whose farewell as the older men ride off hangs in the air – 'So long Wyatt . . . so long Morgan . . . Virg.' Ford holds the shot longer than necessary, allowing us to register fully the boy's youth and spirit. The youngest, left behind presumably because he is whiskerless, James is defined as the soul of the family, his cooking almost as good as Ma's, the bearer of the silver cross for his sweetheart, Cory Sue. His subsequent death represents a murder of the civilised spirit and the feminine, a martyrdom and unspeakable tragedy signalled by the three brothers standing motionless around the body in the dark downpour. The Clantons, emerging from the wet and darkness like denizens of the night, leave no doubt about what has transpired. The die is cast. But if the world is out of whack, the film also proposes that Earp must first give himself to the life of Tombstone before he can right it. Ford insists on paradox: in order to achieve his violent personal revenge, Earp must first become the Law.

'What kind of town is this?' Posed at the outset of the film, this question suggests an enigma, an ambiguity that is in fact largely absent in Ford's deliberate, loving portrait of the Old West and its heroes. Echoing throughout, Wyatt Earp's thrice-uttered question is reinforced by other overheard incredulous or awed remarks: '*Marshalin*'? In *Tombstone*?'; and 'Shakespeare . . . in Tombstone'; and finally, 'Church bells . . . in Tombstone'. That such an untamed America should be able to accommodate law, culture and religion, it is suggested, is something of a miracle. But, of course, the movie enjoys a rich doublethink, a 'wide-awake wide-open' Tombstone just barbaric enough – once Indian Charlie has been kicked out of town and Wyatt installed as marshal – to settle immediately into sedate routines. The transitional moment is charmingly captured in the film's portrait of a schizoid community moved to applaud itself wildly on being addressed as ladies and gentlemen, and to implement a rough justice ('ride him round town on a rail') on being deprived of their Shakespeare.

'Maybe when we leave this country, young kids like you will be able to grow up and live safe,' opines Wyatt at the grave of his brother. But leaving the revenge motif in limbo, the trajectory of the film now moves the action to the saloon, where the new marshal is immediately tested as bringer of the law by subversive elements of the community. Structurally and dramatically, the film proposes that the violent elimination of anarchy is the final act in a historical process that initially involves the establishment and defence of law, culture and religion. The film's key settings and the action played out in them – rowdy saloon, imperilled theatrical performance, half-built church – mirror this transition.

That challenges to Earp's authority are introduced in the person of Linda Darnell's half-breed Chihuahua is an unfortunate example of the racial profiling that runs through much of Ford. Chihuahua's first act on entering the saloon is to taunt the new marshal with a song – 'Ten thousand cattle gone astray' – and thereafter tip off a gambler to the marshal's poker hand. Earp shares the film's incipient racism. Booting drunken Indian Charlie out of town with relish earlier, here he punishes Chihuahua by threatening to send her 'back to the Apache reservation where you belong', and dunking her in a handy watering trough. Wyatt's rude crack appears gratuitous, given that Darnell's Chihuahua seems wholly assimilated into Tombstone's white culture.

Cheating at poker is, of course, a serious business, and the film stresses the importance of gambling to the fabric of the society. Both Doc and Earp will turn away
undesirable cardsharps. Like baseball, poker is an American ritual, a democratic game
that offers a level playing field where cowpoke, gunslinger, rancher, professional and
average Joe can all sit at the same table. A microcosm of society, poker has rules that if
broken threaten the stability of the community. But dubious moral shadings frame Chihuahua's ethical lapse as well. As the scene unfolds, she leans down to kiss the gambler
and then moves around the table to brazenly lift her bared leg to prop a shoe by Earp,
who ignores her. This can be read as a declined sexual overture, with the satiric song and
attempt at cheating that follow efforts to even the score. Certainly, the film does appear
to depict this half-breed character – evidently half-Indian and half-Mexican, and thus
overdetermined as a loser in the period's racist politics – in a harsh light. She will cheat
on Doc with Billy Clanton, threaten Clementine and appropriate Cory Sue's cross, the
signifier of the manifest spiritual destiny bestowed on America's righteous pioneers.
Chihuahua is thus a corrupting force, one of the impurities that must be expunged to
ensure the birth of a new Tombstone.

Yet this border between good girl and bad is too stark. Chihuahua may flirt in the
saloon, but surely she is a singer rather than a whore, and her abject love for the self-
destructive Doc is never in question despite her adultery. Her brash surface
notwithstanding, she is humanised by her transparent vulnerability, gamely wiping her
tears with her skirt as she comes clean. Shot in the back like James and Virgil, Chihuahua
becomes one of the redeeming sacrifices necessary to a new America. But if Chihuahua
is one of those black sheep emblematic of frontier spirit so dear to the director, it is
remarkable how decisively Cathy Downs's Clementine overshadows her. Darnell was

A decorous farewell: Clementine provided Cathy Downs her one memorable character

already a star at this point, while Downs was a second-level performer who was never to achieve even minor stardom. Darnell is given huge close-ups that reflect her stature and the character's sensuality, but the film insists on a respectful distance with Clementine. The dramatic action, Ford's careful staging and Downs's quiet performance all work to elevate the character to a supreme iconic significance.

On his arrival, Holliday also challenges Wyatt's ability to keep the peace. Expelling tinhorn gamblers is not Doc's business, according to Wyatt, who confirms that his duty – repeating the decadent Holliday's ironic phrase – is indeed 'to deliver us from all evil'. Doc immediately draws but backs down when Wyatt's brothers materialise behind him. Disciplining both Chihuahua and Doc in the saloon, with its associations of licence and excess, Earp consolidates his position and the rule of law. Appropriately, the scene ends with the arrival of Eastern culture in the form of tipsy Granville Thorndyke, travelling thespian, 'Mr Shakespeare', the actor in the evening's show.

The Birdcage Theater, like the Bon Ton Tonsorial Parlor, evidences Tombstone's aspirations. That 'Mr Shakespeare' is being held hostage by barbarians, however, indicates how precarious is the progress. Wyatt and Doc look on, and Holliday helps the faltering actor when he forgets his lines. Another paradox appears. The educated man, the man of culture, is impotent to defend that culture: coughing uncontrollably, Doc is forced to abandon his recitation from *Hamlet*, seizing up on the line, 'Thus conscience does make cowards of us all'. The rescue of the actor and the show is left to the untutored cowboy.

As Scott Simmon has argued, the Hamlet theme can be seen to resonate for both Wyatt and Doc.[34] Certainly, this is so for Doc, the divided soul in denial of his past, his identity, his feelings, and of the Ophelia-like Clementine, who represents all of these. A familiar type, the fallen aristocrat (*Stagecoach*'s Hatfield comes to mind), Holliday is a compelling variation, passionately performed by Victor Mature, the consumption a sign of a mysteriously flawed nature. Haunted and self-destructive, a doctor who became a killer, he is drawn to death's 'undiscovered country'. As in his reciting of *Hamlet*, he tries to rise to the occasion to operate on Chihuahua, but with her death will lapse into his gunfighter persona and meet his quietus, white handkerchief fluttering, at the OK Corral.

Simmon's analysis of visual style in *Clementine* seizes on Wyatt's characteristic posture in the film – on the hotel's front porch, leaning back precariously, recumbent – to support the idea of Earp as a homespun Hamlet. Are these images of inaction, passivity, paralysis? Operating within the law, Wyatt resists the impulse to apply wilderness justice, but is arguably killing time. In the shooting script, he acknowledges that Shakespeare had made 'a powerful lot of sense – especially that last about conscience makin' cowards out of all of us', a line that if used would have underscored the parallel between his situation and the gloomy Dane's, the duty to revenge a family murder. Whether the Hamlet theme's relevance for Wyatt registers may depend to some extent on our sense of the film's time frame. Is the film's leisurely pace such that we wonder over Wyatt's priorities? Is there any hint of the character indulging 'the whips and scorns of time, the law's delay'? The action in fact only occupies a weekend – remarkably, given the sense Ford creates of relationships developing, of characters and the community changing.

If attention to the Hamlet theme allows us to see Earp and Holliday as parallel heroes, it is not stretching this point to perceive a shadow text with Doc as hero, a noir *Clementine*. Advertising for the film (both in English and Spanish) that positioned Chihuahua as a fiery femme fatale dominating the smaller images of Fonda and Mature also invited such expectations against the grain of its actual scenario. But tantalising as such alternative readings may be, the values of Ford's film are clear. As with Chihuahua, if Holliday is meant to embody vanishing frontier spirit, there is relatively little sympathy for the character. It is in fact the absence of Ford's strong identification with the losers, so central to the later films, that allows *Clementine* to shine such a bright light on the chosen. At its peak, the film presents a formal procession of Wyatt and Clem to the church in a symbolic marriage of East and West. Intercut with this transcendent passage is a brief visit to Holliday's dark lair, reeking of liquor, lust and despair, where the hung-over Doc histrionically proposes to Chihuahua: 'The Queen is dead. Long live the Queen.'

In contrast to the turbulent Doc who is unable to look at himself, Fonda as Wyatt is a model of balance and decorum throughout the film, loading his poker-chip winnings into his hat, firmly squaring it away in a glass, doing a little dance in his chair on the hotel porch. He shows the same equilibrium with the Clantons, walking stiffly away into the darkness, biding his time. That measured walk will also bring him down the long street at the end, when the clash with the Clantons finally takes place.

'Fonda's pace was Ford's pace,' screenwriter Winston Miller remarked apropos the rapport between star and director.[35] One could add that the pace of Fonda/Earp is arguably the pace of civilisation, the ideal of the socially regulated self. In preparing for the final battle, Wyatt declines the help of the town's mayor and deacon in what he terms is 'strictly a family affair'. If true, this admission would compromise the logic of the film. In the event, however, the officials function as decoys, and Wyatt firmly acts on behalf of the law, warrant in hand.[36] That dust thrown up by the passing stagecoach – *Stagecoach*'s icon for an early America on the move that here had delivered Clementine to Tombstone – should contribute to the finale, tipping the scales against the barbarians, is also appropriate.

Ford's use of deportment to communicate the values of civilisation achieves an expressive peak in the dedication of Tombstone's church. Having defended the law and delivered culture, Wyatt now joins in the dance to dedicate the church – albeit reluctantly, a shy cowboy. A favourite ritual for Ford, the dance marks Wyatt's growing involvement in the community, his stiff, high-stepping style both hinting at a cowboy's awkwardness and embodying the decorum of the new world.

Clementine's heart is the dance of Wyatt and Clem, its beat driving the whole film, a magical moment in the cinema, an icon that contends and codifies at the level of Gene Kelly's solo song and dance in *Singin' in the Rain* (1952) in its affirmation of America. That the episode can so easily be detached from the whole film should not be held against it; the scene in *Singin' in the Rain* also achieves that high intensity saturation of codes, creating a wonderful world of plenitude, the American Dream.

But if the dance is an epiphany, a hymn to harmony, it is just the high point in an ideological operation that everywhere valorizes order and social regulation. A network of themes and codes comes together to create the image of an ideal community, where the meals ('Stowed away a whole skillet of ham and eggs') are as regular as the orderly comings and goings of the stage that provides links to the nation, the occasionally infectious intruder – like the shady gambler resignedly moving on – a minor turbulence in the clear sky, the clear sailing. Ingeniously, wittily, the film constructs a persistent hat code signifying around the poles of civilisation and culture, balance and restraint, or their lack, the frames often resembling still-life compositions organised around huge cowboy hats, sombreros, flowery bonnets, stovepipes, military headgear, a chef's toque, etc. Prominent everywhere, but especially in the saloon, where they are removed only while eating, the hats help to create a formal world, giving the characters weight and personality. Both in individual close-ups and ensemble shots, *chapeaux* dominate the West, Ford's contemplative tableau style creating a signifying force field of sculptured images that rival the *mise en scène* of his exteriors, his landscaping with buttes and mesas.

The various cultural and cinema codes lock into a synergistic construction that speaks the civilising of America, a masterful marshalling of behavioural and iconic laws, editing and musical systems, an orchestration of signs and meanings that reaches its peak in the formal deportment of Wyatt and Clem in their walk to the church. Ford's style has been described as 'realism at its prettiest', an attempt, perhaps, to pin down its poetic swell of meanings. Here our perfumed hero – fresh from the barber's chair, hat smartly squared in the mirror – carefully squires his lady fair from in front of the sun-drenched hotel slowly along its boardwalk, up the hill to the church where, under the open sky and fluttering flags, 'a dad-blasted good dance' is about to commence. In the movie's glorious set piece, Ford's own brother is on the violin under the baton of Russell Simpson's deacon.

Given that Wyatt and Clem's union is so central in the film's network of codes and themes celebratory of a new community, it is understandable why their separation at the end has been seen as its enigma. In this, *Clementine* can be said to resemble the reverse of one of those family melodramas, *All That Heaven Allows* (1956), the *locus classicus*, where the narrative's odyssey of suffering is undercut, a happy ending materialising at the last minute. Here it is the powerful, positive thrust of the film's energies towards a romantic union and closure that is displaced, with Earp and the final moment by the fence – 'Ma'am, I sure like that name . . . *Clementine*!' – then riding off.

In his influential structural analysis of Ford's heroes, Peter Wollen suggested that Earp's progress was an 'uncomplicated passage from nature to culture', that his trajectory was from vengeful nomad to settled, married citizen. Rebutting Wollen, Bill Nichols accused the film of indulging a morbid delaying tactic in its narrative digressions from the revenge motif.[37] The implication was that Ford, like his hero, was reluctant to face the future, and that ultimately Earp remained the outsider. Tag Gallagher's take on the film included a pocket-sized allegorical reading that also stresses a downbeat reading:

> Wyatt Earp (the US) gives up marshaling in Dodge City (World War I), but takes up arms again to combat the Clantons (World War II) to make the world safe. Victory is horrible, and Wyatt must return to the wilderness, to his father (confession; reconstruction), leaving innocence, hope and civilization (Clementine) behind, 'lost and gone forever', a distant memory (the long road) in Tombstone (the world of 1946).[38]

Taking an implicitly post-modern position, Scott Simmon accommodates both positive and negative views, and suggests that the film's conclusion is a blank slate that allows one to see Wyatt's departure as either temporary or permanent, the theme of integration and reconciliation affirmed or broken.[39] Similarly, he suggests that the vision of the film, like that of its hero gazing off to the horizon, may also be both/and rather than either/or – looking simultaneously towards a bright future, and to a glorious past, the film arguably a nostalgia text for its 1940s post-war audience, a Republican dream, when men were men.

Yet such overarching, inclusive interpretations are only possible to the extent that they undervalue the film's basic thrust and formal organisation. The extraordinary sense of order, the harmony of its world, all testify to *Clementine*'s luminous, positive vision. Ford's films are invariably rooted in the flow of history, the inevitability of change, the cycle of life and death. His vision balances faith and loss, love and violence, order and anarchy. Rooted in melodrama, the action often turns on sacrifice and typically mourns the homeless and the lost. The balance can often be strained, the tone dark. In *Clementine*, however, Ford is at a point in his career where his vision of America is a transcendent one, of the garden to come rather than the wilderness that was.

Fort Apache (1948)

All I can see is the flags.

Mrs Collingwood's poignant comment as she watches the doomed cavalry troop ride off in the distance, her husband among them, resonates throughout *Fort Apache*. One of the most faithful members of Ford's stock company, Anna Lee here plays a character who is fatefully bidding her husband goodbye – tragically, given that she holds in her hand news of his transfer. But taken out of its context, the statement also can be seen as a succinct expression of the personality of the film's hero, Colonel Owen Thursday (Henry Fonda), whose blind pursuit of glory proves disastrous, profoundly damaging the military world that Ford lovingly creates. And the line might also apply to the director himself, given the film's argument that the need for national heroes ultimately justifies the cover-up of dishonourable action – the republic for ever! That *Fort Apache*, with no ironic intent, itself exposes the suicidal facts of military action only to record approvingly their transmutation into heroic myth provides an unsettling jolt for most audiences.[40]

To what do we owe the catastrophic behaviour of Thursday, the fort's commander? Introducing herself to his daughter, Philadelphia – 'Your mother was my dearest friend' – Mrs Collingwood is also given the single reference in the film to Thursday's missing wife. The critique that develops in *Fort Apache* evolves out of an isolating contrast between a completely domesticated military existence, for all the fort's allegedly barbaric location, and its leader, who is fundamentally uncivilised despite a surface elegance and culture. In these terms it is not impossible to see Mrs Thursday as the film's structuring absence.

At every turn, the narrative of *Fort Apache* erects vivid characters in the life of the fort to stand as foils to Thursday. Ignoring his outstretched hand, an ungenerous Thursday shows no warmth toward Collingwood, a sensitive fellow officer whose past fall from grace he cannot excuse. A rigid martinet, Thursday will have his every order questioned by John Wayne's second-in-command, an affable democratic type. An icy, remote, class-conscious WASP, the irked Thursday will find himself entangled in an intense domestic squabble with Sergeant-Major O'Rourke, the proud patriarch of a loving extended Irish family. The very embodiment of privilege and personal ambition, he will oppose totally Philadelphia's choice of Lieutenant O'Rourke, a product of West Point but also of the fort's rowdy common soldiers. Most vividly, his cramping will and authoritarian instincts will be set consistently against his daughter's spontaneity, openness and warmth. A final unflattering contrast comes from outside the fort, as the film insists on portraying Cochise, chief of the Apache, as the more honourable man.

Focusing the film's construction of the fort's new commander as dangerously arrogant and by the book, York challenges Thursday at every turn. He disputes Thursday's contempt for the Apache, objects to his refusal to honour negotiations and approaches insubordination in his criticism of Thursday's proposed charge. York's challenges prove correct: far from 'digger Indians', the Apache are estimable warriors; refusing to negotiate with Cochise results in an unnecessary war; Thursday's cavalry charge, classically correct but inappropriate to the landscape and enemy, destroys him and his regiment. Yet in the film's epilogue, reporters discuss a heroic painting of 'Thursday's Charge' that hangs in Washington, with York, the new commander. Lying by omission, York tells the journalists that the painting is 'correct in every detail', and that 'no man died more gallantly, nor won more honour for his regiment'. He then dons a desert cap and barks 'Questions?' – both affectations of Thursday's – before leaving to lead the troop out against the Apache, now ruled by Geronimo. He has not only inherited the command and accepted the necessity of falsifying the truth of Thursday's action, he has also taken on Thursday's role in making war on the Apache.

There is a moment at the height of the last battle when York has ridden into action

Fonda at his most wooden; with Shirley Temple's Philadelphia and Movita Castenada as Guadaloupe

to rescue the fallen Thursday. Exasperated by his attempts to dissuade him from re-entering battle, Thursday tells York, 'When you command this troop – as I am sure you will one day – then *command* it. But until you do …' Ford and Fonda had formed a hugely successful collaboration with *Drums Along the Mohawk*, *Young Mr Lincoln* and *The Grapes of Wrath*. This creative bond had continued after the war with *Clementine* and *The Fugitive*, Ford's modern-day Christ story, followed by *Fort Apache*. Thereafter, the two would not work together again until the disastrous *Mister Roberts* in 1955, which occasioned a complete rupture when Fonda challenged Ford's approach in the filming. Such audacity was unheard of given Ford's authority and famously explosive person-ality, but was understandable in light of the actor's relationship with a role he had performed for three years on Broadway.

But in retrospect Fonda was already being phased out during the filming of the earlier *Fort Apache*. With his youth and passion, Fonda had provided the dramatic core for the early chapters of the American pioneer saga that was emerging as Ford's project. As Orson Welles put it, to look at the actor was to see 'the face of America'. It is difficult to imagine these films *sans* Fonda, so central is he in the creation of their tone, pace and vision. However, as he gained experience, Fonda must inevitably have seemed less pli-able to the director. Certainly, the overall progress of the Fonda hero in Ford's work is away from innocence and idealism towards self-consciousness and rigidity, as the direc-tor increasingly emphasised the wooden aspects of the actor's persona. But generalisations are risky with Ford: ten years earlier, *Young Mr Lincoln* had provided an early opportunity for Ford to explore the unbending side of the actor.

After *Stagecoach*, Ford had barely used John Wayne, turning to him only for another second-in-command role as exec officer Rusty in the post-war *They Were Expendable* (1945). But with the role of Kirby York, Wayne was unknowingly becoming Fonda's suc-cessor (and thus ironically paralleling his character's arc in the film itself), replacing Fonda as Ford's spokesman for the string of outstanding works that lay ahead: *3 God-fathers*, *She Wore a Yellow Ribbon*, *Rio Grande*, *The Quiet Man* (1952), *The Searchers*, *The Wings of Eagles*, *The Horse Soldiers*, *The Man Who Shot Liberty Valance*, *How the West Was Won* (1962) and *Donovan's Reef* (1963). These films, and especially the Westerns, would be instrumental in making Wayne the most popular star of his era and an icon of American identity. Ironically, however, Wayne too would eventually be phased out. In *The Man Who Shot Liberty Valance* he bitterly defers to James Stewart, who is centre stage for the last chapters – *Two Rode Together* and *Cheyenne Autumn* – of Ford's epic narrative of American frontier history.

In *Fort Apache*, the Thursday/York conflict is instrumental in focusing the compet-ing values and ideologies that radiate throughout the film:

Thursday	York
East	West
Europe	frontier
West Point	Fort Apache
book knowledge	wilderness knowledge
individual	family and community
glory	duty

Within this scheme, the overarching conflict of East and West displaces a number of other struggles: white versus Indian, officer class versus soldier, North versus South. That so many of these potentially conflicting personalities and loyalties, which together make up a collective American identity, come into sharp focus during the film's action is a reflection of just how divisive a character Thursday is. In these terms, it is not York who is his opposite number so much as Lieutenant Michael O'Rourke (John Agar), the character who integrates rather than divides, a West Point graduate who knows Indian ways, the rookie officer and son of a non-commissioned officer/Civil War Medal of Honor holder and, ironically, the man who will win Thursday's daughter.

The duality of vision that Ford invariably employs in describing his typical frontier community – at once both wilderness and garden – is here an almost unbridgeable gap. From Thursday we are to understand that Fort Apache is the rear end of the country, the great wrong place to be, 'a ten-penny post' to which he has been 'shunted aside'. The presence of Collingwood (George O'Brien), a failure from the past, reinforces this image. Thursday's first act replaces him as Adjutant – 'Nothing personal, Sam' – after which he offers him a mid-morning drink. Although not fleshed out, the Collingwood/Thursday contrast insinuates a cowardice/bravery theme crucial to the film's interrogation of military values. Collingwood has preceded Thursday in banishment to the isolated fort evidently for a conservative decision smacking of cowardice he had made in their shared past. Thursday had done it differently and 'rode to glory'. Now he too had come to Fort Apache, where a rash decision will destroy his command and yet ironically bring him even greater glory for his 'brave' charge. Thursday explodes when Cochise threatens resistance, and wildly impugns York as a coward for questioning his charge. Thursday's bravery is the suicidal aggression of an unstable, damaged personality.

For all Thursday's bitterness about Fort Apache – 'the end of the rainbow' – what we see is Ford's vision of the ideal pioneer community, an immensely civilised and proud society. Often taxed during his career with the charge that the historical West was not like that, Ford would regularly reply that if not, it should have been. But as his films so often testify, the line between naturalistic representation and expressionist, visionary styling is never absolute.

Fort Apache was also a transitional film for both Ford and its writer, Frank S. Nugent. Falling back on the industry's bread and butter, a Western, Ford was attempting to save Argosy Pictures, the independent production company he had launched with a commercial failure, *The Fugitive*. Nugent was writing the first of a long line of Ford's later films. As film critic for *The New York Times*, Nugent had been a consistent admirer of the director's work, greeting *Stagecoach* enthusiastically, and writing a profile of the director for the *Saturday Evening Post* in 1947. In conversation with him, Ford had shared an idea for a film:

> In all Westerns, the cavalry rides in to the rescue of the beleaguered wagon train or whatever, and then it rides off again. I've been thinking about it – what it was like at a cavalry post, remote, people with their own personal problems, over everything the threat of Indians, of death . . .[41]

Ford had then stunned Nugent by asking him to write *Fort Apache*, which would become the first of the so-called cavalry trilogy, to be followed by *She Wore a Yellow Ribbon* and *Rio Grande*, all based on short stories by James Warner Bellah, and all centred on life in the US cavalry.

This documenting of army life is *Fort Apache*'s subtext, and its enormously attractive feature. We see the fort's veteran officers and new recruits, the campaigns and patrols, the wives and families, the dances and parties. If the vision is romantic, it is justified by being in part that of Shirley Temple's young Philadelphia, whose point of view as a new immigrant to the West structures our own. The tip-off comes when she and her father ride on to the fort after meeting Michael. Hiding her interest from Thursday, she tilts her hatbox lid so that the oval fringed mirror it houses frames the reflection of the dashing young lieutenant as he rides behind their conveyance. Ford gives us an image of extraordinary layering, pointing to her saucy quickness, independence and ingenuity, suggesting her romantic, idealising nature and hinting at her future success in snaring and domesticating the soldier.

Philadelphia's reactions from the outset show good humour and openness, a healthy antidote to her father's negativity. Awakening in her new quarters, she goes out onto the balcony to give us an intoxicating view of the life of a working frontier cavalry post, a dynamic scene in bright morning sunshine of horses being exercised and wagons rolling that seems to reflect her own busy, spontaneous nature. This is again visible when she discovers the poverty of the quarters she and her father have been assigned. Rushing down the boardwalk towards us clutching bonnet and skirt – Ford holding the deep-focus shot – past three lounging troopers, each of whom she greets with a cheery 'Good Morning', a breathless Philadelphia finds Mrs Collingwood and shares her plight. Nothing to it, Emily tells her, Mrs O'Rourke will come to the rescue, whereupon she, echoed in turn by Philadelphia and then the three loungers, all page the fort's matriarch – 'Mrs O'Rourke! Mrs O'Rourke! Mrs O'Rourke!'

The charm of the scene has as much to do with Shirley Temple's spirited performance as with Ford's accommodating *mise en scène*. The former child star, whom Ford had worked with in *Wee Willie Winkie* (1937) a decade earlier, was attempting a comeback in a grown-up role. Her trust in Ford is evident in the full-blooded commitment she makes to her sweet and impetuous character. Like Phil's view from the balcony, the scene provides us with another slice of the fort's domestic life, suggesting its intimate texture and the extent to which the O'Rourke name echoes within it.

The tonic effect of Phil's pell-mell run is matched by the liberating gestures of other characters. The ride out by Michael and Philadelphia through the wide sun-baked expanse of Monument Valley's desert ends badly, with the discovery of the massacred patrol. Even here, however, Ford has O'Rourke double back to sweep up Phil's bonnet in a gallant gesture. Likewise, York's hefting and launching of an empty whiskey bottle from a cliff's edge into the canyon below, the detritus of a good officer's consideration for a hung-over trooper, Pedro Armendáriz's Beaufort. Scenes like these help to define generosity of character and dramatise the frontier's openness.

Such expansive gestures are denied Thursday. The images we retain of him are pinched and mean: the struggle to extricate himself from a broken chair; his reluctant demeanour at the fort's social events; his prissy, pointy-toed dancing. The paragon of gentility and decorum, Thursday is in fact antisocial. His own grand gesture will be the suicidal charge. Thursday represents the triumph of appearances over substance, of the letter of the law, of form. In his pedantic manner, enunciating every syllable, Thursday objects to the tendency of veteran officers to treat the uniform as a site for 'whimsical' expression. He lectures young O'Rourke that if the latter respects a father's rights, he should 'all the more readily bow to my wishes'. Yet if anyone proves whimsical or unbending, it is Thursday.

In Ford's ideal world the military and domestic spheres are coequal and in harmony. This equilibrium is reflected in the balance of his narratives, which alternate and interweave scenes of action and family. Here the film juxtaposes Thursday's assuming of command with Philadelphia's introduction to the fort's social life to unfold its narrative. But the harmony of Fort Apache life – visible in the birthday party for George Washington that his arrival interrupts – is shattered by Thursday. Despite Philadelphia's presence, he is one of Ford's men without women, essentially undomesticated, hostile to the feminine. It is impossible to envisage him in a successful marriage.

'The Colonel's lady', Phil is a young maiden, barely able to control her bonnet. His insensitivity to her needs and indifference to family ideals indict Thursday. In contrast, Wayne's York is an honorary member of the O'Rourke clan – to which he welcomes Philadelphia – who ensures Michael's survival in the final action by sending him for reinforcements: 'And marry that girl!' Ford's analysis connects Thursday's narcissism and lack of humanity to his destructive militarism. In some respects, he recalls a more sympathetic character, Mrs McKlennar of *Drums Along the Mohawk*. Similarly Eurocentric to the core, Thursday is unable to grant intelligence or even humanity to 'savages'. Ford insinuates his critique by ironically framing the turbulent scene in which the combustible Thursday invades the O'Rourke household to retrieve Philadelphia with York and Beaufort's visit to Cochise's camp, where they begin to powwow with great ceremony. The discord Thursday's entrance and authoritarian behaviour ignites in conflicting family allegiances is extraordinary. In a matter of seconds, the two families are riven by disputes, Phil defying her father, Michael proposing, all the O'Rourkes quarrelling, the chaos finally coming to a head when Thursday forgets himself and orders Michael from his father's house.

The critique becomes devastating with his massive blunder, destroying the flower of the American military. Banishing York to the ridge with the supply wagons, Thursday orders him to take O'Rourke with him, which York ignores, taking the line officer rather than the fort's sergeant-major, the son rather than the father, the future of the troop rather than its past. York passes the binoculars to Michael, and he watches his father and four godfathers perish. Ford's use of sound marks the moment as awesome, tragic. Silence reigns as the decimated troop look off into the distance, the thunder of the Apache horses slowly growing as the few soldiers remaining under the wounded Thursday's unsteady leadership are finally overrun. Ford obviously loves these characters, so many of them Irish, and the men who played them, members of his private army. Collingwood's George O'Brien had first worked for Ford on *The Iron Horse* back in the 1920s, while Victor McLaglen (Sergeant Mulcahey) had been tortured into an Oscarwinning performance by Ford in *The Informer*, and had squired Temple in *Wee Willie Winkie* two years later. Jack Pennick (Schattuck) and his squashed visage graces practi-

Ford loves his veterans: Victor McLaglen, Pedro Armendáriz, Dick Foran and Jack Pennick

cally every Ford film, usually as bartender or soldier. Pedro Armendáriz would star in *3 Godfathers*, while O'Brien, McLaglen and Pennick would all reprise their characters for *Yellow Ribbon*. That Thursday's actions destroy them all is perhaps the blackest mark against him in Ford's book.

The film asks who is savage, who civilised? The contrast between Thursday and Cochise apart, the issue also arises with the elegant boorishness of a Mulcahey: 'Get out of my way, Meacham, or I'll break both of your legs – of course with your permission, Ma'am.' Ford's ethnics are never that far from their own barbarism. The vast alcohol consumption of Fort Apache – all the bottles spiking the punch, Mulcahey tipping up the punch bowl itself, the slurred speech of various citizens – is also ambiguous. If Fort Apache is a paradise rather than purgatory, why does the need to escape into booze run so deep?

That Ford is prepared to sacrifice these giants and still authorise a mantle of honour for their ignoble leader testifies to the value he attaches to tradition. Coded as decadent, Thursday cannot survive the encounter with the wilderness. His passing is inevitable, like that of Hatfield or Doc Holliday, part of a process – cauterising, distilling – out of which the nation is forged. At the film's end, we are introduced to an embodiment of the America to come in the form of another of Ford's babes, the offspring of Michael and Philadelphia – Michael Thursday York O'Rourke.

Fort Apache is a film of antithetical energies, a liberal critique of militarism that culminates in a conservative defence of tradition, at once both revisionist and reactionary, a film that employs Ford's dual vision to have it both ways. The cloud of dust that frequently hovers over the film's military actions hints at the ambiguity with which they are seen. *Fort Apache* draws directly on the war fought against the plains Indians of 1876 that resulted in the Seventh Cavalry's pursuit of a large force of Sioux and Cheyenne. Under the leadership of George Armstrong Custer, a battalion of two hundred men were cut off from the rest of his command and slaughtered in the battle of Little Big Horn. Initially hailed as a hero, Custer was also criticised for a megalomania suggested by the writing of his autobiography, *My Life on the Plains*, at the age of thirty-five. This latter view of Custer is reflected in Arthur Penn's *Little Big Man* (1976); the earlier *They Died with Their Boots On* (1941) stars Errol Flynn in more heroic mode.

What Ford's film omits is the fact that the Indians were forced to leave their reservation due to the invasion of white miners after the discovery of gold in the Indian Black Hills territory of the Dakotas. The war that followed was waged by American troops over land, with the cavalry acting as an expansionist arm of US policy. In a familiar strategy, the film's action displaces the imperialist and racist policies of the government onto villainous individuals – Meacham, the 'blackguard', as Thursday terms him, and Thursday himself.

From this perspective, Custer and Thursday can be seen as national heroes whose personal ambition disguised an imperial agenda, their deaths sacrifices that enabled the ruthless pursuit of America's dream of Manifest Destiny. Ford simultaneously exposes the Custer/Thursday myth as bankrupt and attaches Thursday to the noble traditions of the military. Standing at the window, on which ghostly images of the troop are reflected, York looks off and eulogises the army:

> The faces may change, and the names, but they're there, they're the regiment, the regular army, now and fifty years from now. They're better men than they used to be. Thursday did that. He made it a command to be proud of.

By demonising the Apache as savage and inferior, Thursday had given himself permission to surpass them in violence and unscrupulous action, while wrapping himself in the banners of duty and glory. Ford ruthlessly analyses this process, but by an ideological sleight-of-hand suggests that his behaviour was aberrant rather than dominant national policy. Yet what is the purpose of the campaign York is leading against Geronimo as the film ends? Nothing in the film can account for further action against the Apache, given their sympathetic depiction. Suppressing the historical economic determinant for the action leaves the film with a void, which it fills with the suicidal vainglory of Colonel Thursday, whom it finally recuperates. Ford's selective history, allowing him to affirm his idealised America, strains and finally tears *Fort Apache*.

3 *Godfathers* (1948)

'I'm a poor cowboy and I know I've done wrong ...'

As the films of the cavalry trilogy show, Ford found the short-story form very productive as source material to flesh out to a movie's feature length. *3 Godfathers* is another example, although one where expansion is modest. To escape the pressure from studios to repeat successes, Ford often tried to make a smaller picture for himself, as he would

'Bright star of the early Western sky': Harry Carey in *Straight Shooting*

put it. Following the epic *Fort Apache*, with its large cast, complex thematics, dense texture and elaborate set-piece battles and dances, *3 Godfathers* provided that relief.

Testifying to the appeal of its sentimental narrative, five film versions have been made
from Peter B. Kyne's short story, *The Three Godfathers*. First made as a short feature
under the story's title in 1916 starring Harry Carey and directed by Edward J. LeSaint,
it had been remade by Ford with Carey in 1919 as *Marked Men*. William Wyler would
add another version in 1929 floridly entitled *Hell's Heroes*; Richard Boleslawski's version,
Three Godfathers, would follow in 1936. The favourite of his silent films, Ford was
remaking *Marked Men* with Carey's son promoted to a starring role. The personal connection is underlined with the first image, the sun setting behind a rider who guides his
mount to the crest of a hill, gazes off and lifts a hand to remove his hat and scratch an
ear. Anyone who has ever seen any of Carey's films (including his performance as chairman of the Senate in Frank Capra's *Mr Smith Goes to Washington* [1939]) will instantly
recognise the gesture. The dedication reads: 'To the memory of Harry Carey, Bright Star
of the early Western sky . . .'.

Given his imperious temperament, Ford was not predisposed to acknowledge mentors or influences – he would usually mention his brother, Francis, and Griffith, for
whom he had ridden in *Birth of a Nation* (1915) as a Klansman. But he had told
Bogdanovich that 'Harry Carey tutored me in the early years, sort of brought me
along'.[42] Thus the dedication, poetically accurate as far as it goes, hints at a larger debt
in the context of the baby Jesus narrative's own guiding star. Ford had been lucky to

form an association with the older and more experienced Carey as early as 1917, with *The Soul Herder*. Going on to make some sixteen shorts in the 1910s with the star as Cheyenne Harry Henderson, they would work together on more than two dozen productions in all. Typically, the volatile Ford would eventually break off relations with his first major collaborator and sidekick, and never really repair them. It is no coincidence that *3 Godfathers* was produced in 1947, the year after Carey died.

The appeal of the material for Ford is obvious. The film ends on Christmas day as an outlaw staggers out of the desert bearing a baby and guided by a mule and colt, as prophesied biblically. His two sidekicks lie dead in the desert, to which they had all escaped after a bank robbery. Coming on the dying mother, they had delivered the baby, become its godfathers and embraced the mission of its rescue. Much under the influence of Victorian melodrama, silent-film plots often recycled themes of redemption, in which unsavoury rustlers and robbers see the light. Preferring a more realistic style than his competitors, who had made the cowboy a comic or flashy type, Carey had gravitated early to the good-bad hero. *Straight Shooting*, the only Ford/Carey silent to survive, appears exemplary of the formula. A henchman hired by big cattle rangers in a struggle over water rights with farmers, Harry comes into contact with a settler family traumatised by the murder of its son. Responding to the patriarch and his daughter, he joins them against the ranchers. In the original release, *Straight Shooting* ended with Harry bequeathing the daughter to a steadfast rival so that he could ride on to the next hill, still a frontier nomad. In 1925, a reissue offered a happier conclusion, in which Harry pairs off with her. The different finales neatly underline Carey's ambiguous appeal – the character could go either way.

Ford scholars cannot but respond with interest to such a rare early example of the director's work. The idealisation of the victims is to be expected, given Victorian stereotypes, but Ford goes further, creating a holy family with graveyard scenes and a solemn grace celebrated before meals. Interesting, too, is a pictorial style that often frames action exteriors through doors and windows. Such typical Ford designs undoubtedly had their roots in the static camera and theatrical sets of the time. Carey's good-bad character provided another career-long focus for Ford. Are these characters a source of disorder that threatens the stability of the community? Or are they vehicles for justice and progress, a necessary antidote to society's weakness and rigidity? Coordinated with the Western's historical conventions, the morally complex hero could be fine-tuned to order, as happened with Carey in the two endings of *Straight Shooting*.

For Ford, whose work invariably positions the family as the basic social unit, the character tends towards the status of the black sheep. A sentimental construct, fallen, rootless, incorrigible, in Ford's hands the figure could take on any number of complexions, ranging from the innocence of Ringo to the neurosis of Doc Holliday to the tragedies of Ethan and Tom Doniphon; in *3 Godfathers* the complexion is both melodramatic and comic. The struggle between order and anarchy that underlies the black sheep is at the centre of Ford's vision, and accounts for the persistence of the type in his work. Nothing if not a moralist whose heart lies with the family, law, duty and tradition, Ford also strongly identifies with the misfit and the maverick, insisting on society's need for their energy and contribution. It is because Ford is so implicated in both perspectives that the films achieve the complexity and force that they do.

A theme must face resistance in realising itself: the greater the effort to defeat its theme, the more dense and substantial the work. This partly explains why *3 Godfathers*, with its explicitly religious action, is a charming but modest piece. At its richest, Ford's cinema is implicitly spiritual in nature. This is one reason why he found the Western and the settling of America a vital source of material, the Christian nation and the untamed land, the faith of the pilgrims – '*In God We Trust*'. The historical material is rife with characters and structures that can provide symbolic parallels and rise to allegory – the journey and the pilgrimage, the pioneers and the Chosen People, the new settlements and the Promised Land.

Torn between the common man and the charismatic hero, between *Lucille the Waitress* (Ford's first credited film in 1914) and Lincoln the saviour, Ford could always find amenable material in the theme of service. With Ford, what you saw was what you got. 'Just a hard-nosed, hard-working, run-of-the-mill director' who knew nothing about art was the pose – but it fooled no one. That Ford could even try it on was amazing in the face of his extraordinary success with heavyweight material like Liam O'Flaherty's *The Informer*, John Steinbeck's *The Grapes of Wrath*, Richard Llewellyn's *How Green Was My Valley* and Eugene O'Neill's *Long Voyage Home*. Often, such literary projects were delivered to Ford because his style and concerns were perceived as perfect for the material: the betrayal of an Irish Judas; the passing of the old order; the journeys of the dispossessed and the lost.

Ford regularly complained about the philistinism of his producers, but the fact is he enjoyed greater freedom than most. The one sustained period where he chafed under an authority as autocratic as his own was at 20th Century-Fox with Darryl F. Zanuck. Ironically, stretching from 1935 to 1946, from *Steamboat Round the Bend* to *My Darling Clementine*, it comprises a period that produced some of Ford's richest and most personal works. In the face of this enormously successful collaboration, Ford may sound ungrateful, but with Zanuck he was working for a hands-on producer as well as an ambitious and flamboyant impresario. If the studio head brought him material like Steinbeck's novel, he was also a meddler as far as Ford was concerned. Wheeling and dealing for properties, Zanuck would project a whole year's productions with assigned stars and directors, and closely supervise the film-making, visiting sets, viewing the rushes and firing off memos. Above all, he loved the editing process, taking the director's cut and disappearing to emerge later with a trimmed, rejigged or even expanded final cut. Is it a coincidence that Ford declared his independence and formed his own company after *Clementine*? Asked if he was pleased with the outcome, Ford often maintained that he had never seen the film. This is certainly plausible.[43] Given that Zanuck had final cut, Ford often simply escaped to his boat, the *Araner*, sailing off immediately after he had finished shooting. Zanuck had the reputation of being the best cutter in Hollywood: let him do it. In any case, Ford maintained that he edited a film in his head as he shot; the film would assemble itself regardless of who cut it.

Although a former editor such as Robert Parrish, who is credited as sound or sound-effects editor on the five films from *Young Mr Lincoln* to *Tobacco Road* (1941), has supported this contention ('Ford didn't need an editor'), it would seem something of an exaggeration, perhaps a rationalisation.[44] Ford shot at a lower ratio than most, providing fewer angles, but the editor could still have an enormous impact. If it were

Zanuck, indeed, more shooting could be ordered, speeches and close-ups inserted, whole endings changed. In *The Grapes of Wrath*, Zanuck had written and directed Ma Joad's final speech: 'We keepa comin'... We're the people.' Ford had approved. But with *Clementine*, the director had had to give way on his preferred ending, truer to the film's spirit, in which the couple had settled in Tombstone. Moreover, Zanuck had trimmed a half-hour from Ford's version, and had inserted a kiss at the end when a preview audience had laughed at the couple's handshake.[45]

In any case, following the formation of Argosy with his longtime friend and fellow militarist, producer Merian C. Cooper, Ford had decisively changed his production circumstances. Reflecting this, his first film, he admitted to Zanuck, appeared 'not a sound commercial gamble, but my heart and faith compel me to do it'.[46] An adaptation

'Can't you see the star?'

of Graham Greene's *The Power and the Glory*, *The Fugitive* would provide an unparalleled opportunity for Ford to assay the religious head-on. The result, a passion-play allegory set in Mexico in which Fonda's persecuted priest is the object of a manhunt, was a positively medieval effort fraught with symbolism and portentous lighting effects. Argosy found itself in the red.

The Fugitive revealed the downside of a greater freedom from studio pressures and commercial formulas, barriers to push against, build on or subvert that can generate creative solutions. Yet Ford's next project, despite the Western dress, did not constitute much of a retreat. Indeed, the controlling myth in *3 Godfathers* is again the Christian, operating openly in a network of parallels and references: Christmas, the baby Jesus, the three wise men – 'I'm one of 'em!' insists William, the Abilene Kid (Harry Carey, Jr). But more to the point are the miraculous elements, the biblical prophecies and divine interventions. The Kid insists that it is all providential – 'can't you see the star?' Other symbolic elements are more integrated. Stopping at a pool's edge to water horses and fill canteens prior to their attempt on the bank, the three principals are reflected upside down, the shot hinting at their distorted values. Taken on to fuel their impure crime, the water is appropriately soon leaking away from a bag punctured in their escape. An even greater sin, the waterhole at the oasis where mother and baby await them has been wrecked, suggestive of a world in chaos, threatening the extinction of new life. Once in the desert, with their water gone, they will have to work together to extract more from cactus, and ration it jealously, to keep their charge alive. The water is life, renewal, rebirth – holy water.

If *3 Godfathers*, like *The Fugitive*, is dominated by its Christian agenda and lacks the ambivalence that gives Ford's best work its depth, its piety is tempered by its relaxed comedy and pace. A dark melodrama at its base with the survival of the family at stake, the fallibility of its brave heroes, their warmth and humour, make the film a far more popular and accessible entertainment than its predecessor. The familiarity of the Western iconography and of the Ford regulars also contributes. As Bob Hightower, leader of the three desperadoes, John Wayne has his charisma adjusted to ensemble status, presumably because in the company of Jesus all men are humble, including America's number one box-office star. He is here the first among equals, as the godchild's name – Robert William Pedro – makes clear. Armendáriz's character – Pedro, Pete, 'the Mex' – comes last in the string of names. Racism? The actor who had starred in *The Fugitive* and had a major role in *Fort Apache* was a far more established performer than Carey, who was only now joining Ford's stock company.

Given that the film is less about godfathering than stepmothering, its action a shouldering of maternal duties by the desperadoes, it is absolutely logical that Carey's young William, icon of the family and the feminine, should be the film's heart and soul. Does not the Bible prophesy that a child shall lead them? It is the Kid's faith that drives the trio on through the desert, as it his Bible that tells them to head towards New Jerusalem, and that guides Hightower to follow the burro and colt out of Death Valley. William alone knows that it is meant to be – 'You think this is all just chance?' It is Carey's mellow baritone that performs 'Shall We Gather at the River' over the babe's mother, buried at the despoiled waterhole. And the Kid is the first to die, his childhood prayer on his lips: 'Now I lay me down to sleep.'

Not that Pedro is marginalised. Finding the dying mother (Mildred Natwick) about to give birth, the three are unnerved, but it is Pedro who rises to the occasion. Call it ethnic profiling: the Mexican bandit is seen as the most humble, the most reverent, the most in tune with nature. Ford frames him in a shot from within the wagon, solemnly approaching to assist the mother; it is as if he is about to enter church. Minutes after the Kid is gone, Pedro will fall and break a leg. The second martyr, he will ask Bob for a weapon 'for the coyotes', and say a prayer for little Pedro. When a shot rings out momentarily, we excuse the sin – Pedro ends his suffering and meets his Maker, at peace with himself. Wayne's Hightower alone will survive, the most sceptical and worldly, he who had bitterly thrown the Bible away. He will falter, lying down to die, but his comrades' ghosts will nag him on until the mirage or hallucination or miracle – we can take our pick – of the ass and colt to lean on and be guided by. He arrives in New Jerusalem in the darkness, to hear 'Silent night, Holy night'.

All three are reformed, redeemed, reborn. As they go on deeper into the desert, they deteriorate physically, suffering grievously, losing horses, packs, belongings. They describe an ironic but logical progress, their pain the price of being cleansed, the baggage they renounce emblematic of the past's burdensome roles and behaviours. The irony extends to the pursuing posse led by Welcome's sheriff, Ward Bond's wily schemer, Perley 'Buck' Sweet. Plotting his moves like a chess champion, cutting the robbers off from water at every turn, Buck's pursuit is a model of the community's values, an orderly, methodical, efficient process. Yet the closer they get, the more benighted the posse becomes, mistaking the dynamited well as their quarry's work. At the end, when Buck enters the saloon after Hightower, he draws his weapon convinced that he is pursuing a blackguard; tragedy beckons.

He should know better. On arrival in Welcome, Arizona, they and the sheriff, rising from behind the flowers, may have appeared to be on opposite sides of the law, as they are of the fence around his garden. Ford must have enjoyed laying out the scene, with its classic oppositions – the law and the outlaws, the garden and the desert, the settled and the nomadic. But the three had charmed Mrs Sweet (Mae Marsh), especially William, whose mother also used eggshells in coffee grounds. Such traces of domesticity would prove prophetic, as all three readily embrace their surrogate Mama roles and responsibility. Supposedly hard cases, the three have nothing but decent impulses from the start. Noble Bob, like an older brother, tries to dissuade young William from joining in the bank job – it is a sizeable step from rustling a few cows. A model of misplaced loyalty, the Kid will not hear of it – 'I ain't backin' down.'

An unnatural undertaking (they abuse Welcome), the robbery exiles them to the desert, where an early shot shows them arduously climbing a steeply rising hill, an image of disorder and imbalance. Elsewhere, they are staggering silhouettes against the parched land, in the dark despite the merciless sunlight. But it is all a trick of Ford's double-dealing. The good-bad guys, once they have introduced disorder into the garden, will be all good. They will compete comically over the baby's name, refuse their share of water and take pride in caring for it – Bob oiling the baby with wagon-wheel grease, Pedro doing the nappy and William singing lullabies. Their honour and loyalty are never in question: the last wish of a dying mother is inviolable.

The premise is both comical – three men and a baby, the helpless males – and charming, the black sheep being feminised, redeemed, uplifted, entering the garden. A divine comedy and spiritual fable, it is simple, clear, transparent. To dismiss the film on the grounds that it wears its faith on its sleeve would seem ungenerous; study of both Ford and the Western would be the poorer without it. Revealing with unusual clarity Ford's core themes, *3 Godfathers* also demonstrates the genre's mythic adaptability away from the historical.

She Wore a Yellow Ribbon (1949)

'Lest we forget.'

With *Fort Apache*, *3 Godfathers* and *She Wore a Yellow Ribbon*, Ford cemented his collaboration with Frank Nugent, who would go on to script many of the director's later works: *Wagon Master*, *The Quiet Man*, *The Searchers*, *The Rising of the Moon* (1957), *The Last Hurrah* (1958), *Two Rode Together*, *Donovan's Reef*. Throughout his career, Ford naturally gravitated towards the same writers who knew his work and needs. Thus Laurence Stallings shares script credit with Nugent on both *3 Godfathers* and *Yellow Ribbon*, and has sole credit on one of Ford's favourite films, *The Sun Shines Bright* (1953). *Sergeant Rutledge* and *The Man Who Shot Liberty Valance* would both be scripted by Willis Goldbeck and James Warner Bellah, author of the short stories that provide the source for the cavalry trilogy.

Lamar Trotti is another writer Ford worked with productively. Their films together can be seen to constitute a series of Americana subjects: *Judge Priest* (1934) and *Steamboat Round the Bend* (both starring the period's popular folk hero, Will Rogers), along with *Drums Along the Mohawk* and *Young Mr Lincoln*. However, working with Zanuck meant Ford sometimes had relatively little input on scripts. Thus Nunnally Johnson's scenarios for *The Prisoner of Shark Island* (1936), *The Grapes of Wrath* and *Tobacco Road* were all projects on which he did not collaborate.

Such an arrangement may seem more limiting than it in fact was. Ford was offered these films because, however infuriatingly uncooperative he could be, Zanuck recognised the material as ideal for the director. Moreover, Ford's antipathy for excessive dialogue is well known; essential Ford lore relates how he would answer complaints of being behind schedule by tearing pages from the script. Ford scholar Tag Gallagher provides one perspective:

> His movies seem rather to have been conceived directly in visual terms (and not so much antiliterary, as aliterary, in origin). Ford never outlined what he was going to do on paper, and he treated his finished script almost as a preliminary outline. Once on set, huge quantities of pages would be discarded, much dialogue would be improvised, all the staging and cutting (rarely indicated in the script) would be 'invented'.[47]

Ford's own characterisation of the process is useful:

> You don't compose a film on the set. You put a pre-designed composition on film. It is wrong to liken a director to an author. He is more like an architect, if he is creative. An architect conceives his plan from given premises – the purpose of the building, its site, its terrain. If he is clever, he can do something within these limitations.[48]

Before Nugent, by far Ford's most enduring creative bond had been with Dudley
Nichols, beginning with *Men without Women* in 1930 and stretching through some eigh-
teen productions to *The Fugitive* in 1947. Unlike Nugent, who apprenticed with Ford,
Nichols was a veteran Hollywood writer who over a long career worked with George
Cukor (*Heller in Pink Tights*), Howard Hawks (*Bringing Up Baby* [1938], *Air Force*
[1943], *The Big Sky* [1952]), Fritz Lang (*Man Hunt* [1941], *Scarlet Street* [1945]),
Anthony Mann (*The Tin Star* [1957]), Leo McCarey (*Bells of St Mary's* [1945]) and Jean
Renoir (*Swamp Water* [1941], *This Land is Mine* [1943]). Despite this impressive body
of work, as well as his insistent praise for the visual, Nichols has been seen as a literary
writer whose work tends toward the theatrical and symbolic. Yet such tendencies are not
pronounced in the accomplished films cited above, nor in some of his Ford-directed
scripts, such as *Stagecoach*. Nevertheless, Ford's pictorial style does evolve from a silent-
era aesthetic grounded in expressionism during the 1930s and 40s into a more
disciplined poetic realism. Moreover, this early expressionist influence is strongest in
The Informer, *The Long Voyage Home* and *The Fugitive*, all scripted by Nichols. Dominated by an oppressive use of lighting and décor, these films betray a conscious effort to
express inner states. Nichols speaks of the fog in *The Informer* as 'symbolic of the grop-
ing primitive mind' of Gypo.[49] The economic disaster of *The Fugitive*, where he was his
own producer and could indulge his experimental instincts, may have been salutary. In
any case, it would represent Ford's last stand with Nichols.

Just two years after the showy *Fugitive*, *She Wore a Yellow Ribbon* incarnates Ford's
mature poetic style at its purest. The credits feature a yellow ribbon blowing beneath a
crest of crossed sabres, while a classical thematic score that will rework the title song
throughout plays like a spirited overture. The invocation of pageantry and the romantic, martial air could not be more apt. Ford has said that the film was his attempt 'to
copy the Remington style ... to get in his color and movement'.[50] After the crisp, beautiful black and white of Archie Stout's photography in *Fort Apache*, Ford embraces
Technicolor to produce facsimiles of the West's most prolific and accomplished painter,
Frederic Remington. The effect is appropriately emblematic, capturing prototypical
characters and events with a vigour and detail that often fixes the images as a series of
iconic murals. 'So here they are', the narrator tells us at film's end; but what we have seen
is something beyond a photographic record of the nation's horse soldiers. The impulse
we often sense at work in *Yellow Ribbon* is a didactic nationalism, not unlike *Drums
Along the Mohawk*, the making of a picture-book American history lesson. Neither real
nor an official history, it is rather a narrative spine of historical anecdote – the retiring
officer, his tippling top sergeant, junior officers competing for a damsel's ribbon, a failed
mission, a powwow with an ancient chief, a last-minute intervention to prevent hostilities. Cavalry life below glory's radar, as it were.

'*Custer is dead*.' The film's opening narration implies an immediate sequel to *Fort
Apache*, but Kirby York(e) will not return until *Rio Grande* (curiously picking up an extra
letter along the way). Meanwhile, *Yellow Ribbon* cannot but strike us as a conscious effort
to bookend the earlier film with a wholesale contrast of the films' protagonists. Ford's
belief in strong heroes is not indiscriminate: the nature of leadership, a dramatically
juicy question, is often at issue. Certainly, the overarching theme of the trilogy's films
is the question of leadership's proper sphere, the relationship of authority and its

boundaries, the dialectics of ends and means. The cavalry Western's conventions of the heroic military unit isolated on a frontier where law and duty may not always coincide offered an ideal framework. With its hierarchic command, operational missions and complex community of soldiers, family members and civilians, the fort offered Ford a diverse range of personalities and conflicts to explore and dramatise. Thus Wayne's retiring Captain Nathan Brittles could not differ more sharply from his predecessor:

Thursday	Brittles
father in name	father to all
widower *sans* memories	widower still wed
narcissist	selfless
autocratic	benign
lecturer	teacher
demonises the Indian	respects the Indian
precipitates war	prevents war

This pattern of contrasts extends to a wide range of narrative incident, theme and detail. The question of boundaries, for instance, is addressed early on in both films at both official and domestic levels. Paralleling the trespass of the Indians who have left the reservation, in both films the forts' junior officers propose to take young women off the post into the desert. The respective tone of the two scenes is indicative of the films' very different worlds. In *Fort Apache*, Michael and Phil's excursion ends with the discovery of the massacred patrol. Thursday's reaction to the unauthorised outing is outrage, characterising the young officer as uncivilised and forbidding him further contact with Phil. While Thursday's concern is understandable, his rigidity positions him against the values of the community, and raises doubt about his judgment that events will confirm. *Yellow Ribbon*'s couple never gets off the post, with Brittles extracting Olivia Dandridge (Joanne Dru), but allowing Pennell (Harry Carey, Jr) to continue ('*Picnicking*, Mr Pennell?') on his own. Here, as in the film's climax, a genial Brittles prevents possible problems, and amusingly establishes his patriarchal role. As opposed to Cohill (John Agar), his rival who had refused the couple permission to exit the post, Pennell's judgment is put in question, whereas Thursday's excess obscures the issue with Michael.

The education of his officers will be one of Brittles's successful projects. Pennell will give up his dream of going east to pursue an aristocratic life ('Delmonico's'), and will re-enlist. Cohill will take over the command and win Olivia. They learn 'how to cross a river under fire', the film's construct for maturity and manhood. This motif feeds into the major thematic of the film, the primacy of tradition. Cohill will become York; Olivia will be his Mary. At the prospect of their retirements, Brittles's top sergeant, Quincannon (Victor McLaglen), will moan that 'the army will never be the same', but his captain will correct him: 'The army is always the same.' In *Fort Apache*, continuity is maintained at tragic cost with a compromised tradition, a fractured, papered-over history. Essentially a romance and comedy, *Yellow Ribbon* celebrates a harmonious world where storms are weathered, failures transcended, loyalties honoured and merit rewarded.

Thus where notions of bravery had divided *Fort Apache*'s world, loyalty is *Yellow Ribbon*'s – like the army's – glue. '*Lest we forget*' reads the inscription on his new watch, the troop's gift to teary Brittles. 'Forty years a soldier,' he sighs on his last day, but the army also will not forget, calling him back to a chief scout's commission. Tyree will fetch him, the ex-Confederate captain who is ever himself laconically addressing the issue of proper boundaries ('That ain't my department'), sensitive as he must be to the limits of a non-commissioned role. Ford plays a long uncut scene with Tyree and Brittles on horseback in two-shot against the horizon, trusting the ex-stuntman, Ben Johnson, to hold his own with a bemused Wayne as he delivers an extended and incisive analysis in his Southern cracker's accent of what the buffalo's return may mean to the Indian tribes that are gathering – albeit adding that he is not paid to think.

The exemplary soldier, Tyree continues his own fealty to the South and the past. When Brittles's last mission fails to get the women to the Sutro Wells way station in time to defend it and ensure their safe departure from danger, the troop arrives to find a dying Trooper Smith. Delirious, he addresses Tyree as Captain, returning to an earlier life as Brigadier-General Rome Clay, and dies. Emblematic of the South's sacrifice, his heroism folded into the republic's traditions, Smith/Clay is buried with a rebel flag, attended by a grateful Tyree and his ex-Confederate fellow troopers ('We thank the captain'). Ford provides a vintage funeral scene, a massive mesa behind shrouded with fog, reddish in the twilight, as Brittles speaks respectful words over the grave. Apparently a digression, the sombre scene is at the centre of the film's concerns.

Having been torn in *Fort Apache*, the fabric of the military as family is repaired in *Yellow Ribbon*. An early scene features Brittles and his commander, Major 'Mac' Allshard (George O'Brien), sadly reading the names of the dead at Little Big Horn. The list is long. Moments later Brittles is at his wife's graveside performing his regular ritual, watering

Loyalty is the theme

the flowers and telling her 'we had some news today'. He tells her that George Custer and Miles Keough are dead – 'You remember Miles.' In Ford, the army and war are family affairs, the domestic costs always counted. It is indicative of Ford's values that the long central section of the film, Brittles's final mission, should comprise the army's effort to move the women – Olivia and Libby Allshard (Mildred Natwick) – out of harm's way. It is typically a mission that celebrates the heroism in failure, if not the glory in defeat. Besides getting to Sutro Wells too late, earlier they had failed to rendezvous at the relief point to provide reinforcements for a pinned-down patrol, as a badly wounded Corporal Quayne reports. The soul of concern, Brittles swallows and praises a 'good clear report'. The failures are thus multiple, as Brittles tells Olivia, kicking a burning wagon so that its collapse punctuates the point. 'We missed the stage, Miss Dandridge,' he tells her and walks away, suddenly an old man. Thereafter, they will have to 'sneak out' in the darkness to return to the fort. Draining the images of colour, Ford shoots his horse soldiers in dark silhouette against low-lying white clouds behind, the stark black-and-white images of the slowly moving procession creating an eerie effect of statuary, marking the lowest point in the troops' travails.

But there are small triumphs too, as with the celebrated scene of the surgery performed on Quayne, conducted by the troop's doctor (Ford stalwart Arthur Shields) in the back of a slowly rolling wagon in the teeth of a breaking storm. The cavalrymen march forward over the rough terrain, Brittles having ordered a dismount to slow the wagon and to facilitate the doctor's task. An increasingly tipsy Libby – 'Old Iron Pants' – holds the swaying lantern, and shares the patient's alcoholic anaesthetic and a bawdy version of the title song – 'Round her leg she wore a yellow garter'. Lightning crackling overhead, the wagons silhouetted against the stormy sky, it is a larger-than-life drama, with the agitated doctor feverishly working on the delirious, wounded trooper. When Brittles passes word down the line of the surgery's success, the troops cheer and mount up. The brave Quayne is an icon of their mutual love and camaraderie, one for all and all for one. A marvellous set piece, the scene was an audacious coup by Ford, who tells the story of how he ordered his cinematographer, Winton C. Hoch, to keep filming during the storm, and of how Hoch did so under protest and then, ironically, won an Oscar. Disputed by the cameraman, who also worked with the director on *3 Godfathers*, *The Quiet Man* and *The Searchers*, visual triumphs all, the blarney is typical of the maligning and abuse the temperamental Ford often indulged in with collaborators.

An equally exhilarating scene in its way is Tyree's escape from a band of Indians while riding point. Evidence of a more benign Ford, Ben Johnson had been promoted to a small speaking part in *3 Godfathers* after rescuing several people at risk during *Fort Apache*'s production. Exploiting the former rodeo champion and stuntman's skills, Ford has Tyree furiously flee the hostiles in an extended run through the desert with the majestic Big and Little Mitten mesas of the valley behind him, a breathless sequence that ends in a venerable chase climax, the daring leap across a chasm between two bluffs. It is a pleasing divertissement and a small chapter on horsemanship. Scenes like these give the film an affirmative energy that more than balances the darkness and fog, and the plot's small failures. Indulging his usual ambiguous vision, Ford presents a piece ostensibly about life's disappointments that in fact turns out to be a celebration of national spirit – ingenuity, persistence, drive.

Other moments testify to a similar goal: to show America things American. Thus the buffalo are greeted like old friends, the ladies hailed forward so that we can look over their shoulders and experience the awesome spectacle. Ford treats the Indian procession that the party comes across in the same respectful manner: we sense the effort to be true to the Remington originals. The film is about duty, loyalty and tradition, and in its construction bears witness to those same standards. Shooting at eye-level or slightly from below, Ford creates deliberately painterly images of mythic figures. The respect is evident in the rich detail that we are invited to notice: the costumes and lances, the horses and travois. Repeatedly cutting back to the Arapaho warriors from the observing Brittles and Tyree, Ford gives us time to take in the images and register their strangeness and beauty.

We sense a similar objective in the film's treatment of its location. Only *The Searchers* competes with *Yellow Ribbon* in the scale and care of its use of Monument Valley. Again and again, we are given time and opportunity to take in the magnificent scenery, the huge isolated sandstone rock formations rising from the desert floor. As in *Stagecoach*, we do not sense man's puniness in this world but rather an elevation of stature, the forging of a bond and balance between the human presence and the redoubtable environment. The didactic impulse, the desire to entertain by opening a window on pioneer days and ways, is ever present in Ford, but most consistently at work in *Yellow Ribbon*. As the troop slowly winds its way through the desert or mountain chasms, we are treated to long-distance perspectives of the breathtaking spatial coordinates of the West that early Americans had to navigate. At the end of their failed mission, Brittles has to leave Cohill behind at the river to hold off the hostiles so that the women can be returned safely. Ford holds an extended deep-focus shot across the water as small specks of troopers ride towards us from the far distance, its dynamism slowly but inexorably growing as the space diminishes. Again, it is the kind of shot indicative of the desire to afford an audience subtle pleasures and simultaneously teach something about the space, pace and dynamics of travel on horseback. The same impulse is there in the repeated shots of the wagons labouring up grades spilling goods out their back, and the struggle to keep them upright in tight turns and strong currents. Such small delights are not inconsequential to the film's larger ideas. Each such image in the troop's progress is part of the film's chain of meaning, a signifier or synecdoche or, indeed, a snapshot of the pioneer effort and immigrant experience that is fundamental to the nation's history and ideology, the struggle to conquer the environment, to overcome, to become, to accomplish and achieve.

'Romantic, isn't it, Miss Dandridge?' Cohill is bitter that he may be losing the fair Olivia to Pennell and tea parties in the East. But, of course, for the audience, the sarcastic crack is clearly meant to suggest that we are seeing the reverse, an unromantic, unvarnished army life, that of 'the dog-faced soldiers, the regulars, the fifty-cents-a-day professionals'. The narration at the end, sharing in Cohill's bitterness, continues: 'Only a cold page in the history books to mark their passing.' But, of course, the film itself, like so much of Ford, has it both ways, managing to create a day-to-day domestic history rather than an account of famous battles, and yet applying its own romantic varnish despite the pose of realism.

'But wherever they rode, and whatever they fought for, that place became the United

States.' The film ends with an unnervingly direct declaration from the God-like narration of the army's imperialist function, as if to pay with some aggressive lip service for its omission in both *Fort Apache* and its own depictions. Like much of Ford, *Yellow Ribbon* is ripe for ideological critique. The film proposes to tell us how it was – '*So here they are*' – but proceeds to give us a transparently bowdlerised history, a history for the whole family, as it were, a dreamscape. American propaganda? At the centre of the film is John Wayne as Brittles, the touchstone of its values and a paragon of devotion to duty. Rising every morning to inspect the troops, in the evenings he takes his little stool to the grave to report to Mary. He spends his last night in the army asleep in his chair by the three-framed panel of pictures of his wife and daughters, more a small altar than a photo display. At the heart of the film is Brittles's gold watch, presented to mark a lifetime's service from the troop and funded by all the soldiers ('even Hochbauer'). Approaching geezerhood, the captain fishes out glasses to read the inscription and wipes away a tear. Brittles can be seen as an older Captain America (taking over from Fonda's Wyatt in *Clementine*), the benevolent Father, father to the troops, father to his junior officers, father to Cohill and Olivia, and by the end, The Great White Father to the Indians as well.

Wayne was playing a much older man in a role that dominates the film, an ambitious project Ford had offered the actor after seeing him in Howard Hawks's *Red River* (1947), where he also portrays a patriarch. Although Ford had really created the star, he admitted that he had never thought he could act. Facing such scenes of unabashed sentimentality, as when Brittles talks at his wife's grave, Wayne perhaps remembered advice from the director:

> He's not afraid of those kind of scenes ... As a matter of fact, one of the things he told
> me early in my career was: 'Duke, you're going to get a lot of scenes during your life.
> They're going to seem corny to you.' And he said, 'Play 'em. Play 'em to the hilt. If it's
> *East Lynne*, play it.' And he says, 'You'll get by with it, but if you start trying to play it
> with your tongue in your cheek and getting cute, you'll lose sight of yourself ... and the
> scene will be lost.'[51]

Sentimentality is certainly one of the criticisms voiced against Ford by some who object to an excess of feeling. Such strong emotion, however, seems critical to the films' vision, to stories that celebrate faith, loyalty, duty. In the same way, the broad humour he often injects through his larger-than-life Irish also leaves some viewers cold. Again, it is diffi- cult not to see in this 'comic relief' dark hints of the costs of doing the military's business. There is the bottle hidden in the captain's room to provide an obligatory morning nip for the burly Quincannon, who attends him like a stand-in for the departed Mary. And there is the massive violence, however bloodless, of Quincannon's wrecking job on his mates and the sutler's bar. Interesting, too, is Brittles's admission that he has not had a drink 'since that day', looking at his wife's photo; had Brittles sought solace in the bottle?

In *The Searchers*, without a hint of irony, Ford has Ward Bond as a Reverend/Captain of Texas Rangers warn a young cavalry officer that *he* is the dangerous one, not 'those childish savages out there'. In *Yellow Ribbon*, Brittles provides one last exuberant passage by having the troops rousingly stampede the warriors' ponies, averting violence and punishing the proud Indians by forcing them to walk home, like so many naughty children. Earlier he had ridden into the Indian camp to parley with Pony-That-Walks in the hope that the ancient chief could restrain his bellicose youth. Chief Big Tree, who ten years earlier had provided the grotesque Blue Back in *Drums Along the Mohawk*, here delivers one of the most persuasive representations of the Native American in any Western. Ford's trick is that he gives us two old men commiserating rather than cowboy and Indian, the pair defined by a common humanity rather than race. The chief tells Brittles that he has come too late, that his warriors now follow Red Shirt: 'You come with me. Hunt buffalo together. Smoke many pipes. We are too old for war.'

At the end, back where he had started, the film describing a circle rather than the forward linear aggression of *Fort Apache*, Brittles leaves the party in honour of his appointment to go out and report to his wife. He takes up his position by the grave, the fog and low clouds shrouding the valley's mesa beyond, as Cohill and Olivia and the other couples dance inside, inevitably, to the film's title melody. It is, of course, the perfect song for a film that filters history through feelings and conjoins the epic and the domestic.

She Wore a Yellow Ribbon labours in the shadow of *Fort Apache*, the first of the trilogy, whose fissured narrative has proved far more interesting to most critics. This is perhaps understandable: the more complex the work, the more involving we may find it. Something of the same dynamic seems to be at work with the way in which *The Searchers* rather than *My Darling Clementine* is seen by many as the key Ford film. But these preferences also reflect the ideological tilt in contemporary film culture. Like *Liberty Valance*, *Fort Apache* and *The Searchers* are revisionist corrections of the genre's dreams – dreams like *Yellow Ribbon* and in fact the great bulk of Ford and the mainstream of the genre itself. Yet the temper of the times should not be allowed to throw these films into the shadows. At the height of combat over auteur theory in the 1960s, critics of that era were wont to make sweeping pronouncements. Claude Rivette's claim that one could not love the cinema if one did not love the films of Howard Hawks comes to mind. In the same vein, it is possible to suggest that one cannot love the Western if one does not love *She Wore a Yellow Ribbon*.

Wagon Master (1950)

It is illuminating to compare *The Fugitive*, *3 Godfathers* and *Wagon Master*, the cavalry films as I have styled them. All come within three years, and are sandwiched between *My Darling Clementine*, the three cavalry films and a comedy for Fox, *When Willie Comes Marching Home* (1950). Surprising, given their proximity to each other, they are all examples of Ford's smaller, more personal works. Argosy must have been liberating. If *The Fugitive* had bombed, Ford had done his duty and found satisfaction: 'To me, it was perfect.'[52] A sentimental, nostalgic undertaking, *3 Godfathers* allowed Ford to tip his hat to one of his first teachers as well as his religious faith.

Wagon Master would be equally fulfilling. A favourite, with a script largely by Ford himself (although Nugent and Ford's son Patrick are credited), it 'came closest to being what I had wanted to achieve'.[53] The covered wagon and its journey are a basic icon of the Western, the province of simple people, settlers as opposed to the charismatic cowboy or dashing cavalryman. If this suggests ordinary men and not stars, *Wagon Master* put its money where its ideology was, casting Ben Johnson and Harry Carey, Jr in lead roles, likeable character actors who were becoming fixtures in Ford's world. Johnson, the ex-stuntman and cowboy, had performed with distinction in *Yellow Ribbon*, and Carey was fresh from a star's credit on *3 Godfathers*. Nonetheless, essentially they were supporting cast, minor players who fit perfectly into Ford's world, supplying authenticity and colour.

Wagon Master provides a bookend for *Stagecoach*, which it everywhere recalls, from the rustic aw-shucks heroes and the survey of frontier types, to the journey structure and stress on character and geography rather than action. Cheating a little, Ford opens with a pre-credit scene *in medias res* that introduces the Clegg family in a robbery that culminates in the Clegg patriarch, Shiloh (Charles Kemper), apologetically killing a bank teller who had had the temerity to fire on and wound him: 'I wish you hadn't done that, son.' A tease, the brief scene is followed by credits that feature a lively river-crossing by the Mormon pioneers interrupted by a lengthy horizon shot of five darkly silhouetted riders, a subtle prophecy of a confrontation to come. But there will be little violence, even after the fugitive Cleggs have arrived and hijacked the train, until their threat to kill the Mormons' leader, Elder Wiggs (Ward Bond), forces the wagon masters to intervene at the very end. Sandy (Harry Carey, Jr) has been smuggled a weapon – an oversize handgun, a family blunderbuss rather than a gunman's sidearm – by Prudence (Kathleen O'Malley), the red-headed gal he's been flirting with. Like the wanted poster superimposed over the Cleggs' opening robbery, the gun is an iconic reminder of the frontier's violence.

However, such schematic references apart, *Wagon Master* stays focused on its characters and journey, an undeniable source of charm being its broad range of groups and personalities. Capable of the most delicate nuance, Ford was also fond of broad, even vulgar effects, indifferent to violating narrow notions of coherency. Here a wide spectrum of types and acting styles is Ford's strategy in stressing the frontier's diversity.

The heroes – horse traders turned wagon masters – are sweet characters (spiritual relatives of *3 Godfathers*' Buck Sweet), essentially family men at heart. Asked to guide the Mormon train through the mountains, they turn Elder down, but are shortly revealed to be on the fence – literally. They loll on the barrier that runs alongside the trail the wagons are taking. A matriarch, Sister Ledeyard (Jane Darwell), blows her bullhorn, as if calling for help, and the cowboys look at each other: 'We warned 'em, didn't we?' 'That red-headed gal', muses Sandy, and then he breaks into song: '*I left my gal in old Virginny*', and Travis picks it up, '*Fell in 'hind the wagon train*'. They ride off, Sandy to get their horses, Travis to head off the Mormons, who are already going in the wrong direction.

Good-hearted, the cowboys are aware that the train will mark a trail for a hundred families to come, to a valley Elder tells them has been 'reserved by the Lord'. Easygoing and practical men, they are innocent of ideology but nevertheless divine tools, 'the answer to a prayer', as Elder puts it. As in *3 Godfathers*, we are to understand that Providence is providing. The Mormons have the vision and the will, but no practical knowledge; the traders have the know-how, but are drifters. Of all the groups surveyed, however, the wagon masters alone show imagination and openness. They cannot refuse the appeal of families whose lives will depend on their kind of skills.

Coded as nomads, Travis (the traveller) and Sandy (the desert) possess frontier knowledge and can mediate between the settlers and the wilderness. However, the wagon masters have integrated little of the wilderness's brutalising effects; they are not prisoners of the desert. With the impatience of youth, Sandy is eager to use the gun to stop the Cleggs, but Travis – a typical Ford hero – is slower to act, postponing the inevitable until the very end. He will chuck the weapon away with disgust after the Cleggs are all dead. Like the three godfathers, Travis and Sandy are ripe for domestication. At the end, each will be driving a wagon with a lady at their side, Sandy with his Prudence, Travis with Denver (Joanne Dru), a feisty member of the travelling theatre group the train discovers stranded in the desert.

Apart from their fitness for violence, the film's only other nod towards ambiguity in Travis and Sandy's make-up is their inclination towards sharp horse trading. This is forgivable, however, especially in the sale to the town's marshal of a mount that has 'peculiarities or failings', namely the ability to go loco on Sandy's shrill whistle. The trick will come in handy to divert the lawman when his posse happens upon the wagon train in the desert, after the Cleggs have taken it over. Like the other groups, the town's law is seen as self-preoccupied and narrow, drumming the Mormons out of town and proving irrelevant to the real challenges of the film's world.

To the sophisticated theatre folk, introduced in amusing fashion drunk on snake oil imbibed in the absence of water, the wagon masters are rubes. But the troupe in turn appear immoral to the Mormons: Russell Simpson's Adam is all for sharing some supplies and leaving them behind, a death sentence according to Travis. The righteous Mormons themselves had been evicted from town by its marshal for their polygamy. Ironically, it is now the outcasts who are threatening to cast out others. All of these disparate groups are marks for the solipsistic Cleggs, whose loyalty is likewise exclusively

The Mormons: Ford's Chosen People

to their own. These are descendants of *Clementine*'s Clanton family, right down to the whip both patriarchs wield. Ford codes them as satanic – snakes, according to Travis.

Ford sees each group with a sharp eye. Someone as obsessed as he with the clash between social regulation on the one hand, and the 'peculiarities and failings' of individuals on the other, could do justice to them all. Seizing on the Mormons as embodiments of the religious spirit of pioneer America, he portrays them in a fondly critical light. Fordian creatures through and through, they are both conformist and peculiar, their leadership all quirks and contradictions. As the combustible Elder, Ward Bond explodes over the price of a horse, but will be steely-eyed and calm when the Cleggs draw their guns. He and the tyrannical grouch, Adam, are Mormon alter egos: Elder constantly curbs Adam's zealotry, which borders on the inhumane; Adam regularly pulls Elder back from apoplexy. Sister Ledeyard adds a matriarch's compassion and – like a cavalry bugler – succours the troops with her bullhorn. Punctuating the decision to add the show folk to their party, she blows away in time with fife and drum, the latter manned by Mr Peachtree, another cameo from Francis Ford as one of the entertainers.

Like *Stagecoach*, *Wagon Master* celebrates the American frontier's diversity, which here extends to friendly Native Americans as well. There is no 'Mex', as in *3 Godfathers*, no African-American or Asian; the diversity reflects the melting pot of mid-century pre-civil rights America, a brew into which invisible racial minorities of the time did not melt. Playing again on the radical gap between frontier cultures, Ford gets agreeable gag mileage out of the stuffy zealot Adam stomping arm-in-arm with the Navajo visitors around a shadowy campfire to the beat of booming drums. Ford offers an affectionate portrait of the Indian as if to balance against his slanderous projection of them as irredeemably savage in *Rio Grande* a few months down the road.

Until the Cleggs arrive, there is a leisurely flow of colourful incident with the amusing character groups, all in their own worlds. Minor conflicts surface, as when Sandy and a Mormon suitor for Prudence square off. Surprisingly oblivious to the shortage of water, considering they have had to drink the snake oil to keep going, the theatre troupe members come in for discreet chastising from Travis for wasting it. As the community continues on the move, Ford's detailing stresses the fatigue and dry, dusty terrain. The discovery of water, always a sign of renewal in Ford, will relax the tensions and provide a break. There is an obligatory frolic, and some flirting between Denver and Travis, who threatens to join her for a bath. A dance highlights the occasion, the couples pairing off and performing the ritual with great vigour and charm. Ford had used Mormons for the open-air dancing in *Clementine*, and his deployment of the hard-working Mormons as extras in *Fort Apache* had given him the idea for foregrounding them in a film.

At this high point of solidarity, the Cleggs arrive. Ford marks the moment with a prolonged silent montage of the individual members of the two groups in huge close-ups as they size each other up. There are no moral shadings: even without the benefit of the pre-credit sequence, who's who is transparently clear. Surpassing the insensitivity of the Mormons and the show people, the Cleggs are psychotic in their contempt for the rights of others. Ford sketches them in broad, dark strokes. A fraud, Uncle Shiloh talks of Christian charity and genially appropriates Elder's piety – 'the Lord is always providin' ' – while one of his sons cocks a rifle. Two of the brothers are cracked, leering chil-

JOHN FORD: FOUNDING FATHER

dren: bald Ford regular Hank Worden and the hulking James Arness, who would go on to TV stardom in the *Gun Smoke* series. Abuse of an Indian maiden by another of their number results in a whipping by Elder to mollify the Navajo. Inappropriate justice for a Clegg, Shiloh feels, although he himself uses a whip on others. At the end, he will threaten payback, the death of Elder and the destruction of the priceless seed grain the wagon carries, the hope for a new nation.

The trek West, with its challenges and adversity, the transformative encounter with the frontier, will unite the ragtag community, another of Ford's pioneer Americas. The parasitic, godless Cleggs will be eliminated, the show folk will lose their worldliness and cynicism, and the wagon masters will be drawn into the Mormons' dream of a Promised Land. Showing a surprisingly selfless side, Alan Mowbray's snake-oil salesman will insist on following a wagon that has disastrously overturned with his own, as the terrain becomes steep. In turn, he will be surprised when one of the troupe's ladies climbs aboard to keep him company. The journey will educate and mature its various travellers, forging an awareness of common goals, a community on the move, as in *Stagecoach*.

The courtship of Prudence by Sandy will be all a matter of glances, bows and dances. But Travis will have to win Denver, who, like her predecessor, *Stagecoach*'s Dallas, is coded as soiled, and thus cannot afford to risk belief in the possibilities of renewal. Flirting in reverse, a passive-aggressive, she will repay Travis's thoughtful gift of an extra pair of sturdy shoes from Prudence with references to his 'lady friend'. She vows she is not interested – '*That* rube?' But when he begins to propose, she will flee headlong to hide in a wagon, tossing a cigarette after a single puff and with it the veneer of hard-edged cynicism over her all-too-vulnerable emotions.

If the Mormon presence foregrounds the biblical, *Wagon Master* largely avoids the explicit religious symbolism of *The Fugitive* and *3 Godfathers*. Rather, Ford harks back to the iconic style of *She Wore a Yellow Ribbon*, albeit in a sober black and white. The approach is still painterly but with a distinctly lower pageantry quotient. With its attenuated sketch of a narrative, its small vignettes and light-hearted romance, *Wagon Master* appeals for attention through a kind of indirection. There is no war or cavalry, no obsessions or family conflicts – indeed, ironically, the only literal family prominent is the Cleggs.

The stakes are always high in Ford – invariably, the good health of the republic. But although the music of the Sons of the Pioneers that accompanies the river-crossings and mountainside treks is lusty and full-blooded ('*Wagons West are rolling . . .*'), the action is not. Testifying to the reduction in dramatic weight, the pilgrimage here involves no sacrifice or martyrs, no loss of a cavalry troop or a Chihuahua. A string of gentle episodes, jokes and anecdotes, the film achieves a purity that approaches abstraction. It is to be expected that there will be heroic images of the journey, and we are not disappointed with the extreme long shots of the wagons inching along the crests of high mountain ranges. But as in *Yellow Ribbon*, there is a fascination in the small details, the pioneers digging tracks for wagons where there are none, Travis burning off a lariat rope's end, or riding his horse into the river for a bath. The film ends in the Promised Land, with Sandy stealing a kiss from Prudence, the wagon masters and Elder united in song and the final shot of a pony making it to shore.

The film's freedom in its extensive use of music, as in Ford's next production, *Rio Grande*, strikes some viewers as quaint. But few conventions of the genre were as established as inclusion of song and music in the post-World War II era. Modern audiences may be ignorant of the aptly named Sons of the Pioneers: like the singing cowboy heroes of the period, the group was a popular example of the Western's capacity for marrying music to its narratives. Such ignorance can cause viewers to overlook the narrative function of song, as when Sandy and Travis answer the invitation (or is it a divine command?) of Sister Ledeyard's call by breaking into melody as a sign of their joining the train. Ford's films were legitimate horse operas in the sense that they were shaped like musicals, scripted and designed with songs in mind. Asked about dances in his films, Ford explained:

> They're all folk dances, and they're part of the story. I like folk dances; they're very amusing and the cowboys do them very well. Down in Arizona, the Mormons are beautiful square dancers, so we only had to put on a dance and they'd pitch right in and do it wonderfully well.[54]

Crucial in creating a rich sense of a bygone era, Ford's music also celebrates that era. Made with freedom and love, Ford gives us an ancient, fabulous world where those same values are in the ascendant. In comparison, *The Fugitive*, with its tortured priest, seems weighted down with dogma, and even *3 Godfathers*, with its sagebrush Magi, seems more than a touch laboured. Puzzling, almost mysterious in its simplicity and whimsy, *Wagon Master* insinuates its spiritual character gently and diplomatically, while simultaneously expressing delight in its own unique and vital world.

Rio Grande (1950)

'I'll take you home again, Kathleen.'

Although last in the order of the cavalry trilogy's production, *Rio Grande* positions its hero, Lieutenant Colonel Yorke (John Wayne) between *Fort Apache*'s Kirby and *Yellow Ribbon*'s Brittles. Change Brittles's name to York(e) and we have the Wayne officer hero at different stages: the confident assertive young captain in *Fort Apache*; *Rio Grande*'s seasoned, sensitive, vulnerable officer; the ageing veteran in *Yellow Ribbon*, sagacious, relaxed, fulfilled. At the risk of making him sound like Shakespeare, all the ages of man, or at least of Ford's cavalryman.

The political climate is correspondingly different. Each of the characters faces different challenges in the conflict of morality, duty and law, and the military demands with the Indians call for different strategies as well. In the revised order:

> *Fort Apache*: Bitter at Washington's neglect, Thursday abuses his authority in pursuit of glory and leads a charge that destroys his command. The Indians remain in the wilderness, an undomesticated force.

> *Rio Grande*: Despite government strictures that forbid pursuit, Yorke is allowed to make an unauthorised sortie into Mexico. Breaking the chain of command, the troop crosses the border, routs the hostiles and rescues the child hostages.

> *Yellow Ribbon*: Both the army and the Indians are essentially domesticated forces. Chief
> Pony-That-Walks, Brittles's contemporary, is retired, and the bellicose younger braves
> are out-manoeuvred by the captain, who bends the timing of his own retirement in
> order to avoid war. An enlightened government retains his services.

This order illuminates the intermediate status of *Rio Grande*'s Yorke, which goes beyond
age. He is in between, incomplete, a pilgrim, neither totally integrated nor wholly alienated. Like Brittles a caring father as a commander, he leads a tired troop into the
settlement as the film opens. Mindful of the community's gaze, he visibly girds himself
as he approaches the wives anxiously looking for their men. He praises the troopers for
their service, rewards them with access to the sutler's bar and instructs them to cool their
mounts before dismissal. Like Brittles, Yorke is a father to his men. But the father lacks
a family. Where the spirit of his dead wife guided Brittles, Yorke, like Thursday, lives in
a no woman's land, an emotional desert, the result of having been separated from his
wife and son since the Civil War. Kirby had been forced to torch their home, her family's plantation, under orders on Sheridan's march through the Shenandoah Valley; his
Kathleen (Maureen O'Hara) has never forgiven him.

So they are still fighting their own Civil War, except it is a cold war. Washing out of
West Point, Jeff Yorke joins the army as a common soldier and is assigned to his father's
command. Kathleen follows him to the fort, hoping to buy him out of the corps. Thus
the antagonists are brought together, with Jeff between them, after fifteen years, the
ancient wound still unhealed. Jeff replaces Bridesdale, the destroyed home, as a site of
conflict, threatening to perpetuate the schism: 'Ramrod, wreckage and ruin – still the
same old Kirby'; 'Special privilege for the special-born – still the same old Kathleen'.
Their witty, poetic combat neatly suggests how right they are for each other, while defining the danger of repeating the past's impasse.

The film's larger conflict, the struggle to achieve the authority to pursue the hostiles
into Mexico, is actually smaller, secondary, if not quite a MacGuffin. It is simply resolved
when General Sheridan (J. Carrol Naish) gives permission for a 'mission with no record',
as James Warner Bellah's story was entitled. The major conflict that structures *Rio
Grande* is between Yorke and Kathleen. In this, the film is another Ford that marries family melodrama and the Western, a woman's film in so far as it explores issues of identity
for Kathleen, who has chosen her home over her husband, and a male melodrama in its
focus on Yorke's struggle to balance duty and family, heal scars and pull his life together.
One image, in particular, combines these strands of the film's roots and appeal with typical Fordian elegance. It comes late in the film, when a wagonload of children has been
abducted. 'Kirby – those children,' agonises Kathleen. A brief shot captures the mothers
on a ridge above, silent, their long aprons blowing in the wind. The horizon shot, a trademark of Ford's and signifier of masculine action and glory in the genre's iconography,
is here sensitively deployed to suggest the courage and faithful service of these waiting
women.

For Jeff, it is a coming-of-age story as he navigates the tests that will demonstrate his
independence and competency. These compensate somewhat for the paucity of action
in the film generally. Among the new recruits, Jeff has forged immediate friendships with
Tyree (Ben Johnson) and Boone (Harry Carey, Jr). The ex-wagon masters from Ford's

previous film flaunt their Texas horsemanship when challenged by the command's top sergeant, Quincannon (inevitably, Victor McLaglen), to ride in the style of the 'ancient Romans' – standing balanced on two horses as they furiously circle the area and then clear a leap over a barrier. Egged on by his buddies – 'Get it done, Johnny Reb!' – Jeff also has a shot, rides well, but falls at the jump.

He passes a second test with flying colours, giving as good as he gets from a trooper who has spoken ill of his father, but refusing to divulge the issue when Yorke materialises. Dispatched by Yorke to accompany the wagons of women and children being sent out of harm's way, he carries word back to the fort of the Apache abduction of the children. In the final action in Mexico, he, Tyree and Boone sneak into the village church where the children are held, and secure their rescue. Wounded in the action, his father asks Jeff to pull the arrow from his shoulder. Jeff gets it done, earning his spurs as a soldier, acting with authority in a situation where his father and the army had been dependent on him. The arrow's removal has symbolic force – his successful integration into his father's way of life makes possible the family's integration, healing the ancient psychic wounds. Kirby can finally acknowledge their relationship: 'Son ... help me to my horse.'

Ford also structures the other relatively slight military actions to emphasise their relevance for the community and family. Thus the returning troops at the film's opening and close are seen from the families' point of view, and with a fainting Kathleen we come face to face with violence as an Apache attack frees captives. She has never forgiven Yorke for having chosen his duty over his family, the military over her home. Action on the frontier, together with her son's involvement, now forces her to face the importance of the military and of Kirby's role. She comes to realise that service allows no choice. Duty calls.

We accompany Yorke on another fruitless trip to the Rio Grande. The river is the barrier he must eventually cross to achieve his military objective. Camping for the night, he walks by the water at dusk as his soldiers sing softly. Close-ups are relatively rare in Ford; here he had directed Wayne to walk toward the camera, and keep his expression blank, to allow the environment to act. The failing light, the flowing river behind, the plaintive tune – these combine to give the soldier a lonely, haunted look, oppressed by other borders.

Stealthily entering the village and the church where the children are held, Jeff and his mates will fire through apertures shaped as crosses when the attack comes, signifiers of the higher command that countermands the orders of governments. Rousing enough, the action cannot hold a candle to the film's psychological journey. With *Rio Grande*, Wayne and O'Hara were rehearsing for their passionate roles in *The Quiet Man*, which Ford had long tried to set up. A deal with Republic Studios insisted on another film as insurance; Ford fell back on the Western. *The Quiet Man* would be all courtship, stormy and complicated, as its Irish-American hero becomes entangled in old-world customs that prevent him consummating his marriage. Five years later in *The Wings of Eagles*, their union is a strained affair, Wayne's navy pilot an absent father, O'Hara hitting the bottle to deaden the pain of a lonely life. Suffering conscience, Wayne vows to give up his nomadic ways and returns, only to trip on a toy and break his back.

In *Rio Grande*, both of their characters must grow to melt the ice, each accepting that neither has dominion over Jeff. On his arrival, Yorke had immediately addressed the new recruits, promising them a dangerous life, perhaps death. He was talking to Jeff. He next has him brought to his tent, where he coldly affirms the primacy of duty, refusing to acknowledge their bond. The boy agrees – he is there as a soldier. After Jeff departs, Kirby stands in the boy's place checking his son's height, then awkwardly leans back to sneak a look through the tent's opening. It is Ford being cute, sketching Yorke's private inclination – to bend over backwards for the boy. In fact, Jeff trumps Kirby, managing the distance between them better than his father. At each test – the trick riding, the soldiers' fight, the final campaign – Yorke lives and dies with his child, as all parents must. He is a helpless witness, an agonised father as well as a soldier.

Balancing Kirby's painful encounter with the domestic, Kathleen's growth comes through her exposure to the wilderness. Her peace offering to Kirby is the washing of his laundry, a complex gesture. At one level it signals an aristocrat's comeuppance, her renunciation of privilege. Symbolic of the revising of her views, it also foreshadows her acceptance of the wife's role; she has not done her duty to her husband. On arriving, she had trivialised the cavalry's role: 'All this danger to serve people unborn – and probably not worth serving.' But as she shares the army's way of life, experiences danger and sees the threat to the community, she begins to understand the transcendent demands of service: 'To my only rival – the Army.'

Jeff's presence brings into focus the stubborn personalities of both his parents: his father is 'just like you, Mother'. The scene of her entreaties and demands that Jeff resign runs for forty seconds in a single set-up, the two huddled together in the tent, O'Hara producing a single tear on cue, on Jeff's line – 'I refuse to sign it.' The shot demonstrates why Ford rarely delivered close-ups to his editors, aware that their insertion would destroy the psychological intensity. In an earlier moment, Kathleen enters and inspects Kirby's tent, looking at his bed, one hand pressing in on her stomach. There is the sense of pain and a mute eroticism, the remembrance of their life together. A music box's tune stirs feelings – '*I'll take you home again, Kathleen*'. In her reverie, the emotions play across her face, of longing, hurt, sad acceptance.

The gesture of the arm held against the body is the kind of instinctive detail a consummate professional like O'Hara could contribute in her work with Ford. Although he would walk a scene through and rehearse, Ford was famous for avoiding discussion of the material. A mysterious, almost telepathic method steered actors towards a desired result. O'Hara was one of his favourite performers:

> You become so tuned to him, one word of his becomes a volume. You become aware he understands the story and knows how to get it out of you. It's a frame of mind he creates. He puts you at ease and sets you free to think, and you can move easily.[55]

Rio Grande's heady drama arises from the way the characters are conceived. Idealised figures, Kirby and Kathleen are individuals of great purity and epic scale in their depth of feeling and sweep of action. Their righteous wrath and pain are outsize: Kirby counts the days apart – 'fifteen years, two months, seven days'. As in all the cavalry films, the presence of McLaglen's hulking top sergeant confirms the mythic dimensions of the conflicts. A bearer of his commander's past, he is 'the arsonist', Yorke's tool in the torching of Bridesdale: 'And there's the black hand that did the dirty deed.'

Ford turns again to period songs to trigger his characters' recall of the past's sad battles – both personal and national. For Ford, music could create 'auditory images', and in a story so allied to melodrama its expressive power was especially useful. Ford's Western – the sixth of seven he would direct in the decade from 1946 on – would again feature the Sons of the Pioneers. As the Regimental Singers, they serenade Kirby and Kathleen, their love the stuff of song: '*I'll take you home again, Kathleen*'. Except for three brief cuts back to the singers, Ford plays the scene on their faces, both stricken by surprise at the choice of tune. Shutting her eyes, close to tears, Kathleen leans towards a nervous Kirby, who murmurs that the song was not his choice; she wishes it had been.

At dinner with General Sheridan, the singers return to perform yet another tune fraught with memories ('*Glory-O, Glory-O*') of the Shenandoah. The songs define the issues, comment on the action and raise the temperature, but above all they evoke the past, a lived-in history that gives the relationships density and the film its gravitas. Seeing each other again, sharing a world, *remembering* – the present and past come together for the film's characters. *The Man Who Shot Liberty Valance* has been seen as Ford's great meditation on memory. Less spectacular but equally haunting – both for its characters and us – memory also serves *Rio Grande*.

Ford's standard double take on the frontier prevails. We hear stern lectures on the austerity of the cavalry's existence, and see the rough camp of tents and wagons; a creek bed serves as a makeshift prison. Like Tombstone, however, this harsh setting is utopian as well, with its white table-clothed dinners, officers in formal dress and strolling singers. Another of Ford's immigrants, an eye-patched Frenchman, Captain St Jacques (Peter Ortiz), adds a debonair touch.

A key scene tests Kirby. Surprised to discover Kathleen in his darkened tent, he sweeps her into his embrace. Kathleen offers a deal: she is his if he releases Jeff, another

Potentially hackneyed material

invitation to put family above duty. Ostensibly a victory, it would ensure the loss of both; he refuses. With its backdrop of war and its passionate antagonists, the dashing cavalry officer and his highborn, high-spirited lady, *Rio Grande* is perilously close to the worlds of pulp and harlequin romantic fiction. But the material is elevated by Ford's conviction ('Play 'em!') and historical vision.

The demands of duty must be addressed. Kathleen has failed her husband, Kirby has failed his son, the cavalry has failed its mission. Nothing if not another well-made film, *Rio Grande* resolves its conflicts neatly, the borders crossed, the schisms breached. Tyree is a test case for all in the dialectics of law and duty, family and military. Wanted for murder, he has the whole command bending the law to let him escape. Details are unimportant to a feeling Kathleen – a boy like that has to be innocent. A family affair, the killing had to do with a sister's reputation. Threatened with arrest, Tyree escapes on the commander's horse – as if to drive home to Kirby the need to countenance special treatment for special cases, of family over military duty, for once.

'Our boy did well,' a wounded Kirby tells Kathleen as he looks up at her from the travois. She takes his hand and falls in, marching by his side like all the other army wives. She has learned: they also serve who wait their soldier's return. There is a final sun-drenched scene, as the troop turn out to witness the presentation of commendations to Corporal Bell, whose wife had been lost in the Apache attack, and to troopers Tyree, Boone and York. There is also a medal for Navajo scout Son of Many Moons – Ford comfortable with a token good Indian. Threatened again with arrest, Tyree this time appropriates the general's mount and gallops off as a dimpled Kathleen twirls her parasol in time to the strains of 'Dixie', a typically perverse Fordian endnote. The Southern belle has come home: the war is finally over.

The Searchers (1956)

> What makes a man to wander
> What makes a man to roam
> What makes a man leave bed and board
> And turn his back on home?

One of the great journey films, *The Searchers* testifies to the power of myth. The journey is a trans-cultural, archetypal form, mimicking life itself, its rites, passages and cycles. The quest, the going and returning, the tests and encounters – these speak to the mysterious journey each of us makes in our own existence. Myth crystallises the pattern for us by giving it heroic form, inspiring us to meet our own challenges with bravery and honour.

What makes men and women to wander? Is there some higher truth only available to the wanderer? Is it somehow unheroic to settle? Is movement life itself? At the root of the journey film, and fundamental to its appeal, are the dialectics of stasis and movement, constancy and change, settling and wandering, inside and out, home and away. As the many films set almost completely within the community evidence, the Western is by no means always a journey film. Nonetheless, by definition Westerners are travellers, immigrants, pioneers. In terms of the structure of oppositions that make up the Western's spine, it is the classic pairs of the wilderness and civilisation, of the settled versus the nomadic, that define the cultural field within which Americans exist.

Thus for Americans, the appeal of forms like the Western, the journey film and road movie is quite specific, less archetypal than historical. In all cases, this is a matter of family history. Somewhere in each American family there is a forebear, perhaps distant, perhaps recent, who made the choice – courageous? foolhardy? inspired? – to 'turn his back on home'. For these immigrants and pioneers, the act was paradoxical – a leaving of home to find a new home, breaking up a family, embracing loss and dislocation, in hope of a better world. There are no stronger feelings in Ford's work than those arising from a keen sense of that paradox – of the questing that duty can demand and the yearning for home and family, of the lure of freedom and adventure and the pain of dislocation and loss, exile and wandering. In *Stagecoach*, above all, it is the dispossessed Dallas who voices eloquently the yearning for roots and a home: 'Haven't I any right to live?' In *Clementine*, the maladjusted Doc Holliday raises the state of dislocation to neurotic levels. That such turbulence is less a matter of culture and more one of self-knowledge, or its lack, is evident in Clementine's rapid assimilation, the pioneer schoolmarm to be. Literally overnight, the Earps themselves go from incredulous nomads ('What kind of town is this?') to Tombstone's settled authorities, guarantors of order. The deacon is clear on the importance of their role when they beg off attending church: 'Wal, keepin' the peace is no whit less important.' Those who do not keep the peace, however, may find themselves forfeiting the right to belong, if minorities even have that, as both Indian Charlie and Chihuahua discover.

In *The Searchers* the search for home and family is the force that drives all its characters. The epic figure of John Wayne's Ethan, the classic wandering hero, dominates the film. Strangely absent since the end of the Civil War five years earlier, Ethan is a divided soul when we meet him, a mystery figure hovering over the community, returning to a family he cannot join. The back story is denied us, but we are to understand that Ethan nurses love for Martha, who had married Aaron, the wrong brother. Is Ethan punished for his covetousness, or for a sin of omission? Even before the massacre his life is hell. On the evening of his return, he sits on the porch with the family dog and looks back to see the couple's bedroom door swing shut. Ethan is rootless, homeless. Like the Indian corpse whose eyes he shoots out, 'he travels between the winds'. It is this wrong marriage that inflects the tragic action of *The Searchers*, a history that is constantly threatening grotesquely to repeat itself.

Despite its title, *The Searchers* is also the story of two families, the Edwards and the Jorgensens, distant neighbours perched tenaciously on the West's front lines. Their resolve to stay, as opposed to neighbours who have retreated, will prove disastrous. The Edwards family will be devastated, Aaron and Martha, Lucy and Ben, all lost. Only seven-year-old Debbie (Lana Wood) and Marty – Martin Pawley (Jeffrey Hunter), the adopted son – survive, the captive and the searcher. 'Debbie ... Debbie ... Debbie ...' – the name bounces around the cramped space of the opening scenes. Ethan mistakes her for the Lucy of years ago, but the little seven-year-old, standing on a chair centre-frame, is emphatic – 'I'm *Debbie, she's* Lucy!' Ethan hoists her aloft – 'Debbie!' Moments later Martha will remonstrate – '*Debbie!*' – when she charms her uncle out of a 'locket' to match an earlier gift to Lucy. Ethan casually parts with a war medal, which we will next see around a Comanche neck. A stalwart, youthful soldier, Ben gets Ethan's sabre and promptly marches over to hang it in a place of honour on the mantel.

Ford only has a few brief scenes in which to fix so many names, faces and relationships before the Indians come. The Jorgensens will lose grown son, Brad (Harry Carey,
Jr), who courts the elder Edwards daughter, Lucy (Pippa Scott). Imprinting the sweethearts on our memory, Ford has the two younger Edwards children surprise them
smooching: 'Brad and Lucy, Lucy and Brad! Brad and Lucy, Lucy and Brad!' Abducted
with Debbie, Lucy's despoiled body will be buried off-stage by Ethan, who suppresses
news of her death until they come across the Comanche, one of whom wears Lucy's
dress, giving Brad false hope. Revealing her death, Ethan's volcanic rage will explode
when Brad asks: 'Was she … ?' 'You want me to draw you a picture?' Ethan will roar,
leaving it to the boy's – and our – imagination, a strategy Ford employs with the massacre victims throughout. The invitation will prove too much for Brad, who launches a
suicidal charge on the Comanche.

We will not miss Aaron (Walter Coy), husband and father. Ethan barks at the colourless character rudely as he flings him a bag of coins (evidently he is expected to pay his
way); Aaron squirrels it away too hastily. What could Martha have been thinking? Had
Ethan, like Marty who will risk losing his Laurie, been wandering when he should have
been courting? With typical perversity, the director goes to great lengths to get
everyone's name straight for us, but only hints at the history that drives the film. Andrew
Sarris sketched the crucial dynamics of a scene that can be overlooked too easily by inat-
tentive audiences:

The history that drives the film

This bumptious Bond character is drinking a cup of coffee in a standing-up position before going out to hunt some Comanche. He glances towards one of the bedrooms, and notices the woman of the house tenderly caressing the Army uniform of her husband's brother. Ford cuts back to a full-faced shot of Bond drinking his coffee, his eyes tactfully averted from the intimate scene he had just witnessed. Nothing on earth would ever force this man to reveal what he had seen. There is a deep, subtle chivalry at work here, and in most of Ford's films, but it is never obtrusive enough to interfere with the flow of the narrative.[56]

Ford felt he had made it clear:

Well, I thought it was pretty obvious – that his brother's wife was in love with Wayne; you couldn't hit it on the nose, but I think it's very plain to anyone with any intelligence. You could tell from the way she picked up his cape and I think you could tell from Ward Bond's expression and from his exit – as though he hadn't noticed anything.[57]

Bond may have also noticed Martha's earlier interruption of his face-off with Ethan, when talk had veered towards the question of wanted posters – '*Coffee* ... Ethan?' – a valiant attempt to ventilate the suddenly close atmosphere. Dorothy Jordan makes a very believable Martha, the loyal, nurturing matriarch who will collapse like a rag doll on parting with Debbie. But here, with her colour high, she is a woman marked by the sudden bloom of dormant passion.

Ethan is thus one of the most tortured of heroes in American cinema. Ford opined that his film was 'a psychological epic', and epic indeed is the crush of guilt that visits Ethan after Martha is lost to him, the silhouetted character bowed down in the dark doorway after the discovery of her violated corpse. The image is composed and lit with such purposeful design that it would seem too artful were it not for the black weight of despair it communicates. Only a scruffy cowboy, Ethan must nevertheless bear the outsize punishment of the gods like a hero in Greek tragedy. It is as if Martha in some private space, some mind's eye, had been both lover and mother to him, his coveting of his brother's wife – in itself blasphemous enough – an intolerable, Oedipal sin. Ethan rages at everyone, even cutting short the community's funeral services, unheard-of for a Ford hero. If not for his monumental pride ('*That'll be the day!*'), surely he would rail against the heavens, like Job: 'Why *me*, O Lord?'

When the family is massacred and Debbie abducted by the Comanche, their leader, Scar, comes into focus as a distorted reflection of Ethan himself. As if mocking the wrong marriage of the past, Scar has raped Martha, giving flesh to Ethan's own forbidden desires, and will eventually take Debbie as one of his wives to repeat the pattern with Ethan's niece. These monstrous violations are the actions of Indians, savages, red men invading the white world. A cosmic mockery: whose destiny is manifest, anyway?

Given these painfully personal experiences of Indian–white couplings, it is surprising how hilarious Ethan finds the accidental marriage of Marty to Look (Beulah Archuletta), his Comanche 'squaw'. Played for broad comedy, this wrong marriage culminates in Marty callously kicking Look down a hill when she attempts to share his bed, an act of stunning racism by both Marty and the director. If this is a strategy to implicate audiences in the characters' racism, the laughter the scene can generate suggests it is often too successful. Ethan's amused reactions make sense in a film that so clearly defines adoption as one-way, possible only if Indians enter the white world. But as if acknowledging its treatment of her as a non-person and making some small penance, the film shortly thereafter pauses over Look's body in an Indian village raided by the cavalry. 'Aw,' says Marty, 'they didn't have to do that.' Another misbegotten wedding, also in comic mode but far more serious in terms of the film's dynamics, between Marty's Laurie (Vera Miles) and the clownish Charlie McCorry (Ken Curtis), is interrupted at the last minute, rescuing Marty from Ethan's bitterness.

Is there any wonder that at times Ethan appears demented? Consumed by his quest and driven by furies familial, sexual and political, Ethan is a creature of passion, the civilised a thin veneer over the savage beast. Is his pursuit not flight? Does he not pursue himself? Rage is all. At the end of the film, with Scar dead and Debbie recuperated, Ethan will join that gallery of Ford heroes who shape a community they have no place in, the cabin door swinging closed to shut him out. The how-many-children-had-Lady-Macbeth questions that *Clementine* generates do not arise with *The Searchers*. There is no starting over for Ethan, no erasure of the past, no reinvention of self, no America.

The French title captures the soul of the film – *Prisoner of the Desert*. The world of *The Searchers* is not the feminised West of an earlier optimistic Ford. Ethan is not Ringo, Gil, Wyatt, the domesticated hero, settled, married, perfumed. The opening title identifies the year as 1868, but the feel of the film suggests earlier times, precarious years in pioneer history. The immensity of the landscape brooding over the lonely homestead speaks volumes about its vulnerability to savage forces. As Laurie's mother, Olive Carey's Mrs Jorgensen, puts it: 'A Texican is nothing but a human man way out on a limb.' But she goes on to predict the eventual American Eden, 'a fine good place to be'.

The seven-year odyssey in search of Debbie, the Holy Grail, covers all of Texas but never moves far from Monument Valley. Rarely used on such an extensive scale before by Ford, an unearthly barren world, the site is home to the obsessed Ethan, hospitable to his state of mind. The feminine of the French title *La Prisonnière du désert* points to Debbie, but the title seems more relevant for Ethan – although he is perhaps too much at home in the desert to be seen simply as its prisoner. We sense him coming into his own when the posse rides out, Martha and Debbie watching together, and the action shifts to the vast open cathedral of the valley. It is the wilderness, the world of the Indian and of Ethan, who moves through it like its spirit.

Ethan can be seen to define how completely the Western under Ford's direction appropriates the Native American world. Ford was wont to defend himself against charges of racism, and of his indiscriminate use of the Navajo as all-purpose injuns. He would point to the contribution his use of the location had made to the economy of the valley's Navajo reservation, and his acceptance as a blood brother, Natani Nez or 'Tall Leader'. Yet there are other measures of value, of intellectual and spiritual property. What the genre does generally, and Ford's films do in particular, is repeat the original sin, disenfranchising the earliest Americans and stealing their land. The sacred home of the native peoples becomes epic 'Ford country', the challenging landscape that forms the character of the American – the white American – nation. Imprinting the iconic images of red sandstone buttes and mesas on the nation's psyche, Ford was inevitably repeating the original conquest of Indian holy land by cowboy and cavalryman.

Coded as a creature of the wilderness, Ethan darkens the film, threatening to take it over. A big man, Wayne now carried the weight and authority of momentous campaigns into *The Searchers*. Ford and Wayne had been joined for the better part of two decades; the film would be their ninth collaboration. Together they had explored the world of pioneers in *Stagecoach* and the fate of ship-bound wanderers in Eugene O'Neill's *The Long Voyage Home*. After the hiatus of World War II, they had seen naval action in *They Were Expendable*, fought the trilogy's Indian/cavalry wars, and travelled to the Ireland of *The Quiet Man*. Wayne had become an extension of Ford, his vehicle and voice in deeply personal projects. But it is neither his size nor his history that makes Wayne's Ethan such an intimidating presence. Above all, it is the rage that vibrates from the character, the ferocity that cannot begin to face or fathom the essential reciprocity of his and Scar's savagery. In this, he is another, darker manifestation of the same transcendent Eurocentricity that had fuelled Mrs McKlennan, the matriarch of *Drums Along the Mohawk*, crazily nagging the Indians burning her home, and *Fort Apache*'s Thursday in his blind quest for glory. It is again Ford's analysis of how Manifest Destiny operates in personal terms – the Other exists at a lower, sub-human level.

Wayne saw *The Searchers* as a special film in his career, naming a son after his character. Discussing the film, he could at times match Ethan's blind, volcanic rage, as when he had defended Ethan's scalping of Scar to an interviewer – after all, the Comanche 'had fucked his wife', a confusion that fuels all manner of speculation. But *The Searchers* does not belong to an uncivilised Ethan and a savage America. Although it is often seen as a film dominated by its exteriors, Ford repeatedly frames the desert from windows, doors and cave mouths, insisting on the interplay of light and darkness, the wilderness and home. This visual motif reflects the script's own grounding of the action in the community of survivors, the world of love, family and rocking chairs. Nugent had been collaborating with Ford since *Fort Apache* in 1948. His script for *The Searchers* achieves a rich density in its parallel and overlapping chains of characters related by blood, marriage and race, and in its progress into the desert and back, into madness and the final retreat from the abyss.

What does it mean to be alone? Home would not be worth longing for were it not seen by us to be so. With consummate mastery, Ford presents us with two scenes of arrival back to back at the outset of the film that vividly create its parallel worlds. The total blackness of the opening image breaking as the door swings open, the view extending through its frame to the bright desert beyond, reveals the lone rider moving forward in the vast distance. The cabin's inhabitants slowly emerge, each taking up their vantage point as they gaze off in awe at the approaching rider. '*Ethan*?' asks Martha disbelievingly.

It is Ethan. His weary appearance, the ex-army and wilderness-savvy costume, his imposing demeanour – all suggest an actor in history, an autonomous figure, a character of agency. Scar's name for him comes to mind – 'Big Shoulders'. The other burden the figure carries is solitude. Even before we become privy to Ethan's anguished loneliness and self-destructive nature, the opening creates an eerie sense of isolation around the character materialising out of the desert a forbidding self-sufficiency. The atmosphere is oppressive, his reception strangely formal. It is momentous, as if Ulysses or the prodigal son were returning, although not to the fold or – as *Stagecoach*'s Peacock might have it – to the 'family's bosom'.

The contrast Ford erects moments later could not be brighter, as Texas Rangers tracking apparent rustlers arrive, led by a bluff and hearty Ward Bond as Captain/Reverend Samuel Johnson Clayton. Generating enormous dynamism and brio, occupying the head of the table and the centre of the film's frame, Clayton immediately launches into breakfast ('O doughnuts, Sister!'), the family's women buzzing around him as he swears in 'volunteers' Aaron and Marty as deputies, switching roles effortlessly – 'You been baptised yet, Debbie?' The robust spirit of a proud pioneer household, as well as Ford's patently loving approach in creating it, is reflected in the depth of the image and the detail of the décor – the busy dining area and back bedrooms, the furniture and fireplace, the costumes and crockery.

Drawing our eye deep into the frame, Ford has Ethan emerge from a rear bedroom and move slowly forward to greet Clayton and replace his brother ('Stay close, Aaron') in the posse. Ethan and Clayton immediately square off, old adversaries cooling the cabin's atmosphere. Tension goes beyond personality. Ethan stands between Scar on the one hand, and Clayton on the other, between wilderness values and frontier justice – individual, violent, solipsistic – and the community's rational authority, God and the Law, which Clayton combines in his person. Ultimately, it is because Ethan is closer to Scar than to his own culture that he is so compelling dramatically and the film so challenging.

That challenge is incarnate in the film's tough insistence on the rightness of the searchers' mission. Ford richly evokes an ideal pioneer community, only to burn, rape and pillage it, the sky above stained with the blackest smoke. It is an unprovoked attack inviting us to identify totally with the devastated pioneers and the vengeful Ethan. Their cause is just. Complicating things for the audience, however, Ethan gradually appears pathological in his fury, driven by hatred, madness, racism, firing his rifle furiously as if single-handedly to exterminate the buffalo. At the beginning, he barely tolerates Marty, whose Cherokee blood taints him. With Debbie approaching young womanhood and the likelihood of sexual congress with the Comanche, Ethan's quest changes: less search and rescue and more search and destroy; better dead than intimate with red.

Yet Ethan's racism is also the community's. But for Marty – whose own Indian blood provides perspective – the others are all for calling off the search, abandoning Debbie. Should we be shocked that racism infects the whole community? The allegorical swell of meanings basic to the genre, the thrust of the narrative plus the star system's iconic function make Wayne's Ethan nothing less than America itself, a symbol of the genocidal violence that won the West. Ford's great achievement with *The Searchers* is to go beyond *Fort Apache*, beyond where *Liberty Valance* will go, in exposing America's original sin. Using Wayne at the height of his stardom as the vessel for the national sickness, Ford transported his audience into the heart of darkness.

A hymn to America's nomadic soul, *The Searchers* is also Ford's great meditation on its troubled racist history. That the film is itself infected with the virus in its unequal treatment of white and Indian worlds is part and parcel of its complex and extraordinary power. If in some respects the film can be seen as an apologia for the persecution of the Native American, undeniably it can also be read as providing the grounds for an indictment of that action. Ford does not pretend to a moral authority neither he nor the nation possesses to recuperate its pioneers. In his later efforts to confront the issue directly and to pay his and America's dues – as in *Sergeant Rutledge* and *Cheyenne Autumn* – he will be far less successful.

Ideological analyses of *The Searchers* have argued that its great power derives from an unconscious displacement in the film's action of the black/white question in American society, our 'American dilemma'.[58] Alan LeMay's crude novel on which the film is based was published in 1954. Franklin S. Nugent's screenplay, written in 1954–5, made a host of crucial changes. In LeMay, Martin is 100 per cent white, Debbie does not become Scar's wife and ends up with Marty, Laurie marries Charlie, Ethan dies, race is not an issue. Shot in the summer of 1955, the film was released in May 1956, two years after the Supreme Court ruled that separate but equal segregated schooling was unconstitutional. But the suggestion that the film's conflict masks the turbulent reactions to real changes in the law of the land in the period, while suggestive, is in fact unnecessary to an appreciation of the film's relevance. Indeed, the notion that the Indian stands in for black can be seen as repeating the disenfranchising of the Native American, and of blurring the film's focus on the nation's primal events. *The Searchers* does not need to be deciphered: as it is, it remains a monumental effort that takes up America's cross, the racism that scars the national psyche.

As the years go by, marked by changes in the film's landscape and seasons – a winter's sudden snowfall – Ethan becomes implacable. They will find Scar 'sure as the turnin' of the earth'. The cosmic perspective notwithstanding, Ethan is burdened by tunnel vision. In the epic Shakespearian dramatic structure that Ford erects, Mose Harper (Hank Worden) is low man on the totem pole, the holy fool obsessed with his rocking chair providing another mirror image for the mad Ethan. Filled with hatred, yet yearning for the surcease that can only come with love, Ethan's heart will finally crack open as he lifts the Indianised Debbie high to the sky, bringing back into focus the child of his Martha. Jean-Luc Godard captured the dilemma of many a viewer in the politicised counter-culture of the 1960s with his response to the moment: 'How can I hate John Wayne upholding Goldwater and yet love him tenderly when abruptly he takes Natalie Wood into his arms in the last reel of *The Searchers*?'[59] The film's triumph of humanity over ideology was reproduced in Godard and many another audience member of the time, for whom Wayne stood as an icon of reactionary politics.

Ford's design is to force the audience to confront its own racist inclinations as Ethan's extreme state becomes clearer. One of Ford's feminised males, Marty and his judgments are a key factor in this process. One of the screenplay's most ingenious devices, his letter to Laurie returns the action to the community, distancing us from the searchers and filtering narrative incidents such as Ethan's demented attack on the buffalo through their perspective. The letter also provides comic insight into how little privacy a pioneer household offered, as the reading of news of Marty's accidental wedding to Look enrages Laurie and amuses Charlie McCorry, who ends the scene with his eye on her and a tune: '*Skip to my Lou, my darlin*''.

The family is Marty's world, increasing our sense of Ethan as outsider. Marty is consequently central to the comedy, which is designed to provide relief from Ethan's neurotic outlook. Twice the searchers circle back to the Jorgensen farm, and both occasions are seized on by Ford to soften the tone, as Laurie Jorgensen, Marty's impatient betrothed, and her itinerant beaux square off. Postponement of their courtship repeatedly threatens disaster, albeit typically disguised in knockabout violence – as in the mock fight with Charlie that ends in a handshake. The real enemy is out there, not within the family. Gaylyn Studlar has made the point that Laurie, overlooked in many accounts of the film, is a complex character who, as set off against the soft-hearted Marty, complicates the genre's normal oppositions between the passive feminine East and the active masculine West.[60] As Marty prepares to leave for a final rescue attempt, she tells him that Martha herself would prefer Debbie to die with 'a bullet in her brain' rather than be returned after her captivity.

However, the outsize comedy continues to the end. If Ford had cruelly booted Look downhill on her honeymoon, in an act of belated equal justice he has Captain/Reverend Samuel Johnson Clayton punctured in his pompous ass with a cavalry sabre wielded by the impetuous Lieutenant Greenhill. Played by Wayne's son, Patrick, the latter role is one of many filled by a family member in a film centred precisely on that theme, with Lana Wood as the child and Natalie as the grown Debbie, and mother and son, Olive and Harry Carey, Jr, playing mother and son. Appropriately, the film ends with Wayne holding his elbow as he turns away from the cabin, a habitual gesture of the senior Carey, Ford's early comrade-in-arms and the first of his black-sheep nomads.

At the outset very much 'He Who Follows', as Scar dubs him, Marty clearly grows in stature over the seven years of the search, quietly emerging as a balancing heroic figure to Ethan, although obviously lacking the latter's heft. Blindsided by the overbearing Ethan with the fact that his mother's scalp hangs from Scar's lance, he maintains his composure and is not dissuaded from entering the camp to rescue Debbie: '*That* don't change it.' It is Marty finally who rescues Debbie, killing Scar in the process. In another comment on Ethan's leadership, it is Marty to whom Mose gives the crucial clue to Scar's whereabouts. Playing mad to the Comanche so that he can escape, the cracked old geezer gets his reward, his rocking chair and the peace that comes with going home.

Scar also throws light on Ethan. He stands shoulder to shoulder with him, trading insults, the script and staging emphasising them as doubles. They enter his teepee to talk trade, and there, finally, is Debbie holding Scar's lance bedecked with scalps, taken to compensate for sons lost in battle. Both sides have their reasons, both are their own cultures, both are guilty of wilderness justice. The violence is shared, cyclical and interdependent. Brian Henderson argues that the film's kinship relationships undercut this attempt at balance. Indian law, adoption and intermarriage are not acceptable to the white world; there can be only one law, white law.[61] Moreover, if Marty and Laurie represent America's multicultural future, such is only possible because passive Marty is the 'good Indian' – not dead but one who has controlled his sexual urges, in contrast to the libido-driven Scar. This analysis only confirms that Ford cannot altogether transcend his white point of view, which inevitably structures the film's action. The narrative's centring on the white community overwhelms parallels, the massacre of Indians in which Look perishes merely a sketch compared to the horrific attack that opens the film, which exists only in our imagination.

Yet who is the Scar that stands above Debbie signalling the attack, as the little girl looks up in awe? Stripped of its fearful context, the image is a neutral one, perhaps inviting us to fill it with our own racism. Could he be a gentle man (a 'gentleman')? It is remarkable how sane, how well adjusted Debbie is when they find her – '*These are my people*' – a far cry from the unbalanced images of the recovered captives, crazed, gibbering, catatonic, whom Ethan darkly pronounces as beyond the pale: 'They *ain't* white.' Any claim that the film embraces racism and demonises the Comanche must account for Debbie's assimilation and the film's dark portrait of its hero. Among the many contradictions the film explores, including the hero who seeks to save his niece by killing her, there is also the hostage who refuses liberation, who chooses to stay with the alien tribe. Marty is ribbing Ethan about Scar's name for him, 'Big Shoulders', when Debbie crests the sand dunes behind Ethan, materialising out of the landscape like the classic Indian. '*Go* Marty – these are my people.' Ethan pulls his gun.

The eleventh-biggest grosser of 1956, the film received a mixed critical reception but over the years has steadily emerged as a masterpiece of American cinema, in the company of *Citizen Kane* (1941), *Singin' in the Rain* and *Vertigo* (1958). The film has also been held in high esteem by a generation of film-makers, many of whom – Martin Scorsese, Paul Schrader, George Lucas, John Milius, Michael Cimino – have acknowledged direct borrowings. Perhaps the most interesting case is that of the Scorsese-directed, Schrader-scripted *Taxi Driver*. Schrader has said that in discussing their film, he and the director differed over whether to include the scene where Harvey Keitel's pimp dances closely with Jody Foster's teenage whore. They referred to it as their 'Scar' scene, the suggestion being that the one aspect *The Searchers* lacks is evidence of still another family of loving relations, that of Scar and Debbie, the inclusion of which would have driven home the parallels between the races that, as the film stands, remain only sketched.[62]

But this is to ask more than one can reasonably expect. In the end, Ford was a prisoner of his time, as we all are. As it stands, he had brought his historical imagination to bear on an epic level, producing a work of immense power and complexity, tackling contradictions and issues of great moment. Employing the structure of the revenge fantasy, the director had turned it on its head to expose racism's corrosive, self-destructive energies. A bridging film in Ford's career, *The Searchers* looks forward to his last Western, 1964's *Cheyenne Autumn*, where it will be the Indians who go in search of home at the mercy of a savage cavalry. When Ford had made *Clementine* in 1946 he was fifty-one and fresh from service in a hugely successful and patriotic war. Ten years later, after the cold war's McCarthyism, the Korean War and civil rights conflicts, battles at home and abroad, both America and Ford had suffered disillusionment, a loss of faith that would inevitably grow with the imperial assassinations and disastrous war that lay ahead.

The Horse Soldiers (1959)

Early in *The Horse Soldiers*, on the eve of a sortie behind rebel lines, an official photograph is taken of the officers involved, a marker of the historical moment that suggests a possible turning point in the conflict that has divided and bloodied America. Surprisingly, however, Ford's film itself fails to rise to the occasion: despite its setting and subject, a military mission during the Civil War, *The Horse Soldiers* is not one of the director's strongest Westerns.

In *Young Mr Lincoln*, Abe had fought the war symbolically, asked to choose between two pies in a bake-off, two sides in a tug of war and finally two brothers in a murder trial. The foreshadowing had included the storm threatening to break at the end. With *Rio Grande*, 'the late war', as Quincannon termed it, continued to cast its shadow and was re-fought, again symbolically, by Kirby and Kathleen. Although not as successful as his larger Westerns, *Wagon Master* had launched the highly popular *Wagon Train* television series, and in 1960 Ford would contribute 'The Colter Craven Story'. An alcoholic doctor demoralised by his experiences in the war, Craven (Carleton Young) is inspired to perform a vital operation by the example of Ulysses S. Grant, who had risen above disgrace to lead the North and become president.

In 1962, Ford would return to the war (and the Grant story too) directly, in his segment for the Cinerama spectacular *How the West Was Won*. Ford's contribution to the omnibus production (other directors were George Marshall and Henry Hathaway) had an idealistic rustic, George Peppard, going to war and finding himself at the bloody Battle of Shiloh. Together with a Confederate deserter, he eavesdrops on John Wayne's General Sherman as he inspires a depressed Grant (Henry Morgan) to return to battle, and saves the latter by bayoneting the rebel when he pulls a gun. It is vintage Ford material, a vignette of one of America's epic saviours at low ebb, saved in turn by a humble foot soldier. It was also Ford at his most contrary, sabotaging the vast Cinerama screen by concentrating the war into an intimate fireside chat.

But *The Horse Soldiers* would represent his one full-length project squarely centred on the conflict. Ford was known for the exhaustive research he immersed himself in for his films. He had a huge library on American history, and especially the Civil War, an area of special interest. Indeed, how could it not be: what greater paradox exists than that of a divided United States? It is therefore surprising that although *The Horse Soldiers* has its charms, the opportunity does not result in a more focused, substantial effort. The lack is at the film's very centre, and the struggle between Colonel John Marlowe (John Wayne), leader of the behind-the-lines mission, and Major Hank Kendall (William Holden), the doctor attached to his regiment. Marlowe would prefer to leave his wounded to the clemency of the enemy, 'a pretty primitive attitude, medically speaking', Kendall feels. Marlowe rejoins that 'war isn't exactly a civilised business'. But his argument has buried roots: Marlowe's dead wife was the victim of incompetent treatment, and he remains bitter and distrustful of doctors. The conflict erupts immediately when Kendall banishes Ford perennial Jack Pennick as the command's Sergeant-Major Mitchell, on the grounds that the veteran has malaria. The differences grow as the troop rides deeper into the South. When Kendall leaves a wounded soldier to the care of his assistant to deliver a black baby, Marlowe reminds him of his oath to the Union. The doctor counters that he honours a higher oath. The commander promptly puts the medic under officer's arrest for insubordination.

Alongside his quarrel with Kendall, Marlowe is embroiled in a more familiar conflict with a Southern belle, Hannah Hunter (Constance Towers). In an echo of the ancient wounds in *Rio Grande*, Marlowe commandeers Hannah's mansion to rest his troops and plan his strategy. Hannah hates the Yankees but entertains them at dinner, hiding behind a supercilious high Southern manner that becomes outrageous as she offers chicken to Marlowe, bending low to flaunt her décolletage: 'Your preference . . . leg or breast?' Crude and unfair, she is projecting undeserved sexual motives onto the horse soldiers, who from her perspective are no more than quasi-savages. Typical Ford types, both Marlowe and Hannah are prisoners of personal bias that has to be unlearned. Hannah's comeuppance begins when she and her maid, Lukey (Althea Gibson), are caught eavesdropping by Kendall, forcing Marlowe to take them along. The war hinges on the destruction of bridges, trains and ordinance at Newton Station, three hundred miles deep into the dead centre of the Confederacy. How will they get back? The question is raised, but never addressed; the film ends with the troop riding out, their mission accomplished.

Forced to go along, Hannah tries to escape but is dunked in the swamp when her keepers ride her down. It is a humiliating experience – her bloomers hang over the fire – rather than the renewal Ford characters are often afforded in baptismal plunges. Still, it could hint at the character's eventual rebirth. In a familiar narrative pattern, she gradually warms toward Marlowe, who puzzles her with his hostility towards Southern deserters. Reaching Newton Station, the troop engages in a slaughter of Confederate opponents. Marlowe is bitter: 'I didn't want this!' He is a warrior unhappy at war. A prisoner of paradox, his mission requires that he blow up trains, destroying the products of a previous life's occupation as a railway engineer.

Another Ford hero who had lost his woman, Marlowe is a victim of dogmatism but not dementia; he is no Ethan. Hannah will become apprised of the reasons for his bitterness toward the practitioners of medicine, a virtuous, romantic animus. In any case, during the film's action, the posture will fall away as his respect for Kendall grows. When a patient dies (an amputee who has disregarded Kendall's prescription of an Indian remedy disparaged by Marlowe), they square off – 'croaker' and 'section hand' – and each throws a punch, but the war proper breaks out behind them. Narrative logic inevitably requires that the colonel suffer a wound, requiring an amused Kendall to probe for the bullet, removing the poison from the past. Twice in the film, Holden interacts with Confederate doctors, demonstrating that medicine knows no borders. The ambiguous victories and action Marlowe has seen humbles the cocksure military man he was at the outset.

Hannah's own transformation continues when the war comes home to roost, invading her life with the death of Lukey, the victim of a reckless shot from a Confederate. With her death, the schematic ideas and structure of the film become clear. She is the sacrifice, the martyr that helps to bring together North and South, Marlowe and Hannah, their promised union also the promise of a united republic. As in *Rio Grande*, the war has been a kind of lover's quarrel. Unfortunately, this perspective fails to pay even token attention to the black point of view. Lukey's slave status is never addressed; nor is there so much as an exchange about the politics of the conflict, the only reference a knowing remark by Marlowe: 'You Southern people have your own help.' In the kind of enterprising if finally ambiguous casting the director often indulged in, Ford chose Althea Gibson, the first black Wimbledon woman tennis champion, to play the slave maid Lukey. But if this casting was designed to underline the importance of the character as structurally central to the action, Lukey nonetheless has little more than a ceremonial role; we cannot mourn her passing, although the horse soldiers do, empathising with Hannah. But since Lukey's function is essentially one of a structuring absence, these cross-cultural alliances lack Ford's customary dramatic edge.

The death of Lukey, a token character despite the Civil War subject and Althea Gibson's casting

What has Marlowe's hostility towards a sawbones to do with the larger conflict? A side quarrel that he has with another of his officers, Colonel Secord (Willis Bouchey), who has an eye on running for Congress, seems equally distracting. It is difficult to escape the feeling that the script indulges digressive tactics to avoid the issues. A typical Ford hero, Marlowe is caught in contradiction. Possessed by his own prejudice, he is leading a force in a war being fought to free the nation and its victims of a way of life based on racial discrimination. Such parallels make for a tidy structure, but bigotry towards doctors ultimately lacks the force to bring the irony home and point to the tragedy of the war. The logic of the film's structure of prejudiced souls on a cleansing journey into the heart of darkness would seem to demand that Marlowe or Hannah, or someone, suffer from the virus of racism. Is this asking for a different film? In fact, the verbal combat between Holden's liberal doctor and Wayne's rigid militarist plays as if a larger question than the latter's intolerance of doctors is at stake. Given that the Civil War is the canvas, the relationships and conflicts in the foreground of *The Horse Soldiers* seem unfocused. Martin Rackin, who co-produced and co-wrote the film with John Lee Mahin, reported that Ford had the writers working on location as shooting proceeded. Such on-the-fly scripting was exceptional for Ford, and suggests that he may never have felt happy with the project.

For Ford, the war was a complex subject: he often maintained that he had had ancestors on both sides of the conflict. Another of Ford's inventions, the story testified to his relish for paradox, conflicting loyalties and to the fantasy that the Union was embodied in his own person. It is easy enough to line the two sides up in terms of Ford thematic oppositions. If the North was tradition and law, the Union for ever, the Confederacy evoked individualism and rebellion, the nation's heroic black sheep, the nobility of sacrifice and 'glory in defeat'. Ford's romanticism would suggest a slight tipping of the scales toward the recalcitrant South – in contrast to Abe's cheating that favours the law when he has to determine his life's path in *Young Mr Lincoln*.

The film's action bears out this bias. Barring scruffy deserters and the politically ambitious Secord, the film offers no villainy to speak of. But although both sides are seen as courageous and loyal, the South inevitably comes in for special treatment. Spatially attached to the Union force for the most part, the film halves its attention when the troop reaches Newton Station and is attacked. The massacre of the rebel troops, charging full tilt down the town's main street into the withering fire of the North, emphasises their gallantry, the soldiers carrying the Confederate flag falling one after another, the third and last their leader, Colonel Jonathan Miles (Carleton Young). Already marked by sacrifice – the loss of an arm in an earlier campaign – when we meet him, the noble Miles is operated on by Kendall while a tortured Marlowe gets drunk. 'Have a field day,' he bellows at the doctor in twisted logic, as if Kendall is to blame for the carnage.

The South's is perhaps the greater honour, the ambiguous one of devotion to duty in the face of almost certain death. Such suggestions of a suicidal gallantry are also present in the film's other major set piece and its one triumphant moment, the march of the Jefferson Military Academy's cadets into battle. Ordered to make a show of force and delay the Union forces, the school's aged commandant leads children in their dress uniforms forward in a neat, long line. Kids with mumps excused from the action look on despondently from the academy's balcony. A distraught mother (Anna Lee) begs for her son – 'He's all I have left' – and drags the resistant Johnny back home. Moments later, his drum rolls silently down a glade and the boy follows, climbing out of a bedroom window. Asked what to do with one of the kids who have been taken prisoner, Marlowe retorts, 'Spank him!' Avoiding another slaughter, he orders an unceremonious retreat. The use of children in the conflict emphasises its absurdity and domestic character, underlining that the Civil War was a family affair. Marlowe's evasive action also revises his earlier claim: war in fact can be 'a civilised business'; a civil war can be civil.

As a representative episode standing in for the war itself, *The Horse Soldiers'* action did not prove ideal material for Ford. The film's texture is uncharacteristically thin, with little fleshing out. Despite the democratic title and the splendid horizon shots of the troop against the sky, there is little focus on the dog-faced soldiers, the canvas skewed instead towards the officer ranks and their arguments. A single exception is Hank Worden's Deacon, who is instrumental in effecting the escape of the Union troop, leading them through the swamp on a route formerly used by runaway slaves. Another of the director's divine tools, Worden's often cracked character (as in *The Searchers*) is here righteous – '*Lead kindly, Lord!*'

When she had been doing her Southern shtick for Marlowe, Ford had indulged a surprising double entendre in Hannah's offer of a breast or leg. Audiences in 1959 would have enjoyed the joke, which smacks of a self-conscious effort to respond to a more permissive atmosphere. Yet it is hard to believe that the line pleased Ford, even as he puts it to good use. What may have made it possible was that it was a lady in wartime on the attack – all's fair, as it were. Certainly, it is difficult to imagine Ford's male characters behaving with such open sexual provocation. Despite the chemistry between them, Ford had wanted shy Wyatt and his lady fair to part with a handshake. Thwarted by Zanuck on that occasion, Ford here has Wayne take his leave from Hannah, proper, decorous, the soldier reaching down to pull away her kerchief, freeing her hair, and riding off as a bridge blows up behind him.

Sergeant Rutledge (1960)

Nothing testifies to the racism of the Western more eloquently than its exclusion of minorities. Black cowboys worked the range both before and after the Civil War, and it has been estimated that between five and ten thousand of the frontier's 35,000 ranch hands were African-American. Some 180,000 fought in Union blue and over 30,000 perished in the Civil War. Yet the movies, like the history books, buried it all. Edward Zwick's *Glory* received much attention for its focus on the first black cavalry unit in 1989, and Buffalo Soldiers are now the subject of books, documentaries and television productions. Inevitably, however, Ford was there first. The star of *Sergeant Rutledge*, in its title role as embattled top sergeant of the Ninth Cavalry, Woody Strode would return in *The Man Who Shot Liberty Valance* as Tom Doniphon's trusted ranch hand, and a key member of that film's emerging America.

Nonetheless, race is a bedevilling theme for Ford, as for the nation itself. He would righteously object when he was accused of racism and point to his support for actors like Strode and his repeated employment of the Navajo as extras. Critics, however, saw a demeaning attitude at work when Ford cast the black actor as Stone Calf in *Two Rode Together,* unaware that he was half-Indian; Strode would also play a Chinese warrior in *7 Women*. The period's standard practice of one tribe standing in for another or of white actors in Indian roles, as with Henry Brandon's Scar, would look increasingly indefensible as America became more sensitive and identity politics took hold. Above all, there were the films themselves, the mythic depiction of the Indian, the recurrent racial fear, the persistent theme of miscegenation. Criticised for representing the Indian as savage in films like *Stagecoach, Drums Along the Mohawk, The Searchers* and *Rio Grande*, he was also found guilty of rehearsing the stereotype of the noble Indian in *Fort Apache, She Wore a Yellow Ribbon* and *Cheyenne Autumn*. It was difficult to generalise. Depending on the story, he could present the Indian en bloc as a force of nature or develop individual characters. But it was all of a piece: the point of view was inevitably from outside white culture. *Cheyenne Autumn* would be a futile attempt to address this in 1964.

As he approached the twilight of his career, Ford increasingly turned his attention to these issues directly, as his society was. In tackling the subject of the black cavalryman, Ford was nothing if not in tune with his times. Civil rights and desegregation had already begun to convulse the nation in the late 1950s, and would erupt in the years ahead. An adventurous, typically independent-minded project for Ford, *Sergeant Rutledge*'s realisation would prove a challenge. Inevitably, given his age and experience, the treatment of the issues would be conservative and look back rather than ahead.

A genre mix of Western, courtroom drama and racial melodrama, the film has the innocent Braxton Rutledge accused of rape and murder, and defended by Lieutenant Tom Cantrell (Jeffrey Hunter) and a sympathetic witness, Mary Beecher (Constance Towers). Rutledge's military trial is the present-day action framing an extensive series of flashbacks that fragment the past's events, and string out the largely rhetorical question of Rutledge's guilt or innocence. A self-reflexive, distancing strategy, this frustrating structure effectively communicates the constriction and oppression of a minority person's experience trapped inside a prejudiced world.

Ford's presentation of that world predicates the absolute power of the stereotyping that had precipitated the events leading to the trial, and which it is the film's project to interrogate. Standing over a dead young woman naked under a blanket, Rutledge – who has just discovered her himself – had in turn been discovered by the girl's father. As we shall hear in testimony, the girl has been violated and strangled, the gold cross torn from her neck 'a symbol of the purity' destroyed by a 'degenerate'. Assuming the black soldier's guilt, the father had drawn and fired, only to be shot dead by Rutledge, who had then fled.

His colour had thus cast him in a role as the 'degenerate' in a melodrama that the court is now mounting. Developing in narrative fragments, the scenario is shaped by Captain Shattuck (Carleton Young), the prosecutor who elicits testimony from witnesses by censoring the events to support a prejudicial view of Rutledge. Shattuck abruptly ends his questioning of Mary, for instance, just as she recounts how she had entered the isolated train station and suddenly found herself in the clutches of a huge black man. Giving an aptly sensational visual dimension to these interrogative tactics, Ford leaves us with a shocked, wide-eyed Constance Towers, a black hand over her mouth, as the flashback is cut off. Allowed to complete her story by Cantrell, Mary describes how the cavalryman and she had joined forces against two Apache who had killed the stationmaster and were stalking Rutledge when Beecher came on the scene. Mindful of his compromised situation, given the sexual dynamics surrounding white women and black men, the soldier had kept his distance – even trying to forgo Mary's first aid.

Such dynamics are foregrounded in the trial. The courtroom is filled for a voyeuristic spectacle, its front rows occupied by Mrs Cordelia Fosgate, Billie Burke in vintage scatter-brained form, and a phalanx of rouged and bedecked Southern aristocratic fossils. Ford plays the wide-eyed prejudice of the women for comedy, with Cordelia as wife to the embarrassed trial chairman, Colonel Otis Fosgate (Willis Bouchey), who breathlessly testifies that she remembers seeing Rutledge and the dead girl, whom he was teaching to ride, conversing in the store owned by Chandler Hubble (Fred Libby). The atmosphere whipped up by the gossipy women and the apoplectic judge, the rhetoric of the prosecutor and the impressions of a defence on the run construct a world of bizarre extremes, veering between farce and a lynching drama.

Darkening the courtroom to code the onset of flashbacks, Ford employs expressionist techniques of spotlighting and silhouetting that create an apt noir atmosphere. The theatrical styling also extends to key scenes in the flashback action, as in the bare and shadowy railway station where Mary leaves the train. Although Ford's brief vignettes of the black cavalry in action in Monument Valley eventually provide contrast and some relief, the landscape's traditional ideology of freedom and openness is largely held in check within the imprisoning flashback structure.

Was Rutledge infected with the same stereotyping, or was he simply being realistic? Rather than risk white justice he had run immediately. Arrested by Cantrell and taken back for trial, guarded by his own fellow black soldiers from the Ninth US Cavalry, he again flees but returns when he sees the threat of an ambush by the Apache. Asked in the court why he had come back, he struggles to find the words:

> It's because the Ninth Cavalry was my home. My real freedom. And my self-respect. And the way I was deserting it, I wasn't nothin' but a swamp-runnin' nigger. And I ain't that! Do you hear me? I'm a *man*!

A rare use of the racist slur in a Hollywood film of that era, permissible because uttered by a black, the speech was one of which Woody Strode was proud. He had responded to the heroic stature accorded his character:

> It had dignity. John Ford put classic words in my mouth ... You never seen a Negro come off a mountain like John Wayne before. I had the greatest Glory Hallelujah ride across the Pecos River that any black man ever had on the screen. And I did it myself. I carried the whole black race across that river.[63]

The latent hysteria in the trial infects even Cantrell, who strikes the true killer, Chandler Hubble, while on the stand, and bullies him into confessing. Transplanting the uncontrollable animal impulses that belonged to the standard black stereotype, Ford has the white merchant break down and admit it was the way the young girl moved that had driven him to it: 'I had to have her. Help me!' He had seized her, tearing away the gold crucifix from around her neck in their struggle. Reversal is the film's basic strategy: it is a member of the respected white community who disrespects the cross, who is the rapist and killer.

One of Ford's smaller, more personal films, *Sergeant Rutledge* was complicated by the increasingly sophisticated racial politics of the period and the industry's commercial and ideological pressures. Although Strode dominates, the stars as announced in bold credits are Hunter, Towers and Burke; Strode heads the next frame's list of four supporting actors, all members of the black cavalry unit. This is less segregation than the dictates of star voltage, and hints at the inevitable obstacles of a black story told through white characters. The film celebrates Brax's innocence and heroism, but gives more than equal time to the white lawyer who single-handedly exonerates him and the noble white lady who repeatedly stands up for him. The film also must demonise the Apache to make heroes of the black soldiers.

Joseph McBride has suggested that far from upholding 'the stereotype of the black brute', as Thomas Cripps had argued, 'if anything the film could be faulted for playing into the Uncle Tom stereotype':

> In most ways the personification of manliness, Rutledge nevertheless is sexually neutered by the racist strictures of his society. Cantrell bases his defense partly on Rutledge's careful deference to Jim Crow in Mary Beecher's presence. Ford's emphasis on Rutledge's sexless, subservient nature qualifies the message of a film designed to show that blacks should be treated with full equality.[64]

But it is difficult, given the era of the film and its narrative, to envisage a Ford scenario that would have constructed Rutledge as a sexual presence. Nonetheless, such analysis effectively points to the film's lack of nuance in its characters, and teases out the racial complexities Ford's work typically generates.

In part, the difficulties were inherent in Ford's effort to relate the story's period to his own very different and increasingly liberal society. For it is the film's construction of the era's collective mind-set, the extreme imbalance of an institutionalised racism, that gives the action an inflated quality, coarsening the issues and caricaturing the court. Combined with the excessive number of flashbacks that mete out piecemeal the incriminating elements and Rutledge's own story, the film's extremes flirt with alienating the audience on a plane beyond the Brechtian. The problem flows from the attempt to create a historical moment when racism, stereotyping and sexual fears were on such a hegemonic scale that a dispassionate trial was impossible: there could be no question of a black man's innocence.

Clearly, Ford's strategy in the military court's case against Rutledge was to place the white culture on trial. Poised in the classic situation of the accused rapist, Braxton's plight dramatised a process so fraught with prejudice as effectively to discredit the court and invert the action. As with the white rapist, it is the community that is guilty. However, exposing the pronounced racism of events without straining the audience's suspension of disbelief proves impossible. The deflating of the film's bigoted world only perpetuates the overbearing tone and schematic characterisations. It is curious that a drama focused on challenging stereotype should rely so heavily on caricature.

As in *Cheyenne Autumn* four years later, a key source of the film's problems is its failure to integrate its comedy. Ford's typical style was to weave comic characters and episodes throughout a film's narrative, providing layering, nuance and contrast: in *Liberty Valance*'s kitchen – as in Shakespeare's court – nobles and jesters rub shoulders. But in *Sergeant Rutledge*, two worlds collide – the heroic exploits and stark circumstances of the black soldier, and the ignoble buffoonery of the white judges and audience. Comedy is fenced off in characters such as the Fosgates, and in scenes or passages designed to ridicule the white community, while the main action is pitched in an affecting pathos. Given this segregation, the credibility and force of events is weakened, the breadth of approach minimising shading and detailing, and creating a tone of extreme melodrama and morality play – of virtue versus vice. As a result, Ford cannot avoid a righteousness absent in a denser work like *The Searchers*, where the film is implicated in the very racism it critiques. Compared to Ford's other cavalry films, the world of *Rutledge* lacks structural complexity, range and grading. Apart from the unit of black troopers that Ford creates as a warm, proud family, supporting characters and subsidiary themes are few. Mary and Cantrell's relationship is largely tangential.

Ford was far more successful in celebrating the black horse soldiers, the Ninth Cavalry and the myth of its top soldier, Captain Buffalo. It had been the Indians who had named them buffalo soldiers after the animal hides they wore as robes. The original title for the film, 'Captain Buffalo', is retained in the cavalry unit's theme song that celebrates

Woody Strode as 'Captain Buffalo'

the mythic exploits of a black Paul Bunyan, the idealised heroic black soldier of the US Army. As an older trooper explains the name, Ford poses Strode at the crest of a hill, the setting, lighting and low angle presenting Rutledge as a dominating visual presence – he is the incarnation of the legendary figure. These are the strongest images in the film, iconic rather than theatrical. The action in the desert validates these larger-than-life dimensions. Placing service above self, honour above his freedom, Rutledge had lived up to the heroic ideal. At the end, he leads his troop past the white couple whose romance is now flowering. Rutledge is free to ride into the desert, the film closing with Ford's trademark horizon iconography, here employed for revisionist purposes:

> The Negro soldier, the regular, is very proud. They had always been a cavalry outfit, but in this last war, they took their horses away, and they were broken-hearted. They were very proud of their outfit; they had great esprit de corps. I liked that picture. It was the first time we had ever shown the Negro as a hero.[65]

Two Rode Together (1961)

> I didn't like the story, but I did it as a favor to Harry Cohn, who was stuck with the project and said, 'Will you do this for me?' I said, 'Good God, this is a lousy script.' He said, 'I know it, but we're pledged for it – we're all set – we've got Widmark and Stewart signed up'. I said, 'OK, I'll do the damned thing.' And I didn't enjoy it. I just tried to make Stewart's character as humorous as possible.[66]

The result is one of Ford's strangest films, virtually a black comedy. James Stewart's amusingly cynical Guthrie McCabe and his lively friendship with Lieutenant Jim Gary (Richard Widmark), together with the upbeat *Stagecoach*-like ending in which McCabe and the victimised Elena (Linda Cristal) abandon the corrupt Tascosa community for California, provide a light-hearted surface over dark and degrading events. Ford may not have enjoyed the project, but the mere fact that he was prepared to tackle it, as well as the outcome itself, speak volumes about the changes in his outlook over the years. As with *Wagon Master*, the film explores a number of short-sighted, self-oriented individuals and groups; but here precious few rise above their own agendas.

Dominating the film is Marshal McCabe, the West's version of a made man, who gets 10 per cent of everything in Tascosa. Living with, as well as off, the town madam, Belle Aragon (Annelle Hayes), McCabe reclines on the front porch of her saloon with beer and cigar. The hat tipped down over his eyes, the marshal is oblivious to his surroundings. The widow Gomez has given birth, the bartender informs Guthrie, although her man died more than a year ago, a sly joke indicative of the town's morality. Tascosa seems as somnolent as McCabe, its main drag vacant, a far cry from *Clementine*'s busy Tombstone. Yet Ford insists on the comparison. In a reprise from that film, Guthrie evicts two gamblers, his name – like Wyatt Earp's – drawing instant respect. But Guthrie, the company man, has replaced Earp, the community's man. Earp's recumbent position, which had marked his growing integration into the community, is here set against Guthrie's, a sign of the character's parasitic existence. Posed by Ford to recall Earp iconographically, McCabe's profiteering actually suggests closer kin in Doc Holliday, although when we meet him, he evidences little of the gunfighter's tortured sensibility. Rather than an ideal or tragic figure, Guthrie is an ironic hero, flawed and inferior but too funny to be unsympathetic.

Practically an anti-hero, Stewart is remarkable for a Ford protagonist. Perverse and unsentimental, he is amused by appeals to principle. His view of the world is jaundiced, undoubtedly reflecting his own compromised state. In the string of distinguished 1950s Westerns directed by Mann – *Winchester '73* (1950), *Bend of the River* (1951), *The Far Country* (1954), *The Man from Laramie* (1955) and *The Naked Spur* (1952) – Stewart, the pre-war star of screwball and romantic comedy, had reshaped his persona, reinventing himself as a damaged, driven cowboy. Here he borrows the cynicism and ambiguity of those earlier characterisations, but stops well short of the neurotic. Free of emotional wounds, psychological stress or even social commitments, McCabe is refreshingly beyond conscience or convention, the enemy of hypocrisy.

Guthrie's only problem appears to be Belle, whose crowding prompts him to accept an invitation to accompany Gary and his troops to an interview, subject unspecified, with Major Frazer (John McIntire). Breaking the journey, the two sit on a riverbank's edge and puff on cigars, as McCabe explains that Belle conceals a dagger under a garter ('I know', interjects Gary), and has begun to mention 'matrimony'. Shot from a mid-point in the river, the scene runs uncut for nearly four minutes, its relaxed dialogue flowing in leisurely time with the water and effortlessly suggesting the affection and respect the men share. It is Ford at his most elegant, the simplicity and economy of the shot achieving a peak of expressivity.

The serene equilibrium is qualified by professional and ethical differences. The running dialogue between the two men focuses on familiar conflicts – between duty and self, idealism and profit, meagre army pay and the town's 10 per cent – that will structure and colour the action. McCabe's cynicism and self-interest are real enough. At the fort, he is incredulous that the army is appealing to him to lead a group of white settlers desperate to locate captives abducted long ago by the Comanche. McCabe is practically out of the door when the major asks, 'Would money influence your decision?' After a deliberate pause, McCabe replies (with a patented Stewart gulp) that it would absolutely do so, and returns to his seat. But a scout's pay elicits McCabe's contempt. What is a human life worth, the major asks rhetorically: 'Whatever the market will bear,' replies McCabe, the cowboy hero as capitalist scoundrel.

McCabe accepts the job vowing to squeeze a greater profit from the settlers, $500 a head for each captive recovered. The picture darkens as we meet these misguided souls who are hoping for a messiah in McCabe. Inevitably, they are all blind, obsessed, inward-looking. The young Marty (Shirley Jones) is sympathetic – she blames herself for hiding when the Comanche had taken her seven-year-old brother nine years earlier. Then only a child of thirteen, she has never recovered, and even dresses like a boy to replace him for her father. She carries with her the boy's music box, a sign of her allegiance to the past.

Ford rings the changes on the settlers, dreaming of long-lost family members, unrealistic about the obstacles, variously pathetic, corrupt, comical. McCabe gets drunk, bitter at his own chicanery in doing a deal with Wringle (Ford's perennial blowhard, Willis Bouchey) to return a boy – any boy will do – to placate his wife over the loss fif-

teen years ago of their two-year-old, so he can return to his business. When Marty shows
McCabe an old picture of her brother, he launches into a brutal tirade. Does she know
what her angel looks like now? McCabe presses on, unstoppable in his bitter attempt to
educate the settlers. Her brother wears braids and buffalo grease, sports scars and scalps,
grunts Comanche and yes, if given the chance, would rape her. Typically, Ford follows
this searing moment, which returns us to the cross-cultural complexities of *The
Searchers*, with grotesque comedy, as the Clegg brothers (Ken Curtis and Harry Carey,
Jr), moronic rivals for Marty's attentions, square off with the cavalry officer. It is a
measure of the decline in the army's stock with Ford that – although Marty shrewishly
disowns the pair – Widmark's lieutenant is still reduced to brawling with them.

The oafish brothers, together with their father, are searching for their abducted
mother, but once found, she refuses repatriation: 'I'm dead.' Ford's favourite immigrant,
John Qualen, is also on hand, hoping that his daughter Freda will return, but she is
addled, a lost soul. Finally, there is McCandless (Cliff Lyons), whose wife (Jeanette
Nolan) has become unbalanced following the loss of their Toby. When Wringle refuses
to accept Running Wolf, the fierce, troubled Comanche McCabe has brought back, Mrs
McCandless fastens on him, and her husband takes him in. Although his motives are
benign, McCandless ultimately resembles the scurrilous Wringle – any 'Indianised' survivor will do.

After all his passionate tributes to the cavalry, it is remarkable how Ford now paints
the army as self-serving and irrelevant. Captain Frazer is desperate for McCabe's expertise, but ultimately reneges on his deal and jails him. Andy Devine, whom Ford re-enlists
here to serve as the outsize top sergeant, Posey, has little to do apart from suffering cracks
about the grotesque girth that he employs to rescue his lieutenant from the idiot Cleggs
by bumping them into a creek, a far cry from Ford's heroic top soldiers of his earlier
work.

Focusing the army's compromised and ineffectual presence further is Gary's awkward
place in the action. Structurally required to do double duty, he is simultaneously the seasoned leader who heads the troop, as well as the comic junior officer wrestling with
courtship. In this latter capacity, he provides Marty with solace and eventually will be
the vehicle of her redemption. But in the field, Gary is a frustrated sidekick to McCabe,
his impotence emphasised as he watches the cowboy trade the hostiles 'first-class mer-
chandise' – repeating rifles and knives – for the captives. The Comanche chief, Quanah
Parker (Henry Brandon), is arming himself against the recalcitrant Stone Calf (Woody
Strode), whose wife, a Spanish aristocrat in her previous life, McCabe also takes back
with him. Quarrelling again over who is in charge and the best tactics to employ in the
face of Stone Calf's likely pursuit, McCabe draws his gun on Gary, refusing to take
orders. 'Good riddance!' he shouts after Gary, who rides on with Running Wolf to the
wagon train. McCabe lights a fire to set a trap and waits for Stone Calf, whom he
immediately kills when the warrior, armed with a knife, strides into their camp.

Gary's main role appears to be rhetorical, to carry the banner for a more disinterested
way of life in his colloquies with McCabe, and to stand apart from and condemn the
bigoted behaviour of his cavalry colleagues towards Elena. The army, Ford reassures us
through Widmark, is not totally derelict and without principle. But even in his efforts
to assist the desperate settlers, Gary's actions are problematic. An accomplice in passing

off Running Wolf as the Wringles' son, he provides no guidance in transferring the disturbed and uncontrollable youth to the community. Released to Mrs McCandless, the
boy immediately kills the woman once she has cut his bonds. Discovered, Running Wolf
is caught up in the irrational eruption of a mob that is bent on lynching him. In the
havoc, Marty's music box falls and begins to play, arresting the boy, who shrieks 'Mine!
Mine!' as he is strung up and hanged. He was Marty's brother. It is an extraordinary
moment, the identity of an earlier life breaking through the years of another world's
acculturation, the sudden discovery of another self within even as it is snuffed out. It is
Ford mining the cross-cultural roots of America, and deploying the radical contradictions of frontier existence to great ironic and tragic effect.

Although the attempt to reconstitute the broken family is futile, the deaths of Mrs
McCandless and Running Wolf create the psychic space necessary to restore the threat-
ened social system. With her brother's death, Marty is freed of her guilt and obsession.
When first we had seen her, with the arrival of McCabe and Gary at the settlers' camp,
she had resembled a squaw riding a spotted Indian pony. Like both Running Wolf and
Elena, Marty wears her hair in braids, a sign in the film of an uncivilised state. Before
Mrs McCandless can cut his hair, Running Wolf seizes the scissors and kills her, thus
bringing about his own death. Marty, however, will lose her braids when she transforms
from her arrested state into a young woman ready for marriage. In the same way, Stewart is drawn to Elena when, in discussing her appearance, he lifts her braids away from
her shoulders. This pattern is crucial to the overall design: it is with the transition of the
two women and McCabe into the world of the settled that the crisis of the family is
resolved in the film.

An ignoble duel

If one looks at the narrative action of *Two Rode Together* through the lens of Ford's earlier films, despite the reconciliation of its characters, what stands out is the unheroic and defeatist nature of the action. The various groups are all compromised. Ford's usually favoured – the family, the community, the army – treat the captives as interchangeable, lacking individuality. The Comanche expediently abandon whites assimilated long ago in exchange for weapons. The settlers are deluded or cold-bloodedly cynical, the soldiers are marginalised, escorts and onlookers, the cavalry community is loathsomely racist.

The fort's commander taxes McCabe for leaving some captives behind: 'Only God has the right to play God.' But such issues in any case appear irrelevant to McCabe's morality, as in the killing of the Comanche warrior, Stone Calf, when he materialises to retrieve his squaw. Unblinkingly, McCabe immediately fires twice on the imposing figure, who is armed only with a knife. By the genre's classical standards of heroism, the act is one of quasi-murder, akin to firing on an unarmed man. Ford's staging of the scene highlights the practical McCabe's clear-eyed focus on his own ends, but the act's matter-of-factness also emphasises how decisively the issue of combat with 'savages' did not figure in the period's Eurocentric ethics. It is also notable that this abrupt, unambiguously ignoble killing is one of the film's few concessions – together with the buffoonish struggle of Marty's suitors and the grotesque lynching of Running Wolf – to the genre's conventions of physical action. Indicative of the film's pessimism, *Two Rode Together* provides no redemptive act, no violence that resolves conflict and establishes order.

It is principally Elena who makes possible a rescue of the film from defeatism. When she had asked if she could ride with them to the settler camp, McCabe had seen no profit in it and had been offhand, uncaring: 'No difference to us.' But it will be necessary for the self-serving McCabe to convert in order to satisfy the minimal heroic and positivist requirements of the traditional Western. This is credibly achieved in terms of the film's ironic world by virtue of the modesty of that character's reinvention, and its hints of a continued self-interest. When the marshal had boosted Elena's self-esteem, urging her to attend the cavalry dance, he had tentatively styled her braids up, and shrewdly weighed the results. If originally moved by pity, was he now considering her as an investment in personal relations stock? Guthrie will be marrying up, a considerable advance in class on the shrewish frontierswoman, Belle.

Whatever his motives, the dance reveals McCabe now firmly on the side of the angels. Another Ford character trapped in a conflicted role, Elena had reacted to Stone Calf's death with the posture of the bereaved tribal wife, wailing and trickling soil through her upraised hands. Back in 'civilisation', she attends a cavalry ball immaculately groomed, only to be humiliated by the voyeuristic and gossipy cavalry community. The dance is a bastardisation of the Ford ritual, a shameful display of animus and discord, the id breaking through the civilised surface. Ingloriously, Gary and McCabe go from trying in vain to solicit Elena dance partners to stomping and tripping them. Elena comports herself with great dignity, explaining that she had indeed been the wife of a Comanche warrior, had had no children, and that she knows many of them regard her as 'a degraded woman'. Breaking down, she is rescued by McCabe, who explains that Elena had not committed suicide because her religion forbade it, then adds the *coup de grâce*, telling

Linda Cristal's character, Elena, rescues the film from defeatism

the assembly that she has asked to go back, that Elena feels 'she was treated better by the Comanche than by some of you'.

Comedy in *Two Rode Together* is again Ford's strategy for putting the film's best commercial foot forward, disguising the thrust of events towards darkness and tragedy. McCabe's unheroic pursuit of profit in Tascosa and his polemical relationship with Gary, the latter's awkward pursuit of Marty, and the antics of the Cleggs and obese Sergeant Posey – these help to give the film some buoyancy if not the richness of Ford's best work. The lighter tone continues at the end when McCabe returns to Tascosa, only to find that Belle has replaced him. In the film's final devastating comment on declining frontier standards, she has installed McCabe's imbecilic deputy as marshal, an even more grotesque contrast to Fonda's Earp. Seizing on the stage bound for California and its passenger – the 'Senorita', as he calls Elena – as the best deal going, he swings aboard to ride shotgun to the new settlements. The last line from Gary to Belle – that perhaps McCabe had craved 'something he could have more than 10 per cent of' – further contextualises McCabe's actions, and suggests why he may now be up to the challenge of domestication.

In *The Searchers*, efforts at reconciliation had finally brought Debbie home, restoring the Edwards family and reaffirming the white culture's inviolate status. However, in *Two Rode Together*, the thrust of the action suggests that it is best to leave the past alone, to accept loss and suppress memory. This is even hinted at with Elena, who survived her degraded life only because of her religion's dictates against suicide – otherwise, better dead than bedded with red. As with Debbie, however, Ford is unable to explore how oddly such an implication sits with the evidence of Elena's hardly brutalised state, her articulate and graceful survivor.

That the past is best forgotten will be the bitter moral of *The Man Who Shot Liberty Valance* as well. As there, the decline in Ford's belief in traditional values and the future can be read clearly enough in *Two Rode Together*'s departure from the pageantry and ceremonies of his familiar world. There are few iconic signs, no horizon shots, no exuberant chases or heroic last stands. Gone too are life-affirming rituals – meals, sermons, celebrations; only the disastrous army dance remains. Recalling *Stagecoach*, the final image is of Elena and Guthrie escaping, albeit leaving a far darker America behind.

The Man Who Shot Liberty Valance (1962)

It is possible to see *The Man Who Shot Liberty Valance* as the third panel of a great Fordian triptych that enshrines pivotal moments in the progress of pioneer America. *The Searchers* provides images of an early frontier: a worried cowboy's shadowed face looking to the horizon; an isolated ranch burning; a horseman riding into a teepee and emerging with a scalp; a captive being returned. *My Darling Clementine* presents a later historical moment: a drunken Indian being banished; a marshal kicking back on his front porch; a travelling tragedian; lawmen marching to a gunfight. *Liberty Valance* will be later still, a time of conventions, statehood, politics. But the film opens with an even more modern America, ushered in by an arriving train, an appropriate symbol for its triptych panel. *Liberty Valance* puts in place a framing flashback structure, an inspired invention that offers a distance that if not Brechtian nevertheless provides a basis for contemplation of the Old West, and an enquiry into the question of how histories are made.

One dimension of this is the film's insistent emphasis on the present, the site of mystery. Something of moment has occurred, its roots in the past. The characters are silent partners at a sad memorial reunion. Grounding the action of the film as a flashback forces us to relate the past, the robust early West and the Western itself to a contemporary America. A tragic tone prevails: something irreplaceable has been lost. The structure underlines the role of memory: how does reverie relate to history? What is the effect of remembering? How do we construct the past? Of course, Ford is always looking back, the great majority of his work period projects. But here Ford is looking back at characters who are themselves looking back, extending an invitation for the audience to join in contemplation, abstraction, analysis.

Is it a function of memory to idealise, to exaggerate? Is nostalgia inevitable? If *Liberty Valance* appears to be Ford's ultimate personal statement, it is because the film evidences a post-modern complexity, at once nostalgic and critical, a celebration of myth and its deconstruction, a radical recycling, the director's dual vision brought here into its sharpest focus. The film's action is not the generic dramatisation of the violent process by which America was civilised. Rather, it is the revelation of the kind of violence that was required, and its personal and political consequences. In the guise of a horse opera, Ford delivers historical analysis.

Key to Ford's re-imagining of the genre is the film's extreme theatrical style and indoor action, once again confining the Western within melodrama. Although *Clementine* rarely ventures out of town, the imperious geography of Monument Valley in the background is an ever-present comment on the freedom and challenge of early America. In *Liberty Valance*, the action is studio-bound, often in close quarters, intense and pressured. If the past is seen as animated and theatrical, a stage for giants on which a myth is being rehearsed in an appropriate nostalgia ('Things were a lot different back then . . . a lot different'), it also remains a narrative played out indoors, unframed by inspiring landscapes and spectacle. As in its immediate predecessors – *The Horse Soldiers, Sergeant Rutledge, Two Rode Together* – Ford's affirmative rituals and poetic flourishes are missing. So too the genre's traditional liberating action: there are vicious beatings, a humiliating display of superior marksmanship and a murder disguised as a classic gunfight.

Late in the film, its hero, Tom Doniphon (John Wayne), will go berserk, flinging a burning oil lantern against the far wall of the home he has been building in a drunken fury. Although a minor climax by today's standards, the explosive release clearly points to *Liberty Valance*'s closeted world and confining action. Doniphon's is the kind of self-destructive violence symptomatic of the impotent characters of family melodrama rather than of the traditional Western hero. Given that the film is Ford's most elaborate processing of historical events in terms of the domestic, and that its focus is on the exclusion of another of his epic heroes from both family and history, melodrama is an altogether appropriate perspective to bring to bear.

Famous as a meditation on memory, *Liberty Valance* is also Ford's ultimate statement on individualism. The question posed is how are we to remember a giant of the past? The film shows us two views of his defining moment, and affirms the myth over the real, a choice made possible by Tom's heroic martyrdom. But Doniphon is also critiqued. John Wayne was an icon of self-reliance; it was in the very way he walked. Tom's reward for incarnating it so loyally is a wooden coffin and a handful of mourners. *Liberty Valance* is Ford's profound indictment of that fundamental American virtue; held as an absolute, self-reliance is seen as destructive and ultimately self-defeating. Blind to the needs of his lawless historical moment, Tom wants to shield Hallie but not Nora or Anna Lee's imperilled stagecoach traveller or all the other Hallies. Self-reliance without the social devalues the self, personhood, individualism itself; the meek are always at the mercy of force. Tom's solipsism dooms him: his only meaningful action – eliminating Liberty – is belatedly taken and for the wrong reasons. Tom loses Hallie, the Holy Grail, America's spirit, because he lacks moral vision. Ford mourns his passing but insists that the cowboy did not deserve her.

An epic melodrama, *Liberty Valance* compensates for its psychological and spatial confinement by creating a saga of auditory excess and outsized rhetoric. The past is animated and noisy, with Vera Miles's shrilly nagging Hallie, Andy DeVine's whining Marshal Link Appleyard and Lee Marvin's flamboyant Liberty. The climactic territorial assembly features Edmond O'Brien's Dutton Peabody, town drunk and newspaper editor, matching oratorical ham with John Carradine's windy Cassius Starbuckle, cattlemen's lobbyist. Tom delivers pithy, commanding speeches.

In keeping with the bipolar historical vision of the film, the performances in the present-day framework are all low key in contrast to the larger-than-life past. Modern Hallie is silent, frozen, holding herself as if she might break. An aged Link is a shadow of his former self in bluster, if not bulk. Woody Strode as Doniphon's black retainer rises from a bench like an ancient ghost. The generally depressed atmosphere echoes a setting bereft of charm or dynamism. The last major Western of its era to be made in black and white, *Liberty Valance* creates modern-day America as a grey, colourless world, the only source of energy the pushy editor invading the privacy of the mourners.

When I had the occasion to ask Ford what had attracted him to *Liberty Valance,* he immediately replied, 'I liked the story … two people … simple people … in a kitchen.'[67] Who are Ford's 'simple people'? One of the town's social centres, the eatery is the place to be on Saturday night, renowned for the gigantic steaks turned out by Peter Ericson, Ford's loyal Scandinavian immigrant in the person of John Qualen, who will proudly display his citizenship papers on going to vote. Such associations, as with waitress Hallie and cook Nora (Jeanette Nolan) and their ambitious desires to better themselves, imbue the kitchen with all-American trappings. What better place for a broke lawyer to study matters of jurisdiction as he washes dishes to pay his keep – classic American get-up-and-go. In this most theatrical of Westerns, the kitchen is a cramped national stage, not unlike the conveyance in *Stagecoach,* albeit without the inspiring exteriors. Despite the promised face-off between epic heroes posed against momentous political events, it is the scenes set on a humbler stage, the domestic space of the kitchen, that are crucial in exploring the grassroots characters and their personal conflicts that anchor and drive *Liberty Valance*'s action.

A microcosm of early America, Peter's is patronised by its cowboys, individualised in the stuttering Kentuck' and High Pockets, who are bullied out of their steaks by Valance wielding his silver-knobbed whip like a royal prop. Although editor Peabody and Doniphon sit out front, the place of law in the scheme of things is suggested by having the marshal eat furtively in the kitchen and by relegating lawyer Ranse Stoddard to the dishes. Pressed into service to deliver dinners, the aproned dude is spotted by the flashy Liberty – 'Well, looky at the new waitress' – who is lolling at a table with his two myrmidons, as Peabody, ever drunk on words (too), terms his henchmen. Tripped by Valance, Ranse goes down, the huge steaks fly and Tom stands up. It was his steak; Valance must pick it up. The Easterner, Stoddard is uncomprehending: how can a bandit and murderer be allowed to terrorise citizens? How can two men face each other with guns over a steak? Where is the law?

Epic questions are to be decided, matters of historical moment, that will come into focus in the kitchen. As in *Clementine,* we are in a transitional moment: bad men are terrorising the West, resisting the march toward nationhood. The vote for statehood represents the beginning of a collective identity and will, but the community is atomised with no sense of shared ideals; anarchy threatens. Kentuck' and High Pockets weave through the action like a two-cowboy comic chorus, stand-ins for the community at large. Like Devine's Falstaffian marshal, they entertain through their timidity, bullied by Valance out of their dinners, Kentuck' forced to attend Ranse's class because he cut a low card, the two scuttling away from the hapless lawyer in the street as the murderous Valance approaches for the final confrontation.

'Go West, young man.' Horace Greely's famous dictum had brought a lawyer to town, but the law itself is weak, the territory open. Stoddard and Valance, the lawyer and the bandit, statehood versus open range – the conflict is joined. The lawyer intervenes between the two Westerners – he will pick up the steak, and there's an end to it. Except that it is not the end, and the configuration is different – Doniphon stands between Stoddard and Valance – although Doniphon's interest lies not in establishing the law,

Self-reliance becomes solipsism

but in marrying Hallie; he cannot see that the one depends on the other. Hallie, meanwhile, seems strangely impervious to Tom's charm, more concerned that she cannot read. Ford grounds the historical in the personal. Desirous of family but distancing himself from the community, a short-sighted Doniphon lives a contradiction, failing to recognise that he can no longer exist outside of an evolving society. Hallie will choose the lawyer, triggering fateful events. The hard-working frontier waitress is one of Ford's 'simple people' whose love and needs fuel America's journey forward.

Does Hallie repeat Martha's mistake from *The Searchers*, choosing the wrong man? When Stoddard faints in the midst of a tirade against Tom's advice that he arm himself, Hallie angrily glares at Tom – the town could use 'a little law and order'. It is a reproach, for the world that countenances a Liberty Valance is Doniphon's world, too. Tom's proprietal air towards Hallie persuades us of a bond between them, but their relationship is perplexing. Hallie enters the film shrieking at him beneath her window in exasperation for being awakened. Is she fearful that he might have romance in mind? Has Tom really courted her? Kissed her? Tom's own manner with her is oddly formal. When she gets angry, Tom teases her about how pretty she looks, but in response her expression remains vacant. When he reports that he will be leaving town, Hallie answers flatly, prophetically – 'Goodbye, Tom.'

If the kitchen is the emerging America, it is telling how uncertain Tom's place is within it. He comes and goes with the same offhand, breezy air he shows towards Hallie; does he sense that neither is a good fit? He stands with a bemused expression as traffic swirls around him, clearly not in his element, looking too big for the place. Liberty never steps foot in the kitchen. Merely the sound of his voice in the dining room is enough to send the neutered Appleyard out of the back door in unseemly haste. A dandyish bully, a vicious rooster of a man, Liberty's violent entrance into the restaurant makes Hallie visibly flinch back and away. He stares pointedly at her as she beats a quick retreat to the kitchen. He is a wild yet stylish predator, with an air of rampant, aggressive masculinity.

Masculinity is evidently out of place in the kitchen, the America-to-be a more domesticated domain. A resigned figure, the moping Peter has little authority ('Papa, go put on your pants'). Hallie and Nora rail against cowardly Link, Hallie actually pushing him around, but that de-masculinised authority figure is comfortable with the nagging, eating 'on the cuff'. In contrast, the lawyer is gently nursed and nurtured. A vulnerable Ranse needs her in ways that Tom does not – is this love? In any case, she too needs Ranse, who holds out a future. Hallie's behaviour in present-day Shinbone, the pilgrimage to the burnt-out shell of the house Tom was building for her and the harvesting of a desert rose to place on the coffin suggest an unhappy prospect: Hallie had chosen the man she needed but did not love.

That a whipping launches the relationship of Liberty and Stoddard, 'the ladies' man', is suggestive. As weapons go, the whip is the source of spectacularly brutal and personal violence, as in the narcissistic beating actor Marlon Brando receives at the hands of director Brando in *One-Eyed Jacks* (1961). As in its use with slaves, the whip carries the charge of a sadistic domination and invasive punishment that Eastwood exploits in *High Plains Drifter* (1972) and *Unforgiven*. Always restrained in depicting violence, Ford manages to suggest demented brutality in Liberty's punishment of Ranse and Peabody while keeping it all below the frame line.

The beating of Ranse introduces the lawyer to the violence of the wilderness and *its* laws; it is the beating of the editor that finally persuades Ranse to face Valance with a gun. 'Liberty Valance taking liberties with the liberty of the press?' Despite his terror, drunken Peabody cannot resist wordplay on finding himself surrounded. His name a blatant irony, Liberty threatens liberty in all directions – free speech, free press, freedom to assemble, freedom from fear, freedom to vote. His attack on the editor, a key character within Ford's epic dramatic structure, seems inevitable, overdetermined. Opposed to Liberty, he is weak in his alcoholic person and strong in his principled vision. Both the script that grants him histrionic liberties and Ford's expressionist shadow-play *mise en scène* that prefaces his beating privilege the figure. He is virtuous but flawed, like the imperilled republic, one of Ford's holy fools, achieving a Christ-like crucifixion.

Standing between Stoddard and Valance, Doniphon is actually closer to Liberty. Neither has any respect for the rule of law, nor for its advocate in Stoddard, who is 'Pilgrim' to Tom, 'Dude' to Liberty. As those nicknames suggest, both appear jealous of their frontier, dominating its space, interrupting its community gatherings. Facing each other over the fallen steaks, they are like mirror images of overbearing authority and aggressive manhood. Liberty is the toughest man south of the picket-wire, says Tom, 'next to me'. And they are indeed next to each other, although it is Liberty who is the extreme, psychotic version of Doniphon. Liberty throws chairs and people out of his way; Tom will do the same when he has killed Valance and lost Hallie.

Behind Hallie's shrewishness, is there a fear of Tom's intimidating self-reliance and outsize masculinity? It can be argued, as Tag Gallagher has, that she chooses 'security over passion, law over nobility'.[68] But from Hallie's point of view, the choice may appear differently. Her most urgent moment in the film is her confession that she cannot read. Poised in the kitchen like a frontier Mildred Pierce, she is offered opportunity by Ranse, a turning point. In these terms, education may offer its own passion and nobility, as well as adventure and freedom. Hallie chooses the classic path of progress and a reinvention of the self, now offered by a later frontier – 'Go East, young woman!' Does she realise what her sacrifice will be? She becomes Stoddard's prize pupil, helping to run the class and to mother the small ones. But the film is silent about the lack of issue from their union. She will help to birth America instead.

The film makes clear long before such terms became current that the America to come will be a multicultural and diverse nation. Nora, in her thick Scandinavian accent, defines America as a republic where the 'people are the boss … that means us!' She is followed in Ranse's class by the faltering Pompey, the ex-slave who understandably forgets the Constitution's line about all men being created equal. Having Stoddard put up his law shingle outside the newspaper office and teach his reading class next door, the film's spatial logic establishes a relationship between the law, the press and education. Ranse's lecture makes the same connections. Working from an editorial, he defines the need for statehood to protect the future of ordinary citizens, the irony of his own situation escaping him until Doniphon comes with news of Liberty's threatening return.

Pompey's presence contributes to the enigma surrounding Tom. As with the black maids of *Drums Along the Mohawk* and *The Horse Soldiers*, his loyalty to his master throws a positive light on both characters. In the wake that opens the film, Pompey is visibly consumed with grief. He provides back-up ('My boy Pompey, in the window') at critical moments, supplies the gun when Tom kills Valance and rescues him from the fire he ignites in his drunken rage thereafter. Accorded dignity, he is less the genre's classic sidekick and more a manservant ('My boy'). If, as so often in Ford, this accords with the film's era, the director nevertheless also insists on grounding Pompey in the ideological action of the film, his role in Stoddard's allegorical classroom a crucial indicator of the black race's rightful claim to a place in the America-to-be.

That Tom should interrupt the class and order Pompey back to the ranch is therefore especially telling of the ambiguous position he occupies in the scheme of things. He also tells Hallie to go back out of harm's way where she belongs – the kitchen, obviously – and ignores her stern '*You* don't own me'. Tom seems to bring out anger in Hallie, as if she needs to match the scale of the man, fearful of being consumed. When she leaves the classroom, Tom pointedly watches her exit before even acknowledging the others. Perhaps she senses that Tom's investment in her is unbalanced, unhealthy in its denial of a larger vision. Hallie's own long look at Tom's back as he departs down the darkened alley behind the kitchen had come after Ranse's decision to stay. She stands at the door, involuntarily clutching her apron, gazing after him as he walks into the shadows: another prophetic moment.

Like so many of Ford's characters, Tom is a creature of paradox. The logic of his position should be to support open range, rather than statehood and the interests of the 'sodbusters', the contemptuous term he and Liberty both employ for small homesteaders. Yet he launches the election meeting to select delegates to the territorial assembly, only to refuse the nomination – he has 'personal plans'. History traps Tom – he is a contradictory mixture of reactionary values and progressive behaviours. By positioning Tom on the fence, the film makes Hallie's choice of Ranse not only a choice of self-discovery but also a vote for the values of social regulation. Her sacrifice of Tom accords with the West's march into the future, its phasing out of the individual as guarantor of law. In terms of both the Fordian text and the ideological superstructure of the genre, it is clear why Hallie and Tom cannot marry. For Ford, history is the process of law being introduced and defended. As the *Cahiers du Cinéma* collective analysis of *Young Mr Lincoln* had demonstrated, in Ford it is the woman (Lana, Clementine, Martha) who bequeaths the law to the hero, validating his violent defence of the community.[69]

Genre logic thus requires the marriage of the Eastern woman and the frontiersman, Wyatt and Clem the prototypes, a union of culture and wilderness skills. Joining Tom and Hallie, Western man and Western woman, would be to arrest the future. Indeed, as Doug Williams has pointed out, the obvious pair here is Ranse and Tom, an unacceptably queer solution to tradition's demands of a union of law and force.[70] Given Stoddard's coding as feminised Easterner, the genre positions the West's forceful Hallie as his appropriate partner. The catch is that the union is too weak to sustain the community; the crucial covert assistance of Doniphon to supply the Westerner's violence makes civilisation's progress possible.

That the film sides with law, education and nationhood is not in question. Few films, and no Westerns, are more didactic than *Liberty Valance*. The film is an educational document, a revisionist history and a primer in the political process. Ranse's class provides a lecture on political theory; Tom provides a painful outdoor demonstration in frontier practice. Thereafter, we have a lesson in voting procedures – unsuccessfully challenged by Valance – for the selection of Shinbone's delegates to the territorial assembly. The lat-

ter then takes us to the threshold of joining the American republic. No film so methodical in dramatising the democratic process could fail to be committed to its values.

But another lesson the film teaches is that the political depends on the personal. The
apparently lucky shot with which Stoddard dispatched Valance, if it freed Shinbone and
the territory, incapacitates the lawyer. Nominated to represent the territory as the man
who shot Valance, he is overcome with guilt. Enter Tom, a brutish lost soul, like Doc
Holliday on a bad day, visibly out of place. The inspired use of his recall (Ford flashing
back within the overall flashback) lifts the curtain on Tom's brilliant piece of theatre.
The duel between Ranse and Liberty is re-enacted within a lethal triangular *mise en scène*
directed by Tom. A morality play of heroic justice accomplished in a classic gunfight is
performed, but in fact America was born in murder. Tom's memory corrects the play for
Stoddard; the senator's replay animates the events for his audience. But appearances –
'print the legend' – insist on the ideal marriage of law and authority in the lawyer's person: he is the man who shot Liberty Valance. The image is preferred to the real.

Liberty Valance is another woman's film – 'Hallie's Story' – describing her sacrifice for
the future, hers and America's. It is also male melodrama: Ranse gains purpose, love and
a bitterly unwanted fame but at the sacrifice of his own identity, the victim of another's
nobility. Similarly, Tom sacrifices his own values and historical meaning to free the
woman he loves to enter the future she seeks. Killing Liberty is killing his own liberty –
a metaphysical suicide leading inevitably to the anonymous corpse lying in the wooden
coffin. Tom had sensed what he had done after the killing, drinking recklessly and
smashing up the saloon, as if haunted by Liberty's ghost. What Liberty's demise and
Tom's fate represent is the death of the individual spirit that accompanies the institutionalising of the territory. That process is visible in the collectivised body of the
wrangling assembly, and prominent in the shameless exploitation of pioneer history that
inflates the speeches of both Starbuck and Peabody. It is politics that now tames the frontier, a lariat-twirling mounted cowboy a stage prop in the campaign by the big ranchers.

As in *Fort Apache*, the architect of the myths deconstructs them in order to reaffirm
them. Author of so many films that sing the civilising of America, Ford provides a self-
critique and revises his history – the untamed nation required murder to achieve its
civilisation. In *Liberty Valance*, Ford suggests that the mythic properties of the genre as
he developed and articulated them were fabrications. His attitude towards the domestication of the West was different now. The heroic sacrifice of the pioneer is buried,
forgotten, papered over by myth. There is no longer room for the untrammeled individualism that shaped the nation. It is impossible to escape the feeling that in *The Man
Who Shot Liberty Valance* America's greatest film-maker was in fact feeling his age,
increasingly out of place in a Hollywood and America that was rapidly changing.

Cheyenne Autumn (1964)

A blot on our shield.

It is impossible to look at *Cheyenne Autumn* from an authorial and structural point of
view without thinking immediately of all the other journeys – of *Stagecoach* and *The
Grapes of Wrath*, *The Long Voyage Home* and *3 Godfathers*, *The Searchers* and *Wagon Master*. Ford's films, even where their structure is not a journey, are full of departures and

arrivals, epic comings and goings, quests and missions, exodus and exile. Gates and doors are charged junctions between the home and history, fences and rivers are critical borders and tests. Windows, props of melodrama, allow characters to look out and inside themselves, at life's parade.

Epic enough, the journey of the Cheyenne is altogether too autumnal, even wintry, its heroism a dimmed affair. The sad narration hangs over the film far more than its framing use in the cavalry films, and describes no triumph, not even of memory. The Cheyenne reach their homeland, but its attainment provides little light at the end of the film's tunnel. *Cheyenne Autumn* is the logical successor to *Two Rode Together*. That film evoked the barriers to the white captives' repatriation; *Cheyenne Autumn* portrays a tragic futility in the attempts of the Cheyenne. Ford was seventy when he took on the challenge of a return to the ambitious epic journey form. Like his characters, he would find going home again a difficult undertaking.

Returning to the ground of his cavalry trilogy, Ford seizes on the familiar themes of leadership and boundaries, and the conflicts of duty, law and ethics, but here dramatising them in parallel white and Cheyenne worlds that are both declining and compromised in the late-frontier. Leaving the Oklahoma reservation on which they are dying, their numbers reduced from 1,000 to 286, the Cheyenne Nation's epic trek to their Yellowstone homeland 1,800 miles away reaches its nadir when the ill-equipped and divided tribe arrives at Fort Robinson. Refusing to turn back to the reservation, they are penned up in a frigid warehouse on the orders of Karl Malden's fort commander, the rigid Captain Wessels. Dramatising bigotry in another narrative that confronted racial themes head-on, Ford again resorts to melodrama's extremes and scapegoats the character with the incipient racism of a whole system, constructing Wessels as a Prussian obsessed with 'orders'.

Nonetheless, the film accurately reflects what had been the US government's overall policy with the defeated Indians. Attempting to 'restrain' the Cheyenne, Wessels was punishing the recalcitrant Indians for breaking out of land 'reserved' for them, although not the Promised Land reserved by God, as the Mormons believed of their valley in *Wagon Master*. As in *Liberty Valance*, a later frontier dictated a reversal of the genre's ideological structure. *Cheyenne Autumn* describes an attempt by the tribe to reject the journey that had already been enforced on them, one that from the white point of view had them leaving the wilderness for the settled world of the reservation. The Cheyenne saw it differently. The reservation was a savage world: civilisation for them lay in their ancestral lands of the past.

Ford had defined his desire to portray the Indians as 'magnificent in their stoical dignity'.[71] Stoicism, of course, is the province of the defeated, and is thus appropriate for the Cheyenne, whom we first meet standing for hours on end in the searing desert heat waiting in vain for the white man. Waiting with them is the teacher of the Cheyenne children, Quaker Deborah Wright (Carroll Baker), who will be the tribe's advocate and a witness to their Calvary. Deborah's presence, together with her suitor, cavalry Captain Tom Archer (Richard Widmark), provides the necessary sympathetic white perspective to mediate and balance with the racism of a mainstream America. Solicited by Deborah to help the Indians, the cavalry commander, Major Braden (George O'Brien), shares the same cautious, legalistic attitude that Wessels will display: 'My job is to *guard* them.'

When you have lived as long as he has, you learn that 'it pays to stick to your own knitting'.

The Cheyenne unearth guns hidden under fire-beds, arm themselves and leave in the darkness. Ford includes an economic and evocative detail, a sole Indian slowly circling a wigwam as he rolls up its cover. It is Ford at his best, an image both functional and educational, satisfying an audience's anthropological fascination with an ancient culture while marking the sadness of the dramatic moment, the break-up of the home.

Reluctantly pursuing them, Archer is served by an unstable junior officer, Second Lieutenant Scott (Patrick Wayne), whose father had died in a massacre when he was a child, and who consequently looks forward to battle: 'I've waited ten years for this.' Another Ford giant, Mike Mazurki serves as Top Sergeant Stanislas Wichowsky, who is approaching retirement but will re-up despite his distaste for their present mission. Son of Polish immigrants, Wichowsky is reminded too much by the cavalry's role with the Cheyenne of the Cossacks' behaviour in Poland. Both Ben Johnson as Trooper Plumtree and Harry Carey, Jr as Smith are also on hand, with Archer's misremembering of the latter's name a rather tired, not very apt reprise of Colonel Thursday's insensitivity in *Fort Apache*.

The Cheyenne cross the river, leaving the reservation, and dig in. 'What is happening?' Spanish Woman (Dolores Del Rio) asks Dull Knife (Gilbert Roland); he replies deliberately, 'War . . . I think.' The parallel analysis Ford develops between pursued and pursuers is focused by the immaturity of warriors on both sides. Red Shirt (Sal Mineo) looks forward to the combat that he will initiate, firing the first shot. He is the Indian version of the reckless Scott, his wildness evident in the way he flirts with one of Little

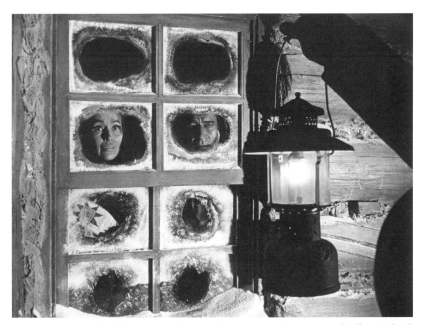

Correcting the myth of the savage: Dolores Del Rio as Spanish Woman and Gilbert Roland as Dull Knife

Wolf's young wives. Typical of the military's irrelevance in late Ford, Major Braden is out-manoeuvred when the Cheyenne stampede the cavalry's horses. He dies, leaving Archer as the ranking officer.

The sudden vacuum in leadership on the white side is balanced by the death of the Cheyenne chief, Tall Tree (Victor Jory), who earlier had collapsed in the heat as he waited for the no-show legislators. Expiring after the battle, he chooses between his sons to bequeath the sacred bundle symbolic of tribe chief to Little Wolf (Ricardo Montalban), rather than to Dull Knife, the impetuous Red Shirt's father. The disappointed Dull Knife will ultimately be unable to accept his subordinate role, and divide the tribe. In a fair effort to match the funerals his cowboys receive, Ford provides a burial ceremony for Tall Tree, his corpse entombed in a cave behind boulders, a horizon shot of warriors standing on the canyon rim above.

Ford frames the tragic undertaking of the Cheyenne ironically, with glimpses provided by Archer's narration describing the white world's reactions. Alarm spreads across the nation as reports circulate of attacks by bloodthirsty savages. Legislation is prepared to shift the Bureau of Indian Affairs from the Department of the Interior to the Army, whom Archer's narration critiques as 'land grabbers'. Secretary of the Interior, Charles Schurz (Edward G. Robinson), extracts a promise that the legislation will be stalled to give him a shot at resolving the problem. Further vignettes add to the picture of red–white interactions. Two Cheyenne beg food from a cattle drive's cowboys, only to be murdered. Ford's revisionism turns a cowpoke ghoulish – 'I shore would like to kill me an Indian'; like *The Searchers'* Ethan, he scalps his victim. Spanish Woman predicts that the buffalo will come, but the hillsides are littered with bones, the buffalo slaughtered by whites.

The parallelism between deteriorating red and white worlds is the film's spine. Red Shirt's open invitations to Little Wolf's young wife widens the rift emerging among the Cheyenne: 'they no longer think as one'. Catching up with the tribe, Archer lectures Lieutenant Scott – it is good to be brave, but 'not to be *too* brave' – and unwisely splits his force, leaving Scott in command of a contingent of troopers. The young officer immediately orders a charge, a debacle in which the humbled character is wounded. The incident suggests the sad state of Ford's army. Eight years after *The Searchers*, where he had played the comical green cavalry officer whose sword ends up in the Captain/Reverend Clayton's rear, Patrick Wayne's officer, although promoted to a significant role remains unformed, immature. In both films he portrays a boyish type in the shadow of his father, a situation John Wayne's son surely knew something about. When Scott returns from medical leave, Archer delivers a line – 'You might make a soldier after all' – but we have seen no evidence of growth.

Although the Cheyenne had two small victories over inept cavalry at the outset, overall the trajectory of the first third of the film is bleak. At this point, Ford changes the film's register completely, with a decisive shift to the white world and point of view in the comic interlude of Dodge City and Wyatt Earp. Ford had obviously seen the Cheyenne fleeing a barren Oklahoma reservation pursued by US cavalry as a yarn of allegorical resonance. True to his roots in the silent era, Ford excelled at vignettes, tableaux and cameos. As his chapter for *How the West Was Won* also showed, he was a master at creating self-contained short narratives, small exemplary episodes marked with his distinctive themes and vision. *Cheyenne Autumn* doubled the process, constructing a comic short piece within a larger tragic episode. But reminiscent of *Sergeant Rutledge*, the effect of a sharp boundary between the pathos of the oppressed racial minority and the absurdities and antics of a warped white community was to create entities a world apart and an overly righteous tone. As in the earlier film, the effect of such extremes was to flatten the director's usual nuanced characterisations and create a largely monolithic struggle.

Like *Two Rode Together*'s Tascosa, Dodge is ridiculed as an anti-community, inhabited by cheats and braggarts. A professional gambler attired in an immaculate white suit, a far cry from *Clementine*'s icon of integrity, James Stewart's Earp wins a duel by shooting an opponent in the toe with a concealed derringer. The only other duel in the film, the inevitable showdown between Little Wolf and Red Shirt in its coda, also departs from the classic form. Challenged, the boy leaps on his horse and rides hard, dismounting on the edge of the clearing, where Little Wolf shoots the boy before he can even set himself. It is a duel fuelled by masculine rage, an affair of revenge rather than honour, a stain on the Cheyenne. Like Guthrie McCabe's killing of Stone Calf in *Two Rode Together*, it is close to murder.

The differing tone of the duels – comic and tragic – focuses the film's strategy of creating parallel universes, one that is ultimately counter-productive to achieving coherency and dramatic force. But the comedy of the Dodge City events does critique the white world somewhat more successfully than in *Sergeant Rutledge*. Brought news of the proximity of 'the murdering devils' by moronic cowboys, the town turns into an anarchic stampede, a mobilisation complete with travelling saloons and madams in a headlong whooping rush into the desert in search of the Indians. Earlier, intent on his cards, Wyatt had ignored a Miss Plantagenet (Elizabeth Allen), who had claimed they had once known each other. As a shot rings out turning the town's expedition into a cowardly mad dash homeward, Earp finds himself struggling to drive his buggy in the crush, as the lady in her bloomers lies upside down on his lap: 'I *did* know her in Kansas City.' The bawdy line rings down the curtain on a comic interlude that flaunts the white world's own loss of honour, courage and mission.

Eight hundred miles on and now north of Nebraska, 'the Cheyenne nation broke apart', Archer informs us. Dull Knife decides that the journey must halt at Fort Robinson to save the women and children from hunger and the cold. His brother rebels and departs, Little Wolf's young wife fatefully abandoning her marriage and following Red Shirt and Dull Knife. Traditional loyalties and duties are lost.

With the arrival of the Cheyenne at Fort Robinson, Captain Wessels hosts a dinner party worthy of *Rio Grande*'s elegance. Deborah and Archer attend, as well as the fort's doctor, another of Ford's Irish alcoholics, Sean McClory's Dr O'Carberry. But there are no serenades, and the affair ends with the arrival of government orders to restrain the Indians, which the captain takes to mean imprisonment. Career risk, first sounded by Major Braden at the outset, comes into focus again as the test all face. 'This will make me a major,' chortles Wessels. His cowardice is contrasted with Archer's initiative in going to seek Schurz out in Washington. Schurz in turn wonders if intervening will be a false move. Ford frames Robinson reflected in the glass of Lincoln's photograph, the faces overlapping: 'Old friend . . . what would you do?'

Trying to break the Cheyenne, ironically it is Wessels who deteriorates. On the other hand, the doctor has stopped drinking and seizes command, confining Wessels to quarters. Too late – the desperate Cheyenne break, fleeing into the wintry desert. However, a final disastrous confrontation is not to be. Arriving like the cavalry of old to prevent a blood bath by the present-day cavalry, Schurz parleys with Dull Knife and Little Wolf and persuades them to trust him, offering cigars.

The still hotheaded Red Shirt draws a bead on the Secretary of the Interior but is stymied by Spanish Woman. Coded as the proud spirit of the Cheyenne, a consummate horseman, Red Shirt is the victim of the white policies that had weakened and divided the Cheyenne Nation, leaving him without a role and identity. His death is a meaningless sacrifice, martyrdom without a cause. Tribal law prohibits the chief from serving if he has taken the blood of another Cheyenne; Little Wolf passes the sacred bundle to his anguished brother and goes into exile. *Cheyenne Autumn* ends with Tom and Deborah and a little Indian girl, teacher and pupil spelling out H-O-M-E. The couple looks off at the riders silhouetted against the setting sun, Little Wolf in a final horizon shot from Ford. His ode to the dispossessed Indian, a poor man's *Searchers*, the film ends with the Ford paradox of a heroic leader losing his home.

There is no attempt by Ford to deconstruct the epic; it simply implodes from its weakened protagonists and abortive action. The Cheyenne achieve the legal and spiritual vindication of a higher moral ground. But their pyrrhic victory is an uninspiring spectacle, a sombre portrait of an impotent people at the end of their rope. For once, the cathedral of Monument Valley provides no ennobling perspectives. The more memorable images are of Fort Robinson's frosty warehouse windowpanes through which the imprisoned Indian faces look. With its ageing warriors, last campaigns and the recycling of actions such as the stampede of horses to avoid hostilities and the last-minute intervention of a benign Washington, *Cheyenne Autumn* recalls *She Wore a Yellow Ribbon*. But the contrast is telling: where the latter celebrates victory in the face of myriad disappointments, *Cheyenne Autumn* records despair and tragic waste despite the epic heroism.

'Hunger bayed at their heels more fiercely than the soldiers.' The film's occasionally rhetorical narration attempts to elevate the action of an all-too-absurd world. Ford had talked of casting Indians in the principal Cheyenne roles, and of having them speak the native tongue rather than English, the language of the oppressor. At seventy, the director was standing on the threshold of a period of great social upheaval, a massive and pervasive ideological interrogation of race, ethnicity and gender. As with *Sergeant Rutledge*, he was attempting to stay abreast of the ethos and pay his dues in his artistic forms of choice, according to his lights:

> I've killed more Indians than Custer, Beecher and Chivington put together, and people in Europe always want to know about the Indians. There are two sides to every story, but I wanted to show their point of view for a change. Let's face it, we've treated them very badly – it's a blot on our shield; we've cheated and robbed, killed, murdered, massacred and everything else, but they kill one white man and, God, out come the troops.[72]

But in truth, Ford had often tried to tell both sides of the story, his images of Indians at times ennobling and respectful. If the approach was romantic and paternalistic, those were the essential terms of his myth-making style. The credits of *Cheyenne Autumn*, shots of a bronzed statue of an Indian warrior on horseback, defined his preferred aesthetic of monumentalising his subjects, but also suggested the dangers of petrification that the film does not altogether avoid.

The timing of Ford's project could not have been worse. The radical event of *Easy Rider* (1969), with its retooling of the genre and discovery of a new audience sensibility, was but a few years away. Ford was focused on dramatising a sad tale of the effects of Eurocentric policies and practices, while wrestling with the pitfalls of replicating such in the work itself. In the end, he would have to make his peace with industrial logic and accept Latin players in the major roles, as well as Sal Mineo, an Italian-American, as Red Shirt. It would be a damaging burden, raising the bar of disbelief's suspension. It is one thing to watch relatively unknown players like Henry Brandon or Woody Strode enact Indians; it is altogether different seeing Hollywood stars like Gilbert Roland, Ricardo Montalban, Victor Jory or Mineo play the Cheyenne. The fabric of the piece was drastically affected, visibly compromising its authenticity.

In 1966 Ford made his last film, *7 Women*, which was received with great appreciation abroad, where a sophisticated film culture brought an awareness of Ford's long career to bear. However, but for a few positive notices, it was dismissed in the USA, not surprising given the habit of amnesiac American reviewers of the time to approach each film as an isolated event.

In any case, *7 Women* was unmistakably a Ford film, most obviously in its resemblance to a disguised Western, with its vulnerable mission menaced by Mongol warriors in remote China, and its group of Christian missionaries whose rescue is effected by the intervention of Anne Bancroft, as the arrogant, cynical Dr Cartwright. More than one viewer was moved to suggest that Bancroft was styling her performance on Wayne, the Ford prototype. What is undeniable, however, is that Ford was working with his usual Western formula of the imperilled community and the heroic, redemptive action that preserves the future. Coming at the end of his career, the film was to provide a felicitous bookend to *Stagecoach*, the earlier, equally significant landmark that had announced his magisterial return to the Western and had launched the series of great works that were to come.

Recalling Dallas and the prostitute that character resembled from Maupassant's 'Boule de suif', Cartwright is the fallen woman on whose heroic action the salvation of the group depends. Fordian paradoxes abound. The one character without faith, the empiricist doctor makes the greatest sacrifice, giving her life so others can live, embracing a suffering akin to crucifixion. The most civilised of characters is forced to mate with the savage, the gross Mongol chief, Tunga Khan (Mike Mazurki). The doctor poisons her enemy and herself, another of Ford's black sheep who departs the community she has preserved. The final image we may remember from Ford's world is of Bancroft, rouged and bedecked like a concubine, making her way with a lantern down the darkened hallway's tunnel to the waiting barbarian. It is Ford's last stand, an apt affirmation of the glory in defeat, of faith's brave light against the darkness.

It is altogether appropriate that Ford's last film should have turned out to be a melodrama centred entirely on women. For those who had received his films without a close

look, it may have appeared ironic that the director associated with the most masculine of genres should have finished with such an anomalous work. From this perspective, it is tempting to see *7 Women* in line with *Sergeant Rutledge* and *Cheyenne Autumn* as a series that attempts to give equal time to, and make penance for, the neglected or maligned minority groups of earlier efforts. In fact, nothing could be further from the truth. In his domesticated West, with its often feminised heroes, its threatened families and emerging Americas, women are celebrated as an indispensable force, major players in an unsung history that his work clearly addresses and corrects.

According to his lights and within the window of his time, Ford celebrated men and women, whites and Others, the majority and minorities. His was a heroic cinema, a luminous and uplifting world of myth and memory. Ford told of characters who did things, who became and achieved, raising families, establishing law, settling communities, building the nation. Over this shining world a second cast its shadow, not one of noir violence and evil, but rather a tragic shadow of life's inevitable pain, sacrifice and compromise. For all the glory, each pilgrimage came finally to the end of the rainbow, a Fort Apache of disappointment, damage and defeat. As a character in a film by the great Japanese director, Yasujiro Ozu, had once put it, life was sad. But each film orchestrated the mix in its distinctive fashion, with its own tempo, beat and rhythm, to sing its praises and laments.

In his work, and especially in the Westerns, Ford gave us the best of both worlds. To cut oneself off from its richness, beauty and music out of a latter-day political correctness is to pay a high price for righteousness. If, as composer Richard Rogers put it, song is as essential to us as food and fraternity, we must be grateful for John Ford. At its best, his melody was set to a programme of idealised images of loving families and loyal brotherhoods, of warm ties and sacred bonds. A new millennium is sensitive to the erotic and patriarchal sources of much of the cinema's visual pleasure. But few in Ford's era or our own have been so blessed as to have no need of his work's fortifying visual pleasure, the state of grace and soulful connection to humanity and nature that Ford's images offer. The fact that the films are grounded in their historical moment with its ideological burdens should not be seen as unfortunate. It is because Ford was so deeply rooted in his time and struggled so tenaciously to understand and honour it that his films achieved their insight, complexity and spiritual force.

Notes

1. In his indispensable *Searching for John Ford* (New York: St Martin's Press, 2001), pp. 480–3, Joseph McBride points out that Ford's ostensibly principled stand was typically counterbalanced immediately in an apologetic note to DeMille, and in a later conversation praising his courageous performance at the Guild meeting.

2. Lewis Jacobs, *The Rise of the American Film* (New York: Teachers College Press, 1939), p. 485; Arthur Knight, *The Liveliest Art* (New York and Toronto: New American Library, 1957), p. 178.

3. Lindsay Anderson, 'The Director's Cinema?' *Sequence* no. 12 (Autumn 1950), p. 8.

Ford's last black sheep: Anne Bancroft in *7 Women*

4. Ibid.

5. Andrew Sarris, (ed.), *Interviews with Film Directors* (New York: Avon Books, 1967), p. 193.

6. Peter Wollen, *Signs and Meanings in the Cinema* (London: Secker and Warburg/BFI, 1969), p. 97.

7. In a 1955 interview originally published in *Cahiers du Cinéma* no. 45 (March 1955) and reprinted in Sarris, Mitry had commented on the 'theme of a small group of people thrust by chance into dramatic or tragic circumstances'. Ford replied:

   > It enables me to make individuals aware of each other by bringing them face to face with something bigger than themselves. The situation, the tragic moment, forces men to reveal themselves, and to become aware of what they truly are. The device allows me to find the exceptional in the commonplace. (Sarris, *Interviews*, p. 197)

8. From a discussion I chaired with Ford and teachers attending a summer school at the American Film Institute at its Center for Advanced Film Studies in Los Angeles on 17 July 1970. In an apparent non sequitur, Ford went on to say that he came 'from a pedagogical family' who had served as the 'heads of the Irish College in Galway', and that his father had been 'a very well-educated man'. This could have been simply a response to the seminar's teachers (some of whom were Catholic nuns), but may also have been prompted by the film's focus on the efforts to educate its 'simple people'.

9. Ford's 'distrust of dominant power structures' is systematically explored in Charles Ramirez Berg's 'The Margin as Center', in Gaylyn Studlar and Matthew Bernstein (eds), *John Ford Made Westerns* (Bloomington and Indianapolis: Indiana University Press, 2001), pp. 75–101.

10. Edward Waterhouse, *A Declaration of the State of the Colony and Affaires in Virginia, with a Relation of the Barbarous Massacre, 1622* (Amsterdam: Theatrum Orbis Terrarum, 1970).

11. Richard Maltby, 'A Better Sense of History', in Ian Cameron and Douglas Pye (eds), *The Book of Westerns* (New York: Continuum, 1996), pp. 34–49. Maltby's essay scathingly critiques Ford, the Western and studies such as this one for perpetuating a racist history.

12. Peter Bogdanovich, *John Ford* (London: Studio Vista/*Movie* Magazine, 1967), p. 83.

13. The presence of Ford's older brother Francis, whose star as actor and director had waned as the younger sibling's had risen, is a frequent, troubling reminder of how problematic Ford's family relations were. Cast in town drunk/holy fool roles, as for instance in *Drums along the Mohawk* and *Wagon Master*, he supplies frontier colour but rarely speaks.

14. Robert Warshow, *The Immediate Experience* (New York: Anchor/Doubleday, 1962), pp. 93–4. 'If justice and order did not continually demand his presence, he would be without a calling. Indeed we come upon him often in just that situation, as the reign of law settles over the West and he is forced to see that his day is over.'

15. Stuart Byron, '*The Searchers*: Cult Movie of the New Hollywood', *New York* (5 March 1979), pp. 45–8.

16. Robin Wood, '*Shall* We Gather at the River?: the Late Films of John Ford', *Film*

Comment vol. 7 no. 3 (Autumn 1971), pp. 8–17; reprinted in Studlar and Bernstein (eds), *John Ford Made Westerns*, pp. 23–41.

17. Sarris, *Interviews*, p. 194.

18. Bogdanovich, *John Ford*, p. 86.

19. Ford's *3 Bad Men* opens with a title announcing: 'Gold on Indian land! The Sioux tribes were given other reservations, and President Grant set a day when settlers might race for possession of the rich lands.'

20. Henry Nash Smith, *Virgin Land: The American West as Symbol and Myth* (Cambridge, MA: Harvard University Press, 1950).

21. Jane Tompkins, *West of Everything: The Inner Life of Westerns* (New York: Oxford University Press, 1992).

22. Bogdanovich, *John Ford*, p. 108.

23. André Bazin, 'The Evolution of the Western', in Hugh Gray (ed.), *What is Cinema?* vol. 2 (Berkeley: University of California Press, 1971), pp. 149–57; reprinted in Jim Kitses and Gregg Rickman (eds), *The Western Reader* (New York: Limelight Editions, 1998), pp. 49–56.

24. Walker Percy, *The Moviegoer* (New York: Knopf, 1961), p. 7.

25. Edward Buscombe, *Stagecoach* (London: BFI, 1992), pp. 12–16, 78–80.

26. Ibid., p. 18.

27. Bogdanovich, *John Ford*, p. 69. 'It was really *Boule-de-suif*, and I imagine the writer Ernie Haycox got the idea from there and turned it into a Western story which he called "Stage to Lordsburg".'

28. Richard Slotkin, *Gunfighter Nation: The Myth of the Frontier in Twentieth-Century America* (New York: Atheneum, 1992), pp. 303–12.

29. Buscombe, *Stagecoach*, pp. 45–6.

30. Editors, 'John Ford's *Young Mr Lincoln*', *Cahiers du Cinéma* no. 223 (August 1970), pp. 29–47; reprinted in Bill Nichols (ed.), *Movies and Methods* (Berkeley: University of California Press, 1976), pp. 493–529.

31. For an account that centres an ideological analysis on Blue Back, see Robin Wood's '*Drums Along the Mohawk*', *CineAction!* (Spring 1987); reprinted in Cameron and Pye (eds), *The Book of Westerns*, pp. 174–80.

32. Robert Lyons (ed.), *My Darling Clementine* (New Brunswick, NJ: Rutgers University Press, 1984), p. 148.

33. Warshow, *Immediate Experience*, pp. 101–2.

34. Scott Simmon, 'Concerning the Weary Legs of Wyatt Earp: The Classic Western According to Shakespeare', *Literature/Film Quarterly* vol. 24 no. 2 (April 1996), pp. 114–27; reprinted in Kitses and Richman (eds), *The Western Reader*, pp. 149–66. Simmon develops his analysis further in his *The Invention of the Western Film* (Cambridge: Cambridge University Press, 2003).

35. Lyons, *Clementine*, p. 143.

36. Changes in the shooting made the decoying largely ceremonial; the impersonations of Morg and Doc by the mayor and elder provide no tangible advantage.

37. Wollen, *Signs and Meanings*, p. 96; Bill Nichols, 'Style, Grammar and the Movies', in Nichols (ed.), *Movies and Methods*, pp. 616–17.

38. Tag Gallagher, *John Ford: The Man and His Films* (Berkeley: University of California Press, 1986), p. 225.

39. Simmon, 'Weary Legs', p. 161. Like *The Searchers*, *Clementine* is a film that has been a focus of an evolving critical field; I trace some of the key studies Simmon refers to in *The Western Reader*, pp. 21–2, p. 31 n. 7.

40. Gilberto Perez argues in his *The Material Ghost: Films and Their Medium* (Baltimore, MD: Johns Hopkins University Press, 1998), p. 249 that the ending's disturbing effect is purposeful rather than the result of confusion, falsification of history or ideological duplicity.

41. McBride, *Searching*, pp. 446–7.

42. Bogdanovich, *John Ford*, p. 108.

43. Ford's claim never to have seen *Clementine* is disputed by George Bluestone. At a retrospective of his films at the University of Washington in Seattle, Ford had left for dinner after speaking before the film, but then returned:

> 'It's okay, they serve until ten', he whispered. We sat through the film and when the famous hoedown scene came on with all its lyrical pleasure, Ford leaned over and said, 'Hey, you know this isn't a bad movie. I haven't seen it in a while'. I noticed he sat with his good eye favoring the screen. (George Bluestone, 'Recalling a 1955 Interview with John Ford' in Gerald Peary (ed.), *John Ford Interviews* [Jackson: University of Mississippi Press, 2001, p. 36]).

44. Parrish is quoted in Gallagher, *John Ford*, p. 463.

45. Joseph McBride discusses Zanuck's changes in his *Searching*, pp. 435–7.

46. Ibid., p. 438.

47. Gallagher, *John Ford*, p. 465.

48. Andrew Sinclair, *John Ford: A Biography* (New York: Lorimer Publishing, 1979), p. 147.

49. 'The Golden Years: Dudley Nichols', in Richard Corliss (ed.), *The Hollywood Screenwriters* (New York: Avon Books, 1972), p. 109. 'I sought and found a series of symbols to make visual the tragic psychology of the informer.'

50. Bogdanovich, *John Ford*, p. 87.

51. Quoted in Sinclair, *John Ford*, p. 147.

52. McBride, *Searching*, p. 440.

53. Bogdanovich, *John Ford*, p. 88.

54. Ibid., p. 86.

55. Sinclair, *John Ford*, p. 168.

56. Andrew Sarris, *American Cinema: Directors and Directions 1929–68* (New York: E. P. Dutton, 1968), p. 47.

57. Bogdanovich, *John Ford*, pp. 93–4.

58. Brian Henderson, '*The Searchers*: An American Dilemma', *Film Quarterly* vol. 34 no. 2 (Winter 1980–1), pp. 9–23; reprinted in Nichols (ed.), *Movies and Methods* vol. 2 (Berkeley: University of California Press, 1985), pp. 429–49.

59. *Cahiers du Cinéma* no. 184 (November 1966); translated in Joseph McBride and Michael Wilmington, *John Ford* (London: Secker and Warburg, 1974), p. 148.

60. Gaylin Studlar, 'Sacred Duties, Poetic Passions', in Studlar and Bernstein, *John Ford Made Westerns*, p. 54.

61. Henderson, '*The Searchers*: An American Dilemma'.

62. Byron, '*The Searchers*: Cult Movie'.

63. Quoted in Sinclair, *John Ford*, p. 191.

64. McBride, *Searching*, pp. 609–10.

65. Bogdanovich, *John Ford*, p. 97.

66. Ibid., pp. 97–8.

67. See note 8 above.

68. Gallagher, *John Ford*, p. 406.

69. Editors, 'John Ford's *Young Mr Lincoln*'.

70. Doug Williams, 'Pilgrims and the Promised Land: A Genealogy of the Western', in Kitses and Rickman (eds), *The Western Reader*, pp. 93–113.

71. Quoted in Sinclair, *John Ford*, p. 198.

72. Bogdanovich, *John Ford*, p. 104.

3
Anthony Mann: The Overreacher

If Christ hadn't risen there would have been no story.[1]

From The Great Flamarion to the Cid, from beginning to end, the characters of Anthony Mann are extreme men stretching out beyond their reach. Rarely is it a matter of choice; as if possessed, these men push ahead completely at the mercy of forces within themselves. Whether demonic or divine, the vessels of a vision or a disturbance, they have little hope of the settled relationships within which most men live. Typically, they are driven to sacrifice or reject the complex ties of family and society; often, they are usurpers.

Given this perspective, it is clear that the significance of Mann's first commercial and artistic success, *T-Men* (1947), has been misunderstood. Location work was always to be important to Mann (*T-Men* was his first project shot outside the studio, by no means commonplace in 1947), and here he seized on the freedom to script and film a subject as he liked. For ten years, Mann had been waiting in the wings, an apprentice to the cheap second-feature. But although its urban atmosphere is notable, *T-Men*'s force flows directly from a structure that requires its young heroes to penetrate a sinister counterfeiting gang. As the married agent, Alfred Ryder consequently finds himself forced to play the role to the hilt, first denying his wife when she comes upon him in a market in his undercover persona, and then his partner, Dennis O'Keefe, who has to support the gang, his own disguise intact, as they destroy his fellow agent. This kind of tragic paradox would always fascinate Mann. In all his thrillers of the late 1940s, he evoked two worlds diametrically opposed, one of innocence and purity, the other an evil domain that extracts a sacrifice in its defeat. Nowhere was this interaction more harshly in evidence than in *Border Incident* (1949), Mann capitalising on the success of *T-Men* by adapting its structure to the subject of an immigration racket operating in the American Southwest. However, here the melodrama was radically extended by an elemental violence, one agent ground into a field by a tractor, the other nearly suffocating nightmarishly in quicksand. If the city never offered Mann the setting to extend his talents, the terrain of *Border Incident*, shaping the narrative and bringing alive the action, clearly did. In a fragmented way (like *T-Men*, the film has a documentary framework), the metaphorical drive of the imagery – especially in its climax, where gangsters march along the rim of a steep canyon through which peasants wind their way to the

Lee J. Cobb in *Man of the West*

slaughter – gives *Border Incident* an almost symbolic level of action. Promising a thriller, Mann delivers something of a cosmic conflict that hints at the play of superhuman forces that can shape destiny.

It was in the Western that Mann was to weld together themes, structure and style to produce his most personal works. The drive towards enlarged character and heightened conflict found its natural canvas in the genre. His first efforts, the downbeat Indian picture, *Devil's Doorway* (1950), and *The Furies* (1950), a reworking of Dostoevsky's *The Idiot*, were dispiriting box-office failures. The first of these, an enterprising and early example of the 1950s pro-Indian revisionist cycle, featured Robert Taylor as an Indian Civil War veteran dishonoured and destroyed on his return to the West. *The Furies* was equally offbeat, a dark melodrama that pitted Barbara Stanwyck against her father, Walter Huston, in a struggle over their huge ranch. Curiously, the film melded the three forms that made up Mann's career – a Western (albeit *sans* any of the genre's traditional action) heavily indebted in its noir styling to the early thrillers but that also looked forward to the heady conflicts over imperial power of the later epics.

But it would be *Winchester '73* that provided a major breakthrough, sparking off the partnerships with Borden Chase and James Stewart, securing Mann's place within the industry and announcing definitively his artistic arrival. In the 1950s, Mann was to be at his most prolific and creative, directing eighteen movies in all, eleven of them Westerns, the great majority of which both bore his personal stamp and enjoyed some commercial success. Throughout the period, Mann was to advance steadily, growing in authority as his distinctive vision found expression, progressively extending his reach over the years to embrace colour, CinemaScope and more ambitious productions, until finally he stood on the threshold of the epic.

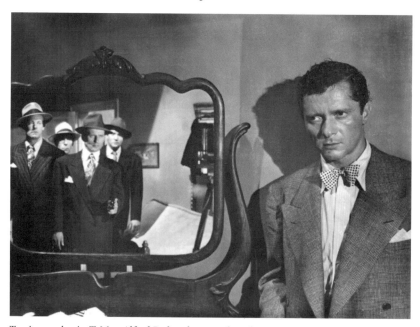

Tragic paradox in *T-Men*: Alfred Ryder plays out the role

Dominating the earlier half of the decade was Mann's remarkable collaboration with James Stewart over eight films. The quality that anchored Mann's respect for Stewart was the actor's dedication, his preparation for *Winchester '73*, for example, by spending hours firing the gun; later Mann was to speak admiringly of Stewart's readiness to do virtually anything, from staging a fight under horses' hooves to allowing himself to be dragged through a fire. This single-mindedness, interlocking with Mann's conception of character, provided the natural vehicle for the director's themes. Animating the obsessive heroes of the Westerns and the idealistic characters of *Thunder Bay* (1953), *The Glenn Miller Story* (1953) and *Strategic Air Command* (1954), Stewart revealed an unexpected emotional range, given his early career of light comedy roles. However, the charming, bemused side of the actor's talent was also important to Mann: in the Westerns, humour expressing the cynicism and softening the violent edge of the character; in the other films, the amusing vagueness and cornball jokes disguising the ruthlessness of a hero callously subordinating the rights of others to his private goal.

Mann's work outside the Western was often uneven, evidence of an unsureness in reconciling thematic drives with material: it is difficult to deify a trombone-player, no matter how good he was. Similarly, *Serenade* (1956), a bizarre operatic study of the threats that modern society holds for natural passion, took Mann to the upper reaches of melodrama, with Mario Lanza living out the tragedy of his stage role as Otello. Only with *God's Little Acre* (1958) and *Men in War* (1957), did Mann in this period approach the vigour and coherence of his best work within the Western. The setting of the Old South, the biblical undertones of the material, the violent conflicts of a divided family close to the soil, these elements in *God's Little Acre*, Erskine Caldwell's bestseller of the period, combined to provide the director with an archetypal cosmos not unlike that of his Westerns. With *Men in War*, Mann was in Sam Fuller territory, following a patrol behind enemy lines in Korea, isolated, exhausted, doomed. In contrast to *God's Little Acre*, Philip Yordan's script provided modest dramatic conflict between Robert Ryan's leader trying to return the patrol to headquarters, and Aldo Ray, whose loyalty to Robert Keith's shell-shocked colonel is rewarded when the catatonic father-figure utters his only word in the picture as he dies – 'Son'. Silent for lengthy passages, the film indulges Mann's pictorial skills and landscape logistics, the patrol navigating between hedgerows, advancing through forests and mine fields, and crawling up a mountainside under fire. Taken together, these very different films sharply highlight the themes and *mise en scène* he would wed in the Westerns.

If the genre was never to be quite the same for his work within it, in films like *The Naked Spur*, *The Last Frontier* (1955) and *Man of the West*, Mann arrived at the summit of his personal authority and expressiveness. The dynamic interplay of the concepts of individualism and communal responsibility within the form allowed Mann to return time and again to the strange neo-classic conflict of passion and duty that was always to preoccupy him. He was never to resolve the tension; and his fascination for the charismatic individual, the superior man, led him finally to the idea of transcendence, and, inevitably, the epic. Crucial, therefore, was the ambiguity of the Western's own attitudes towards these concepts, providing a structure of fruitful tension within which it was possible to achieve an art both personal and integrated. Equally important were the settings of the West, which would allow the gradual refinement of Mann's distinctively physical style and provide an unparalleled opportunity to explore through the dialectic of landscape and hero the interior and finally metaphysical conflict of his characters.

The Hero

> Well actually, he was a man who could kill his own brother ...[2]

Characteristically, the Mann hero is a revenge hero. This is the basic drive with which Mann imbues his characters, regardless of the narrative pattern. At the formal level, revenge is at the centre of only two works, *Winchester '73* and *The Man from Laramie*, although it affects the denouement of three others as well: *Bend of the River*, *The Far Country* and *Man of the West*. If we set aside *Devil's Doorway*, *The Last Frontier* and *Cimarron* (1960) – three films that I propose to consider separately here – this leaves *The Naked Spur* and *The Tin Star*, in both of which the protagonist flees a past of emotional hurt by becoming a bounty hunter. This pattern of denial is a key one, since it is a pure expression of the characteristic drive of the Mann hero. For the revenge taken by the character is exacted upon himself, a punishment the inner meaning of which is a denial of reason and humanity. In general, all of Mann's heroes behave as if driven by a vengeance they must inflict upon themselves for having once been human, trusting and, therefore, vulnerable. Hence the schizophrenic style of the hero, the violent explosions of passion alternating with precarious moments of quiet reflection.

Typically, the hero has a highly developed moral sense, while being at the mercy of

The Mann/Stewart hero: *Winchester '73*

an irrational drive to deny that very side of his nature. The hero also has a strong sense of chivalry, society's cloak for instinct and strong feeling, which vanishes when he is under stress. These tensions, extended in the structure of the films, make the Mann hero a microcosm of the community, where ideals, reason and humanity are always prominent, but below which lie self-interest, passion and violence. Passion, the special quality of the hero, suggests the directions in which he is driven – an assertion of the self above all other things, a movement towards the solitary status of a demi-god, the private and invulnerable world of madness, the total freedom of death. Dark, extreme men trapped in an impossible dilemma, making a neurotic attempt to escape themselves and rise above a past of pain and violence, Mann's heroes are brought low, driven by forces over which they have no control to face themselves, reliving the very experiences they flee.

Like the plaything of a cruel world, the Mann hero is ever at the mercy of paradox and contradiction. Lin McAdam of *Winchester '73* is a model of stability and decorum in all respects except where his own brother is concerned, the mere sight of whom dements the character. *Bend of the River* centres on the attempts of Glyn McLyntock to reject his past as a badman, the character slowly forced into a situation where, his rational exterior shattered, he must destroy a man who shares that past and is virtually a blood brother. Mann was to return to this structure (six years later, in 1958) with *Man of the West*, where the hero is driven to kill both stepbrother and stepfather before he can lay the ghost of his origins and preserve his hard-won status of peaceful citizen. Gary Cooper's Link Jones rarely exhibts the hysteria that Stewart brought to the role, the peak of which occurred in *The Naked Spur*, where, in his efforts to turn bounty hunter, Howie Kemp borders on the unbalanced. Similarly, Henry Fonda's Morg Hickman of *The Tin Star* is a softer character, although his situation is identical to Kemp's. Driven in an unnatural direction, away from the community, the hero is morally ambiguous, his actions carrying a nihilistic undertone. *The Far Country* makes the crisis explicit, Jeff Webster irrationally insisting on his isolation ('I don't need other people') despite the evidence of his commitment to Ben, his older sidekick.

Mann's heroes find themselves outside the community because of deeply personal wounds. McAdam pursues the killer of his father, his own brother, while Link Jones has been torn from society because of his past association with the gang of Dock Tobin, his evil stepfather. Fonda's Morg Hickman has been embittered by the community's indifference that resulted in the death of his wife and child, Kemp has turned to bounty hunting to find the money to buy back the ranch his faithless fiancée sold out from under him, and, more generally, Webster trusted a woman 'once'. The persistence of this kind of motivation – disturbance within the family unit in a distant past – is one source of the compulsive charge the hero carries, and gives the action a predetermined quality. In *The Man from Laramie*, most notably, the feeling created is of an ancestry that inevitably shapes what will come to pass. The Stewart character here, Will Lockhart, has left his army post to find whoever sold the rifles to the Apache who killed his brother. His persistence slowly begins to crack open the sources of evil in the Waggoman family, and old Alec, taking on Lockhart's mission, brings himself face to face with the facts: that Vic, his foster-son, is prepared to murder him, that Vic and Dave, his natural son, sold the rifles, that he himself has brought it all about through his ambition and power.

This psychological action is central to Mann's films and the source of their symmetry and moral complexity. Thus when Lockhart finally confronts his enemy over the rifles, he cannot kill Vic, who is basically a rational, amiable man with some justification for his acts – in short, a man very much like Lockhart. This tension is at the centre of *Bend of the River*, where McLyntock, despite his suspicions, hopes that the Arthur Kennedy character wants to join him in leaving a criminal life behind. But Cole, created in the film almost as an alter ego to McLyntock, slips the other way and forces division. Ironically, before he can be free, the former Missouri raider is driven to take up the stance of his past, preying on the wagon train that Cole has usurped and drowning his friend in a murderous struggle. Similarly, both Morg Hickman and Howie Kemp recreate their past even as they try to bury it. Hickman, an ex-marshal, takes lodgings with a widow and her child and is slowly drawn into the lawman problems of the young Owens. Kemp finds himself involved with Lina, a morally doubtful character whom he comes to care for despite anxieties that are naturally bolstered when she betrays him, forced to it to save his life.

Mann's heroes are always empirical men, distrustful of idealism or generalisation. Facile appeals to principle or feelings are met laconically: 'Oh, yeah?' Simple explanations of suspect happenings – the murder of innocents disguised as self-defence, double-dealing masquerading as the law – generate a similar circumspection. Knowledge is a pragmatic affair, born of experience. Judgments based on appearances are worthless, and meaningful action with all its heavy costs is not entered into lightly. In fact, Mann's characters are reluctant heroes, rarely deciding to act. With Morg Hickman in *The Tin Star*, Mann was able to emphasise the empirical side of his hero, Henry Fonda perfectly embodying the knowledge and skills that only experience can bestow. Oddly domestic for a Mann hero, Hickman is in some measure the most mature version of the type as well. Far removed from the hysteria of a Howie Kemp, Hickman's basic quality is one of resignation, a sad awareness of what the world is like. It is only the character's occasional bitterness that makes credible his occupation, the role of bounty hunter sitting uneasily on one so warmly committed to human worth. Like *The Man from Laramie*, *The Tin Star* is built round a transfer of role and qualities from the hero to a secondary character that only gradually emerges as the focus for our experience of the action. In the case of Alec Waggoman and Lockhart, age, arrogance and power are checked by moral doubt and a drive for the truth inspired by the younger man. But with *The Tin Star*, the pattern is more complex, the idealism of youth being stiffened by the wisdom and power that is passed on by Hickman, who in turn is forced to face himself through the example of Owens. In both cases, the younger man fills out the psychological structure, functioning both as something of a son to the older and as an embodiment of his youth, and in this way triggering action and change.

Mann often deceives by introducing his men as simple, uncluttered heroes, the mood slowly darkening as we notice similarities in temperament and behaviour between hero and villain. Hence Link Jones of *Man of the West*, who appears a country bumpkin at the outset, only to emerge later as capable of the most brutal of acts, savagely beating and tearing the pants off the wolfish young Coaley. The extraordinary power of this famous scene, which culminates in Link not being quite able to strangle his beaten and humiliated opponent with his bare hands, flows again from what I have called the psychological structure in Mann's work. For in attempting to destroy the past that holds him to ransom – tangibly here, in that Coaley is created in the film as Link's successor – the hero is driven inescapably to relive it, the violence and evil that he has tried to bury forced to surface by the situation he finds himself in. Here Mann underlines the moral ambiguity of his hero, giving weight and integrity to John Dehner's Claude, the step-brother who refuses to run out on the crazed Dock: 'I watch out for that old man. I love him, and I watch out for him.'

A similar complexity was achieved by Mann in the first Stewart Western, *Winchester '73*, where the affable McAdam finally gives way to the hysterical hero of the end. The structure here is less elaborate (perhaps because of the limitations of the original material) but effective, the opening contest for the weapon vividly evoking the competition between the brothers as well as identifying the Winchester with their father. Consequently, the brief scene of contorted violence that follows where Dutch steals the gun has considerable force, since Lin is compelled to experience a symbolic re-enactment of his brother's crime and to live through a parody of their childhood relationship, the bigger boy bullying the smaller out of his possessions. The structure is finally resolved as McAdam is driven to re-create the evil of his brother's act – the killing of kin – before he can rest.

If Howie Kemp of *The Naked Spur* and Jeff Webster of *The Far Country* are the most explicit versions of the Mann hero, Jones and McAdam are the most developed in that both are successful in their terms. And finally, we must ask what kind of success it is that accounts for the destruction of a father or brother, and how this equips the character for a role within the community. On this score, the films are mute. The question may appear an external moral consideration, yet it is thrown up by the films themselves and is central to an understanding of the Mann hero. In the films I have been discussing, the central character moves through conflict until at the end he is ostensibly a part of the community. But the paradox here is that his movement is resolutely away from the community, and we rarely witness a process that we could call growth in the character. If there is often a strong didactic tone present – articulated in *The Tin Star*, but more characteristically felt in *The Naked Spur* and *The Far Country* – it is the result of the hero being literally beaten into line; we feel that 'he's learned his lesson'. His old partner shot in the back and he himself nearly shot to pieces, Jeff Webster 'chooses' a revenge that also saves the community. Exhausted from the unnatural struggle to tear his dead bounty from the torrent, crying as he slumps against his horse, loving and loved despite himself, Howie Kemp gives in: 'Do you still want to go to California?' Entry into the community can thus feel like defeat, the hero not so much integrated as exhausted by his compulsion to pursue an unnatural course; not educated so much as beaten by a struggle against profound forces that operate as a kind of immutable law. It is this lack of development on a moral scale, together with the insistence on psychological struc-ture, that gives Mann's world its closed, frozen quality, his heroes their neurotic flavour. If choice is really not possible, then success becomes ambiguous. McAdam exhausted in the streets of Abilene after killing his brother, Jones driving quietly away from his fam-ily's corpses, Glyn McLyntock emerging from a rushing stream that carries his friend's body – these men seem nothing more than empty shells.

Three neglected works, *Devil's Doorway*, *The Last Frontier* and *Cimarron*, are relevant here. Spanning the period under discussion, these differ from the films thus far considered in that they focus on inversions of the typical hero. Essentially, the central characters here are stable, controlled, healthy men; and as such – paradoxically – there is no place for them within the community. Thus in the sadly overlooked and surprisingly tough Indian picture, *Devil's Doorway*, Robert Taylor's Broken Lance, the Shoshone chief who as a Union soldier had won a Congressional Medal of Honor, now finds that under the Homesteading Act, Indians cannot own land. 'Civilisation's a great thing.' Attempts to petition the government fail, and Lance is driven to lead his few braves in a pathetic defence of their home against a local posse bolstered by Union cavalry. His dream of a model community shattered, the idealistic Lance dons his old uniform and moves out into the wreckage to take a bullet and walk, more dead than

Robert Taylor in *Devil's Doorway*

alive, to the officer opposite, who salutes him before he dies. Here Mann had a character of great purity and elemental drive. Society cannot contain such a man, and accordingly the hero is deified, becoming a kind of mythic spirit. As in *El Cid* (1961) ten years later, the film ends on a strange note of dark exaltation – victory through death – and celebrates the uncompromising quality of the character.

This situation is reversed in the very attractive *The Last Frontier*, virtually an imaginative remake of *Devil's Doorway*, where the action is centred on trapper Jed Cooper. Brilliantly created by Victor Mature as a bearish savage, a 'natural man', Jed becomes intrigued with the idea of wearing a cavalry uniform, despite the warnings from Gus that 'calamitous times' are upon them with the approach of civilisation. Cooper is opposed by Robert Preston's Colonel Marston, the natural morality of the trapper soon coming into conflict with the martinet's 'civilised' and neurotic drive towards success. The hero begins by defeating the community, his conquest of the colonel's lady no less than an assault on its very citadel, a fact made clear by the cutting that juxtaposes the scene with a coup by one of Red Cloud's braves, a single-handed attack on the fort. But Jed's act of leaving the colonel to die in a bear-trap when he will not renounce his plans to destroy the Apache at all costs is frowned on by the settlement, including Anne Bancroft's Mrs Marston: 'Not that way.' Unmanned by civilisation but now caught fast in its 'snares', Cooper is forced to accept the self-destructive values of the community. The tone of the film, which has some remarkably funny moments, progressively darkens, Cooper first losing the elemental side of his nature in Mungo, his Indian sidekick who returns to the mountains, and then Gus, the wise voice of reason, who dies at the head of Marston's cavalry charge. The ending (which seems to have been imposed on Mann) is jarringly optimistic, the colonel's wife looking on happily as Cooper, in uniform, salutes the flag. But the statement of the film remains clear: crossing the frontier means leaving whiskey and bearskins, passion and rational simplicity behind.

It is less easy to draw any conclusions about *Cimarron*, Mann's last Western in 1960, about which he felt deeply bitter when, after half the picture had been shot on location, the production was pulled back into the MGM studios and the script altered. Most notably, Yancey Cravat's death heroically fighting an oil fire was cut, the hero dying offstage in World War I in the released version. The mutilations are unfortunate since, as with Peckinpah's *Major Dundee* (1964), the film seems a strikingly personal epic on the origins of America. As the embodiment of the crusader and pioneer spirit of the nation, Glenn Ford tries to balance the roles of restless adventurer and idealistic newspaperman married to a demanding Maria Schell. Shooting off to fight in Cuba for five years, Yancey returns only to vanish again when his wife argues that he should compromise his ideals and accept a shady bargain that would cheat the Indians (whom he has always championed) of their oil rights in order to become governor of the state.

Pegler, the crusading father-figure from whom Yancey inherits the newspaper, and The Cherokee Kid, a young sidekick who has always idolised him but refuses to leave the disreputable life they once shared, represent the irreconcilable sides of Yancey's personality within the structure of the film. A similar opposition exists between Anne Baxter's tough Dixie, an old friend of Yancey's from his whoring days, and his wife Sabra, who is compelled to lay aside her starry-eyed preoccupations with gentility when faced with a crisis, Mercedes McCambridge getting her hilariously drunk as she gives birth to

Yancey's son. Despite the implications of The Cherokee Kid's death and his resistance to Dixie's charms, Yancey is never tamed, and the film celebrates the free expression of his pioneering impulses. The last shot is of a bronzed statue of the hero, his spirit enshrined for ever as a symbol of early America. How much was improvised by MGM executives anxious to bring the sprawling picture to a halt remains an open question. But Mann's original design is clear and supports the general pattern: the values carried by his heroes, and the forces that drive them, do not find an easy home within the community.

The Villain

All Mann's characters exist on a moral and psychological grid, the main determinants of which are goodness and evil, reason and unreason, power and weakness. This is one source of the resemblance between hero and villain, who at the very least share certain characteristics, often a blood relationship. In general, hero and villain are extreme men, the villain a more or less unbalanced version of the hero, and the action of the film is a cancelling out, a neutralising movement towards moderation, compromise and control. This is evidently an ideal state, reason and humanity being seen as attributes of natural order. However, a key source of tension and complexity is that although moral virtue carries the traditional weight of a positive value, it is never seen to bestow power, which remains the property of ambiguous and extreme men.

This structure of resonance between hero and villain is central to Mann's best work. Its lack of force in Devil's Doorway and Cimarron, both relatively social films that centre on racial prejudice, results in a diminished drama. The Tin Star is more successful in this context, although the film is not a major one, nowhere displaying the sense of passionate engagement that is characteristic of Mann. The director suffered some interference on the production; this must have been a bitter pill to swallow, given that making the film had caused a rupture between Mann and both Borden Chase and Stewart, who had wanted him for Night Passage (1957). However, the film does have its qualities, and not the least of these is the conflict between Owens and Bart Bogardus. Portrayed with appropriately unhinged malice by Neville Brand, the latter rises above the stock figure of racist to emerge as a representative of the soft underbelly of society, the hysteria and violence that both the town elders and the youthful sheriff deny in their preoccupation with ideals of decency and fair play. This gives the climax of The Tin Star a fine sharpness, Anthony Perkins bringing a properly hysterical edge to his bullying of the bully. The full effect of the scene, however, depends on our awareness that the hysteria is not wholly feigned, that Owens is confronting himself. The moment is deeply satisfying, since we have been involved with Owens's education; but our pleasure at the success of Hickman's teaching ('Study men – a gun's only a tool') should not obscure the fact that the youth has broken through to a realm of ambiguous power – he has become a killer. The roots of villainy in Mann's films always underline that although society may deny it, the exercise of such power is necessary. But in his best work, Mann goes further, suggesting that the use of that power is tragic.

There is a fruitful tension between these two related ideas that run throughout much of Mann. On the one hand, there is the view that power is neutral. Mann is clearly fascinated by the way in which knowledge and experience, independence and judgment, organisation and physical prowess can be used equally for good or ill. A particularly fine example is Roy Anderson's brilliant use of military tactics in *The Naked Spur* to bring about the liquidation of the Blackfeet so that he can continue with Kemp's party and share in the reward. But the theme is most prominent in the Chase-scripted films, explicit in the first two works and clearly present in *The Far Country* with Mr Gannon, as everyone calls him, whose organisational and administrative skills are remarkable. Using the law to his advantage in Skagway, Gannon sells supplies to miners headed for the gold strike in Dawson – one of his statutes usefully insisting that each miner must carry one hundred pounds of the expensive goods – and then robs and kills them on their return (the pattern recalls *Border Incident*). Both Anderson and Gannon are highly intelligent and rational villains whose presence highlights the 'limitations' – the ethical awareness – of their opposite numbers. As Gannon says with heavy sarcasm of Jeff when the showdown comes: 'We always knew he'd turn into a public-minded citizen.' Some Mann villains – most of the Dock Tobin gang (barring Claude), Ben in *The Naked Spur*, Waco of *Winchester '73* – are so far out, so unbalanced, that they seem unaware of rules of conduct. The insanity we sense in characters like Roy and Gannon, however, derives from the rational and efficient way they break rules they are aware of and disdain. The attractiveness of these characters is that they are so purely out of joint. These more refined versions of the Mann villain – naked power without a moral dimension, self-interest breeding totalitarianism – are persuasive arguments for the existence of evil. Faced with them, a society cannot but sanction force, killing if necessary, the doer freed from blame by virtue of his instrumental role as vehicle for social justice.

Yet alongside this view there exists an older idea that, although it has lost ground, continues to influence our culture, and is persistently at work in Mann's films. I refer to the metaphysical concept, rooted in religion, myth and folklore, that the taking of a life is a sacred act. Essentially brothers under the skin, we kill at our peril, destroying a part of ourselves, staining our hands with the blood of the victim for ever thereafter. *Thou shalt not kill.* The imperative is an absolute one: there are no mitigating circumstances. Within the Western, this ancient precept is present in a corrupted form, the constraints surrounding the killing of a defenceless or weaker man, one of the most tenacious of conventions in the genre. Mann returns to this ritualistic situation often, in both *The Naked Spur* and *The Man from Laramie*, the enflamed hero quivering with hand on gun, but finally turning away in disgust; Link Jones's inability to strangle Coaley is another example. If we are to kill, we require situations in which we do not have to face ourselves, the decision taken out of our hands. In *The Last Frontier*, this issue is at the centre of the action, Mann underlining the fact that even when disaster threatens, social sanctions are not enough to justify execution. The extremity of the act forces a communal guilt unless it has a properly ceremonial or chivalric dress. The horns of the dilemma become intolerably, unspeakably clear with the theme of patricide. What is one to do with an *evil father*? The archetypal and tragic aspects of the crisis are revealed: every man his own Hamlet.

This thematic complex seems to have provided a nexus for Borden Chase and Mann, and accounts for their creative collaboration over *Winchester '73*, *Bend of the River* and *The Far Country*. As a scriptwriter, Chase seems to be an auteur in his own right, his work with other directors marked by the strong thematic interests – the archetypal conflict, the uses of power – he shared with Mann. Thus *Backlash* (1956), directed with little force by John Sturges, nevertheless has an enviable punch, given its narrative built round a hero determined to revenge his father, who was apparently massacred when a partner failed to return with help. Obsessively pursuing his prey, Richard Widmark moves through various adventures to discover the renegade about to ambush and wipe out a whole community; it is, of course, his father. *Red River* (which Chase co-scripted) is also relevant, the action there turning on the rebellion of Montgomery Clift against the older John Wayne figure who has taught him all that he knows. Once again, the conflict is set against a broader canvas, the historic cattle drive, and the continuity of the community is seen as dependent upon the resolution of the struggle between the two men. It is this symmetry of structure, Chase's insistence on a social extension of the personal drama, that provides the marker to the boundaries between writer and director, and assists us in reaching a fuller understanding of Mann's work.

A basic convention of the genre, always in the foreground with Chase, sets hero and villain off through the power that they share. Thus in *Backlash*, a film that recalls *Winchester '73* at every turn, father and son both measure the effectiveness of a gun by the way it rests in the hand. For Chase, prowess suggests a moral ambiguity, and is generally emblematic of an internal disturbance that poises a character on the margins of the community. In turning the skills they hold in common against the villain – who imperils the social structure – the hero thus at once achieves an inner peace, preserves the community and establishes himself within it. A recurrent structure within the Western, apparently constricting and formulaic, this pattern provides a good example of the latitude the genre allows the veteran Hollywood director. Thus for Hawks in *Red River*, the relationships between the characters dominate the action, the community theme remaining abstract. Although the cattle drive is referred to as gruelling and is equated with the salvation of the territory, its epic potential is not realised in the images. The archetypal aspects of the structure are similarly undercut, the patriarchal figure of Walter Brennan functioning primarily as an onlooker and comic relief, the John Ireland character emerging as another professional rather than a kind of brother to Clift, the tragic potential of the Wayne/Clift relationship transmuted into the Hawksian drama of separation from the group. Violence becomes a form of communication – women slapping men, men beating each other to express their love – and the prowess carried by major characters a badge of their professionalism rather than a sign of interior disturbance.

In contrast to Hawks, Mann was to fasten precisely on those areas within Chase's material that allowed for an archetypal extension of the drama. Ironically, in one sense the effect was the same, the socially conscious Chase's interests in the community again fading. Thus in *Bend of the River*, the theme of the need for a rationale for force is not fully developed, young Trey failing to cohere as a character, the motif clouded by Mann's handling of the end. The hysteria with which Glyn replies to Cole's treachery is something more than an expression of the precariousness of the character's ties with the community: Cole's betrayal is like self-betrayal, the betrayal of a brother, unnatural, wounding, and leading irrevocably to the murderous combat of the river.

Winchester '73, much the best of the Mann/Chase Westerns, benefits immensely through the splitting of the villainy between Waco, strikingly created by Dan Duryea, and Dutch Henry Brown. From the beginning, Mann creates an opposition between Lin and Dutch, the brothers holding in common the same skill and shooting style with irreconcilable views of life. But Lin is also set off against Waco Johnnie, the conflict here resulting from their similar psychopathic edge, Lin's functioning in relation to Dutch and Waco – who, as Lola says, isn't 'people' – while Waco's stylish terror operates in reverse, on helpless citizens. Lin's destruction of Waco is consequently a key moment, since it both satisfies our moral expectations and disturbs them, our identification with the hero jarred by the naked violence with which he sets about the villain. This is appropriate, as the death of Waco is only a step towards the more personal duel with Dutch, a structure that, if less pleasing on the formal level, remains true to the drive of the character and gives the film a considerable intensity. Here again, the result is that the social theme concerning the applications of power ('He didn't teach you to shoot people in the back') is obscured, the moral justification for the destruction of Dutch (his own marauding, his ruling of Waco who menaces the social structure) less prominent than the fact that Lin has no choice – he *must* kill his brother. Mann underlines this, as in *Bend of the River*, by making the final confrontation an elemental struggle, the blood pounding in the hero's head as he pits himself against his double high in the rocks. This, together with Mann's emphasis on the villain as a source of unnatural acts, lifts the action free of social or moral contexts. A dark vessel through which blow winds of an immutable justice, the hero restores order, paradoxically and tragically, by descending into the world of the villain.

In comparison with *Winchester '73*, *The Far Country* is formally perfect, yet a minor work. The film is built round a careful set of oppositions: corrupt Skagway and the emerging community of Dawson; the motifs of gold, which 'drives a man crazy', and food, especially coffee, which comes to represent neighbourliness and sharing; Ronda, who balances Jeff in looking after herself, and Renée, who believes that helping other people is part of living. But the key opposition is between the fascistic Gannon, who represents the logical outcome of that half of Jeff that rejects the community, and the paternal Ben, Jeff's partner, who evokes human and democratic ideals. This familiar structure ensures that the resolution of the action – Jeff's solipsism leading to Ben's death, which then drives him to destroy Gannon – has Mann's characteristic intensity. But the source of that intensity remains below the surface, the action of the film finally blurred by the social and moral issues that the script insists on.

However, *The Naked Spur* and *Man of the West*, Mann's most sustained works, are films of extraordinary power, their roots the wholly private quality of the heroes' struggle. Here the relationship between hero and villain is either arbitrary and therefore compulsively necessary – Howie Kemp's pursuit of Ben Vandergroat – or a family affair, as with Link and his stepfather, and thus again dictated. There is no question of larger motives. In fact, the mute intensity engendered by *The Naked Spur* springs precisely from the paradox that although Kemp may be doing something socially useful, he is transgressing natural law: he is *unclean*. In both films, the threat of villain to community is not at the centre of the action, the social order only suggested by the figures of the brutalised women, Lina and Billie, and the petty thieves, Jesse and Beasley.

(Next page) Stewart with Arthur Kennedy in *The Man from Laramie*: alter egos, blood brothers, doubles and doppelgangers

The latter figures are evidently examples of the harmless scoundrel – carpetbagger, morally unstable prospector – that the society can accommodate. Basically good and likeable men, the characters' flaw is that they are weak. These men, like the community itself, are far removed from the world of hero and villain, the world of power. And for Mann, power is something more than Chase's expertise, or the capacity for good and evil it bestows. Clearly this is involved, as are the key drives of ambition and pride: 'I knew Madden couldn't take him,' says Gannon with some satisfaction as he prepares to face Jeff. But finally, the essential otherness that hero and villain share is a mysterious extremity of nature, a singularity and integrity of spirit.

Mann consistently heightens and exploits aspects of ritual and legend behind basic conventions of the genre – skill in battle, knowledge of the savage, fearlessness in the face of the unknown – to give his major characters an almost magical quality and a mythical stature. Hence the competition for the perfect weapon, the brothers matching each other shot for shot until the hero wins with the perfect shot, blowing a hole through a postage stamp pasted over a ring thrown in the air. 'It worked, didn't it?' asks Roy Anderson, emerging from cover after the last Indian is dead. The massacre is so total that finally it seems less a demonstration of efficient tactics than a display of diabolical power, a kind of black magic. Even in *The Tin Star*, where the drift of the script is to demystify the figure of the gunfighter, shifting attention from mechanical skill to human qualities, Mann nevertheless gives Fonda a mysterious aura, making of him the solitary keeper of the keys. In this light, Owens's education becomes an introduction to secret rites, an initiation, a passing on, again, of magic. The same idea is there in *Bend of the River*, where Laura admires the song of night birds, and McLyntock and Cole sardonically agree as they listen to the Indians approaching the camp; moments later the men melt into the landscape to defeat the Indians with their own methods. Men at this level instantly recognise each other: 'I'm gonna like you,' opines Gannon after a remark or two from Webster. Gannon having stolen Jeff's cattle, Jeff steals them back, and the two men jockey expertly in the dark, aware of each other's every move, as lesser men die. 'You act as if you belong with those people,' exclaims the incredulous Sam Beasley as Link savagely digs a grave outside Dock Tobin's squalid shack. Ordinary men soon sense the differences.

Hero and villain. The kind of possibilities these structural elements presented Mann is most clear in *Man of the West*. Like Peckinpah's *Ride the High Country*, the film is built round the tragic implications of the growth of civilisation; like that work, it is a personal achievement of the highest order. The film is remarkable for the integrity it allows its characters: not only Julie London's Billie, whose own precarious defences must be stripped away; or Beasley, whose cowardice is irrationally overcome when he steps in front of the bullet meant for Link; or Claude, whose sense of loyalty we are forced to respect, thus qualifying our relationship with Link; but also 'that old man', the resolutely evil Dock Tobin himself. Lee J. Cobb's liking for the grandiose for once served a director well, and through him Mann was able to create his greatest character in the figure of the demented and totally corrupt old bandit frozen in time. The extent of the character's depravity comes across with an almost horrific force when Link and Dock face each other after all those years, and we learn what kind of past our apparently timid hero has had. Mann gives the scene in the old shack a black, oppressive atmosphere, Cooper standing silent and powerless surrounded by the grotesques, Trout, Coaley and Ponch, as his stepfather greets him:

> You been eating good? ... you ran out and left me ... I put a piece of work into you ... you were my property ... do you remember Uvalde? ... eleven thousand dollars ... you held him, I took off the top of his head ... I could have pushed your guts through your back ... every idea in your head ... look at these pigs ... there's no guts any more ... NO GUTS!

The end of the film sustains the strange honour that grows up around Tobin. With all of his 'sons' dead by Link, himself one of their number, having raped Billie as he must, since she functions in the action as Link's woman, with the knowledge somewhere in his demented brain that Lassoo ('It rings in my head – *Lassooo!*') is no longer a thriving mining town his for the picking but, like Dock Tobin, a ghost – he stands atop his lonely mountain, a figure of tragic force, and watches his son – caught in an equally tragic situation – come to kill him. An unforgivable, absurd line from Cooper – 'I'm gonna take you in' – is corrected immediately by an exchange that crystallises the dilemmas of the two men: Link wildly rushing up the incline – 'You've outlived your time'; Dock lumbering wildly down from the crest – 'Kill me ... you've lost your taste for it.' Integrity intact to the end, Tobin forces his stepson to destroy him, firing wildly and continuing the demented soliloquy that is his basic mode of expression, until he is finally silenced.

Throughout the film, Mann creates a complex sense of tragic inevitability, making sure that Dock and Claude communicate to us their awareness, brought home to them by Link, of themselves as anachronisms, and consequently of Link as their fate; this in turn balanced by Link's growing realisation, Hamlet-like, of what he must do. This awareness is strongest where the brothers, Link and Claude, finally resolve their issues in the landscape of the past, the ghost town of Lassoo. A tour de force by Mann, the scene, beginning with Claude's 'I want to see you, Cousin', and Link's response 'Over here, Cousin', is shot with immense authority, the scope frame following and containing all the action, culminating in the classically pure shot of the two brothers above and below the porch of the worn-out bank, both wounded bloodily, Claude shouting, hysteria in his voice, 'You have to come to me', Link answering, 'It finishes here, what you've always wanted.'

Mann's evocation of evil in the film is extraordinary: at one point, even the moon seems to glower. Tobin's gang is a marvellous assortment of gargoyles: the mute Trout, played as a crazed child by Royal Dano, who is allowed his two pitiable howls as he runs to die on the outskirts of Lassoo; the wolfish Coaley; Robert J. Wilke's dumb oaf, Ponch. John Dehner's more rational Claude rightly stands outside and above these Shakespearean appetites and buffoons. But over all presides Dock. When the main title of the film appears, the scope frame balances it against Cooper astride his horse like a statue. But this is one of Mann's deceptions: the film itself leaves little doubt over who is the man of the West.

Mann's response to the Western was not a response to history, as with Ford and Peckinpah, but to its archetypal form, the mythic patterns deeply embedded in the plots and characters of the genre that can shape and structure the action. Although little interested in the simple oppositions of the traditional Western romance, it was precisely these elements that allowed Mann to turn the genre to his purpose, hero and villain transmuted into protagonist and antagonist. Mann's fascination with the superior, charismatic individual found a rich outlet in the form, if no easy solution. The hero, his sanity at stake, enters the world of ordinary mortals only through a kind of metaphysical suicide, destroying the mirror of his magic, the incarnation of his pride and ambition. The villain finds his release only through madness and death.

The Community

For Mann, the community is the family. It is this equation that accounts for the hero's ambiguous status on the edges of the society, the passion and power of the character, the private and violent nature of his struggle. This is clearest in *Winchester '73* where the theme of the family organises and sharpens the action, although the episodic movement ensures some diffuseness. Dodge City, where the brothers compete for the rifle, is portrayed by Mann as a homely place with children much in evidence, a community ruled over by a fatherly Wyatt Earp. Thereafter, the action moves with the Winchester as it passes from Dutch to a gun-runner to the Indian chief, Young Bull, who promptly trains it on the young couple, Steve and Lola, travelling to look at a possible home for themselves once they marry.

Seemingly irrelevant in the movement of the film, the couple is central to its action, the tawdry Lola and the cowardly Steve both trying to find roles within the society by becoming a family unit. This structure is extended by Mann's treatment of the troopers in the besieged camp, whom he creates as a group of young boys away from home under the guidance of Jay C. Flippen's fatherly sergeant-major. Here, in one of Mann's finest scenes, before the dawn attack of the Indians, all the characters speak to the theme of putting down roots, building a family, having a home. The structure is finally rounded out by Waco, who dashes Lola's hopes by killing Steve and terrorises a family with whom he takes cover, their homestead burned to the ground as a result. Waco is a usurper and stands with Dutch, who in killing his father has left the community irrevocably; Mann places the character in sharp opposition to 'people' by having him ridicule normal relationships, casting Steve in the role of housewife, brutalising Lola by imposing a grotesque caricature of a love relationship on her.

Waco dies, appropriately, in the main street of town. But Lin and Dutch confront each other, as they must, in the brutal landscape outside the community. The central paradox in Mann is that although the values of the community are always at stake, the community itself is powerless, its forms and institutions inadequate to the threat. This perhaps accounts for the pathetic figures of Steve and Lola, their incarnation of an ideal at its weakest; Mann himself might have said he was only being realistic. Certainly, the consistency of his treatment of the community throughout all the films is remarkable. Typically comprised of children, old people and adolescent, sexless girls, the social order is always highly vulnerable and easily corrupted. In *The Far Country*, for instance, Dawson is a marvellous collection of old wrecks. Mann treats the citizenry with real affection, giving the old cronies, Ben and Luke, a moral awareness and stature, portraying Hominy and Grits, the spinsters who run the restaurant, as warm, tough human beings. Here, as with the community elder played by Jay C. Flippen in *Bend of the River*, a variation of the patriarch who often accompanies the hero, Mann nicely communicates the tenacious, enduring qualities of the community. But as the action of the films always makes clear, these qualities are essentially helpless when faced with naked power.

At his most pessimistic, Mann suggests that the community exiles or destroys its best features, anarchy and evil disguised as order forcing out reason and humanity. This idea is clear in *Devil's Doorway*, where the ending suggests that the society is committing suicide. Similarly, *The Tin Star* demonstrates how the community brings about the death of its very soul – the saintly Doc McCord – by denying the existence of evil that its own attitudes create. This is, of course, the dialectic at work behind the bounty hunter, a figure Mann clearly found fascinating. Mann must have responded to the tragic potential of the situation: the hero thrown from the heavenly community like a Miltonic angel, to land, wounded and bitter, in some hellish landscape. 'Evil be *thou* my good.' Scratch many Mann heroes, in fact, and you find something akin to the sensibility of the bounty hunter. The process of alienation was described with great force by Mann in *The Last Frontier*, like *Devil's Doorway* a film that makes a frontal attack on the values of society. Mann tempts us into tight identification with his comically frank, uncluttered hero and consequently compels us to experience the community as he does, as an irrational, suicidal world. A civilised man can jeopardise a whole community, can order a murder through an intermediary. But simply to kill a man face to face, even though he is a cancer within the society, is the act of an animal. For a man simply to take a woman, destructively joined to another, because he loves her – this too is not correct. What defeats Jed finally is the idealism of society, its insistence on theory and chivalry in the face of evil. For the unnat-̄ ural passion of a Marston, the society has traditional modes of expression; but the purity of a Cooper must be destroyed before he can enter the community. In such a world, the pragmatic, empirical man, the physical, visceral style – these are lost.

Mann's vision of the family as microcosm of humanity is profoundly ambiguous: the highest good, the source of all evil. Working within the Western, Mann over the years was able to clarify and shape his area of interest, inevitably seizing on the tragic and epic potential of the theme: the modest *Winchester '73*, inherited by Mann in 1950 when Fritz Lang left the project, extended into the grand designs of *The Man from Laramie* in 1955 (*God's Little Acre* coming in 1957), *Man of the West* in 1958 and culminating with the mutilated *Cimarron* in 1960, after which Mann naturally moved into the full-scale epics of the Cid and Rome. Relevant to all of these works is the theme of usurpation, the cosmic conflicts of dynasty that are at the centre of classical tragedy. This is perhaps most prominent in *The Man from Laramie*, Mann and his scriptwriter Philip Yordan clearly attempting a loose reworking of *Oedipus Rex* within the genre. The structure of the film places the roots of the evil many years back, in Waggoman's passing over the woman he loved – the tough, tired Kate who still waits for him – to marry a wealthy Eastern woman instead. As a result of this unnatural act, their one son, Dave, takes on not only Alec's tragic flaw of ambition but a feminine weakness as well. The evil spreads, the ambitious Vic repeating his stepfather's pattern in his relationship with Barbara Waggoman. The fateful figure of Lockhart, reminding the old man of the furies that torture his nights, enters the scene to trigger the drama that must be played out. Inevitably, the only beloved son dies, the body brought home at dusk, the whole universe mourning with the king for his heir.

With *Man of the West*, Mann returned directly to the terrain of *Winchester '73*, the hero driven tragically to preserve the ideal of the family by destroying its evil incarnation, redeeming the macrocosm by crucifying the microcosm, saving the world by giving himself. The charge provided by the archetypal cycle at the heart of all myth, the death and rebirth of the hero, always in evidence with Mann's work, is particularly strong here. But in *Cimarron*, adapted by Arnold Schulman from Edna Ferber's novel, Mann had material that while offering an epic theme was to prove less tractable in terms of his own interests. Inevitably, the film has a profound ambiguity at its centre, since the epic design demanded that Yancey be married (the only Mann hero of the Westerns to be so, visibly, and consequently much less on the margins), while also carrying the incorrigible, questing drive of a free spirit. The result is that *Cimarron* veers in tone from national epic to domestic drama, the marriage between Maria Schell and Glenn Ford frequently recalling the tense Stewart/Allyson relationships of *The Glenn Miller Story* and *Strategic Air Command*. An ironic paradox, rather than a tragic dilemma, emerges: the community is created and defended by the individual finally too footloose to stay within it.

Mann's tendency was always to work towards the heightened drama of family relationships; he bemoaned the lack of courage in producers who would not allow him to make Lockhart still another son to Waggoman, Billie the wife of Link. Thus the almost unholy force of that modest production, *The Naked Spur*, stems in part from the resemblance of the five characters to a malignant family bent on murdering each other at the first opportunity. Mann gives Janet Leigh's Lina the quality of a waif tagging along behind an older brother who fills the shoes of her dead outlaw pa. Ben functions generally as the eldest, evil son positioned serenely above the struggles of Howie and Roy, yet inevitably determining the direction in which they move. A querulous old grandad to them all, Millard Mitchell's Jesse fills out the structure.

By creating these relationships in the context of a parable, the situation drawing on at least two ancient and powerful myths – Christ in the wilderness and the theme of the rewards of acquisitiveness embodied in the classical situation of three men squabbling over gold – the whole held together by the journey structure (always central in Mann because of the pattern of death and resurrection it implies), Mann achieves an extraordinary intensity. The complex of associations gathers around the characters, Ben functioning at once as the gold that creates the destructive divisions among the other three and as a more personal temptation for Howie, the devil to his tortured Christ. Bent on destroying himself, Kemp swings violently from still moments with Lina to his more obsessive posture, unable to trust, to lean on anyone. The great power of the ending of the film is its unrelenting toughness, Howie still refusing to recognise that Lina is the Holy Grail, not the gold of Ben's body, despite the evidence of three ugly deaths. Begging Howie to leave the corpse, Lina is beaten down, accepting that she will marry him whatever he does. 'But why . . . tell me why? I'm gonna sell him for money.' Finally unable to become inhuman, Kemp collapses against his saddle and cries.

The typical structure in Mann's films presents a spectrum of character ranging from representatives of the social order, highly rational and humane, through to the crazed and evil opposition. The hero stands at the centre torn between the two worlds. What makes his tragic struggles to rise above himself so credible is the fragility, the dependency and the blindness of those values he is called upon to defend. Reason, humanity, democracy – these may be virtues; they are not necessarily power. There is an overwhelming feeling in Mann that nice guys always finish last. The knowledge of this makes

Mann's heroes the neurotic men they are, accepting the role and responsibilities of being a nice guy with the greatest reluctance.

Landscape

> A Western is a wonderful thing to do because you take a group of actors who have acted on the stage or who have acted in rooms and now you take them out into the elements, and you throw them against the elements and the elements make them much greater as actors than if they were in a room. Because they have to shout above the winds, they have to suffer, they have to climb mountains . . .[3]

For Mann, all the West is a stage, but especially its mountains, streams and forests. The agrarian ideal, so central to Ford, has little relevance for Mann's work: the fecund valley, the frontier homestead – these are largely absent. Mann's West is the wilderness, 'way up in that far country' where the passions he deals with can find expression, his conflicts their resolutions. It is in the name of the furrowed earth and a world where neighbours are possible that his characters finally act; but the universe they inhabit is one of rushing rivers and the lonely, brutal rocks of the snowline.

If Mann's cinema is pre-eminently a cinema of landscape, it is because through landscape he communicates a view of life. For Mann, space is concrete and continuous, shaping action and determining outcome. On a minor key, for example, it is striking how in *Bend of the River*, Mann creates the sense of a community on the move and blending with the terrain. His sketch of the community putting down roots is only that, brief images of land being cleared, over which we hear Jay C. Flippen's commentary – surprisingly, given Mann's commitment to pictorial values. These are more characteristically in evidence in the fine scene where the riverboat can go no further, the men slowly transporting the supplies through shallow water on to the beach. The architectural sense informing the use of location and colour is impressive, the scene caught carefully in long shot, the eye driven through space from the shore along the line of porters back to the *River Queen*.

Action scenes in Mann always take on force by being set in locations that give us a sense, physically, of what is going on. Small details sharpen this, the rockslides at the outset of *The Naked Spur*, like Ben's ugly target practice on the dead Jesse's boots at the end, increasing our awareness of the situation. Always we are given a tactical understanding and therefore a greater involvement with the action. It is this principle that informs the great care that Mann takes in setting up the ambush of the Blackfeet. As Kemp's party approach a small glade, the deep-focus shot reveals the Indians behind them in the distance cresting a small hill on the trail and disappearing from view. Moments later, the Blackfeet gallop in to rein up as Howie and Lina, Ben and Jesse slowly move across the glade, Mann cutting from close-ups of the nervous faces back to the Indians, and then panning from the side of the trail with the group, so that as they pass us and approach the forest's edge, we see Roy buried in the shrubbery, rifle to hand. The bounty hunter's party pull up, turning, and now the Blackfeet move peacefully through the clearing, Mann repeating the pan so that our vantage point is again Roy's as they pass, only to be caught in the middle, his hail of fire behind, Kemp's party ahead. The massacre, shattering for us in its efficiency, in retrospect appears inevitable.

But at a deeper level, Mann's landscape provides a correlative for the drive and conflict of his characters. The physicality of Mann's style creates a world that is hard and punishing towards moral disorder, unnatural, extreme behaviour. Justice emerges not from within the individual soul or through a social dialectic: standing outside and above man, there exists a cosmic equilibrium, a natural law that demands a paying of dues. This is the meaning of the rushing torrents at the end of both *Bend of the River* and *The Naked Spur*, the swirling rivers of an immutable justice that spirit away the vice of an Emerson Cole, a Roy Anderson. In *The Man from Laramie*, the cache of rifles is at the lip of a spur, accessible only by a steep ascent that doubles back on itself along the cliff-face. During the film, we watch as all the characters pit themselves and their horses against the terrain, driving precariously against space and ground to achieve their desperate ends. The spur dominates in the resolution of the action, Dave dying at its crest by his stepbrother's hand, Vic savaged by the Apache near its base, the buckboard of rifles forced over the lip by Lockhart to hurtle to their destruction below. But a key moment is the slow yet relentless ascent of Alec Waggoman up the tortuous path that culminates in the frenzied Vic being driven to push the blind old man over the edge. Ironic, terrible, but finally liberating, the act lays bare the evil, Waggoman dying and reborn through his fall.

  The Far Country also takes on force through Mann's use of landscape to evoke a universal justice. 'It can do things to a man – make him crazy.' Luke's paean to gold is interrupted by the roar of the avalanche of snow that sweeps down from the heights of White Pass across the mountain trail, an awesome assertion of natural forces that brings low the self-willed Ronda, who has parted company with Jeff's group, driven by her haste over the icy slope. Jeff's solipsistic drive to leave Dawson to Gannon's tyranny invites a

The Far Country on location: 'The elements make them much greater as actors'

similar intervention by fate. The two men, Ben complaining about having to travel to
Juneau by raft to avoid Gannon, unpack their goods at the river's edge, the surrounding forest and hillside crowding in on them. Seconds later, Ben is dead and Jeff has had
his comeuppance, the result, as with Ronda, of an anonymous and implacable attack
from on high.

Where the traditional imagery of the Western intersected with Mann's preoccupations,
offering an image through which he could express and focus his themes, was in the recurrent visual motif of a man alone in landscape. But for Mann, the landscape was specific,
the man, time and again, on a mountain. Great height is always important to Mann, a
clue to the reach and conflict of his characters on the one hand, the transcendent forces
of justice that they defy on the other. In a superficial way, the scene in *Bend of the River*
where Glyn, Cole and Trey fire down from a cliff pocket onto their pursuers works to
differentiate the three men, Glyn easing off once the attack is broken, Cole firing on with
relish, Trey asking why stop? But the real force in the scene stems directly from our sense
of how exact and cruel is the justice that is being visited on the greedy townsmen below.
Study of the topography of *Bend of the River* repays itself, illuminating the deceptive
movement of the film, in which Cole, by his act of defying the community – leaving his
better impulses in the form of the savagely beaten McLyntock to perish atop snowy
Mount Hood – becomes a tragic figure. The hero in turn becomes an omnipotent force
firing down from high up in the terrain, blocking Cole's every step. Creating him only
as gunfire, movement and a voice in the landscape, Mann suggests the spirit of an
implacable justice working itself out through the figure of McLyntock.

Occasionally, Mann heightens the action by an ironic use of landscape. Hence the
openness of the range Will Lockhart covers as he rounds up Kate's strays, the great plain
stained moments later by Dave Waggoman's evil act, blowing a bullet through the hand
of the incredulous hero. The scene recalls an earlier moment, and one of Mann's most
impressive uses of space and terrain, where Lockhart and his men are quietly loading their
wagons on the edge of a sprawling sea of salt. A large body of riders appears, a far-off
speck in the distance, as the men work on in the tranquil sunshine. Mann holds the shot
an audaciously long time, its depth of field ensuring a gradual build-up of foreboding as
the group slowly makes ground at a dead run round the curve of the salt flats towards
Lockhart, the director finally releasing the tension, panning hard with the dark riders as
they thunder past on the ridge overhead to rein up. Mann's control over the changing
tone of the scene is total, arming us with a suspicion of the violence that may occur, only
to disarm us – as Lockhart himself is disarmed – by the hysteria of what does follow.

But more typically, Mann exercises the expressive potential of the medium to create
a pathetic relationship between man and environment; inevitable, given his view of the
protagonist as microcosm of humanity, social order and justice as attributes of natural
law. Thus in the opening scene of *The Man from Laramie*, the landscape seems to brood
over Lockhart as he explores the location of his brother's death. The scope image –
Mann's first and strikingly assured use of the wide screen – is filled completely by the
crater in which the silent hero stands, the lip of the terrain behind curling round and
above the solitary figure who bitterly fingers a dusty cavalryman's hat in the growing
twilight. Structurally, the treatment of the moment is particularly important, since it
looks forward to the later scene where the body of Dave is brought home, the dark

images supported by a moaning chorus, the last act of the drama beginning with a grieving Alec Waggoman now cast in Lockhart's role.

At its most dynamic, Mann's style takes on an expressionist edge, resulting from his unremitting concentration on interior conflict. Rarely articulated, the action characteristically flows below the surface to break out in strangely malignant scenes of great physical intensity. It is this subterranean drive that gives much of Mann's work a static, disembodied quality, as if a private obsession were at work on the material rather than being disciplined and put at its service. At times, Mann's cinema reaches an electrifying pitch in the relentless way it focuses on the unnatural struggle of extreme men, trapped in the ugly, unyielding rocks of a horrific landscape. One of the great pleasures of *Winchester '73* is that the nervy contest for the rifle with which the film opens is only a play, a parody of what must happen but cannot here, since the passions at work are contained by the community. Only away from 'people' – in the private world of open space – can the cataclysmic release of those deep, violent drives take place, civil strife between brother and brother, men from the same womb filled with hatred, sacred family blood being redeemed. Mann's treatment of the final confrontation in *Winchester '73* gives it a concrete quality, the wind whipping over the brothers as they try in turn to bury each other in the brutal rocks, the punishing, merciless pressure of the rifle shots shattering the air and throwing up a choking dust. This physical intensity, together with the ritualistic exchanges of the two men over their father as they fire, gives the scene a force that mounts to a psychic peak. The terrain is so coloured by the action that it finally seems to be an inner landscape, the unnatural world of a disturbed mind.

Dramatic Structure and Style

Well of course violence is a very strange thing. If you follow all the great plays, whether they're Greek, Shakespearean … heads roll. Most gruesome … even in *King Lear* when they jab Gloucester's eyes out with the spurs. I haven't done that yet, I use the spur, though, the naked spur for a weapon. But actually this is true of great drama, that it needs violence because the audience is sitting there and they are experiencing things, and then in order for it to take hold the dramatist really needs … to express an emotion, for the character to go through something that the audience feel for.[4]

The Mann hero functions as a scapegoat. The scenes of greatest force in his films are always where violence smites the hero, who, like Job, seems to have done little to deserve it. Will Lockhart, the least ambiguous of Mann's revenge protagonists, suffers most. Where Kemp, Webster and Hickman have turned their backs on the world, and where McAdam, McLyntock and Jones turn on their own kin or kind, Lockhart is a more familiar figure, seeking the revenge of a brother who died at the hands of strangers. Yet the revenge drive, which normally requires no validation within the genre, vibrates in Mann with primeval significance, operating as a flaw in the hero, who is seen to raise himself up and presume to judge. As the action of the films makes clear, this form of hubris is tantamount to self-destruction, the impulse embodied in the sudden, unnatural violence the hero both expresses and suffers in the course of his struggle. A cosmic revenge is visited upon the revenger. Lockhart, roped and dragged through a fire, must watch helplessly as his wagons are burned and his innocent mules destroyed, must stand, pitiable and horrified, as a bullet is shot through his hand. A particularly strong thread in all of Mann is the ritualistic idea of violence as a punishing test that the hero must be mercilessly exposed to and cleansed by. So McAdam must be left bloody and alone atop his mountain, Owens must 'walk through the nettles' of his encounter with Bogardus. In cameo, the idea is there in *Devil's Doorway* with Jimmy, the little Shoshone boy who passes his painful initiation test, returning from above the snowline with the claws of an eagle. For Mann, we learn only through suffering, experience and environment bending and beating us into shape. Education – life itself – is pain.

This tragic pattern is the core of Mann's art. The punishment that the hero sustains in his obsessive pursuit of a villain who is a projection of himself is in turn visited upon us; for we have projected ourselves into the hero. Mann had come to Hollywood from Broadway; with him he brought a sure knowledge of the importance of a pure line of narrative action and a dramatic structure that evokes both a personal and universal conflict. If the dialectics of tragedy are not wholly realised, if we do not emerge from a Mann movie having experienced horror and pity and having finally been cleansed, it is not because Mann did not try. Like Hitchcock, Mann puts us through it, forcing upon us a relationship with the hero despite unsettling doubts, then finally smiting us – and the protagonist – from his position, godlike, outside and above the action. If the morality is an overweening one, the understanding of medium and audience is impressive.

The hallmark of Mann's style is a mobile camera, moving fluidly with the action, its pace and direction dictated by the drive of the character. Will Lockhart moves off from Barbara Waggoman's store in a barely controlled, infinitely determined march towards the corral and Dave some distance off, the camera receding smoothly before him, the intensity of its concentration and the relentlessness of its retreat creating the meaning for us. The style, always evoking a sense of the continuity and physicality of space, is also marked by the close-up, evidence of Mann's commitment to passion and an expressive cinema. 'Look at it!' screams Dave, brandishing his bleeding palm in Lockhart's face, the hero held fast by two Barb cowboys. The camera moves down to Lockhart's quivering hand, as Dave strips away the glove, the gun poised and cocked – and then glides upward with the explosion to a tight shot on the violated, ashen face. Mann's cinema has often been seen as a notoriously violent one: it is therefore odd how little, relatively speaking, violent action there is. The secret, as all the old Hollywood veterans seem to know (see *Psycho* [1960] or *Rio Bravo*), is to allow the whole to be coloured by one or two parts. Thus, in what is arguably his most arresting moment, the first meeting of the brothers in *Winchester '73*, much of the violence in Mann is a violence of atmosphere, not a blow struck or a gun fired. What both men know – that their guns hang in Earp's office – disappears in the frenzy of the moment, the brothers simultaneously slapping leather with electric speed. The image of Stewart, his face ablaze, fairly quivers with murderous intent.

Mann naturally shies away from cutting for his effects, treating the frame itself as a stage within which the action can be played out. The recurrent use of deep focus enhances the effect, as the eye is drawn into the situation to locate the key elements of the drama. As Lin grapples with a villain on the sidewalk, across the street the bank is being robbed by Dutch, Mann sharply extending our suspense by forcing us to look through a violently bucking stagecoach in front of the saloon in an effort to spot the brother. The world created is a morally ambiguous one, protagonist and antagonist balanced on the same plane of action. Time and again, two men – always two men – held tightly within the frame savage each other in a river, a dark cave, under the hooves of horses: in *Man of the West*, the horizontal line of the porch divides the image cleanly, Link above, Claude below.

A rich contrast to John Ford in many ways, Mann followed the old veteran in the common cause of a visual cinema, in which pictorial values are paramount. The kinds of conflict and the terrain itself are vastly different, but the style in both cases unfailingly roots the action in the sweep and pull of landscape. For Ford, this broader canvas provided the structure through which he could express his poetic vision of America, in the process carrying on almost single-handedly the romantic mainstream tradition of the genre. For Mann, space was cosmic, the camera ever standing back to place his characters in a continuous and elemental reality, Prometheuses chained to their rocks. His contribution was in its way equally unique, the incarnation of his tragic world darkening the genre as no one else had. His neurotic characters and their extraordinary violence were a strange personal gift to the Western, extending its frontiers for both audience and film-makers that were to follow. The sensibility at work was a peculiar one: highly modern in its preoccupation with psychology and violence; oddly anachronistic in its fascination with the austere morality and art of Classical Greece and Elizabethan England. Remarkably, the Western allowed the welding of these elements and the expression of Mann's own troubled dialectic surrounding the individual and the cosmos.

Last Years

> What is learning anything? It is doing something, however tawdry it may be. I've made some tawdry films, I've made some fair films, I've made, I think, a few good films … but all of it was a process of learning.[5]

Few directors could have moved to the epic with surer credentials than Anthony Mann. In its way, the step was to prove as momentous for him as his coming to the Western, resulting in a great triumph, *El Cid*, which was acclaimed everywhere, and the most crushing of defeats, *The Fall of the Roman Empire* (1964), which was roundly condemned by all. Yet the two films are less black and white than that (except thematically), the vigour of the first balanced by the discipline of the second. Few of his generation, responding to the pressure of Hollywood's confused commercial climate of the late 1950s, weathered the transition to the epic so well.

With the form, Mann seemed at last to have arrived at ground he had been moving towards throughout his career. Apart from the archetypal conflicts that structured the films, there was an unheralded opportunity to focus on key ritualistic situations – the joust, torture by fire – against the backdrop of epic landscape. Mann seized on the potential, scenes such as the exhausting sword-fight of the challengers and the resurrection of the Cid, the punishing test of faith undergone by James Mason's Greek philosopher-slave and Marcus Aurelius's sombre funeral in the falling snow, moments of memorable quality. Yet although the achievement of these works is considerable, neither film achieves the consistency and power of his work within the Western. It may be that Mann did as well as he could, given the size and demands of the form. But finally there lurks the suspicion that he was always at his best when the narrative structure threw up models that allowed for archetypal extension, rather than the particularised situations themselves:

The Naked Spur or *Man of the West* rather than *Hamlet*. It was in the act of reaching that Mann became alive, impregnating his material, frequently tired and worn, with passionate meanings. Getting there, Mann may have discovered he had little to say.

Either way, Mann withdrew into silence. *The Heroes of Telemark* (1965), Mann's final, ravishing tribute to the snowline and his homage to the silent cinema, was a slender work. Centring on the old themes of the costs of being human and the emotional education of the hero – here compelled to move away from the rational posture that he shares with the Nazis – the action is somewhat mechanically followed through, finally dwarfed by the beautiful silent scenes of warfare in the majestic white Norwegian landscape. *A Dandy in Aspic* (1968), Mann's last film, the veteran dying in the final stages of shooting, achieved snatches of intensity despite the restrictions of an urban setting. Here Mann returned, perhaps appropriately, to *T-Men* territory and the counterpoint of character of the Westerns, building it round a new version of his hero, a tired Russian double-agent anxious about his identity, reaching out to feel, hopeful of escape from a ruthless past and a cold war world of power. The structure is embodied in the opposition of the hero, Eberlin, to Gaddis, the British agent, a mechanical, emotionless man. Ordered by the British to murder himself – in his Russian persona – Eberlin finally does so, shooting Gaddis and thus destroying his past even as it destroys him, Gaddis's car running him over on the airport tarmac.

When he died, Mann was planning *The King*, a reworking of *King Lear* set in the West. Mann seems always to have worked at an intuitive level – both his career and the films are a hymn to American pragmatism – and he may have come to feel that in returning to the form he might recover the drive and direction of earlier periods. Certainly, it is difficult to escape the view that Mann had lost his way in the 1960s. In a sense, it could be said that with the epic, Mann had used himself up, not only exhausting appropriate forms but his themes as well. There is a desperation about his embrace of the emerging genre of the spy movie, as if a sense of his irrelevance to the contemporary context had been borne in on him. Yet Mann would always be a prisoner of his empiricism. Despite the shifts of form and subject, there is finally a compulsive, strangely static quality about his career, a lack of growth and development that, perhaps inevitably, parallels the action of many of the individual films. Like his heroes, Mann tested himself all his artistic life; yet the disturbing questions that can both cripple a career and open new vistas may never have been faced, perhaps could not be posed. But for a time, Mann had touched the heights: his place is assured.

Retrospective

Mann's fate has been one of neglect. Despite the radical re-evaluation of the American cinema that took hold in the latter part of the 20th century, Mann has received relatively scant attention given his very sizeable contribution. If one compares his status with figures of analogous stature and achievement such as Nicholas Ray, Elia Kazan or Sam Fuller, he appears decisively overlooked. Longevity can be a factor: Ray, Kazan and Fuller, Frank Capra, Billy Wilder, Douglas Sirk, finally even Jerry Lewis, clearly benefited from avoiding an early demise, as suffered by a sixty-one-year-old Mann in 1967. In an age of increasing visual sophistication and post-modern nostalgia, of film festivals, retrospectives, celebrity lectures and organised tours, even modest figures enjoying a ripe old age like Boetticher, Andre de Toth and Joseph H. Lewis have occasionally found the spot-light. On the other hand, mere survival does not guarantee work or kudos, as Arthur Penn has discovered. Moreover, Peckinpah provides an interesting contrast, achieving what amounts to critical deification despite leaving the scene prematurely.

As cinema studies has become increasingly institutionalised over the past three decades, book publishing has also made a quantum if uneven leap forward. This is to say again that particular directors – one thinks immediately of Hitchcock and Peckinpah – have become a heavy presence on the bookshelf, while others, depending on status, fashion or perceived utility, have received modest attention, or may remain largely unexplored. Surprising given his long and productive career, Mann would fall completely into the latter group were it not for Jeanine Basinger's *Anthony Mann*, the most sustained study in English of the director. While joining the consensus that locates the Stewart Westerns and *Man of the West* as the cornerstone of the director's achieve-ment, Basinger nevertheless covers his early work and especially the noir period in considerable detail, as well as devoting a chapter to the two strong non-Westerns, *Men in War* and *God's Little Acre*, and another to the epics. However, it is the study of the Westerns that provides the main focus. Basinger erects her own rigorous structural analyses of the narrative components of the basic Mann plot and of the recurring char-acters, as with the hero, 'the man with a secret'. She also usefully explores the tripartite interaction in Mann's overall narrative design of interior conflict, landscape and dra-matic/emotional arc. An ardent admirer of Mann, Basinger provides a wealth of close analysis, scholarship and information.

But even in his own time, in contrast to Peckinpah or to contemporaries such as Kazan and Ray, Mann's work never dominated his era. If his obsessed, neurotic cowboys trapped in their noir conflicts resonated with 1950s America, the films in which they appeared, invariably highly successful commercially, never received more than passing attention. Only the French had seized on him early. With his impeccable taste Bazin had held *The Naked Spur* up as the anti-*Shane*, praising Mann's Westerns for their 'novelis-tic' approach that explored traditional themes with originality, psychological insight and 'an engaging individuality'.[6] If Bazin's emphasis on psychology and the novelistic tag suggested a literary experience, Jean-Luc Godard corrected such a reading in his effu-sive review of *Man of the West*:

> Each shot shows that Mann is reinventing the western. *Man of the West* is both course and discourse, beautiful landscapes and the explanation of this beauty, both the mystery of firearms and the secret of this mystery, both art and the theory of art; the result is that *Man of the West* is quite simply an admirable lesson in cinema – in modern cinema.[7]

Notwithstanding the poetic obscurity of the writing – so typical of *Cahiers du Cinéma* in its heyday – it is possible here to discern Godard's enthusiasm for the deliberate, studied quality he saw in Mann's visual style. In interviews Mann repeatedly defined as his goal a heightened, more intense realism that dictated his strategy of filming on location and pitting the actors against their environment. Images were more important than words – the audience needed to *see*. With reference to *Man of the West*, Mann had said he strove 'to accentuate the hieratic aspects' of his characters, 'like on a medallion'.[8] Time and again, he would refer to the enlarging effects of majestic or savage settings for tragic characters driven by inner torments – landscapes worthy of a Western Oedipus or Macbeth. Echoing the French, Andrew Sarris had also commented on this formal thrust:

> Anthony Mann is a style without a theme. His Westerns are distinguished by some of the most brilliant photography in the history of the American cinema, and yet it is impossible to detect a consistent thematic pattern in his work . . . Curiously, Mann's visual style is the American style which most closely resembles that of Antonioni in the literal progression through landscapes from the vegetable to the mineral . . .[9]

This concentration on Mann's visual style found its most extreme expression in the 1983 Paul Willemen essay, 'Looking at the Male'. Willemen believes that 'in one sense, Mann's stories are mere excuses to replace one image by another, pretexts for the renewal of visual pleasure'. He seizes on one shot in particular as emblematic of Mann's style – Gary Cooper sitting astride his horse during the first thirty seconds of the credits for *Man of the West*. Cooper takes a chaw of tobacco, then swivels round and peers off into the distance. 'The image and the figure in it are simply there to be looked at, to be enjoyed as pure pictoriality.'[10] The implication here is that Mann's images are not designed initially or principally to serve the narrative, but rather to extend an invitation to contemplate their visual phenomena – the hero, action, movement. A subtle reading, but is this an experience that is unique to Mann? The registering of a charge of visual pleasure that may go beyond narrative function in the Western is surely familiar. To discuss images generated by a 'cinematic writing' that is made up of 'camera movements, light, color, the inscription of figures into landscapes . . .' is evocative not only of Mann but of Ford (whom Mann revered) and Boetticher as well. Visual pleasure is a staple of the genre.

Willemen's analysis is too subtle. He dismisses the 'glaringly coherent thematic unity' (which had eluded Sarris), the psychological, archetypal and elemental conflicts that structure the drama and settings. The notion that the images are pretexts for observation and aesthetic pleasure treats them as if subjects for an easel painter. 'The images always draw attention to themselves, never as fodder for the eye, but always "eye-catching", arresting the look. Spectacular in the true sense of the word.'[11]

The distinction implied but not clearly focused here between the merely picturesque and the spectacular provides a useful insight into Mann's style, although not necessarily one that Willemen had in mind. Many a Western, like calendar art, promotes a sentimental romance of forms, vistas and views, insulating the viewer from the physical reality of the world. We are encouraged to stand back and 'see' life as if it had the reassuring design and proportions of a painting or photograph. Despite Willemen's contention that Mann goes beyond the 'fodder' or eye-candy of the picturesque, it is not clear how 'the pleasure of seeing the male "exist" (that is walk, move, ride, fight)' arrests the look, nor how the psychological space we are placed in differs from the comfortable spectatorship created by the picturesque.

In fact, the hallmark of Mann's style is its physical intensity, its brutal, mineral, ground-level point of view, and its vividly concrete treatment of space. Spectacular, these images can also be said to be literally sensational, jarring the jaded viewer with direct physical and kinetic experience. The images we recall from Mann are not still-life studies

of a man on a horse looking off, but rather dynamic frames: the hero marching precipi-
tously forward as the camera recedes; driving a horse precariously up the side of a
mountain; slapping leather to draw a weapon that isn't there. Above all, there are the
recurring images that led me to label the Mann hero the 'overreacher', the desperate
struggle to climb against gravity, against nature, against the odds, the unforgiving,
jagged, naked spurs that stud the landscape of these films. The regularity with which
such scenes launch, punctuate or culminate action (all three in *The Naked Spur*) gives
them the force of a rite of passage and of a ritualistic suffering.

Most physical of all, of course, are the bruising fights under horses' hooves, the struggles against rushing torrents, the pain of wounds brutally inflicted. In my view, it is this
heightened physicality of Mann's style, the 'realism' that he always aspired to, that arrests
the look, not its 'eye-catching' spectacles. Mann is much closer to a sculptor than a painter
in the way his images work with density and gravity to register physical sensation directly,
both on the hero's and the viewer's body. Mann insisted on these moments as essential to
escalate the stakes for hero and audience, to give a greater stature to the driven Stewart
hero. It was part of the strategy of achieving the hieratic, lifting the action to a mythic and
heraldic level, a notion that again suggests a sculptor's approach – 'like on a medallion'.

Willemen's interpretation of Mann is really driven by his focus on the violence, 'the
unquiet pleasure of seeing the male mutilated', rather than simple images of the hero
walking or riding. Psychoanalysing the films, he finds these spectacles arresting for the
way they play out a sadomasochistic dynamic of savage beatings that signal a repressed
homoerotic fascination. Insisting on these psychosexual undertones as the film's true substance, Willemen reduces the archetypal drama that drives the action and generates the
images to window-dressing. Paying an impolite lip service to the dramatic reality of the
films constructs it as a kind of mystified conscious content, misleading the films' audience. The 'real' content is the pure (or impure) imagery and its Freudian undercurrents,
the symptoms of the film's unconscious, where its true significance and meanings reside.

Willemen throws out the baby and leaves us with but snapshots. Nevertheless, despite
the disproportion of this argument, aspects of his reading suggestive of a troubled masculinity in Mann's hero are useful. Borden Chase's description of the narrative construct
both he and Mann shared – 'a love story between two men' – captures the homosocial
matrix of the films, but also hints at its potential for the homoerotic.[12] The threat of
such – Willemen's 'anxiety' – resonates in particular scenes in Mann, although not where
the character simply 'exists'. Rather, the threat materialises in specific moments of
ambiguous dramatic interaction, as in the opening of *The Naked Spur*, where Stewart
nervously looks over his shoulder as he begins to climb the sheer mountain wall before
him. 'I'll be right behind you,' opines an arch Ralph Meeker, not at all reassuring.

Dennis Bingham builds usefully on Willemen's thesis in his study of masculinity by
centring analysis on Stewart's career and star image.[13] Bingham locates Stewart's work
with Mann as crucial to his post-World War II efforts to break with the boyish, feminised
persona of the 1930s comedies, and create a more mature manhood in keeping with his
wartime military experience as a decorated Army Air Force colonel who had commanded
a squadron and flown thousands of hours of bombing missions over Germany. Bingham
relates this effort by the actor to the Mann–Stewart hero's brutalising struggle against
commitment, morality and community. The tortured state of the character is seen as

stemming from the cost of this performance, an acting male, an amoral masquerade that events conspire finally to crack open, revealing the character's truer nature. This gentler, more civilised essence is also in evidence when the character is unguarded, either raving deliriously or in a reflective moment, as when in *The Naked Spur* Stewart talks lovingly – the rain falling at cave's mouth on coffee cups providing a tinkling soundtrack – of the satisfactions of 'working the land' and 'bringing in the cattle'.

As we have seen, Mann's driven heroes are always in contradiction, nomads in conflict with their yearning for the settled. This familiar analysis of the hero's conflict is reconfigured by Bingham's focus on Stewart's evolving and ambiguous star persona in terms of gender, which adds force to the notion of a homoerotic subtext. Within these terms, Stewart's effort – both in career and in character – can be seen as a struggle to deny the feminine, the hero embodying a compromised masculinity. Beyond the typically edgy relationship between hero and villain, Bingham points to other elements and details that can be seen to bolster such an interpretation – the heroes' reliance on feminised geezer sidekicks, and the resistance to aggressive women and preference for the boyish – as in the noirish Ruth Roman versus the asexual Corinne Calvet of *The Far Country*. Bingham even suggests that the cowboy's typical outfit of chaps open at the crotch foregrounds the Stewart hero's genital area, a costume that protests the character's maleness. *Man of the West* can also be related to this analysis. There Gary Cooper remains detached from the warm overtures of a needy Julie London, and as payback for Jack Lord's forcing her to strip, brutally beats and strips *him*. Picking the fight by taunting Lord, Link turns his back and insists that Coaley come at him from behind – 'He's good at that.' As far back as *T-Men*, Mann had depicted closely bonded heroes rejecting married status and pursuing a manhunt in bathhouses.

Man of the West: ambiguous dramatic action

A more recent analysis by Douglas Pye of masculinity in Mann argues less for an ambiguous gender but rather suggests 'the collapse of fantasy' (as his study is entitled), the fantasy being that of the genre's heroic male agency. Disputing the claim that Mann responds more to archetype than history, Pye traces the way in which the films can be seen to describe a trajectory for the Mann hero that is reflective of a closing frontier. As the wilderness and its possibilities of the unknown shrink, the hero is forced into the still open northwest corner of America (*Bend of the River*) and on to Alaska (*The Far Country*), to final confrontations in ghost towns (*Man of the West*) and to defeat by civilised values (*The Last Frontier*). Pye argues that the geography traces a dead end that the character also faces in a choice between an increasingly brutalised, neurotic state outside the community and an emasculated existence within the settled. The crisis is fuelled in Pye's view by the ideological contradictions inherent in American culture that are reflected in the genre's traditional oppositions between a manhood defined in relation to the wilderness versus the community coded as feminine. Pye quotes Martin Pumphrey's encapsulation of the dilemma: 'How far can masculinity survive contact with the feminine sphere?'[14]

I do not share Pye's argument that Mann is interested in the Peckinpah paradigm of the hero tragically beached by a receding frontier. Even in *Man of the West*, the one film where the historical time frame is prominent, it is decisively overshadowed by Mann's focus on the hieratic aspects of his characters. But the argument positing the impossibility of masculinity, in conjunction with the accounts by Willemen and Bingham, confirms that Mann's cinema offers a fruitful site for an interrogation of the genre's ideological operation with reference to gender.

Further psychoanalysis of Mann's films can advance them as exemplary of the genre in obsessively rehearsing an Oedipal journey basic to the Western that parallels the social, psychic and sexual trajectory of men in the real. This analysis supports the ideological critique exemplified by Jane Tompkins's *West of Everything* that sees the Western as reassuring its audience as to what constitutes manliness.[15] The heroic quest and combat that frame the action are seen to symbolise proofs of masculinity, defined as a self-reliance free of dependency on the feminine. Often the hero nurses a wound inflicted in the past by a woman, suggestive of the trauma of separation from the mother. The violence of the genre, and especially the punishing fights and painful woundings, can be interpreted as forging bonds of manhood, and demonstrating a rejection of the feminine. As Willemen argues, dominant patriarchal ideology disallows a voyeurist contemplation of masculine physical beauty. Signs of implication in the homoerotic or the feminine for both characters and audience must therefore be displaced and masked by violence. We cannot look at the male body without blood, fear or pain.

In this account of the genre, the pairings of hero and villain, hero and sidekick, function to provide character conventions that explore different aspects of the masculine. In Mann, the use of blood brothers or doubles is a particularly key structure. As in *Bend in the River*, joining forces allows a closeness forged in battle that, rather like sports, forestalls uncomfortable questions about intimacy. Bingham quotes Stewart and Kennedy, the ex-bad men, as they enunciate with a small, bemused emphasis Stewart's plans to take up '*farmin*' . . .'. Later, as innocent settlers remark on pretty bird calls, the two wryly identify the Indian signals they both recognise as '*redwing orioles . . . from Canada*'. Such is the edginess with which true males dance around and mock the feminine.

From this perspective, focused in the extreme by Mann's films, the Western can be faulted for a failure to explore and define a masculinity that challenges mainstream ideology. But, of course, to apply this psychoanalytical diagnosis to individual patients – the movies themselves – is perhaps to find that the genre is not unilaterally sick. Certainly, Mann is by no means exemplary of the Western's gender dynamics, as Ford's domesticated frontier amply demonstrates. Moreover, as in critiques of the latter's racism, it is easy to bring a multicultural perspective to bear judgmentally on work produced a half-century ago. More to the point is whether contemporary culture and the art of the future can begin to provide a masculinity defined as inclusive of the feminine instead of opposed to it, models of men able to acknowledge among themselves attraction, desire and intimacy unmarked by blood and violence. In the meantime, we have Mann's work, whose neurotic heroes given a psychosocial reading can be seen as the maladjusted victims of a distorting macho universe. Such latter-day interpretations, however, do not invalidate the auteurist and thematic analyses they build on. Instead, they flesh them out with additional depth and a contemporary significance. Mann's archetypal subject – the blood brothers, the noir hero and his doppelgänger, Cain and Abel, Oedipus and himself – are now given another guise, that of the masculine and feminine.

Notes

1. Paul Mayersberg interview with Anthony Mann for the 'Action Speaks Louder than Words' edition of the BBC series *The Movies* conducted while Mann was in the UK on pre-production for *A Dandy in Aspic* in 1967.
2. Ibid.
3. Ibid.
4. Ibid.
5. Ibid.
6. Andre Bazin, 'The Evolution of the Western', in Hugh Gray (ed.), *What is Cinema?* vol. 2 (Berkeley: University of California Press, 1971), pp. 149–57.
7. Tom Milne, (ed.), *Godard on Godard* (New York: Viking Press, 1972), p. 117.
8. *Cahiers du Cinéma in English* no. 12 (December 1967), p. 48.
9. Andrew Sarris, *American Cinema: Directors and Directions 1929–1968* (New York: E. P. Dutton, 1968), p. 98. Sarris quotes himself from an earlier 1963 commentary.
10. Paul Willemen, 'Anthony Mann: Looking at the Male', *Framework* nos. 15/16/17 (Summer 1981), p. 16; reprinted in Jim Kitses and Gregg Rickman (eds), *The Western Reader* (New York: Limelight Editions, 1998), pp. 209–12.
11. Ibid.
12. Jim Kitses, 'The Rise and Fall of the American West: Borden Chase Interviewed', *Film Comment* vol. 6 no 4 (Winter 1970–1), p. 17.
13. Dennis Bingham, *Acting Male: Masculinities in the Films of James Stewart, Jack Nicholson and Clint Eastwood* (New Brunswick, NJ: Rutgers University Press, 1994), pp. 49–68.
14. Douglas Pye, 'The Collapse of Fantasy', in Ian Cameron and Douglas Pye (eds), *The Book of Westerns* (New York: Continuum, 1996), pp. 167–73.
15. Jane Tompkins, *West of Everything: The Inner Life of Westerns* (New York: Oxford University Press, 1992), pp. 58–67.

4
Budd Boetticher: Rules of the Game

Boetticher stands alone. There is much about this director's life and art that encourages this romantic notion. Where Ford, his roots deep in history, was to achieve a great respect within the industry, where Mann, sustained both by his experience of the stage and a natural empiricism, over the years collected three reputations (at home with the thriller, the Western and the epic), Boetticher appears a diminutive and isolated figure working in the shadows, trying to create his art wholly out of himself. Often he has been likened to Hemingway, his work and career hovering between tragedy and cliché, only an unyielding integrity apparently forestalling the parody that his much-publicised individualism invites.

His bizarre entry into the world of movies as a bullfighter is now well known, Boetticher swapping his apprenticeship as a matador for a Hollywood career in 1941 when he was taken on as technical adviser for Mamoulian's *Blood and Sand*. Ten years later, after a string of small pictures, Boetticher shot what he has described as the largely autobiographical *The Bullfighter and the Lady* (1951), John Ford assisting the John Wayne production by cutting the film and ensuring a prompt studio release. Always self-conscious, the director marked the film as a milestone by changing his credit from Oscar Boetticher, Jr, to Budd. Yet the breakthrough was minor: if the contract with Universal that followed offered a base and more substantial performers, the production conditions for the adventure films and Westerns that now occupied him remained cramping and unsympathetic.

In 1955, Boetticher had a second opportunity to undertake a personal project in *The Magnificent Matador*, easily his most ambitious production thus far. However, it was with the small Western that followed this highly uneven work (and the taut thriller, *The Killer is Loose* [1955]) that Boetticher's career finally clicked. *Seven Men from Now* was the first of a brief cycle of Westerns that were to emerge over the next four years. Highly successful commercially, these little films would bring a measure of critical recognition in France, at least, where Bazin hailed *Seven Men from Now* as an 'exemplary Western'. After a half-dozen of these, between each of which Boetticher was shooting footage for his long-cherished third bullfighting film about the renowned matador, *Arruza* (1972), the director went on to make *The Rise and Fall of Legs Diamond* in 1960. Then he left for Mexico to complete his project on Arruza, who was a close friend. Astonishingly, the commitment to complete this personal production resulted in an eight-year exile before

Ride Lonesome: existential landscapes

Boetticher was free to return, taking up his Hollywood career with yet another small Western.

Hollywood and Mexico, bullfighting and the Western, these are the polarities of Boetticher's world and point to the profound ambiguity at its centre. On the one hand, there is the deepest commitment to a highly romantic individualism: life is seen as a solitary quest for meaning, an odyssey, action as a definition and expression of the self that is its own reward, compromise of personal integrity as indefensible. On the other hand, there is Boetticher's chosen profession, the corporate and glossy public world of an industrial art, the Hollywood cinema, within which he was buried (his two original projects apart) for fifteen years. Perhaps only his competitive drive, the desire to do everything as well as possible, sustained him throughout this troubled, directionless period.

The contradictions inherent in Boetticher's position are clearest in his success. *Seven Men from Now* led directly to the Ranown cycle of Westerns, all of which were produced by Harry Joe Brown (Boetticher himself was often associate producer), and which comprise the core of Boetticher's achievement. All the films starred Randolph Scott, Brown's partner in the venture, and the more substantial works – *The Tall T*, *Ride Lonesome*, *Comanche Station* – were scripted by Burt Kennedy, whose first effort as a screenwriter had been to adapt his Western novella (of the same title) for *Seven Men from Now*. A reading of this story is instructive for any student of Boetticher's films: most of the situations, incidents and dialogue that would be developed and refined later in the cycle are already present here.

Robert Stack in *The Bullfighter and the Lady*

However, I am not suggesting that the films are not Boetticher's own. As Kennedy himself has pointed out, the scripts were as much Boetticher's as his; moreover, to examine the novels adapted by Charles Lang and Boetticher for *Decision at Sundown* and *Buchanan Rides Alone* is to recognise a pattern of meaningful changes – in particular, hero and villain being given a parallel stature – falling into place. In his own career as a director, Kennedy decisively revealed a sensibility far removed from the irony, discipline and stark confrontations of the Ranown cycle. Often shamelessly quoting from the earlier scripts (see *Return of the Seven* [1966]), his work has tended to a broad, often vulgar comedy (as in his two most successful movies, *Support Your Local Sheriff* [1968]/*Gunfighter* [1971]), which suggests the common ground that sustained this fertile collaboration. But in any case, if Boetticher's overall career has been a broken and artistically uneven one, the consistency of its thematic and formal preoccupations, from *The Bullfighter and the Lady* to *Arruza*, from *Seven Men from Now* to *A Time for Dying* (1969), seems undeniable.

Yet the Ranown cycle (my use of this term encompasses *Seven Men from Now*, which in fact was a Batjac production) was crucial to Boetticher in two ways. First, it offered an enclave within the industry in which he could operate, a structure characterised less by studio bureaucracy than by the personal style of individuals who shared a common respect working together in a small outfit. While sheltering Boetticher from the destructive confrontations – the impulse to square off against the whole industry – that his individualist ethic exposes him to, this arrangement also offered him the opportunity to arrive at a meaningful form. Boetticher's obsessive return to the subject of bullfighting is ample evidence of his belief in the validity of the matador, the ritualistic encounter with death providing action that is both personally and artistically meaningful. However, the completeness of the commitment to individualism, if privately sustaining, confines the film-maker: how to dramatise a static world, action that is neither growth nor change? Here again Mann was the more fortunate, his heroes compulsively reaching out. Perhaps nothing testifies more eloquently to the flexibility of the Western as an artistic model than the fact that it should have been so important in the development of two such disparate artists committed to starkly contrasting conceptions of character and dramatic action.

The sheer appeal of making Westerns for Boetticher is obvious: like Ford, he is a man of the outdoor life most at ease in good male company. As with Hawks, this extends into an ethic of physical action that is evident in the films: stunts and chases, careering buckboards and skirmishes with Indians, these are always shot with exuberance by Boetticher. But more importantly, at an ideological level the Western is deeply attractive for Boetticher in its insistence on an archaic world where the ambiguous drama of individualism can be played out. Although not a man of the West like Peckinpah, Boetticher is fascinated by the idea of the frontier: it is this that explains his sojourns in Mexico, metaphorically speaking the last stronghold of the American West. However, the vulnerable men and women and the isolated swing stations that characterise Boetticher's frontier have little to do with history. Boetticher's West is quite simply *the world*, a philosophical ground over which his pilgrims move to be confronted with existential choices wholly abstracted from social contexts. Where Mann had self-consciously edged the revenge Western towards tragedy, Boetticher intuitively reversed the movement, gradually stripping the form of its revenge drive (and the metaphysical ethic it carries) to arrive at the structure of the morality play and the fable. Unsupported by virtue, tradition or the community, Boetticher's characters confront their destiny nakedly. However, we are deceived if we consider them to be in control of it: sustained only by an idea of themselves in the face of a mocking meaninglessness, the characters are helpless, doomed to play out their absurd roles in the tragicomic game of life.

The Ranown cycle gave Boetticher a stable base and creative relationships that allowed him to refine his form, the films growing deeper and more personal until with *Ride Lonesome* and *Comanche Station*, the controlled objectification of tensions and the appropriateness of form and style approach perfection. But above all, his Westerns are a series, Boetticher demonstrating more dramatically than most artists how an understanding and appreciation of the single work can grow through knowledge of earlier and later works. Moreover, his achievement, although it is not inaccessible to all but the connoisseur, does require for its full impact an awareness of the fine adjustments he makes within the form. And this provides the final paradox. For if the Ranown team and the Western gave Boetticher the latitude and structure through which he could create the ritualistic play that he finds meaningful, the results could never be fully satisfactory for the director. Boetticher's romanticism demanded that he rise above the industry and its genres rather than function there *mano a mano*, that single-handedly he create the *apocalyptical* work, the original masterpiece, his *magnum opus*. Living out the myth of his individualism to the hilt, Boetticher cut free from the constraints and disciplines of the industry to find himself, like his characters, moving through bewildering and dangerous experiences, a commitment to personal style finally little protection. Boetticher's account of the wild adventures of those eight years, *When, in Disgrace*, inevitably expresses his sense of vindication and triumph in never compromising or quitting his task to return to Hollywood defeated. In this light, it may be that Boetticher will want himself to be measured by the qualities of *Arruza* finally, rather than by those works whose stature and meaning depend on tradition, and to which I turn now.

The Ranown Cycle: Themes and Worldview

Boetticher's Westerns can be difficult to distinguish from each other, given the recurrence of plots, locations, performers, even names. Therefore, it might be useful to begin by briefly summarising the films:

Seven Men from Now (1956)

Stride (Randolph Scott) tracks the seven men who held up the Wells Fargo station and killed his wife in Silver Springs. In the desert he meets and escorts an Eastern couple, the Greers, and is joined by two outlaws, Lee Marvin and Donald Barry, who are after the stolen gold that Greer is secretly transporting. After Indian attacks and the death of the killers, Stride guns down Marvin in a face-off.

The Tall T (1957)

Losing his horse in a bet that he can ride a bull, Brennan (Randolph Scott) hitches a ride on a stage driven by an old friend, Rintoon, which carries the honeymooning Mimses and is mistakenly held up by Richard Boone, Henry Silva and Skip Homeier. Brennan and the woman, who is an heiress, are kept alive while word is sent to her father. Undermining the trust of the outlaws in one another, Brennan separates and kills them.

Decision at Sundown (1957)

Bart Allison (Randolph Scott) and Sam (Noah Beery, Jr) ride into the town where Tate Kimbrough (John Carroll), the man who had an affair with Allison's wife before she killed herself, is about to be married. Interrupting the ceremony with a promise to kill the groom, Allison takes cover in a stable with Sam. The brutal murder of the latter – in part the result of Allison's rejection of his friend's attempts to describe his wife's other infidelities – affects the cowed citizenry, who disarm the villain's henchmen, thus forcing a fair fight between Allison and Kimbrough, which is cut short when Valerie French shoots her lover in the shoulder to save him.

Buchanan Rides Alone (1958)

Riding into corrupt Agrytown, Buchanan (Randolph Scott) is arrested with Juan, a young Mexican of a wealthy family who has killed Roy Agry for molesting his sister. While the Agrys try to cheat each other of ransom money, the hero's death is averted by one of the gang, Pecos, who commits himself to his fellow West Texan, the two then freeing Juan. However, Pecos is killed and the two recaptured, escaping finally to engage in a shoot-out, where members of the Agry gang find themselves caught in crossfire on a bridge. Carbo (Craig Stevens), Simon Agry's henchman, inherits the town as Buchanan rides off.

Ride Lonesome (1959)

Brigade (Randolph Scott) arrests Billy John (James Best) and returns him to town slowly, since he is really after Billy's brother Frank, who long ago hanged Brigade's wife. The hero is joined by two outlaws, Pernell Roberts and James Coburn, who want Billy because an amnesty has been declared on any who bring him in, and by Mrs Lane (Karen Steele), whose husband has been killed by Indians. After the death of Frank, Brigade and Roberts face off, but the hero relents and leaves Billy and Mrs Lane to the outlaws, who carry on without him.

Comanche Station (1960)

Cody (Randolph Scott) buys Mrs Lowe (Nancy Gates) from the Comanche and in returning her to her husband, who has offered a large reward, is joined by Claude Akins, Skip Homeier and Richard Rust. Homeier is killed by Indians and Rust by Akins when he refuses to ambush the couple. Killing the villain, Cody then returns the woman to her husband, who is blind, and rides off into the mountains.

The perennial evocation of Hemingway does little to illuminate Boetticher's work; if we must look for literary parallels, Chaucer seems more appropriate. Above all, Boetticher's films are comedies, deeply ironic works, but comedies all the same. In contrast with the tragic world of Anthony Mann, Boetticher's small films are bittersweet reflections on the human condition. Within this perspective, Chaplin and Lubitsch seem as relevant as Ford and Hawks for an understanding of Boetticher. Serious anatomies of the inadequacies of different attitudes to life, his movies exist as parodies of the morality play, insisting on a sophisticated relationship with the audience, an agreement to reject simplistic notions of good and evil and to recognise that violence and injustice are less the property of malignant individuals than of the world itself. No one ever feels the impulse to hiss a Boetticher villain. Created with great care, these most human and sympathetic of men are almost always invariably blasted, to our sorrow. That these charming rogues must die is an index of how hostile and finally absurd the world is.

Typically, the hero is both a victim and a product, an expression of this world; indeed often, it seems that he functions as its tool. The variations in the hero, and his development, can be seen if we group the films as follows:

1. *Seven Men from Now* and *Decision at Sundown*: In both of these, the hero's wife has been killed relatively recently. In the first, characteristically, the hero has withdrawn into coldness (tempered somewhat by guilt at having been indirectly responsible for his wife's death), which makes him seem rather inhuman. Lee Marvin's stylish lust for Annie Greer forces the hero to intervene, the growing involvement softening the character. In *Decision at Sundown*, an earlier, less mature version of the hero has become virtually unbalanced, a dark and tragic figure in Mann style. Here the action forces the hero to see that his revenge is meaningless, the character riding out bitter and alone, close to the ground later heroes already inhabit.

2. *The Tall T* and *Buchanan Rides Alone*: In both of these, the heroes are jaunty, philosophical men going about their business and suddenly surrounded by danger. The first, one of Boetticher's finest works, begins as a broad comedy and rapidly darkens with the deaths of Rintoon, Hank and Jeff, his small boy, whose bodies are thrown into a well. Here again, the hero withdraws into a granite-like circumspection, only relieved by his relationship with Mrs Mims. In the second, the hero remains jaunty and something of an irrelevance, the tone consistently comic (barring the death of Pecos).

3. *Ride Lonesome* and *Comanche Station*: Here the roots of the action go back a long way. 'I most forgot,' says Frank of his hanging of Brigade's wife. In the second film, the abduction of Cody's wife by the Indians is ten years old; yet the character persists 'all the time alone, all the time in Comanche country'. In these works, the closest to the original structure of *Seven Men from Now*, the character is now absurd.

It was Bazin who first pointed out the resemblance of Randolph Scott to W. S. Hart: certainly Scott's archaic presence is a crucial factor in the films. An actor with an innate sense of his qualities and range, Scott had begun to restrict himself to Western roles early in the 1940s. Like the Mann/Stewart films, the Ranown cycle gave a fillip to a declining career, the films intelligently structured around the star to ring the changes on a presence that could evoke anything from a cheerfully optimistic pragmatism to the unbending stoic reticence of a beleaguered man in the twilight of his days.

In general, the Boetticher hero as created by Scott can be said to possess (or be moving towards) a great serenity, the knowledge that we are fundamentally alone, that nothing lasts, that what matters in the face of all this is 'living the way a man should'. Especially in the later films, the hero has had it all – love, position, security – and lost it all. This makes the figure oddly anachronistic, a man who continues to assert values out of an image of himself that has its roots in the past. The essence of the hero is the knowl-

The Tall T: 'Some things a man can't ride around'

edge that action is both gratuitous and essential. Revenge is meaningless, since the wife is dead; yet it is necessary because it is evidence of a way of life that the hero embodies: 'Some things a man can't ride around.' This stoicism arms the character with a grace that forms an impenetrable armour against the temptations and threats of life. In this context, despite the ironic tone of the films, the absurd plight of a hero often menaced or held in bondage, there is finally a great dignity about the figure. The villain, for instance, always knows that there is no way of achieving his goal apart from 'going over' Scott: if the hero can be taken from behind, his code demands that he be confronted. The character has no magic; he is not the perfect shot or the fastest gun: only in *Seven Men from Now*, the loosest because the first of the series, does Scott have a mysterious expertise, felling Lee Marvin in the showdown like a dazed bull. More typically, the hero survives through intelligent calculation and a capacity for self-control in facing danger. Thus, at the outset of *Ride Lonesome*, Brigade rides into Billy John's camp to find himself surrounded by a gang in the rocks. Turning the trap to his advantage, Brigade simply threatens to kill Billy on the spot, putting his own life on the line, unless the men are ordered away. The opening of *Comanche Station* is equally forceful, Cody moving through an arroyo, the crests of which are suddenly covered with Comanche. Instantly, the figure dismounts and unpacks trade goods, gracefully gesturing up to the Indians like a matador before his judges, his 'cool' unblown and intact.

This equilibrium, an essential expression of the hero's integrity, springs from his complete knowledge of the world through which he moves with the precision and skill of a dancer. The opening of Boetticher's original scenario of *Two Mules for Sister Sara* establishes a characteristic version of the hero:

It's rock country and the bleached-white spires burst jaggedly up through the desert sand in a wavering line opposite the setting sun, from south to north, where they grow in stature and seeming dignity to eventually jut their way into becoming a part of the Sierra Madre. As we scan the terrain we discover an almost imperceptible movement mostly hidden in the long evening shadows tight against the rocks. Zooming closer we recognize the figures as a lone rider astride his horse; followed by a pack-pony, who trots to keep up with the long-legged animal before him. The saddle horse is a blood red roan; a thoroughbred . . . The man is tall and lean, dressed in the colors of the desert and the rocks. The tans, and the browns, and the grays of his tight-fitting outfit are only broken up by the black and yellow beaded Indian moccasins which he wears instead of boots. The plain leather holster of his Colt revolver is thong-tied tight down just above his right knee, and his long-gun, a Winchester, swings slightly with the movement of his animal, in a dirty canvas scabbard attached to the saddle just behind his left leg. A new leather case containing U.S. binoculars hangs from the saddle's pommel. And now we get our first real close look at the man himself. It is impossible to determine his age. He could be thirty, or maybe even forty, but we'll never be sure because the wrinkles around his eyes and at the corner of his tight lips could have come into being from the desert sun. He wears his sweat-stained hat low down over his eyes to shade them from the fading light, but there is a sparkle of all-consuming awareness in those eyes that makes you feel certain that not even a lizard mor'n half a mile away could skitter across the sand without his knowing which way it was headed. Unpleasantly there is an aura of meanness about the man. Watching him you smell the sticky odour of hate that seemingly envelops everything around him except his horse. But in spite of the meanness that you feel, or the suspicion that his deep-rooted loathing includes even the sand and the rocks, you are suddenly overwhelmingly aware that the man is all-over, downright, beautiful. Even the slight movement of his body as he swings his head and shoulders around to check his pack-pony is cat-like and deadly . . .

A somewhat darker figure than usual, the hero here is typical in other respects. Riding easily through the world to which he belongs, the character carries everything that he needs with him. He is invulnerable so long as he is alone: once he meets with others, he will insist on travelling in the open, aware that he is now exposed. Although danger lurks everywhere, it is most common where the desert offers the illusion of safety or life: at a deserted swing station, a green oasis, atop a ridge or in a cave. The terrain is barren and hostile, a cruel and empty landscape, permanent and unchanging, that dwarfs the figures who move through it for a time. 'A man needs a reason to ride this country. You got a reason?' Suspicious of all he meets, the hero himself needs no reason: the desert is his domain. While others sleep, the hero sits erect and alone, ever on guard.

In both *Seven Men from Now* and *The Tall T*, the hero admits that he is afraid, and he and the heroine are allowed to touch, the audience offered the possibility that at the end they have come together. If the heroes of *Decision at Sundown* and *Buchanan Rides Alone* are both fearless in their different ways, they are not allowed to kill their antagonist (Kimbrough, Carbo), and thus are softened despite the absence of women. However, in *Ride Lonesome* and *Comanche Station*, we cannot believe that the hero experiences the emotions that we do. Here nothing is possible between the hero and heroine, the decorum unbroken, the distance unbridgeable. In these works – especially the second, where he destroys the villain – the hero has ceased to be a man altogether. In his purest expression, the core of the Boetticher hero is apparent, the figure existing as a spirit rather than a person, a way of life rather than a life. An abstraction, the hero represents an unrealisable ideal, an experience and knowledge of the world so complete that the character is finally as impervious as the rocks around him. But if it were possible to become like Boetticher's Scott, we would hesitate. A man beyond all human ties, the character is impotent, never initiating action, ever passively responding. There is no drama in the figure, for this has been played out in the past (*Decision at Sundown*): every encounter now is simply the occasion for a ritualistic reaffirmation of a choice forced upon the hero long ago.

This absurdity in the character's position is the source of the duality that Boetticher exploits in the films. At times, the hero is the very butt of the world, tossed about like a leaf, tragicomically at the mercy of life. At others, the character is the world itself, as relentless as the landscape, as regular and predictable as the seasons. This interplay accounts for the comic range of Boetticher's work, which extends from the farce of *Buchanan Rides Alone*, where the hero is bewilderingly shuttled in and out of menacing situations repeatedly, to the bitter irony of *Decision at Sundown* or *The Tall T*. However, regardless of the mode of the film, the hero himself remains a source of amusement. In order to survive, the character has had to adopt a colourless and severe style, the main feature of which is a laconic frankness. Where others, like Mr Mims, shoot their mouths off, and where the villain, Richard Boone, for example, often *needs* talk, the hero knows that language can be dangerous: 'A man can talk himself to death.' Villains are ever confessing to Scott that when 'a man gets halfway, he oughta have something of his own, something to belong to, be proud of'; the hero replies stolidly: 'They say that.' Where the villain comments in detail on the desirability of the woman, Scott agrees: 'She ain't ugly.' Using in a very disciplined way the cracker-barrel tradition of humorous observation that runs through the Western, Boetticher creates the hero as a plain dealer, a sophisticated yet rural figure, a Will Rogers with six-guns. In the same vein is the character's quaint courtliness, even when angry dismissing the heroine with a sharp compliment: 'You cook good coffee – good-*night* Mrs Lane!' A source of great humour, these qualities also contribute to our sense of the fabulous in the character, evoking a code by which he lives despite his circumstances. This is even clearer in the blunt, gritty aphorisms that are infrequently wrung from him: 'A man oughta be able to look after his woman.'

If half of the Boetticher hero is a sad clown, the other half is a killjoy. The basic deception in the films of the Ranown cycle, and the key to their dramatic structure, is that the Randolph Scott figure is the hero only in a technical sense: it is the villain who is our true hero. Boetticher's villains are so important that one can claim the stronger they are, the stronger the film, tracing a slowly descending curve from *The Tall T*'s Richard Boone through the three journey films (Roberts and Coburn, Akins and Rust, Marvin) to *Decision at Sundown*, which only really comes alive when John Carroll has to muster the courage to face what he feels will be certain death, and *Buchanan Rides Alone*, where Craig Stevens's Carbo is as amusing and marginal as the hero himself. Here Boetticher forsakes characters of integrity to play with the Agry family, whom he creates as humours in the medieval sense, farcical expressions of ignorance and greed. Even the weak *Westbound*, a bad script that Boetticher shot reluctantly for Warners in 1959 so that he could make *The Rise and Fall of Legs Diamond* the following year, is enlivened by its heavies, Andrew Duggan and Michael Pate.

Typically, Boetticher's villains differ from the Scott figure in their comparatively flamboyant style, ever sporting a shocking touch of green or pink, a colourful Indian armlet, a fancy draw. Within the community, this impulse can produce a villain that has the splendour of a peacock: the immaculately tailored Carbo among all the sweaty Agrys, Kimbrough in his white shirt complete with ruffles. Where the hero is ever ready to 'say out in words' exactly what he means, the villain is as likely to tell us a story, which soon begins to sound very like the situation that the characters are in: 'Once knew a gal looked just like you, Mrs Greer.' Cocksure of himself, Lee Marvin tells his tale with great charm, virtually ravishing Annie verbally in the process, and wholly disrupts the ritual of shared coffee, while the hero sits helpless. It is this narcissism, the need to entertain and dazzle, that is often the villain's undoing. Above all, the character must dominate, imposing himself and taking on the world single-handedly. Thus Marvin and Akins both shoot down their minions ruthlessly; Boone is cheerful on finding Silva and Homeier, the 'animals' as he calls them, both dead.

Yet Boetticher insists that the villain shares a certain integrity with the hero. This is evident in a strict rule of the drama whereby the Scott figure is saved by a gratuitous act of the villain's: thus Lee Marvin guns down one of the killers about to shoot Stride in the back; Boone keeps Brennan out of the well; Pernell Roberts bluffs Billy into dropping the carbine he holds to Brigade's middle; Akins rides into an Indian attack to help Cody: 'It seemed like a good idea.' The villain knows that his act will not matter when the final confrontation comes; yet his idea of himself compels a rescue of the man who may (and usually does) destroy him. Some Boetticher villains are darker than others: where Marvin and Akins seem driven by self-aggrandisement – to be the top gun, the head man, 'number one' – both Boone and Roberts are trying to retire from outlawry, to find 'a place' and escape being 'all the time alone'. The great power of these works follows from poising the major villain in the existential moment that is essential to Boetticher; in both *Seven Men from Now* and *Comanche Station*, locating this drive to 'cross over' within essentially innocent characters (both Greer and Dobie turn their backs on evil and are promptly riddled with bullets) results in a drama of less force.

This action, together with the structure of Boetticher's films, may suggest that this vision is a moral one, the films resembling 'floating poker-games', as Andrew Sarris once called them, in which each character must decide how to live. But, fundamentally, the action of the films is a dialogue between villain and hero that masks the attempt of the villain to become the hero, a reaching out for the power or experience that the hero embodies. Whether a dark figure or not, Boetticher's villain remains a deeply attractive individual for us – we understand him in a way we cannot the hero – and the films stand finally as celebrations of this character, who attempts to create action in a way that the static Scott cannot: 'I couldn't have enjoyed the five thousand if I'd done you that way.' It is bitterly ironic that the thrust and style of the villain make him vulnerable by exposing him to the very ideal he aspires to. At the end of both *The Tall T* and *Comanche Station*, the villain stands with his back to Scott, safe for the moment; in the earlier work, the point is made explicit, as Richard Boone walks carefully to his horse and then rides out alive. But finally, in both cases the character – a man of great life and wit who has given us much pleasure – turns to confront the world and an absurd, relentlessly dour justice that utterly destroys him.

At various points, Boetticher insists that the villain can survive if he resists the pull of narcissism to embrace meaningful relationships. This is, of course, implied by the hero, who, while resolutely alone, carries the scars of past involvements. Tate Kimbrough, a figure who clearly looks forward to Legs Diamond, is only saved by Lucy's act of love, wounding him as he faces Scott and thus forcing him to accept his need for her. Carbo, who is allowed to emerge as the headman of Agrytown at the end, perhaps deserves this for his steadfast loyalty to Simon Agry in an atmosphere rife with intrigue and betrayal. Certainly, Pernell Roberts, the one character who survives to enjoy a life of amnesty with Karen Steele, alone among the major villains enjoys a relationship of real warmth with another character, James Coburn's Wid. However, given the dialectic of the hero and the thrust of the villain, it is not surprising that Boetticher's view of social relationships is ambiguous. Marriages are pathetic, shattered by death, betrayed or weak; even the optimism of *Ride Lonesome* diminishes if we consider that Roberts may be on the threshold of the cycle through which Scott has passed. In *The Tall T*, Mrs Mims has married a cowardly carpetbagger to escape her loneliness; in both *Comanche Station* and *Westbound*, the husbands are cripples, dependent on their women. As with Mann, characters often muse on a pastoral future, 'a place' just north of the Sonora, just west of the Pecos. Yet the typical community within the films is that of the campfire, the only ritual that of the meal, people passing the coffeepot. Groups never exist in Boetticher, the action almost always developed through a series of dialogues. Sitting on guard in the shadows, the hero is visited first by the heroine and then by the villain; the minor villains talk, perhaps interrupted by their leader, who then passes on to the woman.

The villain shares a certain honour with the hero: Claude Akins in *Comanche Station*

A similar ambiguity cloaks the heroine. The scripts insist that the woman is important because she assuages loneliness and offers meaningful contact – she is the keeper of 'the place'. However, this spiritual view is undercut as the films unwind, the heroine invariably taking on overtones of great physical desirability. Boetticher's women always suffer indignities, forced to stand in a downpour, tripping into mud, ducked in a water-trough; yet they come out sparkling, their often tattered clothes hugging their bodies. Even Maureen O'Sullivan's homely and ageing Mrs Mims takes on sexual qualities sharpened for us when, humiliated, she bares herself to tempt Skip Homeier to his death. However, it is Karen Steele who is Boetticher's definitive heroine, at once a good-natured, warm companion and a hard sexual object.

Inevitably, Boetticher's individualism naturally moves towards its close neighbour, the Hawksian ethic, and a separating out of the men from the boys or, in Boetticher's terms, the aficionados from the crowd. If weaker characters in Hawks aren't 'good enough', in Boetticher we could say that men who 'run on the gentle side' lack *cojones*. Thus, although the films insist on a dignity for hero and villains, this does not extend to a Willard Mims, whose name sums him up. Similarly, even if Boetticher's women do not have to become men to be taken seriously (as Hawks's must), they remain somewhat on the margins, their shifting persona reflecting the drives of hero and villain. Living within the desert, speaking true, functioning man to man – these imply accepting a love that finally can be crippling. Trying to top the world, to sparkle, to be the man, this can mean using the woman mechanically, the individual attempting in vain to remain invulnerable.

The Ranown Cycle: Form and Style

The moral of Boetticher's films is thus a simple one: everyone loses. Life defeats charm, innocence is blasted. The world is finally a sad and funny place, life a tough, amusing game that can never be won but must be played. If Boetticher's films can darken to near-tragedy, the pessimism is always held in check by an innate response to the absurdity of it all, the way in which we are forced to take up roles in a farce. It is this comic awareness in Boetticher that is behind what appears a natural classicism, a fascination with formal aspects of the drama and the terrain on which it is played out.

Boetticher clearly takes a sympathetic delight in the way in which his characters always find themselves under the gun, often trapped in the middle of a circle of stress. In the journey films, which almost invariably culminate in the setting of an arena, this action is constant. The group is at once under the threat of a hostile environment (Indians are all around them) and functions as a source of menace internally for the hero, the dramatic action a mirror image of the world the character inhabits. Often the action itself seems circular or cyclical, the hero failing to advance on ground he commands at the outset. The foundation for the very production of the Ranown films, this key cyclical movement structures many of Boetticher's earlier works as well. Hence *The Cimarron Kid* (1951), Boetticher's first Western, opens with the hero's release from prison and ends with his arrest; *Seminole* (1953) begins and closes with the Indians resolutely independent of the white man; *The Man from the Alamo* (1953) opens with the departure of the hero from the fight against Santa Anna and ends with his return. In both *Decision at Sundown* and *Buchanan Rides Alone*, Boetticher plays with this movement within the plot very self-consciously: in the first, Allison is visited in his besieged stable by a parade of interested parties; in the second, the Agrys, their henchmen and Buchanan all change places as they conspire to achieve their ends.

This impulse at a formal level accounts for the great elegance and grace of Boetticher's work. Typically, *Seven Men from Now* opens *in medias res*, Scott creeping through the desert to come on two of his wife's killers sheltering in a cave on a stormy night. In the morning, Scott moves out through the sun-bleached terrain to crest a rise and discover the Greers, their wagon mired in the mud. After a scene of great delicacy, the men washing the carthorses in a limpid pool as Annie bathes around the bend, the oasis is left behind, the party moving on deeper into the desert. After its light-hearted opening, *The Tall T*, although not a journey film, takes on a similar movement. In both *Ride Lonesome* and *Comanche Station*, the construction and pace are tightly controlled, the action unwinding with spellbinding formal rigour, the films finally resembling pure ritual. Seizing on the cyclical pattern of the journey Western, the alternation of drama and lyricism, tension and release, intimacy and space, Boetticher gradually refines it to arrive at the remarkable balance of an ambiguous world poised between tragedy and pastoral comedy.

The meaning in a Boetticher movie resides less in its bright moments of good humour or its dark moments of violence, than in the continuum, a seasonal movement, a perpetual interplay of light and shade, success and decline, life and death. Spiralling through day and following night, the drama remains ever in the foreground, the settings changing religiously as different stages are reached on the journey, yet somehow not changing at all, the desert finally the dominant place. Thus *Ride Lonesome* moves through three days and nights, the company pushing on over dangerous open vistas of arid country each morning and afternoon to cluster in the dappled dark of an evening camp. If dusk is often a kind, contemplative time for talk of the future, danger rides in bright and early at sun-up to temper hope and throttle dreams. There is one moment in particular here that with great economy and resonance seems to express the heart of Boetticher's world. As the party moves out from the swing station after the visit of Indians who hope to barter the dead husband's horse for the wife, the camera follows them from inside the building. The dark outlines of the roof and porch frame the image, the eye drawn out past the silhouetted horse-rail to the bright clearing, the rocky hills and misty mountains beyond. In the left-hand corner of the scope frame a water-vase hangs from the porch roof, gently swaying. Four times the eye is drawn across the frame as the group ride out in single file, each character moving into vision from the right and trotting across out of sight to the left, the camera panning with the last rider to frame the whole group as they move into the desert. This briefest of images has a narrative function – the shot is repeated when Frank and his gang approach the station later – but the composition and lighting are so delicate that finally they are a pleasure in themselves. The tension between static black border and bright rhythmic play within is so fine that ultimately the image has the quality, the essence of Boetticher, of an animated still life.

At moments like these, Boetticher achieves a formal rigour and philosophical nuance that recall the most unlikely of parallels, the Japanese master Yasujiro Ozu. Certainly, a common factor is the evocation of a sadly ephemeral life in a world, beautiful in itself, that remains apart and unchanging. Landscape in Boetticher always has a conceptual weight, signifying a lonely and hostile universe. Often this relentless primeval world is bordered by a lush, green Arcadia: both *Seven Men from Now* and *The Tall T* move from a pastoral setting into the desert; *Ride Lonesome* and *Comanche Station* reverse the pattern. However, always in Boetticher there is a formal interest in landscape, an observation and delight that give the images a decorative value. Often what we have is very like a painting, the characters moving over brutal terrain in the foreground, the middle distance a wall of jagged spires, the great peaks of the Sierras in the misty background beyond. As Bazin was quick to point out with reference to *Seven Men from Now*, the very texture of the rocks, like the faces of horses, gives Boetticher a pleasure that he communicates directly to his audience.

This aesthetic delight in pattern, colour and movement – simply, in creating beautiful images – is paralleled by Boetticher's joy in playing with the recurrent elements of his form. If these films strike us as highly civilised works, it is because of the studied awareness with which certain rites are enacted. Nowhere is this more in evidence than in the fact that Boetticher worked to a formula: of course, *Seven Men from Now*, *The Tall T*, *Ride Lonesome* and *Comanche Station* are essentially the same film. Moreover, both *Decision at Sundown* and *Buchanan Rides Alone*, which have structural similarities, can be seen as loose transpositions of *The Tall T* into the setting of the community. The word 'formula' is important and must be insisted on: often it is the heaviest club in a critic's armoury, reserved for the mechanical and repetitive. Yet Boetticher's movies are both personal and refreshing precisely because of their given structure, which frees him to achieve his distinctive ironic and comic effects.

Any view of Hollywood, any theory of mass culture, that excludes a Boetticher must be a sadly impoverished one. But it would be euphemistic to describe this level of popular art as unpretentious. In a genre only the epic tip of which drew consistent attention in his era, Boetticher's small films were very nearly the bottom of the iceberg: co-feature-length formula exercises built round a minor star in the tradition of Tom Mix, Roy Rogers and Hopalong Cassidy. Yet Boetticher's care is admirable, the direction never inflating into solemnity nor lapsing into slackness, but meeting the material head-on with obvious affection. Burt Kennedy's tendency as a scriptwriter to repeat (and steal from) himself in playing on time-honoured patterns of the Western could not have found a better home. Responding with sympathy and wit to ritualistic elements, Boetticher achieves a range of cosmic expression that provides the basic tone of his pictures:

1. Verbal play: repetition, variation, reversal and surprise are of course fundamental to comedy, and a feature of Boetticher's own scripts as well as those with Kennedy. 'Buchanan's the name,' announces the hero cockily everywhere he goes in Agrytown, clearly asking for the trouble he gets. 'Do you want to hear the rest of the story?' Lee Marvin endlessly asks as he sits grinning over his coffee at the Greers and the silent Scott. 'I'd hate to have to kill you' – 'I'd hate to have you try': some such formulaic exchange often passes between hero and villain. Similarly, a rhetorical question is amusingly undercut: 'Do you think I love him any the less?' – 'Yes, M'am.'

2. Play with settings and props: the pleasure Boetticher derives from landscape often results in a sharp contrast of tight places – caves and crevices – and vast open country, the scope frame filled with desert on which small dots move. On many occasions, we

can sense that these settings function as a stage. Characters are always passing each other either cups of coffee or guns, a measure of how abstracted the action is from social norms, but also a source of paradox and irony (as well as movement within the frame). Villains throw the hero a gun, but show little respect for the ritual of the meal. In *Buchanan Rides Alone*, both Juan and the ransom for him function somewhat like props that the villains can never bring together. Juan's dancing horse (one of Boetticher's own, trained in *rejoneo*) also weaves in and out of the action.

3. Play with character: Boetticher often achieves a broad comedy while establishing his characters, which, given the violence that follows, colours the action with a sad irony. The clearest example of this is *The Tall T*, where the opening rapidly introduces us to a whole range of juvenile genre elements: a jaunty hero thrown from a bull; a venerable Gabby Hayes of a mule-skinner in Arthur Hunnicutt's Rintoon; an admiring lad who asks the hero to buy him some striped candy; his lonely, talkative father who runs the swing station. Created with great warmth, the characters are rapidly destroyed, save for the hero, who has to face the real bull of his world in the form of Henry Silva. Minor villains in Boetticher are always affectionately treated and are a source of both gentle humour (often they do not know their age but are 'mostly young') and great jokes. Hence in *Comanche Station*, Rush and Homeier agree that although it may be desirable to 'amount to something', the price of actually *working* would be too high. Homeier, insisting that all it would get a cowboy would be a decent burial, is left floating in a river moments later. James Coburn in *Ride Lonesome* is surprised that his partner of five years' standing actually likes him: 'I never knew that.'

4. Play with situations: I have already referred to the disciplined way in which Boetticher structures action around dialogues that break the journey; also to his play with the situations of confinement and release, a delightful example of which occurs in *Ride Lonesome*, where James Best holds a carbine to Scott's stomach, unsure of whether it is loaded, while Roberts trains a gun on *him*. *Decision at Sundown* opens with a sight gag, Scott a bearded tough who orders the stage he is aboard to stop at gunpoint, only to get off rather than rob it. Boetticher always inflects confrontations in an original fashion. Hence the murder of Clete by Marvin, who then lights his cigarette from the one still smouldering in his sidekick's mouth, a comic act that nonetheless darkens the character for us and prepares us for his shocked death at Scott's hands. More typically, endings in Boetticher partake of a delicate irony: Boone in *The Tall T* escaping but forced to turn back by his respect for both Scott and himself; Frank in *Ride Lonesome* facing the hero's exquisite revenge – Billy strung up to the same tree from which the wife was hanged. Grave-digging scenes are always light years away from John Ford, the only 'words' a few jokes from the villains as they dig away in a scruffy corner of the desert.

Predictably, Boetticher's humour can be cruel where weakness or cowardice are involved. Thus, although we hear a lecture in *Decision at Sundown* on how none of us can face ourselves as we really are, this does not alter the pleasure we get from the breaking of the whiskey bottle hidden in Zaron's pocket, the smug preacher exposed as a drinker. In the same way, we relish (or seem to be asked to) the way in which both Andrew Duggan and John Carroll are forced to face the righteous figure of Scott without their supporting henchmen. Certainly, the death of Willard Mims in *The Tall T* is surprisingly funny, Boone gently reassuring the character, then brutally giving the order (*'Bust him, Chink!'*) and showing genuine surprise at the suddenly widowed woman's grief. Similarly, the impulse to play with the audience in Boetticher can sometimes slip over the line into a manipulating or conning of the viewer. Thus, if the crippled Mr Lowe at the end of *Comanche Station* is dramatically right, given his introduction after the death of Akins, he is nevertheless something of a clever trick in answer to the questions the film itself sets about the husband. The irony of a prostitute dressed as a nun, the mask in place until the very end, also seems an unnecessary gimmick.

But characteristically, Boetticher plays the game according to the rules, his respect for both audience and form evident in the way in which he disciplines his own experience in the service of the material. Thus, although there are echoes of the bullfight in Scott's attempt to ride and win a seed bull in *The Tall T*, the scene owes less to the tradition of the *corrida* than to that of the rodeo, evoked at the outset, where cowboys struggle with a bronc that bursts through the corral dragging our hero behind it. Given Boetticher's preoccupation with bullfighting, one might have expected him to deepen the picture's tone, making the encounter more expressive of his themes. However, to have done so would have been to violate the drama, which here requires the hero be established as amusingly philosophical in the face of setbacks. The imagery of bullfighting often colours Boetticher's films, invariably coming into play where its rituals meaningfully coincide with those of the Western. In *Comanche Station*, Indians ride in on the hero with spears at the ready like *banderillas*. At the end of *Ride Lonesome*, Frank charges Scott, who stands like a matador ready for the kill. The carcass of Chink, like that of a dead bull, is dragged out of sight by a horse; moments later Boone's final charge ends with hands clutched to head as he wheels blindly, tearing a rough curtain from the mouth of a cave. Everywhere in Boetticher, men turn their back on a gun – the majority at their peril. However, such moments, evidence of the personal nature of Boetticher's art, do not depend for their effect upon our awareness of the underlying metaphor, the action growing out naturally from the narrative, which he treats with the utmost respect.

It is in the interaction of Boetticher's commitment to character and drama and his distinctively geometrical style that we have the final expression of the game. If often we feel that we are watching a play within a play, it is not only because Boetticher's art, like sport, rests on inventive variations within the narrowest given limits. Nor is it wholly due to the way in which the films (recalling the action of Shakespeare's dark comedies) trace near-tragic patterns within a comic structure. Above all, the quality flows from the great tension of character and behaviour realised with a vivid particularity within a formal discipline that moves towards abstraction. Boetticher's gifts as a film-maker – intelligent dramatic organisation and a creative use of actors, a fine sense of composition and pace – typically create a world that is both close and distant, action that is open and yet predetermined.

Always Boetticher uses the actual lifestyle of his performers (rewriting his scripts once the cast is set) to achieve a vigorous life within the drama. Developing with an elegant

The Tall T (top) and *Comanche Station* (bottom): echoes of the bullring

mathematical precision, the action pyramids, growing peaks of tautness alternating with a leisurely lyricism. The camera moves fluidly within the group as it makes its rounds, pausing here and there to record the play of issues, the counterpoint of character, within a static frame. As the figures move through landscape, Boetticher stands back to fix them in the depth and perspective of eternity. Often, as it dollies with the characters, the camera gradually brings into focus the black blur of danger on the horizon. Men are free to move; the world is hostile.

If finally nothing is possible but the game, we must be grateful that with these films Boetticher found a playing field and ground rules when he most needed them. The strange accident of the Ranown cycle at last allowed the experience of fifteen years of professional attack and frustrated authority to find direction and purpose. Working consistently within a shared traditional form, ideal for the expression of his private world of a questing individualism, Boetticher slowly arrived at a personal tradition in the small, glittering morality plays that emerged. At his best, he achieved here a remarkable formal and dramatic control, *The Tall T, Ride Lonesome* and *Comanche Station* recalling the delicate perfection of finely cut gems, immaculately drawn miniatures. Working at virtually debased levels within the industry, Boetticher nevertheless found the ritual, at once personally sustaining and publicly meaningful, that he required.

Departure and Return

For Boetticher, action exists only at the level of the individual: hence the absurd dilemma of existence, each man both a bullfighter and a bull. Strikingly, the villains of the Ranown cycle ride on the scene like matadors, flanked by their *banderilleros*, the darker ones committed to any encounter that will prove them '*el numero uno*'. However, for the hero, whose scars, intelligence and poise are evidence of that status, these men are sleek, brave bulls, narcissistic animals that charge into the arena completely unaware that others exist, shocked to discover their own vulnerability.

This internal dialectic is expressed in a very pure form in *The Rise and Fall of Legs Diamond*, made immediately after the Ranown cycle and a rare example of Boetticher being given considerable freedom (so long as the film kept its distance from the facts) in a different genre. Consequently, the opening promise of the film ('This is the way it happened'), although supported by sleazy 1920s jazz, journalistic titles and a resolutely period look, is soon betrayed by Boetticher. Any idea of exposé is left far behind as the film moves forward wittily and gracefully, like its dancing hero. Legs Diamond's great quality, his strength and weakness, is his complete egotism, and we watch in fascination as he dazzles all with his footwork, exploiting his style and charm to get higher and higher up the ladder. Beginning with Karen Steele's humble, naïve Alice, whose emotions he plays on brazenly ('I'm lonely'), Legs cons a host of characters in order to get close to Arnold Rothstein, the king of gangsterdom. Both 'A.R.' and his mistress, Monica, fall for Legs's patter ('I'm a young man trying to get ahead') and are quickly discarded, Diamond soon reigning supreme from his base at the Hotsy Totsy Club where his first appearance had been as a dancer. At this point, Legs seeks to free himself of ties that make him vulnerable, condemning his consumptive brother by refusing to pay medical bills. The moment is crucial: when he and Alice return from their comical tour of Europe's cinemas, Legs finds himself alone and facing the syndicate. Turning to

Monica in his desperation, Legs is betrayed to hoodlums, one of whom masters his fear sufficiently for the kill.

The great flaw in this impressive work is its jarring shift of tone from elegant comedy, which is the film's basic mode and is admirably sustained from the outset, into the dark, tragic vein of its last few minutes. That the film flies apart here is due wholly to the traditions of the gangster picture that are not amenable to Boetticher's philosophical preoccupations. Within these conventions, Legs's fall is partly historical, his old-style individualism overtaken by the corporate capitalism of the underworld boardroom. To some extent, Diamond's need to confront individuals man to man, to dominate through the personal encounter and to avoid all forms of organisation makes this resolution meaningful. However, the drive of the script and action is at a deeper level: 'As long as one person in the world loved you, you were safe ... that was the magic.' Like a narcissistic matador or a stereotype of the movie star, Legs feeds off the image that he projects and that is reflected back by those he exploits. Movies bore Legs because he lives one, his life one long game that he plays brilliantly, adopting whatever persona – small-town lad, sycophant, hero, lover – the situation requires. In this light, the tragedy of Legs is that, like the entertainer, he realises too late that without an audience he has no role. Thinking that the game can be won – that he can achieve immortality – Legs loses by eliminating all the other players.

This philosophical thematic, while clarifying the action of the film, does not excuse its broken quality or the moralising of the end. Legs is the one Boetticher character to get an epitaph: 'He never loved anybody ... that's why he's dead.' The decline of Legs is altogether too arbitrary and mechanical, the ravished innocence of Alice, while delicately expressed in the film, finally an insubstantial judgment on this charming Boetticher rogue. Thus the central confusion in the picture is between the classical structure, which demands a tragic, precipitate fall, and Boetticher's attempts to satisfy it by having an invulnerable villain, who is the hero here, defeat himself. Not surprisingly, the result is that *The Rise and Fall of Legs Diamond* is mostly rise.

It would be tempting to see this elegant film as Boetticher's bitter farewell, the action in these terms a private parable about success and failure in the smart Hollywood jungle. But in going to Mexico, Boetticher was not renouncing his past; nor did he know he was leaving for eight years rather than eight months. Simply, *Arruza* became both a test and a debt, a proof of himself and an obligation both to his original idea and to the famous matador. Not surprisingly, therefore, the long-awaited *Arruza* is an important work in every respect: a deeply personal film, a valuable record, a moving experience. It is Boetticher's labour of love, a personal tribute, and the outcome of fifteen years of planning and effort.

In tracing how Arruza comes out of retirement on two occasions – first as a *rejoneador*, later to fight in Plaza Mexico – Boetticher celebrates one of the greatest performers in the ritual that has been so important in his own life. The action in the arena is treated with great care, the point of view changing fluidly to follow the beauty of the rider and his horse circling endlessly before the bull, the corridas themselves, models of grace and courage, quietly observed by the respectful camera. Boetticher's sense of humour gives the film characteristic warmth, the commentary guying Arruza for thinking that the most expensive horse must be the best (the mount, like a Boetticher hero, turns out to be wary of circular enclosures). The film records the amusing tests administered to the cows, playing with the faces of jealous matadors, disgruntled at Arruza's skill. Dominating the picture, Arruza is evoked in simple, idealised terms, his family sketched in the background.

The style and movement of the picture, despite its documentary nature and the narration, recall the Westerns, the action shifting regularly from quiet lyrical moments at Pasteje, Arruza's bull-breeding ranch, to the high drama of the arena. The farewell appearance is exemplary, the audacity of the *rejoneo* giving way to an extraordinary series of passes, the man a graceful statue as the bull charges past repeatedly, culminating remarkably, as Arruza kills the bull according to Boetticher's plan for the camera. The film opens with an elegant series of zooms in on matadors of the past enshrined in statuary surrounding the plaza, a motif that recurs when Arruza visits the empty ring before deciding to return a second time. This imagery is extended by the freezing of the final frame – Arruza radiant as he circles the ring with his trophies on high – after we have heard that the matador died, meaninglessly, in a car crash some months later. But, the narrator insists, no man is dead while he is still remembered.

In 1951 with *The Bullfighter and the Lady*, Boetticher had seized on a sure dramatic structure in using his own experience, the film tracing the growth to maturity of a young American learning to fight bulls. The action of *The Magnificent Matador* was less successful, a melodrama describing a top matador's flight from the ring to escape having to introduce his illegitimate son to the bulls. The tautness of the opening here was eventually betrayed in a relaxed scene where Anthony Quinn tries to tell the boy laconically sipping soup that he is his father: 'Yes, I know, Matador.' Moving through what seem to be obligatory scenes for Hollywood bullfighting films – the matador pursued by an American woman, the drawing of the bulls, scenes of prayer before the corrida – the film comes alive only in the tour of Pasteje, a sequence of extreme long shots on the black dots moving over a range drenched with sharp, pure sunlight, culminating in Quinn's fight with a bull against the timeless setting of mountains and sky.

If *Arruza* in many respects transcends Hollywood treatment of the subject, if the film must stand as a fine work, its power is nevertheless diminished (as in the latter picture) by the nature of its fundamentally static hero. For while capturing for us the most dramatic moments of isolated action, *Arruza*'s own dramatic action is motion. Like the Scott hero, Carlos Arruza is complete and serene when we meet him, the film only recording countless confirmations of who he is. Inevitably, the single most important and dramatic moment in Arruza's life – his absurd death – occurs off-stage and is denied by the film.

In twenty-five years as a film-maker, Boetticher has made many small movies, only a dozen or so of which have been Westerns. However, in the eyes of both the industry and criticism, he had existed only within that genre. With *Arruza* at last completed, Boetticher seemed prepared once again to accept and work within this role, his return to Hollywood marked (self-consciously as always) with a small Western shot on the eighteen-day schedule typical of the earlier pictures. Moreover, the film emerged from a production context that in many ways recalls the Ranown cycle, with a small company of mainly veteran actors and stuntmen (except for two or three featured newcomers), one of the director's favourite photographers, Lucien Ballard, and as producer,

Boetticher's friend, Audie Murphy, appropriately enough a venerable star – like Scott – of the Hollywood B-Western.

His in every detail from original script to final cut, *A Time for Dying* is even more studied in its play of formal and dramatic elements than many of the earlier works. Thus the film describes a perfect circle for all of its principals: the aspiring gunfighter, Cass, dying outside the brothel from which he saves Nellie at the outset; Nellie herself returning, again alone, to the setting she fled; Billy Pimple, with his outriders, drifting back into the rocks and trees from which they appeared to confront Cass in the beginning. The film also has both an overture – Cass's rescue of a rabbit from a rattler ('Run, little feller, run for your life') ironically establishing the film's theme of unprotected innocence – and a coda, the final images of a second young Nellie making for Mamie's, which announces the beginning of another cycle.

Although the landscape here is Arizona ridge and cactus rather than California's jagged Lone Pine rock formations, dramatic site of all the Ranown films, the interplay of barren open range and pastoral forest faithfully evokes Boetticher's world of the morality play. His two pilgrims are mocked by the cycles of freedom and confinement, hope and humiliation, through which they move. Ironically, the couple suffers and Cass dies, not because of his disruptive heroism in saving Nellie and foiling the bank robbery. Rather, it is his foolish bravado and exhibitionism in killing the rattler and his sharp-shooting in the saloon that lead to the encounters with Billy, his fancy gunplay for Nellie attracting Jesse James and his boys. Although James warns the couple to stay clear of Silver City, Cass stubbornly rides on, to meet more of James's men, who surround them and steal Nellie to dress up their party in the attempt on the bank.

Having stopped the hold-up, Cass hears applause for the last time. He is called out into the street by Pimple (or William C. *Cootes*, as he insists), a second-rate matador in comparison with the stylish '*el numero uno*' of Audie Murphy's James. Original as ever – the two men are comically caught with guns at their back – the final confrontation is made explicitly theatrical as well, Cass and Billy standing in spotlights on the empty stage, their faces half-masks of light and darkness. The comedy ('Billy, that girl pull a hammer down on you, I'll blow her husband's head clear across the street' – 'Ben, this girl pull a hammer down on me, it don't do no good what you do with her husband's head') recedes, the play growing dark with the snake's revenge on the rabbit, the innocent *novillero* making the final discovery of what life is about in his meaningless death.

'One of those fellas always loses.' An inane circle of violence, an absurd but compulsory play of comic suffering, Vinegaroon's game of rock, scissors and paper describes the action of the film and the core of Boetticher's ironic vision. Vinegaroon itself, less a town than an extension and summary of the world through which the couple move, is presided over by the spectacle of Victor Jory's Judge Roy Bean. The ruler of the game – this funny, monstrous old man, an evil clown – is a brilliant expression by Boetticher of life's absurdity. A humour in the tradition of the Agrys, the character of Bean at once evokes drunkenness and sloth, greed and self-love; but above all he is variability itself. Sternly lecturing youth on its presumption one moment, nostalgically reminiscing on a Lily Langtry he has never met the next, brutally hanging an apple-cheeked lad, benevolently forcing a marriage on Cass and Nellie, the Judge's justice is a series of acts, a bit of comedy followed by a bit of tragedy, each 'turn' followed by a break for the audience to visit the bar. Casting those who come before him in roles within the play according to his mood, this bitterly farcical figure takes a particular delight in gently passing his verdict on the sweet youth, Sonny, whose crime has been to ride a horse into Vinegaroon:

> Time will pass, and seasons will come and go. Soon, summer with her shimmering heat waves on the baked horizon . . . then, fall with her yellow harvest moon and the hills growing golden under the sinking sun . . . then winter with its biting, whining wind and the land mantled over white with snow . . . and finally – spring again with its waving green grass, and heaps of sweet-smelling flowers on every hill . . . BUT YOU WON'T BE HERE TO SEE NONE OF THEM!

In returning to the form after nearly a decade, Boetticher had evidently wanted to update his style, to keep abreast of where the Western had been. Hence the slight flexing of muscles with the zoom lens, the slowing of action at key moments. But this last, in particular, is evidence of a thoughtfulness on Boetticher's part; often he has suggested the innocence of a Lumière in allowing the interested audience a careful view of the West's small dramas, the pulling out of a wagon from mud, the nursing of a sick animal, the rodeo. Neither do the traces of Peckinpah in the film, nor its air of being a conservative parable about youth and violence, detract from its quality: *A Time for Dying* has more to do, of course, with *The Cimarron Kid* (where it is a young Audie Murphy who is disillusioned by the world) than either *Ride the High Country* or Berkeley.

The flaw in this fine film lies elsewhere. Boetticher's great quality has always been his narrative power, in particular his realisation of strong characters, a firm foundation on which he could play creatively. *A Time for Dying*, as with *Two Mules for Sister Sara* (which was also scripted while in Mexico), departs sharply from Boetticher's traditional terrain in concentrating on a love story. And the film fails, finally, because its quirky hero and the surprisingly hard Nellie at the centre of the action never truly marry. The looseness flows less from its cameoed villains than from the failure of its heart to come alive; *The Tall T* is deeply moving because we *care* if Boone dies.

Boetticher had had two careers. The great Ranown pictures and the original, distinctive *Arruza* comprise a substantial achievement. But a third cycle was not to be. If *A Time for Dying* had been a test of Boetticher's ability to connect with the new audience, its quick disappearance clearly spelled failure. But of course Boetticher had arguably never connected with the audience in any major way. From the beginning he had toiled in the depressed B-movie levels of the industry, breaking through to modest personal films in both his bullfighting dramas and the Ranown series. The latter, genre co-features with the established Scott as star, had provided shelter and modest success, but little industry recognition. Ironically, with the accomplished *Legs Diamond* signalling the possibility of meaningful work at another level, Boetticher had left Hollywood to take up the fateful challenge of making *Arruza*.

Endgame

Budd Boetticher passed away in early December 2001 at the age of eighty-five. He had outlived Burt Kennedy but only just, his former scriptwriter's death at seventy-nine coming ten months earlier in February. Both had had their last hurrahs in 2000. *The Tall T*, for many the best of the Boetticher/Kennedy films, had been added to the Library of Congress annual list of twenty-five 'classic or historic' works designated for preservation. The company was particularly distinguished: *Apocalypse Now* (1979), *Five Easy Pieces* (1970), *GoodFellas* (1990), *Little Caesar* (1930), *President McKinley Inauguration footage* (1901), *Shaft* (1971), *Why We Fight* (1943–5), *Will Success Spoil Rock Hunter?* (1957)...

More kudos followed. The restoration of *Seven Men from Now* by Batjac and the UCLA Film Archive resulted in a retrospective of the key films at New York's American Museum of the Moving Image as a run-up to a tribute and screening of *Seven Men* at the New York Film Festival. Although frail, wheelchair bound and hampered by weak short-term memory, Boetticher made appearances at both New York and Berkeley's Pacific Film Archive in the spring of 2001.

A viable director for considerably longer than his old partner, Kennedy had been feted at the Autry Museum in 1997 with a book signing to mark the publication of his memoirs, *Hollywood Trail Boss: Behind the Scenes of the Wild, Wild Western*, not surprisingly a volume as genial and anecdotal as his films. Kennedy recalled the beginnings of the work with Boetticher that ironically would result in far more critical recognition for him than any of his other assignments:

> When I finished, they said, 'Well, why don't you write a screenplay for Duke? I had this title that I had used on a story years before, and had never made or sold it: *Seven Men from Now*. I took the title, they gave me an office and a legal pad and pencils ... They

On the set of *Seven Men From Now*: John Wayne, Randolph Scott and Budd Boetticher were paying me $250 a week for six weeks. I needed two more weeks to finish, and they said, 'Okay, you can have the two weeks but we're not gonna pay you. You can use the office and the pencils and paper ... I spent two weeks without pay and I finished. The total cost to them was $1,500 ...

Jack Warner read Seven Men and loved it, and said he wanted Duke to do it. But Duke was right in the middle of doing *The Searchers* at the time ... They gave it to Joel McCrea, who didn't want to do it. They gave it to Robert Preston, and I don't think Bob ever read it, because he didn't like Hollywood too much at the time. Then they gave it to Randy Scott, who in turn hired Budd Boetticher to direct. *Seven Men from Now* was my first picture and was very well received. I went on to get Duke to buy an Elmore Leonard short story called 'The Captives', which he paid $5,000 for and for which I did the screenplay.[1]

Comparison of Leonard's story, reissued in a recent collection of his early shorter pieces, with *The Tall T* confirms Kennedy's magpie instincts and practice.[2] In fact, practically the whole script is taken from the story. The king of crime fiction, Leonard is renowned for his mastery of vivid and pithy dialogue, amply in evidence in the novels and film adaptations of *Get Shorty* (1995), *Jackie Brown* (1997) and *Out of Sight* (1998). His practice is to write sparely and never qualify utterances with adjectives, strictly holding himself to 'he said', and forcing the line itself and the exchange to carry tone and create character. The result is very close to film dialogue. Nevertheless, it is unnerving to find so many of the sharp lines and telling bits credited to Kennedy's script and Boetticher's film verbatim in the original. The story opens with Brennan being picked up in the desert, the lost bet with the rancher Tenvoorde that costs him his horse a back story that is fleshed out in the film. But once Rintoon has picked up the hero and the honey-mooning couple is introduced, most of the exposition and main action comes straight off the page. Many of the film's effective lines are Leonard's:

> You-all drop your guns and come on down ... Gently, now ... Chink, I swear you hit him in midair ... I was waiting for that old man to pull something ... You didn't have to kill him ... I would've, sooner or later ... I'm asking this man ... He's a talker ... You know what's going to happen to you? Put him in the well ... Chink, bust him [transposed in the film] ... How many did that make? I'll tell you this: yours will be from the front ... I don't care what happens to me ... Listen, you're as much woman as any of 'em.

Small scenes added by Kennedy include the important discussion between Frank and Brennan as the latter strips meat from a carcass that establishes Frank's desire for 'a place' and to be free of his immature companions. In a later moment crafted by Kennedy, Frank tires of Chink's talk of 'hurrah gals' who are 'wild as mountain scenery' under an exterior 'quiet as Sunday', and seeks out Brennan, who is not sympathetic: 'You run with 'em.' These additions develop the Brennan/Frank relationship significantly, preparing the ground for the screenwriter's most important intervention. Apart from dramatising the lost bet over the seed bull at the beginning, the most significant change in the script is the transposition of Chink and Frank's deaths. The story reserves Chink's killing for the culminating action to punish him for his murderous role. However, by trading in this greater emphasis on vengeance, Kennedy and Boetticher were freed to build up Frank further and maximise his potential as Brennan's peer and adversary. A crucial change, it cemented the film's toughness, complexity and irony.

In the final analysis, Boetticher is a cult director. Articles that have appeared from time to time over the past four decades dispute this characterisation. Boetticher has had innumerable tributes and retrospectives at specialised venues stretching from Berkeley to Chicago to London and beyond, supported by press releases and journalistic accounts that declare him one 'of the major glories of the cinema'. In conjunction with the screenings of the restored *Seven Men from Now* and *The Bullfighter and the Lady* (John Ford's original cut augmented by some forty minutes), laudatory essays appeared in a number of journals, including *Sight and Sound*, *Film Comment* and *The New York Times*. In the latter, Richard T. Jameson remarked that the Ranown cycle 'constitute one of the most elegant and esteemed bodies of work in American film' (3 September 2000). Obituaries claimed that film historians rank him as one of the handful of great Western directors.

But the truth is that Boetticher is the property of a small group of devoted film scholars. Despite the kudos generated by art house appearances and screenings, Boetticher's small movies hardly exist within the larger cultural picture. Even within the realm of Western scholarship, it is not unusual to find accounts of the genre that contain only a passing reference to his work. Scholars of the Western as epic commentary on America's history or as ideological discourse often ignore Boetticher. It is telling how little sustained attention he has received since his discovery and the studies of the 1960s. Boetticher has continued to be undervalued and overlooked.[3]

Karen Steele is often the object of Boetticher's gaze; here with Ray Danton in *The Rise and Fall of Legs Diamond*

Why is this so? The B-level scale, the absence of Hollywood glamour, is surely an obstacle. Perhaps more to the point, however, is the miniaturist aesthetics of the cycle, the theme and variations approach, remaking or reworking the same film. This tactic, plus the stripping down of the genre to its bare essentials, creates a rarefied air, a kind of purity. The genre is distilled and honed down to its essence, a spiritual vision embodied in stark images – men facing death, bodies in a well, a hang tree burning. Writing in 1954, Robert Warshow had described the genre as 'an art form for connoisseurs, where the spectator derives his [sic] pleasure from the appreciation of minor variations within the working out of a pre-established order'.[4] Although understandable in light of the low regard in which the genre was held by the literati of his day, Warshow's characterisation hardly made sense given the Western's great popularity with mainstream audiences. If the formulation obtains at all a half-century later, after the further mainstream successes of Peckinpah, Leone and Eastwood, it applies to Boetticher.

In her famous essay on visual pleasure and the male gaze, Laura Mulvey had quoted Boetticher on women's roles in his films as defining of mainstream movie narrative gender dynamics:

> What is important is what the heroine has caused to happen, or what she represents; what she inspires in the hero, whether love, or fear, or even indifference and how he behaves in consequence. She herself is of no importance.[5]

But Mulvey, in her analysis of how women are objectified by the cinema into voyeuristic spectacles, failed to indict Boetticher himself for the unabashed quality of his comely Gail Russell and Karen Steele heroines, etched at times with the innocent prurience and good-natured eroticism of the Coca-Cola ads and Varga pin-ups of the period. Is it because Boetticher is too modest a target and patently too formalist in his priorities that he has gotten a free pass with feminist and racial perspectives, as if his films were inoffensive ideologically? If indefensible, the director's utilitarian treatment of both women and Indians is in keeping with the essentialist approach, the reduction of the genre to its brilliantly clear, pure focus on a modest humanity facing cosmic questions of meaning and existence. It is perhaps because Boetticher's films are too unambitious, too unpretentious, too unproblematic, too sane, that they can be overlooked. In the postmodern world, there is no success like excess – recycling, genre fusion, exaggeration, special effects. The dominant appetite is for pathological characters, dystopic visions and bravura action, for horror, science fiction, neo-noir, melodrama and diverse hybrids of the same. Within such a context, it is no surprise that Boetticher hardly exists.

But if Boetticher's films in all their charm, intelligence and spiritual force still await a wider audience and greater critical attention, it is true that they nevertheless have had their impact and influence, however circumscribed. It is to be hoped that this will increase as the films find greater accessibility in different formats. Anything that prolongs the life and increases the accessibility of these outstanding movies is most welcome. Boetticher's brief moment of extraordinary creativity in the 1950s left a remarkable legacy for which we must be grateful.

Notes

1. Burt Kennedy, *Hollywood Trail Boss: Behind the Scenes of the Wild, Wild Western* (New York: Boulevard Books, 1997), pp. 6–7.
2. Elmore Leonard, 'The Captives', in *The Tonto Woman* (New York: Delacorte Press, 1998), pp. 16–53.
3. Bazin's insightful reception of *Seven Men from Now*, 'An Exemplary Western', in *Cahiers du Cinéma* no. 174 (August–September 1957), is reprinted in Jim Hillier (ed.), *Cahiers du Cinéma: The 1950s: Neo-Realism, Hollywood, New Wave* (Cambridge, MA: Harvard University Press, 1985). Sarris's brief entry on Boetticher that characterised the films as 'floating poker games' first appeared in *Film Culture* no. 28 (Spring 1963), before publication in his *American Cinema: Directors and Directions 1929–1968* (New York: E. P. Dutton, 1968). In 1965 Peter Wollen published 'Budd Boetticher' in the *New Left Review* no. 32 (July–August 1965) under the pen name Lee Russell; the essay is anthologised in Jim Kitses and Gregg Rickman (eds), *The Western Reader* (New York: Limelight Editions, 1998). In the spring of 1969, I produced a dossier, *Budd Boetticher – The Western* in conjunction with a retrospective at London's National Film Theatre; the first edition of *Horizons West* was published later that year. An essay by Paul Schrader on Boetticher first appeared in *Cinema* vol. 6 no. 2 (1971), and is reprinted in Kevin Jackson (ed.), *Schrader on Schrader* (London: Faber & Faber, 1990). An early interview with Boetticher appeared in Eric Sherman and Martin Rubin (eds), *The Director's Event* (New York: Atheneum, 1970).

   In 1978 Manny Farber, film critic and painter, combined his interests in a still life in his 'auteur' series entitled *My Budd*, which according to Bill Krohn is in part a response to *Horizons West*'s account of Boetticher. Both Farber's painting and Krohn's commentary are on the internet. A useful overview of Boetticher's career by Barry Gillam appears in Jean-Pierre Coursodon (ed.), with Pierre Sauvage, *American Directors vol. II* (New York: McGraw-Hill, 1983). 'A Time and a Place: Budd Boetticher and the Western', an appreciation by Mike Dibb with a special focus on Lone Pine, the director's favourite location, is in Ian Cameron and Douglas Pye (eds), *The Book of Westerns* (New York: Continuum, 1996). *Framework* vol. 43 no. 1 (Spring 2002) contains an extended interview with Drake Stutesman, in which the 85-year-old Boetticher looks back at his work. In 1999 the *Hollywood Reporter* announced that Arnold Schwarzenegger would star in a remake of *Seven Men from Now*, but Schrader's upgrading of Kennedy's original to *Nine Men from Now* was shelved when Schwarzenegger finally decided on *Collateral Damage*'s (2002) very similar plot instead. Boetticher can be seen in a small role as a judge in Robert Towne's *Tequila Sunrise* (1988).

4. Robert Warshow, *The Immediate Experience* (New York: Doubleday, 1962), p. 99.
5. Quoted in *Visual and Other Pleasures* (Bloomington: Indiana University Press, 1989), p. 19. Boetticher's written reply was to a question from Bernard Tavernier in *Cahiers du Cinéma* no. 157 (July 1964).

5
Sam Peckinpah: The Savage Eye

I have never made a 'Western'. I have made a lot of films about men on horseback.

What does Sam Peckinpah mean? The director had made his comment in 1969 to then critic Paul Schrader in response to his suggestion that *The Wild Bunch* (1969) was not a Western 'in the sense of *Ride the High Country*'. Schrader was distinguishing between a film in which 'an antiquated code' was still valuable and a world bereft of that code.[1] This distinction between traditional and revisionist forms has often led commentators to suggest that the latter are not true Westerns or are anti-Westerns or that the Western is dead – as if the classical is the whole of the genre.

The quote marks around 'Western' in Peckinpah's declaration are suggestive: advocates of the director who repeatedly refer to the Western *films*, rather than simply the Westerns, reinforce the snobbish hair-splitting suggested here. Like the quotation marks in the director's claim, the persistent qualification of 'films' is meant to hint at profound difference, evidence of a polemical and transparent strategy to lift the film-maker clear of any relationship with the common oater, horse opera and shoot-'em-up.[2] Both the director and his advocates are at pains to distance him from the 'conventional Western', as if there are other kinds, as if challenging or subverting conventions is not using them. These films, we are to understand, really do not belong to a genre; they are *sui generis* – Peckinpah films. The increasing emphasis the films themselves gave to the director's credit by virtue of placement and punctuation ('If they move – *kill 'em!*') bespeaks a similar reach for a unique artistic status that practically amounts to a claim to ownership. We may sense such an attitude as well behind the perennial battles Peckinpah had with studios and producers.

Is Peckinpah then like Howard Hawks, whose films are equally accomplished and personal regardless of genre? Whose *Rio Bravo* is closer to the flyboy drama *Only Angels Have Wings* (1939), the noir romance *To Have and Have Not* (1944) and the big-game adventure movie *Hatari!* (1961) than to the Western *High Noon* that inspired it? Not so. Peckinpah produced a remarkable series of original and passionate Westerns, but he failed to show a commensurate personal force and mastery in his lesser efforts in violent melodrama (*Straw Dogs* [1971]), the gangster film (*The Getaway* [1972]), the thriller (*The Killer Elite* [1975], *The Osterman Weekend* [1983]), the war film (*Cross of Iron* [1977]) or the comedy/road movie (*Convoy* [1978]). The irony of Peckinpah's disdain for the

Charlton Heston in *Major Dundee*

generic Western is that his great achievement absolutely depended on it. A conflicted soul in personality and ideology, half-classicist, half-modernist, Peckinpah was ideally positioned to emerge as a post-modernist giant of the genre. As in Sergio Leone, Peckinpah's work everywhere speaks 'the already said', in Umberto Eco's phrase. Although some would dispute it, I think it impossible to discuss the achievement of either of these filmmakers without reference to the other. The cumulative impact of their work, Peckinpah attacking from within the core themes and constructs of the genre, Leone operating from outside, would radically change the Western, in effect reinventing it.

The evidence of his filmography thus suggests that if Peckinpah elevated the genre, he in turn was elevated by it. A Wellesian, Peckinpah aspired to dominate artistically, to transcend, to be the American cinema's heavyweight champion. Given that Peckinpah's own roots were in the West, the frontier's heroic canvas and masculine codes provided an apt setting for this effort. Although it is possible to see the more modest, elegiac *Ride the High Country* as Peckinpah's most fully realised work, it was in responding furiously to the dilemma of his anachronistic heroes in *The Wild Bunch* that Peckinpah produced his crowning achievement. A defining work of the tumultuous 1960s, the film is a majestic effort at the level of the American cinema's master-works, many of which also allegorise a fallen nation in flawed protagonists: *Citizen Kane, It's A Wonderful Life* (1947), *Sullivan's Travels* (1941), *My Darling Clementine, The Searchers, Taxi Driver, The Godfather* (1972).

But although *The Wild Bunch* has the undeniable freshness and force of an original work, its power arises from its epic articulation of traditional frontier mythology, the genre allowing the director to raise his violent characters trapped in contradiction to the level of national epic. Like America itself, Peckinpah's flawed heroes look back to a visionary past of principles and loyalties now compromised and broken. Fallen idealists, at once the elect and the damned, these scarred characters are unable to live coherent lives in a changing world. As with Ford's characters, Peckinpah's heroes are rooted in history – their own and the land's – and like the later martyrs of his predecessor, they are unable to reconcile individualism with the social.

Both of the early works, *The Deadly Companions* (1961) and *Ride the High Country*, are redemptive and restorative, the latter looking like the grand finale to the classical Western. In Ford, *The Searchers* is the key bridging film, its epic stand-off between the obsessions of the individual and the demands of history marking a turning point in its director's journey away from the faith and transcendence of the early films. In Peckinpah's more concentrated, less prolific output, *The Wild Bunch* is the dark tragedy that provides a bridge from *High Country*'s bright lucidity to the nihilism and despair of his last Western, *Pat Garrett and Billy the Kid* (1973). In these three films, the core of the director's distinguished contribution, the progress is rapid towards a bleak vision of America as a landscape wherein authentic identity and action are impossible. Without a meaningful role, heroism becomes anarchic and self-destructive. As with the groundbreaking efforts of Arthur Penn's *Bonnie and Clyde* (1967) and Leone's *Dollars* trilogy, Peckinpah was taken to task for the excessive violence of his films. Such sensitivity in the guardians of the era's culture towards these early post-modernists was clearly justified. In Peckinpah, the extreme savagery of the world and its characters signals the primacy of passion over reason, and fuels a critique of society that achieves a genuinely oppositional force. Peckinpah's deepest responses are to the spectacle of a doomed individualism.

Like Ford before him, Peckinpah mourned the crossing of the frontier into the modern. Ford's response to this changing world ultimately had been to the sacrifices that made an ambiguous salvation possible, the redemption rather than the blood. If Peckinpah shared the older figure's spiritual and tragic vision, his emphasis was distinctly different within the dialectic of the sacred and the savage. Ford's violence was ritualistic and mythic, necessary to birth the nation and bring the community into focus. Burdened by a more radically divided sensibility and darker social vision, Peckinpah fastened on an embattled masculinity and the desperate violence that remained its only vehicle for expression, and that gave his work its critical edge.

It was in his attack on the desensitising norms of screen violence that Peckinpah's contribution came into focus. In *The Wild Bunch*, the *mise en scène* works at moments of bloodshed to create something akin to what Maya Deren called vertical poetry, the expression of an inner reality through the distended exploration of a key event, the action slowed down to mark it as high-pitched and subjective. Peckinpah's montage strives to look at violence both from within and without, to allow us both to experience it directly and yet to stand back, to register the blood and slaughter plus the fact that it is being presented in aesthetically pleasing forms. Peckinpah corrects generic representations by communicating a gory reality in his bloody images, and yet suggests that we all have an appetite for it. In doing so, he comes perilously close to celebrating violence as an essential rite of manhood, transformative, intensifying and elevating existence. Peckinpah's heroes appear to experience a transcendent joy and satisfaction in living and dying at an intensity of pitch unknown to most of humanity. The complexity of response, visceral and moral, is what makes the experience so disturbing. There is a kind of epic theatre here designed in part to elicit a critical awareness: the audience is compelled to experience the thrills and the brutality, the sustained excess ideally keying spectatorship's uncomfortable insight into its own complicity.

Given his obsessive focus on an unbalanced manhood defined through bloodshed and alienated from a meaningful social role, Peckinpah's great flaw, inevitably, was his inability to explore and dramatise the feminine. There are few proofs of love to balance the codes and tests of masculinity; women and the family are marginalised and often victimised. Peckinpah is sometimes seen as cinema's tortured Van Gogh, a creative artist who could do no wrong. Thus even the brutalisation and rape that regularly threaten his heroines are advanced as proof of the director's democratic treatment of women, who have to face the same savagery that defines the male. Peckinpah did not look down on women especially, we are told, but had 'a low opinion of humankind in general'.[3] However, this stretch of logic hardly addresses the imbalance of the typical Peckinpah narrative's emphasis and action, with its heroic structure of deep respect and intimacy between men. Complementing these damaged and alienated heroes, it is logically and inevitably woman as whore that is the director's ideal, at the centre of a warm fantasy in his only comic Western, *The Ballad of Cable Hogue* (1970). However, in the more violent films the grace notes of warmth and love Peckinpah insinuates are rarely between men and women. As in Anthony Mann's work, the adversarial relationships of his heroes are marked by intense looks exchanged at key moments, the male gaze that is a sign of the love that can only be expressed in combat.

As Dave Blassingame knees an opponent in *The Westerner* (1960), the Englishman gasping that the blow is against the rules, the hero bellows: 'IT'S NOT A GAME!' Samuel Fuller's description of the cinema in Godard's *Pierrot le Fou* (1965) – 'a battlefield' – could well stand for Peckinpah's view of life. Certainly, his West is the dialectical frontier that runs between brutalising instinct and self-defining discipline and action. The quest for personal identity is here equated with a movement towards inner peace and salvation. The Garden and Desert are not images of temporal life, but states of spiritual being, a choice for all men. To see Peckinpah merely as a moralist is to simplify and blur his work. There is an undeniable moral commitment in his insistence on self-knowledge as a prerequisite for meaningful action (*The Wild Bunch* is nothing if not moral); but in the end, his unremitting vision of tortured souls caught up in an odyssey of self-exploration is a spiritual one.

In this, as in the Old Testament quality of many of his characters and images, we may sense a strong current of Puritanism, an inward concern with the struggle for deliverance from all evil. At times, Peckinpah could create an Edenic cinema of great charm, intimacy and pastoral lyricism. These qualities, so prominent in *Ride the High Country*, were again uppermost in *Cable Hogue*, which had launched a second phase of his career after the obsessive efforts of *Major Dundee* and *The Wild Bunch*. As these two works made clear, Peckinpah's other great strength was an epic and tragic sweep rooted in the commitment to test American tradition against present realities. If Peckinpah appeared John Ford's bastard son, it was because as an artist he was caught between the dream and the mango, the vision and the violence. The radical quality of his work – so evident in the distance between Ford's cavalry and his, between the activity on the horizon of Ford's heroes and Peckinpah's Wild Bunch, between the humour of Ford's stock company and that of the younger man's repertory (Warren Oates, L. Q. Jones, Strother Martin, Ben Johnson) – arose naturally and inevitably from a deep personal romanticism that he fought every step of the way. And it is this tension that gave his cinema its distinctive allegorical quality, the present igniting the past, the promise and pain of America brought alive on the screen.

Peckinpah's rare quality was the formal invention he brought to the service of his ambitious thematic range. In this, as Alan Lovell pointed out, he at times suggested the stature and scope of a Jean Renoir. That he made good his effects followed from the great care he exercised over every aspect of the production, from casting to cutting. This concern resulted in significant detail in the finished work – the raven on Henry's shoulder, the portrait of Lincoln in Dundee's office, the handbill on Lyle Gorch ('Rapist; murderer') – which gives it his characteristic richness. His response to landscape typically revealed a careful geographical sense, while simultaneously creating an unearthly terrain, a Dante-like world over which his tortured characters move; here especially, his distinctive, virtually baroque colour sense comes into play. Peckinpah's style was marked by a heightened, often florid imagery held in check by the editing. Although the imagery is often continuous, with its own depth and play of light – as in the village sequences in *The Wild Bunch*, so reminiscent of Ford – Peckinpah's was a cinema of montage, the flow of cutting both honouring and distending time, bridging all the elements of his action.

With a historical sense that demanded the creation of character and community in the round, a social awareness that forced a contemporary relevance and a metaphysical perspective that ordered all, Peckinpah's was an arresting cinema that forcefully positioned him as a dominant creative force during his era. Working within the 'American genre, *par excellence*', in André Bazin's phrase, he used the language of the Western to explore and dramatise themes and conflicts obsessing the American sensibility. If this had been a traditional function of the Western, Peckinpah had brought the genre up to date.

The Deadly Companions (1961)

The perspective of a dual vision at once historical and metaphysical, in which the individual is both located within a continuing society and stretched on the rack of a spiritual quest, immediately makes clear why Peckinpah has been so dismissive of *The Deadly*

Peckinpah felt straitjacketed in his debut, a personal project of star Maureen O'Hara and her brother, producer Charles B. FitzSimons

Companions, his strange and impressive debut as a Hollywood director. Ideal for a Mann or a Boetticher, A. S. Fleischmann's property flows wholly from the archetypal base of the genre, a psychological revenge fable that describes a demonic wasteland through which its haunted characters move. Restrained from doing more than tinker with the script, Peckinpah left the picture after the first cut and dubbed it an 'unworkable project', a surprisingly cavalier attitude given how much of himself he managed to get into the film. A serious director will always crave total freedom, stretching from the script through the final cut to embrace even the sales campaign. But if a director is one whose ancestors were pioneers (and perhaps Indians), who learned biblical verse in his childhood from his father, a rancher and a judge, surely we must ask what greater freedom – in the first place – can he have than the opportunity just to make Westerns?

The Deadly Companions is an astonishing first film, Peckinpah wholly dominating the material and overcoming the considerable problems of odd psychological elements (the scar and powerless shooting arm of the hero, the coffin, the ghost town), some weak dialogue and a shortage of physical action. If he looks back on the film as a compromise, given its ahistorical world, nothing is more revealing for the critic than how a director compromises. But whatever Peckinpah may say, *The Deadly Companions* could not but have involved him imaginatively given its movement of a journey into the past, its theme of the interior struggle with the temptations of savagery. Treating the psychological elements lightly (only the scar now mars the film) and evoking an infernal landscape, Peckinpah creates the action of a spiritual odyssey, Yellowleg (Brian Keith) and Kit Tilden (Maureen O'Hara) deeply troubled characters driven to redeem themselves and establish secure identity.

As they move into the arid, cactus-ridden Apache country, Peckinpah locates the party within the CinemaScope frame precisely, underlining the conflicts at work. The angry Kit sits alone on her buckboard with its sad cargo, while the man who has accidentally killed her son rides alongside in earnest dialogue with her. Hanging on behind are the jeering Billy and Turk, figures out of their past, waiting like vultures for their prey. In obsessively driving on to bury Mead next to the dead husband that Gila City has never believed in, Kit is trying to break free of her brutalised life. Steve Cochran's Billy is all style and bravado, ever ready to manhandle the woman and reduce her to an animal, keeping him at bay with a rock. Successful as this figure is, Chill Wills's Turk is on a different plane altogether, a gross shambling barbarian decked out in buffalo coat and Indian beads, constantly rubbing up against buildings and cactus. The richness of this character goes a long way towards evoking Yellowleg's dilemma, to rid himself of the seven-year obsession to scalp the man who all but scalped him on a Civil War battlefield, without sacrificing what damaged sense of identity he has left, without himself spiralling down to the level of a savage.

Peckinpah brilliantly objectifies this interior conflict in the latter, extraordinary half of the film. Once the villains have left the couple, the buckboard rounds a bend, and suddenly beyond it on a high crest a stagecoach is silhouetted against the sky driving full tilt and pursued by yelping Apache. The suddenness of the action, the distance, lighting and framing of the shot are highly dislocating: what is happening? As the stage rolls down the hill to veer crazily round a pool before tipping over, we see that it contains a number of Indians dressed in shawls and bonnets, thus transforming the scene into a drunken parody of the action in which the stage was acquired. Peckinpah's realisation is vigorous and intelligent, sharpening the bizarre quality that runs throughout the film, his personal edge giving the moment a disturbing complexity. Who is chasing whom? Who is Indian, who is white man? The shock we experience, the crisis of blurring lines between savage and civilised roles that the characters face, is then counterpointed in the mysterious struggle that we witness between Yellowleg and the lone Apache who now begins to haunt him, the ghostly figure trailing and teasing, a constant invitation to join in a violent duel.

However, if this were all, *The Deadly Companions* would not be the fine work that it is. The great achievement of the film is that while evoking the private conflict of its characters, it also describes a moving love story. I use this sentimental phrase specifically to underline Peckinpah's resistance to the tug of psychological and archetypal drives in the script. Through Brian Keith (the fine actor whom Peckinpah had used as Dave Blassingame in his TV series, *The Westerner*) and Maureen O'Hara, Peckinpah makes good dramatically the human implications of the tensions within his characters. Frozen in a posture of righteousness, unable to give or take, Yellowleg and Kit tear at each other like animals. 'You don't know me well enough to hate me!' shouts Yellowleg when Kit lashes out at him with a whip. The slow and exhausting process by which the two come to know each other and themselves is finally the bedrock of the film, Peckinpah building on this action surely to flesh out his theme. Alone in a wild and primitive landscape, the man and woman gradually recognise their need, each other's humanity, and begin tentatively to reach out. The movement of the film (clearly looking forward to *Major Dundee*), whereby the characters progressively take on the appearance of Indians, the couple stolidly marching through the Apache country dragging their burden behind them on a travois, is finally broken with their arrival at Siringo and the delicate imagery of the woman picking flowers in a dusty corner of the ghost town, the man's face transformed by a rare smile. As Kit had laid Yellowleg's ghost to rest, blasting down the lone Apache when he wriggles into the cave to stand above her like a primeval spirit, so internal logic demands that Yellowleg destroy Billy, a meaningful symmetry that is absurdly withheld in the final cut. As the picture stands now, it is Turk who kills his protégé, thus altering Peckinpah's ending, the director unlucky from the beginning.

American films have often described a love that is painfully earned: Maureen O'Hara perhaps reminds us of Ford's *Rio Grande*; we can look back as well to Howie and Lina of *The Naked Spur*. If we move further afield, there is no shortage of distinguished examples: Fuller's *Pick-up on South Street* (1953), Kazan's *Wild River* (1960) are but two. Much rarer in the American cinema, however, are films that wed this action to a convincing process of socialisation, evoking the pain of the individual forced to grow into an awareness of others, the animal becoming a social animal. Throughout the work of so many American film-makers, there flows a deep stream of anarchy, a subversive current that insists that society is too oppressive, love is impossible, living with other people is impossible, community is impossible. In Peckinpah, the anarchy is public and makes up one-half of the man, as with America itself, his continuing struggle with it objectified for us on the screen. In his later films, the battle is tragically lost; but in *The Deadly Companions*, Peckinpah's most optimistic work, it is painfully won.

Ride the High Country (1962)

There is no need to advance claims here for *Ride the High Country*. The great acclaim
enjoyed by this work, so richly deserved, has if anything obscured the consistency of
Peckinpah's achievement. If *The Deadly Companions* can be seen as a pilgrimage, and
Major Dundee as a crusade, *Ride the High Country* takes the form of a temptation. In all
three films, it is a dialogue that shapes the dramatic action, the structure here linking
the two ageing ex-sheriffs who have begun to travel different roads in their response to
a society that they helped to create and where they are now out of place. Falling on hard
times for Gil Westrum (Randolph Scott) has meant a surrender to forces destructive to
his identity: a cheating sideshow 'Oregon Kid', the pragmatic Westrum cheerfully cari-
catures himself, his red-bearded, satanic cowboy a falsification and a denial of the past
that he shares with Steve Judd (Joel McCrea). This old man, in contrast, clings desperately and absurdly to his past in a world of cops, horseless carriages and Chinese
restaurants. Judd has also been damaged by the encroaching anonymity: pathetically tipping his hat to the noisy holiday crowd that awaits the spectacular race of horses and
camel, the man has a bearing immeasurably above the frayed cuffs of his present condition, the bars and brothels of his immediate past. With the embattled pride has come
righteousness, a high sense of moral mission and an obsession to honour all contracts.
There is something very akin to desperation in the character's severe treatment of
Westrum when the attempt on the gold is made. The bankers would not be hurt by the
loss – 'Not them, only *me*!' shouts Judd, smiting the baser instinct before him. The temptation is confronted, disarmed and held – cruelly, we feel – in check: the companion of
all those years makes the rest of the journey bound tightly.

   Through his creation of key locations, Peckinpah disturbingly evokes the forces that
threaten meaningful existence. Once the party has left the world of balloons and belly
dancers that Westrum and his protégé, Heck, move through so easily, the action shifts to
the Knudsen household. Through R. G. Armstrong, the brooding figure to which he was
again to turn for *Major Dundee*'s Dahlstrom, Peckinpah creates one of his most impressive characters in Joshua, a dark, inward, finally incestuous figure whose response to the
complexity and violence of the world has been to withdraw completely. The enemy of
feeling and instinct, the Knudsen household is deeply repressive, the girl Elsa (Mariette
Hartley) stunted and hiding herself in ill-fitting men's clothes, growth and self-knowledge finally impossible here. However, if both Westrum and Heck are cramped and out
of place in this setting, Judd is not, as his reply to Elsa makes clear. 'My father says there's
only right and wrong, good and evil, nothing in between. It isn't that simple, is it?' – 'No,
it isn't; it should be, but it isn't.' If the two characters are not cut from the same cloth, Judd,
swapping proverb for proverb with Knudsen at the dinner table, understands from first-
hand experience the forces that drive the man. Peckinpah's great writing skill is perhaps
at its peak in abuse: the end of the film, where the Hammonds, 'red-necked peckerwoods
… damn dry gulchin' Southern trash', are stung into defending their family honour
openly is a typical example. But equally impressive is the mastery over prose with an Old
Testament ring, here delicately linking Knudsen and Judd: 'Levity in the young is like unto
a dry gourd with a seed rattling round inside.' Appropriately, Judd's own judgment earlier,
if no less righteous, locates the character in time rather than absolute standards: 'Boys
nowadays. No pride, no self-respect. Plenty of gall but no sand.'

The pastoral purity of the Knudsen farm and the overweening morality of its master faithfully delineate the spiritual centre of Steve Judd. In this context, the humbleness of his present task, the purgatorial quality of its movement from the home of self-righteousness to the Sodom and Gomorrah of Coarse Gold, and then painfully back – these are entirely correct. The party, now increased by the fugitive Elsa, discover just how mean the job is when they reach the mining camp. No grand sum here but a few thousand dollars, largely from the whorehouse that dominates the camp – as Kate points out, its real gold mine. Balancing and complementing the Knudsen household, Coarse Gold is a brutish world of violence and excess. Instinct incarnate reigns supreme ('Have fun, Honey') as the lamb goes to the slaughter, Elsa joined to the Hammond brothers. In a world of moral grotesques and animals, it is Westrum who functions efficiently, unscrupulously destroying the judge's licence to marry so that the court must release Elsa. However, it is Heck, seeing the girl as a person rather than an object, who prompts the act, Westrum forced into it to save his manpower for the attempt on the gold. With a cruel legalistic detachment ('the problem is you're legally married to Billy'), Judd himself remains rigidly committed to his own contract, prepared to accept the mining camp's justice even if it reduces Elsa to the status of an animal.

A network of detail, clustering round the figure of the girl, gives the action of *Ride the High Country* a delicate resonance. As she rides through the twilit camp at the head of her weird wedding procession, it is her mother's gown that she wears, the mother at whose grave Knudsen prays daily, its stone bearing the inscription: 'Wherefore O Harlot, I will judge thee as women that break wedlock and shed blood are judged.' Marriage is a difficult business, life is complicated: Judge Tolliver, a man clearly broken by it all, knows: 'People change . . . the glory of a good marriage doesn't come in the beginning . . . it comes later on . . . it's hard work.' For Judd, the commitment to a life of hard and good works has meant the sacrifice of home and family, the girl Sara Truesdale, whom Elsa resembles, left far behind to a comfortable life with a farmer, spawning grandchildren now. For the likes of Judd and Westrum, history allowed no choice. Seen within this perspective, the character of Elsa is at the very centre of *Ride the High Country*, the soul of its action, her growth (the girl finally accepting a suitable costume) faithfully paralleling Judd's own progress. The delivery of the innocent from the savage forces that threaten her, the commitment to her value – these together with the redemption of Gil and Heck describe the rediscovery of a whole life.

With great vigour Peckinpah highlights the choices that men face through the deaths that await them. When the Hammond brothers attack, Sylvus circles up behind to find Heck waiting to shoot him brutally in the chest. Blasted down into a sitting position against a rock, Sylvus looks up uncomprehendingly as Heck takes the rifle and departs. Living on for a few seconds, the cold mountain wind sweeping over him, Sylvus sits there blinking, and then pitches over to die in the dirt. It is a lonely death in a barren, savage place: barbarous and meaningless, it is the death of a wolf. The discovery of Knudsen's end is even more unsettling, Peckinpah playing tightly on the nervous hens who cluck in the barnyard adjoining the grave where the farmer prays, then cutting to zoom in from below on the bloody face, eyes frozen open and staring. The Hammonds revealed within the house, the violation of the hens by Henry's raven, these underscore our sense of the precariousness and inadequacy of Knudsen's compromised stance in life, both a denial and celebration of death that has finally claimed its disciple.

'Just like the old days'

At the end, we have the passing of Judd. Rising up from the ditch 'just like the old days', the partners face the struggle head-on and in the open. Like Christian soldiers they march into battle, Peckinpah cutting away to reveal the confusion in the animals that they face; then Judd is dying. Heck and Elsa, the future, are spared the pain of a good-bye, Westrum sadly taking his own farewell to leave the old man alone in the shadow of a great tree in the yard. Peckinpah frames the last shot with the greatest care, placing us directly behind Judd so that we share his last look away from the Knudsen household and out past the yellow and russet leaves of the forest to the far horizon, where the high country in all its savage majesty stands. Then Judd lies back and dies.

If nature is in affectionate sympathy at the end, it is not because a god is dying: the elegiac tone of an autumnal world marks the passing of the old order. Like *Major Dundee* three years later, *Ride the High Country* is finally about America. The movement of the film describes not only a spiritual quest, but a whole history as well ('that time in Lincoln County'), a way of life torn between the ideals of a manifest moral destiny and the instincts of a pragmatic imperialism, a romanticised self-interest. Discussion of this great work has often erred in relegating the Scott figure to a secondary role, despite his magnificent charge, like the cavalry in early Ford, to join the party in the ditch, his equal place in the gunfight, his survival. But these two heroes are masks for the same face, expressions of the same spirit, the spirit of the American West. Judd and Westrum, judge and cowboy, vision and violence: Peckinpah insists that both were necessary in a savage land.

Major Dundee (1965)

One of Hollywood's great broken monuments, *Major Dundee* is a landmark in the Western. With characteristic audacity, Peckinpah, in his third film, attacked an epic theme of such deep personal significance that his career itself would be thrown into jeopardy. The film was originally intended to be up to an hour longer than it is at present. Although trimmed and truncated throughout, it lost important scenes or major sequences that can be briefly described here:

1. The film was to open with B Troop, having failed to locate Sierra Charriba after two months of tracking him, en route to the Rostes ranch, where they join in a Halloween party. These scenes, which were to be shot last and as a result were never shot at all, would establish Ryan (our narrator) and Beth Rostes, who enjoy a brief flirtation, Lieutenant Brannin, the scout Riago and the Rostes and their younger children, one or two of whom scurry about dressed as Apache.

2. Then the real Indians come. The massacre, a long and violent one, was omitted because the producer could not accept an opening that postponed the introduction of the major characters for twenty to thirty minutes. Its absence works to heighten the obsessive quality of Dundee's pursuit of the Apache.

3. In returning to Fort Benlin from the scene of the massacre, Dundee and C Troop recapture Tyreen, the Hadley brothers, Jimmy Lee Benteen and Sergeant Chillum, seizing the manacled Confederates in a stream as they flee the jail. A brief exchange between Dundee and Sergeant Gomez reveals how, as a child, the latter had been stolen by the Apache, riding with them for two years against his fellow Mexicans.

4. After Jimmy Lee Benteen's baiting of Aesop, a scene where Dundee breaks out the whiskey as a reward to the men on their conduct crossing the river. Two toasts are made – one by Sergeant Chillum to the Confederacy, the other by the preacher, Dahlstrom, to the Union – which results in the whole command spilling their whiskey except for the mule packer, Wiley.

5. As the command moves out to the Mexican village after the river ambush, a long scene where the men fall about laughing hysterically but silently, as Dundee tries in vain to get his mule to move.

6. Footage from the night of the fiesta, including a drunken scene where Dundee and Tyreen relive their West Point days, and a knife-fight between Potts and Gomez, half-serious and half-staged, in which the two men express a kind of love in their testing of each other, the crowd of soldiers and Mexicans watching admiringly until Dundee breaks it up, revealing himself as the outsider, as the only one who does not understand.

7. Scenes of Dundee's breakdown and drunken wanderings in Durango, including a long montage of his memories of all that has happened. Also, drunken moments of pleasure between Gomez and Potts as Tyreen rescues Dundee.

8. The discovery of Riago's mutilated corpse strapped to a tree by the Apache, Potts insisting that Dundee himself cut down the scout whose loyalty he has doubted throughout.[4]

From this perspective, it is clear that the released version is a severely damaged work that Peckinpah could only look back on with pain and misgivings. However, for all this, in my view the power and meaning are still there, the structure and imagery clear, the deeply personal statement of the film undeniable.

Peckinpah is fond of describing the thematic continuity of his work in terms of a pre-occupation with losers (he produced and directed a TV play called *The Losers*), misfits and drifters. Certainly, the work of few directors is so peopled with characters who are emotionally, spiritually or physically crippled. However, more precisely, Peckinpah's characters suffer from not knowing who they are: above all, it is the quest for personal identity that provides the dramatic action of his films, a quest seen both in terms of a meaningful confrontation or dialogue with the past, and a tortured struggle to achieve mastery over self-annihilating and savage impulses. In *Major Dundee*, these themes inform the conflict of jailer and jailed, of Dundee and Tyreen, two characters who share a troubled history and an uncertainty about their role. Tyreen has been three men – Irish immigrant, cashiered Union officer (Dundee casting the deciding vote), Confederate rebel – and now stands or falls by the romanticism of his posture, that of the complete cavalier. The style is visible in his first appearance, where Dundee asks for volunteers from the Confederate prisoners to join the band he is assembling to pursue the Apache. In torch-lit darkness, we see the manacled figure – arms crossed and head low, a mar-tyred Christ – as he makes his noble gesture: 'It's not my country, Major. I damn its flag and I damn you. And I would rather hang than serve!' A feather cocked in his cap, Tyreen remains true to the style throughout (Richard Harris has been much maligned for giv-ing a strong performance here): in his fanciful encounters with Senta Berger's Teresa, in his perverse refusal to break his promise to Dundee (his enemy at both private and mili-tary levels), and in his personal execution of O. W. Hadley, one of his men who had deserted. Although Tyreen insists often and rhetorically that he will serve only until the Apache are taken or destroyed, the confusions inherent in his position trap him fatally. In the final battle with the French Lancers, it is the gallant Tyreen who is mortally wounded saving the hated Union colours when they fall, then dying grotesquely in a single-handed charge against the lances of two hundred French reinforcements. Recall-ing the passing of Steve Judd in *Ride the High Country*, Tyreen dies the way he lived, in a magnificently romantic gesture that undoubtedly serves its purpose; the French charge broken, Dundee and the few survivors slip into Texas and safety.

Having fought 'his own war' at Gettysburg, Major Amos Charles Dundee now finds himself a jailer as the struggle between North and South rages on. His obsessive pursuit of Sierra Charriba also soon takes on the quality of a private war. In general, Peckinpah's heroes are complex, paradoxical figures. Moral rectitude – originally the very quality that shaped the traditional heroes of the genre – is often what they suffer from, charac-ters so committed to living by the book that they seek to embody its very spirit. It is the ideal of perfection, the sense of being the elect, that can animate the Peckinpah hero, the power of the protagonist rooted less in ethical considerations than in something akin to a metaphysical imperative. In so far as they can break free of their righteousness to a sense of their own imperfection, Peckinpah's characters can grow and achieve self-knowledge. But if – like Dundee and his forebear of *Ride the High Country*, Joshua Knudsen – they do not, they are trapped in a destructive pattern ever moving from the peaks of judgment to the troughs of guilt. Before he is through, the major, not a pretty character, decimates his command, destroys a Mexican village, provokes a war with neutral French forces, and leaves a bloody trail of death and destruction stretching far behind him.

The pursuit of the Apache can resolve nothing for Dundee, since it functions as a headlong escape from placing his own house in order. The major himself seems to hint at this when Teresa, the Austrian widow, asks him why men must forever be fighting: 'War is simple . . . men can understand it'. Women can be important in Peckinpah: where they know who they are and what their role is, they can positively assist in the men's search for understanding and equilibrium. Here Teresa, a mature and sophisticated woman, freely gives herself to Dundee because she wants to feel alive, to escape the destruction that is everywhere. This gift exposes Dundee – the major, breaking with the book, has gone beyond his own pickets to make love by a languid pool – and forces upon him the fact of his own fallibility. Betraying the woman, Dundee spirals into a sodden purgatory to land in the garbage of the streets of Durango. Wallowing in his guilt, it is the major's turn to play the fallen Christ, the swing of the pendulum elevating Tyreen, who now goads him back into action. Ironically, earlier the major had pronounced on the lieutenant: 'He is corrupt . . . but I will save him.'

Although Tyreen is ever there to accuse him and force a self-awareness – when Dundee compulsively buries his dead after the Indian ambush, at the pool with Teresa, in the gutters of Durango – the major is finally trapped within his idea of himself. Less of the elect than of the damned, Dundee can find no peace or freedom in his crusade to 'smite the wicked'. When Sierra Charriba and his warriors have been laid low, Dundee and Tyreen again confront each other, only to be interrupted by the attack of the French. Their dialogue unresolved, Tyreen falls in the fighting, and the major survives to carry on with his own war. The final image is a disquieting one, the bloody remnants of the command pushing on into the cactus-dominated prairie.

This account of action at the level of character makes *Major Dundee* sound more coherent than it is. Even if we allow for the elisions resulting from extensive production cuts, the twists and turns of the narrative remain deeply disturbing. To gain a grip on *Major Dundee* as a whole and extend the levels of meaning that I have been discussing, it is necessary to attend to the total conception of the work, one of immense ambition and intelligence. For here Peckinpah explores his themes within a framework that makes a monumental attempt to lay bare the roots of America as a nation: the quest for personal identity is anchored in, and informed by, the parallel and overriding theme of national definition. Ever in the background of the great epic painting that *Major Dundee* resembles is the Civil War, and the confusions that both its principal characters face are rooted in that background and are of a peculiarly American nature. Dundee, a man of Southern birth, has turned on his own kind to fight for the North, an act clearly in accord with the legalistic character of the man. Tyreen, the Irish potato-farmer and former Union officer, has joined the rebels.

These contradictions are reflected in the force that Dundee assembles to pursue the Apache. Settlers and renegades, Union soldiers, Confederate prisoners and black soldiers tired of sweeping stables, horse-thief and preacher, veteran Indian scout and innocent bugle-boy, inexperienced lieutenant of artillery and Mexican sergeant at home with the Apache, the anomalies and divisions of early America are starkly evoked here. As they ride out and Dundee asks Ryan for a tune, the Confederates strike up 'Dixie', the blue-coats respond with 'The Battle Hymn of the Republic' and the civilians bring up the rear with 'My Darling Clementine'. If the snatches of the latter point to Ford's film (which Peckinpah admires), it is more than appropriate. Although the vision here is tragic rather than pastoral, a dance of death rather than a wedding, Ford and Peckinpah belong to the same tradition of the national epic, stretching back through *Union Pacific* (1939), *The Iron Horse* and *The Covered Wagon*, to *Birth of a Nation* itself. Given this genealogy and the film's structure, it is right that the threat emerges in racial terms: 'You're for-getting your manners, nigger.' Temporary solidarity vanishes when Jimmy Lee Benteen taunts Aesop, the command instantly splitting into opposed camps. The force stays together only because the impulse to savage each other is held in uneasy check and given other outlets. '*Until the Apache are taken or destroyed.*' Ringing out like an incantation in the film, the phrase takes on greater significance in this context. For if Dundee can only define himself through his righteous mission, his command, like the new nation itself, is only held together by a single-minded drive to destroy the common enemy. Led by tortured men at the mercy of self-annihilating impulses, the crazy-quilt company wheels blindly, slowly acquiring a shared bloody past, gradually achieving definition as a group, if not identity. At this level, the real action of *Major Dundee* is the freezing of the command in a barbaric posture, and this Peckinpah communicates brilliantly.

It is in these terms that the movement of the film, concentric rather than linear, must be seen. At the fort, we enjoy a comfortable relationship with the familiar situation of an ambitious officer with a shady past and the prospect of a pursuit of Indians who have taken hostages. The crisp pace here, together with Charlton Heston's authoritative Dundee, naturally arouses expectations in us of action that will have purpose and direc-tion. However, once away from the fort, all this is gradually but totally undercut by a series of dislocations so disturbing that they have the effect, finally, of giving *Major Dundee* the air of a bitterly artful parody of the traditional cavalry picture. The recur-rent features of this form are familiar: an undermanned company (or settlement), while torn by internal conflicts, functions as the heroic unit in achieving the group objective, the defeat of the faceless hostile. If the form has been brilliantly inflected by both Ford and Mann (*Fort Apache*, *The Last Frontier*) to make deeply ambiguous statements, nowhere has it been so relentlessly undermined as in Peckinpah's hands. Pushing the structure to its breaking point, Peckinpah both stresses the divisive tensions within the group and renders the objective wholly meaningless, except in so far as it serves to chan-nel savage impulses. By placing the defeat of the Apache immediately prior to the French attack, Peckinpah defines it as a minor climax, compressing the action into a relentless barrage shot head-on largely from middle distance, the overall effect being to create an odd vacuum at its end.

The presence of the French is a particularly disturbing element. Just what, we won-der, are they doing down there, in Mexico, in this movie? Yet the structure of *Major*

Dundee demands their presence, since it is the challenge they pose – at the US border – which makes clear the violent American identity that Dundee and his men have achieved in their pursuit and extermination of the Indians. Once across the river, Dundee will again ask his bugler for a tune and this time, as the picture ends, there will be no war of opposing melodies. Peckinpah takes great care to establish the French, with their colourful uniforms and martial sense, as a force that carries traditions and a past, a distinct identity, thus highlighting the primitive character of the Americans. When Dundee threatens an attack on the French garrison at the Mexican village and its commander replies that international law is being breached, Sam Potts, the scout bearing the ultimatum, stolidly replies: 'The Major ain't no lawyer, Sonny.'

'But who do you answer to ...?' Dundee's shortcomings, his compulsion and lack of self-knowledge, are highlighted within the structure of the film through Michael Anderson Jr's humble Ryan and Jim Hutton's bumpkinish Lieutenant Graham. Growing in stature as the film progresses, it is Graham who holds the command together when Dundee breaks. On the night of the fiesta where both Tyreen and Dundee, the prisoners of their styles, waltz with Teresa, Graham interrupts to join the woman in an uninhibited Mexican dance. It is Ryan, on the other hand, whose sensible diary of events is used as a commentary throughout, an ambitious device Peckinpah employs both to distance us further from the action (as with the assault of the film's violence) and to give the work the appropriate tone of a chronicle. Ryan also has a relationship of great warmth and simplicity with a Mexican girl – kissing her goodbye sleepily before the whole company until the major orders him to 'put it in the saddle!' – which acts as a foil to the impotent Dundee/Teresa affair. But in spite of all this, and the fact that it is Ryan (who has a personal score to settle with Charriba, since he alone escaped the massacre) who destroys the Apache chief and not Dundee, neither of these characters finally emerges as substantial positive alternatives. Simply put, the two men strike us as innocent. It is difficult to believe that either has a past, that the securing of a mature identity that Peckinpah insists on does not lie before them. If these men have made a beginning, they have yet to travel through the terrain upon which all of Peckinpah's heroes live, the struggle with destructive impulses out of which independent and meaningful action can come.

In *Major Dundee* this struggle is embodied in the complex interaction of Indian and white man, a key motif woven through the fabric of the film with great skill. Treating the Apache in a ghostly and ritualistic way, Peckinpah creates them both as an objective evil and as a savage direction open to all men – an interior potential. Thus the effect of the brutal Apache massacre, the aftermath of which opens the film, is balanced by the cavalry's eventual liquidation of the Indians, the inhuman treatment of the Mexicans by the French, their exploitation by the Americans and, last but not least, the butchery of the end. The structure is made morally complex by the historical fact, insisted on, that the Apache have some justification – 'It's their land ... all of it' – which places in perspective the 'civilised' behaviour of both old world and new. Peckinpah underlines the moral ambiguity by his use of costumes that function ingeniously as masks throughout the film. Lean, brown and breech-clouted, the Rostes boys return to hum happily as they demonstrate their skill with bow and arrow. Moments later, as he reconnoitres the river, Tyreen only barely saves himself from Apache disguised as Union soldiers by realising the trick when they fail to respond to his whistled 'Dixie'. Although they don Mexican clothes from time to time, the command itself become increasingly like the Apache as the film progresses, a fact underlined by the trap that is finally sprung on the Indians, together with the bloodiness of the final river battle. This complex interplay is extended structurally through the rituals that recur in the film (the Halloween party that was never shot, the Christmas Eve gathering in the ruins, the fiesta) and that are always the prelude to slaughter, the two rites brought together in the final battle, savage, gory, but a triumph nonetheless.

At the heart of the ideological structure of *Major Dundee* are three key characters, none of whom are simply Americans. There is Riago, who says disgustedly of himself that he is no longer an Apache, like Charriba, but a Christian Indian; and there is Mario Adorf's Sergeant Gomez, a Mexican who functions with the skills of an Indian; both of these characters suffer as a result of cuts. But above all there is Sam Potts. In trying to elicit an understated performance from James Coburn (in which he clearly succeeded), Peckinpah is said to have told the actor repeatedly that he was playing a 'pro'. However, in terms of my analysis, it would be more accurate to say that Potts is the one character at Dundee's own level who knows who he is and what his role is. A figure of resolute independence and intelligent detachment ('Everyone else seems to be doing it,' he remarks when Dundee wonders why an Indian should turn against his own people), the character is vital to Dundee, ever pointing his direction. But where others in the party serve out of inner compulsion, blind allegiance or the threat of execution, Potts has the capacity for choice. Hence the strange power of that amusing moment when Potts and Riago entertain the camp on Christmas Eve with a 'high-spirited, brotherly bout of wrestling' (a moment that would have been reinforced by the knife-fight between Potts and Gomez at the fiesta, now cut). Part of the scene's quality comes from our awareness of how appropriate this savage fight is as entertainment for the command, since it is a parody of the instincts they hold towards each other. But more than this, what is striking – for the command as well as us – is that we are watching men secure enough in themselves to be able to choose violence as an entertaining exercise and pure expression of self.

Sam Potts is crucial to an understanding of Peckinpah. A kind of half-breed, a squaw man, a man of the mountains, Potts, like the apocryphal Daniel Boone or Bill Cody, stands between savagery and civilisation. Indeed, this dialectic comes to rest within the figure, its marriage shielding the character from the destructive righteousness of a Dundee or the nihilistic romanticism of a Tyreen. But in Peckinpah's view, history is not made by those who have found their personal salvation. The tragedy of *Major Dundee* is that the whole man is a cripple, that the one-armed scout, serene and aloof (wholly so from Teresa), is finally almost irrelevant, an observer and an accomplice in actions springing from the tortured soul of Dundee, caught fast in his private limbo and yet dictating the course of events, the blood bath from which America is born.

The Wild Bunch (1969)

The characteristic quality that stamps Peckinpah's work is its disturbing edge. This is clearly evident even in much of his early television direction, which deservedly has its own reputation. The surrealist jolt that so much of Peckinpah communicates flows from a particular way of seeing and experiencing the world. Luis Buñuel once observed that 'neo-realist reality is incomplete, official and altogether reasonable; but the poetry, the mystery, everything which completes and enlarges tangible reality is completely miss-ing'.[5] Different from Buñuel in many ways, Peckinpah nevertheless reveals a similarly all-embracing vision, a total response to the world. I am not suggesting direct influence here (although Peckinpah thought *Los olvidados* [1950], the one Buñuel film he had seen, a superb work); it is from Don Siegel, with whom he worked on a number of films starting with *Riot in Cell Block Eleven* (1954), that Peckinpah originally learned most. However, Peckinpah's preoccupation with the existence of savage and destructive instincts, with the consequences of their repression or free play, and with the night-marish struggle necessary before balance and identity can emerge, clearly anchors him in terrain artists within the Surrealist movement have been traditionally concerned with.

The surrealist edge thus derives from Peckinpah's realistic worldview. In an increas-ingly liberal 1960s, many American movies underwrote the notion that evil resides not in our stars, nor ourselves, but in our environment. Peckinpah insisted that men can be animals, that fate is inside us, that evil exists; that America's posture in the world, her power and menace, owes not a little to the existence of that evil. From the outset, Peckinpah resolutely demanded the material and conditions to make this personal state-ment. However, that he felt that he had been constrained from achieving his goal with *Major Dundee* was clear in his triumphant return to the cinema after nearly four years (given over to more TV, as with the remarkable *Noon Wine* [1966], and to scriptwriting and planning) with what was a second and, on this occasion, completely realised *Major Dundee* in *The Wild Bunch*.

After the carnage

At the outset of this extraordinary work, there is a shocking image that directly evokes the world that is to be explored. Scorpions struggle in a sea of killer ants, children gaily watching, as the Wild Bunch disguised as US soldiers ride into Starbuck. While dramatically preparing us for the action that is to follow, the image also describes the relationship between Peckinpah's characters and the society through which they move. And we must not forget the children: above all, the moment introduces a network of detail that is crucial in the film, a structure in which innocence and cruelty, laughter and barbarity, idealism and blood-lust, exist side by side. Like birds on a string, children are part of a violent world. In particular, Peckinpah insists on the point in Mapache's Agua Verde, a mother suckling her babe nestled between cartridge-belts, riding the tortured body of Angel round the courtyard. In the final, indescribably bloody massacre, a small boy becomes a gleeful participator, shooting Pike Bishop in the back. The action here balances the opening, the hail of fire between bounty hunters and the Bunch tearing the innocent ranks of the Temperance Union literally to bloody bits, Peckinpah returning time and again to the children who are the massacre's spectators. Peckinpah's own small boy, Matthew, stands in the middle of it all, his arms round a little girl.

Within this perspective, it is wholly appropriate that the action of *The Wild Bunch* is played out – once again – with civil war in the background. For it is the fathers, sons and brothers (the women too) of the same people who entertain the Bunch so gracefully in Angel's village who eventually destroy Angel and his comrades. Man's twin capacities for love, joy and brotherhood, for destruction, lust and bestiality, is what *The Wild Bunch* – like all of Peckinpah's work – is finally about. And it is this central preoccupation that accounts for his abiding affinity for Mexico. Where Boetticher responds to that country as an arena in which individualism still flourishes, Peckinpah loves it for its special place below the American waistline. If the United States has been quick to deny death and violence by institutionalising them, to rob love of meaning by romanticising it, Mexico (like Buñuel's Spain) shows little inclination to do either. Hence, in Mexican history and culture, Peckinpah finds action and ritual that he sees as universally significant in its candour. One measure of this is Peckinpah's respect for John Huston's *The Treasure of Sierra Madre* (1948), from which *The Wild Bunch* borrows so freely for its structure and the important character of Sykes. Hence too the emphasis in the film on ceremonies (invariably accompanied by richly evocative Mexican music) that Peckinpah creates as tribal rites, most notably the generous farewell Angel's villagers give to the Bunch, the funeral procession for Teresa, and finally the march of the Bunch itself to the slaughter at the end. The range of Mexican characters that Peckinpah achieves is also relevant. The birdlike grace of Pike Bishop's prostitute is balanced by the toothy, carnivorous accountant of the *federales*; the gentle wisdom of the village elder who tries to teach Angel discipline is matched by the grotesque honour of Mapache, who cuts his throat.

As Tector Gorch observes when the group is about to cross over: 'Just more of Texas as far as I'm concerned.' The world that Peckinpah creates is a continuous and morally complex one: Harrigan and the vulpine bounty hunters, the innocent US Army recruits, the revolutionaries, the *federales*, the women and children, all have their roots in Peckinpah's metaphysical dialectic. However, as always, his vision forces a confrontation between what he feels to be essential drives in human nature and the social costs of a failure to understand and control them. At the heart of the structure that I have been describing is the Wild Bunch itself; and Peckinpah's great achievement is to create these men both as a microcosm of the elements in conflict and as vividly particularised characters in time. The historical moment of the film is crucial: if *Ride the High Country* is an elegy on American individualism, if *Major Dundee* enquires into national identity, in *The Wild Bunch* it is the male group that is Peckinpah's subject. Properly understood, the film is criticism: of the American idea of the male elite, of the professionalism and incipient militarism of a Howard Hawks, of the slick evasions of a *Bridge on the River Kwai* (1957) or *The Professionals* (1966). *The Wild Bunch* is set at a point in time when society is increasingly institutionalising and rationalising the function of the unsocialised group. In terms of the radical structure of the film, the criminal is being supplanted by a criminal society. What distinguishes Peckinpah's 'heroes' from those who pursue them and those they traffic with is an extraordinary violent expertise and a fragile code of brotherhood, the two elements of their identity as the 'Wild Bunch'. If the Gorch boys are appetites and instincts, they are not vultures like the bounty hunters. Above all they are brothers, sharing a natural relationship rather than living out of principle. The threat their greed and violence pose to the unity – and hence the identity – of the Bunch is appropriately expressed through the constant friction between them and the two key characters, Sykes and Angel. Embodying the past and the conscience of the Wild Bunch, the old Sykes is created by Peckinpah as a mocking ('my what a Bunch') liability, ever threatened by Tector, finally left to die in the mountains when wounded by the bounty hunters. Angel is similarly opposed to the Gorch boys by virtue of his impulse (as in the assistance he provides to his village) to extend the ideal by which the Bunch tries to live. Outside law, society, politics – 'we're not *associated* with anyone' – the Wild Bunch have but two choices for survival: they can give way to complete brutalisation by serving a corrupt society, or they can embrace the vision and future that Angel's simple communism offers. The tragedy is that the Bunch does neither, belatedly making the right choice for the wrong reasons.

At the centre of the group are Pike and Dutch, both holding it together and in the trust and affection of their relationship embodying the spirit that allows both Angel and the Gorches to belong. Of course, the Bunch are not moral men: Dutch's self-deception ('we don't *hang* nobody') should not obscure the evidence that is everywhere before our eyes. In particular, Peckinpah emphasises that the Bunch attack women, Bishop trampling a young girl in his escape from San Rafael, the Gorches callously using them, Dutch shielding himself with a woman in the final massacre. Angel apart, the Bunch has no honour, only a way of life that is shared. Central to meaningful survival is discipline. *The Wild Bunch*, like *Major Dundee*, develops through a structure of divisive moments of impending violence alternating with rituals of celebration (especially drinking and shared laughter) that reunite. And what dooms the group finally is not only the fact that they cannot change; neither can they sustain their ideal of a disciplined unity.

It is Pike Bishop who is in every respect the leader of the Wild Bunch; and Bishop, like other Peckinpah heroes, is a crippled man burdened by his past: 'When you side a man you stay with him ... if you can't do that you're worse than some animal.' Bishop

(Next page) '*The Wild Bunch* is America'

asserts a value and an idea of himself that he is forced at every turn to compromise. 'Why didn't you tell me he was your grandson?' That the slow-witted Crazy Lee, left behind to die in Starbuck, is of Sykes' blood ironically points the issue, Bishop betraying the very history of the group. The execution of the blinded Buck, the acceptance of Angel's fate, the abandonment of Sykes himself: these acts develop the pattern of counterpoint between ideal and reality. The irony of the entrance of the Bunch, and their masquerade as a unit of soldiers, grows in this context. For Bishop, this pattern has a special meaning, the vehemence of his commitment to the code informed by failure in the past ('being sure is my business'), Deke Thornton left behind when a trap had been sprung on them in a bordello. Peckinpah's characters are always caught in the grip of their own instincts, the demands of man's law, the dictates of God's. The tragedy springs from the fact that we cannot serve them all. Hence the strange bondage of Thornton, Harrigan's 'Judas goat', bound by his word to see his closest friend dead. At the end, Thornton marches straight to Bishop's body and silently takes his gun: both recording the end of an era and an act of love, the moment also marks Thornton's freedom.

'Angel dreams of love, while Mapache eats the mango.' Like Elsa of *Ride the High Country*, Angel is the spiritual centre, the innocent vision, the imperilled values of the world of *The Wild Bunch*. Angel's complete loyalty to himself and 'family ties', his killing of Teresa in the lion's den, his commitment to 'my people, my village, Mexico', these can only describe a world of action for Bishop that his own life touched and departed from. The idea is sustained by another aspect of Pike's past, his love for the woman he hoped to marry blasted by her husband out of malice rather than jealousy, Bishop himself still limping from that wound of long ago. The quiet moment Pike shares with a prostitute before the final battle extends this delicate network of meaning, the scene carrying a bitter sense of what could have been, and suggesting a capacity for love untapped. The scene also recalls Pike's escape from the bordello, the wounded Thornton left behind. In this light, Bishop's decision to return for Angel is classic Peckinpah action, the movement of a man into his past, a reassertion of identity, an honouring of the most important of contracts, with one's self, God's law.

The great force of *The Wild Bunch*, as with *Major Dundee*, flows from its attack on the audience through Peckinpah's brilliant orchestration of the romantic drive of the genre, in which the viewer is both exalted and violated. With the ominous march of Pike and Dutch, Lyle and Tector back into Agua Verde to confront Mapache, the transcendentalism of *Ride the High Country* is left far behind. As the group steps out past the drunken soldiers and the huddled family groups; as our whole world hangs in suspense after the death of Mapache; as the bloody slaughter begins and grows and grows; as Lyle howls out his joyful song of blood-lust; as the Gorches die, their bodies endlessly dancing in the air; as Pike and Dutch finally expire after having 'done it right this time'; as the bounty hunters sweep in to observe in hushed tones that history has been done ('T.C. – there he is . . . there's *Pike*'); as the film ends and Peckinpah, still unable to leave them, reprises the Wild Bunch to stop the picture with their ride out under the sunny trees of Angel's village – during and after all of this we cannot but experience the most painful confusion of feelings. *The Wild Bunch* succeeds in arousing in us precisely the world that it explores: an atavistic pleasure, a militant glee, a tragic sense of waste and failure. A work of great audacity, *The Wild Bunch* was a violent gauntlet at the feet of the liberal establishment of America. With this bleak and desperate film, the dialogue is now finished, the vision dead.

If the group honours its bond, if the spirit embodied in Sykes and Thornton is free to find what had always been its proper home ('even the worst of us . . .'), in the revolution, it is the unrelenting nihilism and despair, the absurd gratuitousness ('Why *not*?') of the action of the Wild Bunch itself that we are left with. For the Bunch it is too late, and history – its own way of life compromised rather than extended in a changing world – has gone too far. Finally, the group acts not for Angel's values – the 'dream of love' – but for the dead Angel, their own inadequate code, the past. More simply, they do what they do because there is nowhere to go. The Wild Bunch represents a way of life, a style of action, a technology, with no vision, no values, no goals. The quiet battle cry of the group is, ironically, 'Let's *go*': but we can only ask where? In this context, although this great work is not a structured parable like *Major Dundee*, we must see in it another chapter in Peckinpah's deeply troubled commentary on his country. *The Wild Bunch* is America.

The Ballad of Cable Hogue (1970)

Take him, Lord, but do not take him lightly.

If *The Wild Bunch* was to be Peckinpah's richest and most disturbing expression of his morally complex vision, *The Ballad of Cable Hogue* provided an opportunity for a reworking of the pattern in an experimental style that wed a number of narrative and formal structures. Launching the film, Cable's suffering in the desert and dialogue with God announces an ironic biblical/religious focus that is furthered by the arrival of David Warner's rascally preacher, Joshua, a complicated character whose calling includes a hands-on bringing of comely young women to God. This complex spiritual motif informs the film's main dramatic action, Hogue's progress from embittered and revengeful pilgrim to frontier capitalist after his discovery of water in the desert. As in Ford, the characters and action offer the allegorical resonance of a nationalist narrative of progress towards the settled, as romance blooms between Hogue and Stella Steven's hooker, Hildy. But this idyllic, dreamlike relationship offering the promise of married life in San Francisco materialises only to be blasted by the hero's death under the wheels of her limousine.

However, it is the act of betrayal between partners and the revenge theme it sires that provides the actual genesis of the film's world. Opening the film in a sharply focused pre-credit sequence is the double-crossing of Hogue by his prospector brethren, Taggart and Bowen, who abscond with mule, guns and water to leave their partner to die in the desert. In this privileged expository moment, Hogue is constructed as a loser and maligned as 'yeller' – he actually had the advantage on the pair after they make their initial move, but is lulled into foolishly putting up his gun. Cable is thus established at the outset as small-time, damaged, an ironic hero victimised by disloyalty, the ultimate sin in Peckinpah.

Although the setting is the desert and not the Sierra Madre, and the treasure is water and not gold, as with John Huston's film the action evokes the biblical parable, the falling out of the three thieves in the wilderness. However, Cable is not infected with greed, and if the treachery of his partners diminishes him, his Job-like suffering in the vast emptiness of the desert provides recuperation. Bowen and Taggart – Peckinpah regulars

Strother Martin and L. Q. Jones, respectively – improvise a song of Hogue's defeat as they move off, but it is the film itself, awash with music, that is Hogue's ballad, including the apt tune that swells beneath the credits – *'Tomorrow is the Song I Sing'*. As Cable begins to march off, the camera tracks back to reveal the awesome cathedral of the West that lies before him. With wonderful economy and invention, Peckinpah tracks his fallen protagonist in a split-screen, freeze-framed credit sequence that memorialises Hogue's epic suffering as he wanders for five days without water. Framing his isolation against the majesty of the wild American West, the images describe an epic spiritual odyssey punctuated by respectful but increasingly querulous complaints to God about the direness of his plight. The magical discovery of water finally caps the process whereby this lowly clown is transfigured into the charismatic proportions of an American Adam.

It is this positivist thrust that the film thenceforth builds on, the revenge theme abandoned, but for the running moral disputation with Josh and Hildy, until the end. Leaving vengeance behind, the film develops a highly satisfying Robinson Crusoe-like narrative action. A busy film, *Cable Hogue* regularly laces its scenes of moral colloquy and romance with the ongoing work of creation and housekeeping that the establishment of the waterhole as stage-stop calls for. 'You have built an oasis,' Joshua tells our hero, and he is soon enlisted as Cable's man Friday, although we are unclear what their deal is, if any. If seen with affection as ground-breaking American pioneers, the prospector and the preacher are hardly ethical icons, or like the Bunch, exemplars of loyalty.

Joshua is a lecher, ready to turn his clerical collar (and pants) in the direction of any inviting skirt. For all his theatrical sermonising, one of his deepest moments is his awe at God having given women breasts, a preoccupation he shares with other, usually less 'civilised' Peckinpah characters. But if he is ever ready to grope Hildy, even as Cable is protecting him from a cuckolded husband, he is also quick to lecture Cable on the other's denial of feelings: 'You love that girl, Cable.' The film approves of Joshua, who is seen to answer to a higher morality. His womanising appears a mark of his worldly wisdom about life and its priorities, about love and vengeance. Peckinpah obviously enjoys turning his normal take on the gospel as a repressive force inside out with this randy carpetbagger priest.

In contrast to Joshua, Cable is nothing if not focused and inflexible. A typically righteous Peckinpah hero, Hogue is driven by the desire to repair the scarred self-image of his past, insisting that everybody pay their dues and get their just deserts. Hogue's ethics, however, are impelled as much as Josh's by self-interest, as in the immediate commodification of his discovery – 'my water'. Starting up his business, he makes a killing with his first customer, who dies during their dispute over the dime Cable is charging for a drink. A Scrooge-like capitalism also hovers over his dealings with Josh and Hildy – despite his tributes to her 'ladyness'. It is this narrow self-interest, his brooding over the hurts done him, that fuels his obsessive fix on the revenge that will close him off from the redemptive power of love until it is too late. Hogue fails to see that it is Hildy and not the water who is finally his salvation, and that the logic of his good fortune should suggest a forgoing of revenge.

If Hogue deserves his ballad, it is not because of his humanity or stature, but rather because of his ground-breaking enterprise. Warts and all, Hogue is the film's prototype American businessman. In his typical style that marries romanticising and downsizing,

Peckinpah's disreputable, antisocial and mercenary roughneck provides a quirky model of America's founding fathers. Dominating the action, Jason Robards's Cable is a nuanced character of biblical shadings, hinting at both the darkness of Cain and the virtue of Abel. In what can be seen as a comical spin on Ford's *The Man Who Shot Liberty Valance*, Peckinpah situates the reprobate hermit as a humbler Doniphon-like figure, lacking vision yet instrumental in turning America's desert into a garden. But if we are to talk of Ford, it is also *My Darling Clementine* that *Cable Hogue* recalls, both films employing a revenge structure of indirection to frame their nation-building and romance.

Clementine's poetic vision of the civilising of America is embodied in the progress of its hero from cowboy to keeper of the peace. A similar development thoroughly compromises Cable's status as desert rat and hermit. Declaring his isolationism, Cable tells Hildy, 'in town I'd be nothing', failing to realise that the town will be coming to him, as both he and the desert are reclaimed. Rarely venturing 'amongst 'em', Cable's uncouth, oddball status is confirmed when he visits Deaddog to raise a grubstake and register his claim. Arousing hooker Hildy's ire when he runs out on her, Cable generates a havoc that brings the town and its prayer meeting to its knees. But is this tramp the same sober citizen we encounter later in the film? Here it is not law or love but capitalism that drives the transition, Cable's deals with the bank and stage company the turning point. Thereafter, the American flag is prominent in a half-dozen scenes that frame the transition from prospector to entrepreneur, as Cable's scruffy clothes give way to formal suits. The arrival of Hildy – the film's construction of the whore as an immaculate lady, a goddess of the desert – prompts a parallel spring-cleaning of the way station.

If there is no Shakespeare coming to this budding Tombstone, Joshua's arrival on the heels of Cable's opening for business lends a pseudo-uplifting and theatrical tone to the proceedings not unlike *My Darling Clementine*'s travelling thespian. Their conjunction signals a symbiotic relationship between capitalism and ideology, the result a spurious, self-seeking, Christian gospel-cloaked imperialism. A pious snake-oil salesman, Joshua provides a complex moral perspective on Cable, but has no important narrative function until he delivers his friend's funeral oration at the film's climax, explicitly evoking the grand myth of Manifest Destiny in the image of the humble Cable 'stumbling out of the wilderness like a prophet of Old'. For performing this crucial ideological function, crowning the desert rat with God's blessings on American empire, the film firmly bequeaths Joshua equal stature alongside its hero.

The two men are complementary in their contradictions: while Joshua continually holds forth about sin, he is obsessed with screwing anyone he can, just as Cable forever rants about his pound of flesh while at bottom remains a fair-minded soul. Together with Hildy, Josh carries on a running debate with Cable, a familiar Peckinpah structure, to focus issues of love and adultery, loyalty and revenge. If this discourse does not quite make up a spine, as in the earlier films, it is partly because of the script's refusal to develop a traditional dramatic resolution – perhaps having Cable rescue the imperilled Hildy from the clutches of Taggart and Bowen. *Cable Hogue* is not a classical Western; indeed, its charm is that it gives traditional characters and narrative material a distinctly modernist spin.

Cable and Josh provide further contrast in their respective visits to Deaddog. Cable is lucky to find a sharp capitalist in the bank manager prepared to look beyond his clownish bumbling. Out of place in the elemental desert, Josh is at home exploiting appearances in the civilised world, as in the mock-preacher's seduction of a moronic, self-deluding young wife. But the narrative positions them both as losers when Hildy has left the station, a matched set in their black-and-white costumes as they mourn the girl who 'cuts right through . . .'.

The key moment in defining and linking this odd couple comes earlier, however, after Josh had watched Cable solemnly raising the American flag for the first time, and then had helped him service a stage's passengers with a desert coq au vin of rattlesnake, brown squirrel and suchlike. The 'call' is on him and Josh is headed for town. Cable and the preacher shake hands in a formal parting, recalling a similarly ceremonial gesture when they had met. But here the salute celebrates not only good fellowship but also the success of what is in some ways their joint enterprise, the way station that Josh has dubbed Cable Springs. The parity is insisted upon by the self-conscious symbolism Peckinpah indulges, posing the two before the flagpole prominent in the background that bisects the space between them, holding the shot, the stars and stripes aloft as they shake hands. They are heroes, the image insists, America's pioneers and pilgrims, although the vehicles of a revisionist Manifest Destiny of greed and lust rather than law and God.

The nationalist thrust of the proceedings is nevertheless insisted on by the prominence of the flag that Hogue had solemnly accepted from Slim Pickens – an apt iconographic standard-bearer as Ben, the film's friendly coach driver – to mark the official status of the stage-stop. Thereafter, Peckinpah persistently structures Cable's deepening relationships around the ritual of raising and lowering the flag, the solitary ex-prospector doing his duty as Josh and Hildy come and go, and as they carry on their colloquies. The flag is especially foregrounded – both lowered and then raised, exuberantly – to mark the arrival of Hildy, who, like *Stagecoach*'s Dallas, had been invited to leave Deaddog by the town's 'good people'.

In *Clementine*, Ford implies the civilising effects of the heroine through indirection, as with Earp's haircut and the 'sweet-smelling stuff' the barber applies. Peckinpah, however, has a full-blooded relationship to work with, and he celebrates the joys of domestic life in a warm, bright montage that accompanies the couple's duet of 'Butterfly Morning'. Relaxed, intimate, life-affirming, the images describe a ripening love in days spent collecting eggs, cooking, and harvesting the spring's water. Cable offers her a desert flower, and Hildy takes a sunny, open-air bath that is comically interrupted by the early arrival of the stage. This sweet vision of the bliss of a shared housekeeping is vividly created, only to be abandoned – Cable is not fully housebroken. On his arrival, Josh had offered himself as Cable's redeemer, but it is the town hooker who is the real bridge to a new life, and it is a perversity of the film that the possibilities are so eloquently represented, only for its short-sighted hero to lose out on them. In the face of what Hildy offers, the macho claim and old Western saw that 'some things a man can't forget' seems pitifully inadequate; but the mean-spirited capitalist, who insists on keeping moral as well as financial accounts, lets her ride away.

This inaction generates multiple ironies. In the film's final act, our hero will get his revenge – at least in part – with Taggart's killing. But maturity strikes as he realises that he no longer has an appetite for vengeance and makes his other nemesis, Bowen, his heir. Thereafter, Hildy's return prompts both his final reformation and his death, paradoxically brought about in trying to save Bowen, of all people, from the path of her run-away limousine.

If the image of a cowboy trying to hold back the modern world's automobile is an apt icon for the genre in general, it is, of course, especially relevant for Peckinpah's work. Although a small man in stature and vision, one of the director's ironic heroes, Cable is a successor to the line of tragic Western protagonists whose exploits contribute to an emerging state in which they have no place. Peckinpah's comic spin on these themes achieves a fine balancing act, allowing the hero both to strive in the masculine realms of empire and revenge and to enjoy the feminine domain of love; to sustain both sides of the binary of nomad/settled superimposed on him until the very end, the hermit who falls in love, the prisoner of the desert who becomes its housekeeper, the avenger who turns the other cheek.

But finally Hogue must expire because like all Peckinpah's heroes he cannot cross over. 'Prisoner of the Desert' – the French title for *The Searchers* – is a more apt description for Ford's martyrs than for Peckinpah's outsiders, who fit comfortably within the wilderness, and whose problem comes when they are forced or, in Cable's case, tempted out of it. If the two directors share a commitment to the black sheep, the vagrant and the loser, it is typically Ford who brings alive with great warmth the family and home from which they are exiled. Peckinpah, for once, does something very similar in *Cable Hogue*, satisfying precisely because it captures a rare moment in his work wherein domestic space is created and blessed. Inevitably, however, it is a mirage, Cable's doomed dream.

End of an idyll: Jason Robards and Stella Stevens

Cable is the West's last adventurer, and he fits uneasily in a world of deals and office jobs where bosses rule. Leave it to Peckinpah to make a comedy about the impossibility of his tramp's transition into the modern world, and of sustaining love and freedom. In *Clementine*, the American flag fluttered above the church and the dance of the townspeople, honouring its community. In Peckinpah's film, it flies above the barren desert way station, celebrating the nomadic and underlining the transience of a world in which it is impossible to sustain meaningful ties and loyalties.

Cable Hogue thus provides a comic spin on Peckinpah's deconstruction of the frontier. Wrapping the hoariest of stereotypes – the scruffy prospector, the hooker with the heart of gold, the lustful preacher – in the American flag is Peckinpah's comic strategy for his redefining of the spiritual birth of a nation. It is once again the director at his most rabble-rousing, anarchic and self-consciously provoking. America, land of the free, is the land of hermits, whores and hustlers. A modernist take on *Stagecoach* perhaps, but in contrast to Ford's classical symmetries, *Cable Hogue* is all deceptions, digressions and discord. The diverse narrative strands are punctuated by an absurdist comedy that, rather like the violence of the earlier films, plays with spectator expectations and invites a distanced perspective.

In *Cable Hogue*, however, the emphasis is on a world not so much brutal as out of joint, the comedy effectively disguising the fact of an existence that is bleak, incapable of sustaining love. The main action of *Cable Hogue* is its evocation of a historical 'progress' towards a world of despair camouflaged by the romance that ultimately functions structurally as a digression. Like Godot and one of his stooges (Lucky?), Cable and Joshua occupy the centre of the film and its basic location, Cable's desert enterprise. Bringing onto this stage-like setting a fraudulent preacher in David Warner's unsettling stick-like figure corruptly quoting scripture to mask his own lust, Peckinpah creates a quirky critique of humanity's ethical systems. Blessed Hildy's arrival challenges the solipsism and cynicism; her shining mission is to extend love and hope, and an offer to redeem the tramp. 'Nobody owns Hildy,' Cable tells Josh, suggesting that the harlot is a free soul; he is unable to perceive the woman's gift, the growth of his personal desert into a garden. Finally reaching out to her, Hogue will realise that he is too late as the limo's wheels grind him into the sands.

Joshua's entrance had been the first of a series of narrative and stylistic jolts the director would administer. These would culminate at the end in the limousine's crushing of the crusty pioneer's last-minute hopes for renewal. Peckinpah loved to engineer the collision between primitive setting and modern technology. Here motorcycles and high-powered automobiles invade the desert, the latter filled with a laughing party of sightseers zipping past a desperate Bowen begging for help. Along the way, this shock strategy flirts with becoming playfully Brechtian when Cable first encounters Hildy, his hunger for whom is comically established through the delirium of seeing the Indian on a five-dollar bill grin up at him, and by repeated gross zooms into her cleavage, crotch and rear. A Keystone Cops fast-action technique adds to the self-consciousness, when the demure hooker runs in sped-up fashion after her bath from an approaching stage to prevent exposure of her charms. However, these have not been forbidden the audience, who glimpse her nipples bobbing above the water, along with an earlier rear-end shot as she undresses alone; whose POV, we wonder?

The bomb-thrower, the anarchist, the provocateur, Peckinpah clearly relished the use of crude and distancing strategies such as this aggressive indulgence of the male gaze to offend a spectatorship his films often seem to envisage as piously liberal and – in a phrase more recently coined – politically correct. Even in a milder comic register, shock tactics were always a favourite strategy of Peckinpah's. In many ways his freest film, *Cable Hogue* reveals a director clearly interested in extending his stylistic range and playing with his audience on a variety of levels.

Pat Garrett and Billy the Kid (1973)

'I believe you know of me …'. Jack Elam's Alamosa Bill – wall-eyed, black-bearded, a 'character' – introduces himself to Lincoln County Marshal Pat Garrett, then proudly listens as his fame is recounted, how he had 'killed old G. B. Denning last year at Silver City for calling you a cheat at monte'. 'That'd be me …', replies a pleased Alamosa, taken aback seconds later on being drafted for the hunt for Billy the Kid. Played stylishly by a dapper James Coburn, Garrett is getting a shave and has just asked an oddly derbied Bob Dylan, sitting and drinking at a nearby table, who *he* is, only to receive the puzzling reply, 'That's a good question.' Earlier still, we had heard Garrett instruct an errand boy to alert his wife that he would be home for dinner …

If this conjunction of badge, barber and bride would seem to point to a comfortable fit for Garrett with the settled life, the film everywhere complicates such notions. Although the film pauses with Pat at the picket fence in front of his house, a return home seems less the occasion for his critical inspection before the barber's mirror ('Do me up good this time, Guiseppe') than his meeting with the governor, an elegant turn by Jason Robards, who greets him with slick musings about the 'fabulous melancholy' of rainy New Mexico evenings that hopefully bring one closer to 'some greater design'. However, the only design that the film bleakly maps is that of the increasingly destructive impact on the West of a squalid capitalism – incarnate in the governor's mealy-mouthed guests – whose goals are achieved through Garrett, arm-in-arm with the governor, and his grudging service to Chisum, giant rancher and creature of the state's money and political interests that are closing down the frontier.

This is the power structure the film defines as authorising the manhunt and murder of William Bonney, a charming bad-boy Christ who kills people, a tarnished icon of independence and freedom as constructed by Kris Kristofferson's soft performance and Peckinpah's direction. A film suffused with its own fabulous melancholy, *Pat Garrett and Billy the Kid* is a languorous dirge, a drifting death-poem, a post-modern lament for an earlier America, an Edenic time pre-dating our worthies' situation when life meant more than image and reputation ('That'd be me'). Peckinpah's vision of the closing frontier peoples it abundantly with outsize characters of renown such as Pat, the Kid and Alamosa – originals, eccentrics, one-offs – but the authentic life, the autonomous self, are no longer possible. Style has replaced substance, the frontier a stage with a cast of drifters, unhinged, heroes without a referent. A rich tapestry of the West's final days, *Pat Garrett* is Peckinpah's ultimate statement, the tragic moment frozen, his final Western, his farewell to the Western.

In this ultimate elaboration of their historical plight, Peckinpah's characters find themselves in a world defined by compromise and betrayal, where the genre's mantle of heroic identity is a lie. 'How good is he?' is a question often asked in the genre, ethics and expertise combined. Here we see the reality, the practice of social contracts such as the ten-step duel the film puts forward as the standard format for regulating violent conflict. Ironically, cheating itself has become a given. Alamosa Bill whirls round to shoot on the count of eight; Billy has turned on three. At the end, Billy will get similarly unsparing treatment from Garrett. The West is a combat zone where neither law nor honour exist, life a cockfight. Billy shoots people in the back. There is no gold to be saved, no Elsa or Angel to rescue, no bad guys – only the range war with Chisum, but that's lost.

For all the echoes of Christ, Billy is as compromised as Garrett, as trapped in a righteous narcissism, a saviour without a cause. The film's prologue/epilogue structure, which records Pat's murder twenty-seven years after the film's main events, has led some critics to see the action as if from his point of view, and to install him as its tragic hero.[6] But as the title, the to-and-fro of the narrative and its even-handed depiction of its epic characters suggest, the film is balanced equally on the shoulders of both men, ambiguous and ambivalent characters caught in a no-win deal, a historical Catch-22.

For men of charismatic authority and individual style, a life with honour and meaning is no longer possible, neither within the community nor on the shrinking open range. Trying to cross over, as befits his grey hairs, Garrett has become alienated, reminded by everyone of his compromised identity in serving Chisum. How dark this character becomes for us – an undertaker doling out death left and right – is quietly captured towards the end of his quest, in a gentle tableau that barely survived the studio's scissors. Resting in his manhunt by a river, Garrett's attention is drawn by gunshots from a barge floating downstream, a family aboard, a bearded patriarch firing at a floating target from the bow, womenfolk cooking behind. It is an image of the fragility and instability of the frontier community, a family at once both settled and transient, who appear to be living out Sheriff Baker's dream, 'to drift out of this damn territory', its vulnerability thrown into stark relief when Garrett has a shot at the target, and the man aboard fires back. Garrett then takes aim, and the world of these strangers, drifting by on life's current, hangs in the balance. But the deadly Garrett refrains, the barge drifts on and we are thankful that Pat's presence does not inflict a gratuitous violence on this family – as Billy had on the trading post's homesteaders, who provide a mute audience for his murder of Alamosa in their front yard after the meal they all share.

Pat's icy isolation is balanced by Billy's barely civilised life with cronies and whores, true to a meaningless bunkhouse existence, cynical, indolent, ever liquored-up, rustling Chisum cattle to recover back pay, all that's left. This narrow concern with personal cowboy justice bespeaks a self-absorption equal to the marshal's. Children are often in evidence around the Kid and his bunch, an ambiguous motif interwoven to suggest a kindred youth and hope, but indicating a lack of maturity as well. Neither man has a larger vision, something 'to back off to', in the words of The Wild Bunch's Dutch. Peckinpah takes the Western's stock melodrama of heartless corporations circumscribing free men of action to its ultimate, both characters allowed a limited space for manoeuvre, a stage that makes for gestures rather than authentic action.

Peckinpah is no populist. Where John Ford foregrounds the foot soldier, the common man, the family in tension with the razzle-dazzle of a Liberty Valance, ordinary people in Peckinpah's West are the anonymous underlings who have to live with snotty bosses, as in *The Wild Bunch* – 'It's not what you *did* I don't like' – who survive by 'standing in my own good hole', as the scurrilous sad sack Garrett turns over to Sheriff Cullen Baker puts it. However, if the director's heroes generally belong to an elite, *Pat Garrett* goes further, exploiting the genre's incipient dandyism to suggest 'characters' in the late-frontier's shrinking outlaw society that carry the knowing air of celebrity and fame. These men occupy a charged space, a hyper-reality within which they play out their roles in a drama of historic proportions. As Alamosa lies dying, he consoles himself – his name will be included in reports of Billy's doings. Similarly, a bewigged Richard Jaeckel – another familiar face – on being pressed into action by Pat: 'I hope they spell my name right.' In contrast, we have Slim Pickens, the emotional epicentre of the film as Sheriff Baker, lumbering down to die by the river, supported at a respectful distance by Katy Jurado, the genre's Latin firebrand here recycled to mourn the passing of the West's last honest man, who shares the wisdom she first expressed about civilisation's discontents long ago in *High Noon*: 'This town is not worth it.' Employing a favourite strategy for contrast, Peckinpah crosscuts from the fading sheriff at the river's edge to Garrett manoeuvring for a shot at a talky Black Harris, on the roof above, who is trying to distract the marshal with a running chat recalling their arrival in the country: 'How long ago was that, Pat?' Meanwhile, as he dies, Pickens and Jurado exchange soulful looks, but are silent.

If that silence registers as protest, it is perhaps because the main business of language in the late-frontier appears to be its endless narrativising of the 'colourful' and violent events of a largely shiftless cadre, collectively constructing 'history'. There is no author of dime novels in *Pat Garrett*, no foregrounding of the myth-making process, as in Arthur Penn's earlier treatment of the legend, *The Left-Handed Gun* (1958). Centred on Billy, as its title suggests, Penn's impressive debut was a Western of uncommon psychological complexity – 'Oedipus in the West', as its director put it. Peckinpah's characters do not achieve analogous psychological depth, but then they are poseurs, inauthentics, in a world where even the ambiguous honour of revenge is not possible, as it had been for Paul Newman's tortured Billy.

Rather than document the formal construction of the myth in print, as both Penn's film and Eastwood's *Unforgiven* do, what the film provides instead is a vivid grassroots experience of the process, a preoccupation with events and their audiences ('Rode in from Seven Rivers to see you get hanged'), a pervasive telling of stories, anecdotes, histories, incidents, jokes and gossip, constantly flowing around the action and creating a kind of instant nostalgia, a nostalgia for the present, as it were. 'That's a good story, Bell,' Billy tells Matt Clark's runty deputy, the first of a large cast of supporting players behind Garrett. Bell has been describing a 40-mile trek he once made after his horse 'locoed' on him, but primed with a six-gun discovered in the outhouse, Billy is ready for darker tales, and asks if J. W. knows how his friend Carlyle died. Although Bell has already heard about it, Billy wants to tell it his way, how he 'shot him three times in the back – blew his goddamn head off', and having brutally set the stage, does the same to Bell, in a typically show-off self-reflexive turn.

We hear innumerable frontier stories of death and dying – of Eben, who drowned trying to escape a posse; of US Christmas, the old man who expires in a ten-step with

John Jones who had stepped on his new boots; of a horse-thieving Jace Sommers dead by an artfully placed rattlesnake. We see how events are kept alive in the memory, how stories are formed and circulate, how an oral tradition operates, reputations are made and a heroic world, a mythology, grows up, a mythology that the film itself is both mourning and critiquing. Like *The Man Who Shot Liberty Valance*, *Pat Garrett* suggests that there is a gap between the shiny legends and the facts, between fame and greatness. The word cannot be trusted because signifier and signified have separated, image and action, aesthetic and ideology are disjunct. And it is this haunting, incipient schizophrenia that gives the film its angst.

There is a preoccupation with image, style and reputation in *Pat Garrett*. As the capitalists at the governor's table make clear, a developing territory cannot be seen to accommodate the likes of a Billy the Kid. A danger less for what he does than what he represents, Billy is a signifier of an individual freedom and social anarchy of the past that threatens the new order. A writer interested in modernist reworkings of American myths, as in his screenplay for Monte Hellman's *Two-Lane Blacktop* (1971), Rudolph Wurlitzer had produced a script for *Pat Garrett* that posited heroes who knew they inhabited a myth.[7] This attitude is visible in the film in the bearing of its characters. As opposed to the upright stature and moral drive of Joel McCrea's Steven Judd in *High Country*, Peckinpah gives us a languid stardom in *Pat Garrett*, characters who exhibit a kind of glamour. They look, they pose, they make speeches, they are legend. Inhabiting a cozy old-world global village, these privileged members of a frontier pantheon are introduced by Peckinpah in freeze-frame cameos over the film's credits that immortalise this bunch, all insider looks, jokes, one-liners and tall tales ('So Pat said . . .'). Were ever images and characters so deliberate in the genre, actions so mannered? Towards the end of the film, when Billy has returned to Fort Sumner after aborting his escape to Mexico, he greets Beaver with a languid left hand, a Hollywood handshake on the frontier. Self-consciousness is everywhere.

This self-consciousness was evident in Peckinpah's intended design for the opening of the film, an associative montage worthy of the Russians that erects a future (1908) time frame in which Garrett is being murdered by the capitalists he has served in his own murder of Billy. Intercut at the outset with the present-time (1881) action of the chicken-shooting show Billy is putting on, the action returns at the end as a fatal come-uppance for Pat after he has killed Billy. This complex structure establishes the treacherous modern world in bleak sepia, then bleeds in the rich colours of the film's present, underlining how the dialectics of the actions are being paralleled across the years by match cuts of the shootings, which suggest that Billy and Pat are tied together in a strange kind of double-murder/suicide. A flashy conceit that encapsulates the film's action – the death of the individual spirit at the hands of a corrupt corporate law – the frame is the kind of Brechtian brainstorm that was forever pitting the director against his producers to act out battles that often seemed self-consciously to mirror the struggles and defeats of the characters in the films.

Three years earlier, the relatively modest, quirky *Cable Hogue* had suffered an indifferent release by Warners, its studio confused at the absurdist antics of a Mutt and Jeff in the desert. Like *Major Dundee* and *The Wild Bunch*, however, *Pat Garrett and Billy the Kid* was another ambitious Peckinpah epic doomed to traumatic final cuts against the wishes of its director, caught up once again in a power struggle with estranged MGM executives and producers. Along with the framing device, scenes of Garrett and boss Chisum and of Garrett and his wife also vanished, together with numerous other bits, some sixteen minutes in all. The result was a disastrous reduction of the film. In cutting away the frame, a flashback structure was lost that enunciates the basic theme of looking back, and the first hint of the key motifs of doubled characters – mirror images – and of suicide. Equally damaging was the loss of the dandyish affectation inscribed within the freeze-frame credits that introduce some of the 'players' striking poses and theatrically over-enunciating, as well as countless twists, tweaks and trims throughout, the total effect of which would produce an infinitely less stylised, more conventional film, diminishing the languorous, mournful, dreamlike tone.

After its disappointing reception, this release version was eventually followed by another cut, bowdlerised for broadcast television, of 103 minutes. An unstable text, *Pat Garrett*'s afterlife is complicated, the experience of the film modified depending on whether one is watching film or video, 16mm or 35mm, mainstream TV or cable.[8] Thankfully, a version closer to the director's design at 122 minutes is available on video, although still minus two small scenes involving Garrett – with a bitter and unhappy wife, and with a hooker he abuses to locate Billy (which is in the release version). Mourn these cuts we must, but in my view their absence is not crucial. The male-oriented world of the Western in any case allowed Peckinpah to marginalise women (often having them provide vivid cameos, as with Jurado), and his work, especially if we take into account their representation and treatment in his other movies, clearly is bound up with a cult of masculinity.

Borden Chase, author of so many key Anthony Mann-directed scripts as well as Hawks's *Red River*, once defined the relationship between two men as 'the greatest love story'.[9] For Peckinpah, that love is always threatened. A dominant theme, loyalty provides the master-code of value, loyalty to oneself, loyalty man to man, loyalty to codes, contracts and commitments. Loyalty to women is not an issue. But loyalty is an impossible ideal, the films tracing the contradictions and fallibility of the characters. Indeed, the action of many of the director's films begins under the sign of betrayal, original sin in Peckinpah. Jean Renoir once said that the auteur makes the same film repeatedly. It is possible to discern in Peckinpah a master-text, all his work interconnected through and radiating out of the central binary of loyalty and betrayal, and the parallel motifs of giving one's word, signing contracts, honouring friendships, bonds and commitments, set against breaking faith, compromising, double-crossing, selling out, whoring. At its highest pitch, as in *Pat Garrett*, the drama of such ties and their transgression within the masculine sphere can express the depth, complexity and intensity of a love relationship. Asked why he doesn't kill Garrett early on, Billy ponders, then replies: 'He's my friend.' The sense of a private bond being violated is so intense that it has led some critics to speculate on the presence of a radical gay text struggling to surface in Peckinpah.[10]

Such speculative subtexts are understandable, given the fraught air surrounding Peckinpah's antagonists. *Pat Garrett*, in particular, with its self-conscious theatrics and insistent mirror-image motif, lends itself to a quasi-autobiographical reading – Billy and Pat as co-stars in a glum saga directed by Garrett against his wishes for Chisum's producer (Barry Sullivan moving over from his role as director in Minnelli's *The Bad and the Beautiful* [1952]). Garrett as auteur of the show within the show – an ominous, exemplary text for the enlightenment of the territory – is a resonant notion, given his calling of the shots throughout. Within this perspective, Pat's meeting with Billy at the outset is perhaps less a warning than a provocative invitation to join the production, play the game of art, narrativise together. The master of *mise en scène*, Pat will shortly thereafter direct the action at the cabin's siege from on high – like a Ford or DeMille – but also show a flair for up-close, intimate scene-shaping, such as the later semi-comic humiliation of Billy's cohorts at a poker table, culminating in the killing of Holly. As befits the mind that holds the whole scenario, however, Garrett also displays a more deliberate, introspective side, increasingly hesitant, slowing the pace, contemplating, resisting the final action. In contrast, either with story or song, target practice or duel, Billy is always 'on', the exhibitionist, perfect for star billing. Actors rarely look beyond their role, however, and at the end Billy, the naked, jilted lover, appears not to have realised how the action would play out, that he had been cast by his friend in a snuff film.

The aloof, imperious auteur and the madcap drinking buddy, the whore and the stand-up guy, the two halves of a perennially schizoid film-maker are objectified here. This ultimate post-modern conceit centres on Peckinpah casting his own shadow in Garrett, egging his surrogate on at the end in his cameo as the coffin-maker, and contemplating the treachery and murder that lie ahead at the hands of an ungrateful 'business' in the frame's final dumb show and curtain, the director accurately foreseeing his own future marginalisation and failures. To entertain such a reading is, of course, not necessarily to give credence to its image of the auteur as tragically compromised victim. It is tempting to speak sympathetically, as Paul Seydor has, of Peckinpah's films suffering 'mutilation' at the hands of 'money men', of *Pat Garrett* coming in, for all the vicissitudes of its production, '*only* twenty days behind schedule and $1.5 million over the original $3 million budget' (my emphasis).[11] But the truth is that the director was frequently unable to sustain the collaborative relationships essential to the quasi-industrial system of mainstream feature film-making. Peckinpah's early breakthrough successes coincided with the broad diffusion within the film community of auteur theory, as it was mistakenly called, and in so far as the premise of the director as author was seen as a theory of production rather than a critical method, its impact may well have been unfortunate within Hollywood.[12] Certainly, Peckinpah's films and career stand for nothing if not a belief in the absolute primacy and authority of the gifted individual. That Peckinpah was aware that this was a doomed model, as the dramatic action of his films suggests, appears not to have deterred their director from aggressively attempting to live it out. In this, he differed sharply from his early mentor, Don Siegel, who lived by compromising wherever necessary to make the best film that he could, a policy that acknowledges Hitchcock's famous maxim – 'Ingrid, it's only a *mooovie*.' In contrast, Peckinpah conceived of his work as an original and personal creation, 'A Sam Peckinpah Film', signed on occasion with a witty self-reflexivity that literally, portentously, inscribes the director within the manly world of the film, as with *The Wild Bunch*'s freeze-framing on his name and the line, 'If they move, kill them!'

In *Pat Garrett*, the credit is actually withheld until some three minutes after the producer's, until Garrett lays the gauntlet before Billy – he is asking the Kid to leave the territory, but if necessary will make him go – at which point Peckinpah freezes the image and imprints his name as author, branding the charged masculine space that his characters inhabit. It is hard to believe that in Rudy Wurlitzer's script, the two only meet at the very end. Peckinpah insisted on the opening scene where the two friends come together at Fort Sumner in the bloody, outrageously callous target practice – how jaded these worthies! Immediately introducing the duelling dramatis personae of the legend that provides the film's structure, the scene also reinforces the circular form of the framing device in the action, since Garrett will return to the fort for the showdown. The opening is also impressive for its nuances, balancing good feelings stemming from a shared past ('We did have some times') and underlying hostility as their paths now diverge, the beheading of the chickens immediately establishing aimless (for all the marksmanship) and spectacular brutality as a norm. The threat implied by Pat's gunfire interrupting Billy's is soon made good by the marshal's message: 'The electorate wants you gone.' Moving to the door of the saloon, Garrett stops and glances back, a pregnant, theatrical moment as the two trade threats and loaded looks, members of the bunch standing about, watching and listening to the *mano a mano*.

'How does it feel, Pat?' This question, put to Garrett by Billy, resonates throughout Peckinpah, and points to the ambiguous nature of the law, to how someone still 'half-outlaw himself' can become righteous overnight, the system behind him. Looking at Garrett posed against the sky above Billy's cabin in his immaculate black business suit, the spectre of death and capitalism, a cigar jutting from his smiling face, a rifle balanced on his hip pointing to the sky, one would have to say it must feel pretty good. If Pat is in 'poor company', as an equally posturing Billy will tell him, arms half-raised in a

Billy performs

crucifixion shot borrowed from Penn's film, Garrett's pose up on high among the cactus communicates nothing so much as a personality convinced of his absolute right to rule over the landscape he inhabits.

Everyone strikes poses in this world. When Pat's ambush mortally wounds the half-pint Bowdre, and he, Billy and O'Folliard hunker down in the besieged cabin, Peckinpah provides a measure of just how self-conscious their larger-than-life act is by having them deal out a hand of poker while the bullets fly around them. A recurring notion in Peckinpah is that life is just a game, albeit a deadly serious one. This scene paints the frontier's players as eccentrics revelling in romantic whimsy, and suggests that when it was time to fold, they could go out in style, material for narrative. Played straight, a ploy that exaggerates the macho heroism, the scene presents the poker as a nihilistic affectation, the players themselves the only audience (apart from us) for their 'cool' performance, and especially that of the scrappy Bowdre, whose vision is so blurred that he cannot see his cards, and who consequently makes himself available as a decoy to draw fire.

As Robert Warshow pointed out, poker is a basic convention of the genre, a signifier of the inner serenity of the Western hero, of his grace under pressure. But in the degraded and decadent world of the late-frontier, such ideals can hardly survive intact and are here mocked in their excess, rendered even more absurd in a later scene where Garrett's search for Billy leads to an encounter with Holly, Beaver and Alias in a bar presided over by a thoroughly obscene Chill Wills. An invitation to poker there gets everyone to the table, but Garrett then draws his gun and indulges a showy, contemptuous power-play, forcing Alias to club Beaver unconscious, pull Wills's hat down over his eyes and then stand by a shelf bizarrely reciting the contents of cans ('Plums . . . beans . . . succotash'), while Holly is compelled to drink himself drunk and make a fatal lunge for his knife.

Ironically, the earlier poker game with Bowdre and O'Folliard continues with Billy's incarceration, stressing the paradox of it all (like Billy dining with Alamosa before he kills him), the friendships continuing across the roles dictated by the law. Here the hands are played with Garrett and J. W. Bell under the vengeful eye of R. G. Armstrong, recycling his zealot's act from *High Country* as the hammy, demented Deputy Bob Ollinger. Here too, the poker is subverted, Bell folding a strong hand out of pity, as Billy's gallows outside provides a swing for a bevy of typical Peckinpah kids, innocence and death hand in hand. Once Garrett has left, however, it is Bell, shot in the back as he tries to run from Billy, and Ollinger, dead by his own shotgun and the sixteen thin dimes it holds, who are executed, not Billy, who continues his witty performance ('Keep the change, Bob') for a fascinated community of groundlings with his improvised song delivered from up in the window, as he frees himself of his manacles. A far cry from the traditional, unifying melodies of the genre – memorably, everywhere in Ford, of course, and in Hawks's *Rio Bravo* – this solo ballad typically celebrates Billy himself and the towns he has seen, none of them as 'lowdown' as Lincoln.

Where did the weapon Billy finds secreted in the toilet come from? Theories include Pat himself, not such a radical notion if we bear in mind his ambivalence, the desultory pursuit and the possibility that he is following his own script. Or perhaps it is 'the people?' In keeping with his legend, Billy is seen as a populist figure dropping in on homesteaders for dinner, friend to the Mexican sheep herder, Paco, whose death at the hands of Chisum's henchmen will fatefully turn Billy away from the border and safety. Here, as Billy starts his ride out of Lincoln, he discovers that the horse he has been supplied by the old Mexican peasant he has pressed into service is wild enough to unseat him. Cavalierly confiscating a superior mount, and tipping its stunned owner the bloody $1.60 in Bob's body, Billy again begins to ride out, but then stops, turns and rides back to the same peasant, who is still holding Billy's poncho. A strange little encore – all smug smiles and deep glances by Billy – the retrieving of the poncho has the Kid grandstanding as a friend of old Mexico, a true democrat for all his charisma and the contempt expressed for Lincoln and its gawking, more 'civilised' citizenry assembled in all their finery for a different show – his hanging. Finally, he does ride out, the whole town watching, and the Dylan score soars on cue to accompany a cosmic shot of Billy heading out to open range, an extended exit that eulogises this outlaw hero, rather like the serenade that underlines the ride out by the Bunch from Angel's village, marking it as legendary.

Thereafter, the film neatly contrasts the journeys of its principals. Pat gets his hair cut, and then Peckinpah's design has him heading for his wife, the governor and Chisum – to all of whom he is accountable now that he is, according to Billy's jeer, 'a working man'. In contrast, Billy heads out into open country and returns to his bunch, reclaiming his bed and whore from a resigned, lesser mortal, Harry Dean Stanton's Luke. Refreshed, a perky Billy arises bright and early to kill three bounty hunters over breakfast, during which he tells a story about another duel, that rambling narrative's similarity to the film's own drift and violence underscored by the rhyme of the two showdowns, the 'let's get to it' of Billy's yarn extending a parallel invitation to the three silent visitors in his audience. Always the ham, here again Billy is self-reflexively staging and performing deadly action, his narrative a frame and punctuation for the duel, during which he also makes the acquaintance of Alias.

In casting Bob Dylan in an unscripted role and using his score (although he was finally unhappy with the music's pervasiveness), Peckinpah was boldly challenging his audience to make connections. Music was, of course, the dominant artistic voice of the period's counter-culture, and Dylan its soul. By employing Dylan alongside Kristofferson and Rita Coolidge (barely recognisable as Billy's girl after cuts), both of whom also evoked anti-establishment culture, Peckinpah erected a dialectical relationship between his film's characters and events and those of the period. America's youthful protesters were like the West's last heroes, at the mercy of corrupt law and ruthless institutions, and the fate of Billy the Kid and his boyish bunch provided a mythic parallel for the victimisation of an idealistic counter-culture in its struggle against the government and its Vietnam policy.

Jarring the illusion, kicking the audience out momentarily, Dylan's presence here has the distancing effect Peckinpah often aimed for in his work. Much commented on, Dylan's iconographic potency combined with his lack of function opens an oddly disproportionate, privileged space in the film. He is 'Alias', an enigma ('That's a good question'), vacant, a cipher, Mr In-between. To understand Alias, it is helpful to see him in the film's overall design as positioned in opposition to its other privileged figure, Sheriff Baker. Always committed to casting for character, Peckinpah had turned to another

veteran Western performer, a minor star of the genre in Slim Pickens, for Sheriff Cullen
Baker, and had again, as with Alias, riffed on the script to enlarge his scene, in one fell
swoop communicating a way of life unto death.

If Baker is to help Garrett go after Black Harris, he tells the marshal, he wants payment
– but when it comes to it, he puts on his badge and flips the coin back. Baker is thus constructed as a figure loyal to himself and a lifetime of service and integrity. A good soldier
(as his costume suggests), Baker is defined by the past, the bearer of an identity now
threatened by his duties to a law that serves the corporate powers creating the new West.
Heartsick, yearning for surcease and escape, for the possibility of drifting with life's currents, Baker is destined never to use the boat he has been building. Mortally wounded,
he heads for the river, sits on its bank, dies, Dylan's mournful music cueing a whole
world's passing. An ultimate signifier of loyalty, Baker's meaning is doubled in his partner, a wife who is also a deputy, a deputy who is also a wife, Jurado canonised for her own
faithful service, the tears streaking her face as she watches her man expire, respecting him
and the moment with her distance, but riding shotgun to the end.

All tics and twitches, a quirky Chaplinesque immigrant to the wild West, Alias has no
past and no ties, walking off his printer's job in Lincoln after witnessing Billy's flashy
performance and sizing up Garrett and his answering moves. No spouse for Alias; in
fact, he strikes us as pre-sexual, adolescent, epicene. He is thus a good fit with Billy and
his bunch, sharing in the romance and adventure, the childishness and humour. Indeed,
the film insists on its construction of Alias as Billy's double – the two swapping lines
ritualistically – as an image of the pure child in Billy, a mirror of 'the Kid', Billy's soul,
balancing the parallel reflection that Pat provides of a more worldly, 'grown-up' manhood, ageing, housebroken, funereal, a shadow of who he had been.

Where Baker unwillingly backs up Garrett, Alias volunteers his services, knifing one
of the bounty hunters, a sidekick for Billy in their turkey-hunt hijinks. However, if
Dylan's presence is a means of underscoring the anti-establishment spirit of the film, his
fate within the diegesis as a signifier of uncertain identity, drift, the future, is both bleak
and blank, Garrett making a stock boy of the character and using him to deliver mess-
ages ('Boy!'), like Lincoln's errand boy (played by the director's son, Matthew). Another
icon becoming capitalist tool, a yuppie witness to 'history', Alias is prominent in privileged close-ups as a spectator, grimly looking on to the end.

That history, *Pat Garrett* insists, is the suborning of the best spirits and skills of the
West in order to destroy it. If Baker's service and death are the axis of the film, it is
because of the characters that cluster together in a supporting system around him – their
coercion by Garrett making up *Pat Garrett*'s spine – a gallery of venerable icons richly
evocative of the genre, testifying to Peckinpah's determination to construct the West here
as a paradise lost, a sad landscape peopled by diehards and has-beens, the oppressed survivors of the genre's wars. Pickens and Jurado, Elam and Jaeckel are joined by other
classic personalities – Chill Wills's grumpy Lemuel and Emilio Fernández, *The Wild
Bunch*'s Mapache, as Paco, as well as other ageing players such as Elisha Cook, Jr, fall guy
in *Shane*, and *The Wild Bunch*'s Dub Taylor, both cruelly beaten by Poe, the capitalists'
lackey, to give up Billy's whereabouts. As befits a cattle baron and the corporate overlord above this old-world power structure of reluctant retainers and vassals called on to
end Billy's threat to the modern era, Barry Sullivan as Chisum aptly presents a face less

coded (although still familiar from Sam Fuller's *Forty Guns*). Similarly, as his main agent, James Coburn's ambivalent Pat Garrett can be seen as neatly poised iconographically between the heroic past and a self-serving future, *Major Dundee* and *In Like Flint* (1967).

In contrast to this iconographic classicism drawn on to incarnate the Old West and its executioners, the modernist strategy of 'making strange' suggested by casting relative newcomer Kristofferson, in his first Western role, and Dylan and Coolidge as the rebellious younger generation is further supported by a cameo from scriptwriter Wurlitzer as Tom O'Folliard, as well as the presence of little bespectacled Charles Martin Smith as Bowdre, both of whom die at the cabin siege. L. Q. Jones and Harry Dean Stanton apart, Billy's bunch also includes a number of other less familiar performers, newer faces such as Kristofferson band member Donnie Fritts as Beaver, Richard Bright as Holly and Luke Askew as Eno. The blankest slate of all is John Beck's Poe, a character without character, who has been forced on Garrett in an ironic comment on the genre convention of the sidekick, cruel payback for tracking Billy, and whom Peckinpah ironically provides with a white horse.

The death of the West is thus played out in a systematic elimination of the youth and frontier spirit of a community at the hands of its older generation, who are thus destroying themselves. The extent of this suicide is vividly apparent in a civil war in which Bowdre and O'Folliard are killed by Garrett's posse, Sheriff Baker is killed by Black Harris, Black Harris and Holly are killed by Pat, Billy killing Bell, Ollinger and Alamosa, Pat killing Billy and Poe killing Pat. This self-destructive logic is everywhere in the film, in its frame and narrative structure, in Billy's half-hearted attempts to escape, and in Garrett's typically self-dramatising act, blasting himself in the mirror after he has killed Billy, the image of who he used to be.

The stress on a declining, decaying and decadent world continues through its vignettes of grizzled old geezers, all reluctant accomplices, as the film drifts towards its end. After Baker and Lemuel, and the two greybeards Poe bullies, there is also Rupert, the sleazy bordello owner who reclines on his bar and supplies Garrett with four whores; Peckinpah's absurdist fantasies of sexual excess flaunt a typical invitation to his critics to construct him both as sexist and racist in the 'scandalous' composition of a five-way sexual sandwich, a cheerful, sanitised orgy in which two white hookers are accorded the honour of an armpit, while two dark-skinned women are assigned a Garrett leg, and twirl each other's nipples.

Shortly thereafter, there is Jaeckel's Sheriff McKinney, sourly chewing his whiskey, but for whose survival we will be grateful. The action will culminate at old Pete Maxwell's, with doddering old Pete doing what the very old do – reliving his glory, repeating old stories, talking to himself – as Pat and Billy describe a final dance, Pat going in, Billy coming out, Billy's lovemaking ('Jesus!') his final act before the marshal kills him. And, of course, we must not forget Will the coffin-maker, whom Garrett encounters as he finally approaches Pete's, Death walking in the blowing mist brushing up against a ghost, another icon for the insiders, another Brechtian joke, Peckinpah himself working on a small coffin –- for the classical Western, surely. Like Godard's winking appearance in *À bout de Souffle* (1960) where the director points the cops to Belmondo, Peckinpah here directs Garrett on his way ('Go on – get it over with'), and thus acknowledges his own complicity, his crucial role in the murder of the myth.

Dead Ends

Writing about Peckinpah in 1969, I argued that on the evidence of his first four films, all Westerns – *The Deadly Companions* and *Ride the High Country*, *Major Dundee* and *The Wild Bunch* – the genre was crucial to the director, that it made possible the distinctive allegorical richness of the films, the vivid and penetrating commentary on America past and present.[13] Now weighing Peckinpah's overall career, taking into account all his work outside the genre, I find no basis on which to alter that early claim; indeed, if anything, the case for Peckinpah's special relationship with the Western is immeasurably stronger, arguably self-evident.

If Peckinpah's films can be read as post-modern texts, it is in part because they look back with romantic longing at characters who in turn are perpetually looking back ('We had us some times, didn't we?'), characters forever in 'the day after', barbed wire everywhere, El Dorado lost, the movies nostalgia films twice over, the director, characters and audience all implicated in a Narcissus-like play of gazes and reflecting surfaces. However, Peckinpah's Westerns are anything but escapes to a hermetic past. The director's basic narrative strategy was always the insistence on the closing frontier, 'the times are changing' a line that runs through *Pat Garrett* like a mantra, as it does in much of Peckinpah's work. This *fin-de-siècle* clash of old and modern worlds provided conflict that could stand in for contemporary wars, allowing Peckinpah to celebrate a mythic ideal of America set in the past, and to construct and critique a brutally violent modern world, authorising the director to throw his bombs. It was because Peckinpah occupied his own frontier, torn between the romantic traditions of the classical form and the sensibility and instincts of a modernist, that he was able to turn the form on its axis, inflecting the genre with great originality and force to reflect the turmoil and divisions of a new era.

Peckinpah died in 1984, aged fifty-nine. In some twenty-three years, he directed only fourteen features, of which six were Westerns, *Pat Garrett* the grand finale, another broken monument. The director could not have known these would be his only efforts within the genre, nor how badly he would miss it. Peckinpah's allegiance to the form would be apparent in the reworking of its characters, themes and settings in much of his other work. There is, of course, the rodeo film, *Junior Bonner* (1971), the modern banditry of *The Getaway* (1972), the revenge-driven Mexico-based *Bring Me the Head of Alfredo Garcia* (1974) and his penultimate film, *Convoy*, the white-trash trucker movie set in the Southwest with its motorised cowboys. And, of course, there are the recurrent elements – the theme of threatened identity, the masculine codes of behaviour, the preoccupation with savagery and violence – that are reworked in the early, spectacularly controversial *Straw Dogs*, as well as the war film, *Cross of Iron*, and the political thrillers, *The Killer Elite* and *The Osterman Weekend*, Peckinpah's last hurrah.

Junior Bonner (1971) and *Bring Me the Head of Alfredo Garcia* (1974)

It comes as no surprise that the two strongest works outside the genre proper rework the Western in contemporary forms, expressing the contrasting sides of Peckinpah's bipolar artistic personality. Although a drastic contrast in subject and tone, *Junior Bonner* and *Bring Me the Head of Alfredo Garcia* both illuminate the increasingly desperate situation of the Peckinpah hero as the frontier recedes. A charming film, *Junior*

Bonner's piquant tone depends in part on our shaky respect for its anachronistic, arguably arrested, ageing rodeo heroes, father and son, whose family is constructed as the site of a divided America. At one level an affectionate documentary of Prescott, Arizona's Frontier Day and the world of the modern rodeo rider, *Bonner*'s action is set against bulldozers wrecking the old family homestead to make way for a new West of mobile homes. Steve McQueen's laconic Junior follows his father Ace (Robert Preston) in refusing to compromise with modernity, as opposed to brother Curly (Joe Don Baker), who is hawking the trailers.

Junior Bonner ends with Ace abandoning Ida Lupino's feisty, long-suffering wife Ellie for a new frontier in Australia, honouring a threadbare life's pattern of poetic dreaming. Having scored a victory over a mean bull and furnished Ace's stake for a new territory, former rodeo champ Junior limps on to the next town in pursuit of further tests that will allow him to define himself, to state what and who he is. These, we understand, are existential heroes left over from the Old West risking life and limb at the head of the parade, lonely icons of a heroic masculinity. 'Seen one rodeo, seen 'em all': perhaps defensively, the film rehearses an ancient insult, but challenges it with sharp montages, split screens and slow-motion action of the bronc- and bull-riding tests of skill and bravery.

But the charm of the rodeo, of Bonner senior and junior, and of the film itself finally wears thin as we catch glimpses of the narcissism and bathos that lurk beneath the romanticism of both its characters and action. What *Bonner* insinuates through its conflicts and behaviours is a retrograde fear of the feminine and the family, a romance of the irresponsible, and a celebration of violence as love. Junior sucker-punches his brother through a plate-glass window for disrespecting Dad, but the love-tap only requires two band-aids. Not a drop of blood is spilled in an interminable old-time Western bar-fight, a comical homoerotic ritual love-in that rages on while music, poker and dining continue on its margins. A revealing film, *Junior Bonner* has no villains, just an America being paved over, and a couple of tired heroic hold-outs, like Peckinpah and the film itself, manfully flirting with absurdity.

In contrast, there is *Bring Me the Head of Alfredo Garcia*, the director's most aggressively experimental, surrealist and personal work, a pastiche of *The Searchers*, in which Warren Oates incarnates Peckinpah himself as a desperate, demented hero holding aloft the symbol of a triumphant bestiality – or, alternatively, the head of John Ford, whose tomb he has burglarised – a film so challenging in its grotesquerie that for many it accomplishes what at times seemed to be the director's ultimate goal, total audience alienation.

As if to make penance for *Bonner*'s heroic chauvinism, the Western's codes of masculinity are savagely satirised in *Garcia*. The frontier's promise of opportunity and new beginnings, the American Dream of the reinvention of the self, is rehearsed here in the tarnished hope for an escape from mediocrity. *Garcia*'s Bennie is no hero but rather the consummate loser, a two-bit peckerwood, a not-so-innocent ugly American down and out in Mexico, a scruffy refugee from a John Huston movie, a savage waiting to happen. Casting has never been more definitive: Warren Oates is ideal for a man too small for life's challenges, a ham-and-egger, the ironic hero par excellence. In so far as it is naturalistic, the film is bizarre but finally uninteresting, its protagonist too brutish and limited, too short-sighted in sacrificing the love of a warm and gracious woman for

Bring Me the Head of Alfredo Garcia: Warren Oates's Bennie awakens in a grave with his dead lover

ghoulish bucks, too stupid to keep Garcia's head from rolling about in the car, too obsessed with talking to it to transfer it to the trunk and escape the stench and flies.

But, of course, the film is less a realist fable than an ugly noir fairy tale allegorising modern manhood and national experience, an abstract road movie featuring empty roads and roadside massacres. A devastating pastiche, *Garcia*'s lounge-lizard hero, in his desperate need to better himself, to 'be somebody', recalls the ambiguous model of *On the Waterfront*'s (1954) Terry Malloy. With his immigrant roots, its director, Elia Kazan, understood that desperation too well, the motor force that drove him to name names before the post-war House Un-American Activities investigations, an act that saved a career but also scarred it for ever.

Bereft of principle or even imagination, Oates's Bennie also sacrifices love for profit. In an altogether too familiar pattern, the film's action turns on the sacrifice of the feminine, a Peckinpah ritual enacting the stripping and threatened rape of the woman, her betrayal and ultimate death. Peckinpah layers the key scene with complex ironies: the couple seek romance under the stars, only to be accosted by outlaw bikers; an onset of conscience in a boyish Kris Kristofferson forestalls the rape; the woman subsequently begins to give herself freely; Bennie's escape from his captor at that precise point frees him to 'save' Elena by killing her abductor.

The key irony is, of course, that the action turns not on the rape but on the woman's readiness to betray her lover. Is this possibly her strategy to ensure they survive? Or is Peckinpah indulging stereotypes – the Mexican Elita (Isela Vega) so passionate and compassionate that she opens her heart wide to one in need? Or so emotional and impulsive that she eschews reason? The distance on the scene's staging provides no help in reading the moment, as opposed to the layering of self-disgust we sense in the extreme close-up on the hysterical laughter of Angel's girl, Aurora, who had betrayed him with Mapache in *The Wild Bunch*. Either way, the conception of Elita's character here typically involves her prostitution by the director, her willingness to betray her betrothed muddying the film's morality, as does the hero's crab-infested crotch that he discovers after sleeping with her.

Peckinpah often described himself as a whore doing what he was told in the Hollywood machine. No more disingenuous pose was imaginable, but it served to allow a defence of his preference for hookers in his women (being 'true' to his period), and for the dramatic action that often featured woman's complicity in her own prostitution. The master-text here, of course, is *Straw Dogs*, an effort that has been defended as a masterpiece by some despite the overpowering reek of calculation in the film's characters and action. Peckinpah's interpreters have regularly bemoaned his references to Robert Ardrey's theories of the savage, suggesting they allowed critics to see *Straw Dogs* as a thesis film in its construction of events. But Ardrey or not, it is impossible to ignore the way in which its characters serve a basic premise and predetermined outcome rather than the possible surprise of independent action.[14]

There is finally something of the thesis film about *Garcia* as well. Although much of the film's action is unpredictable, and not least its scurrilous hero's resurrection from Garcia's grave, Bennie's lethal progress seems finally preordained. *Garcia*'s hero blazes an unholy trail of death and destruction that culminates in the revenge he takes on its original source, Emilio Fernández's Mexican overlord, El Jefe, before himself expiring with both Garcia's head and a million bucks beside him in his bullet-riddled vehicle. A new-wave modern Western/action film looking ahead to Robert Rodriguez's trilogy (*El Mariachi* [1993], *Desperado* and *Once Upon a Time in Mexico* [2003]), it is the absolute polar opposite of the director's earliest success, the classical *Ride the High Country*. There are no majestic mountains here, no sublime, only a flat landscape and a degrading, nihilistic and perverse journey that demonstrates how low humanity can be. In contrast to the passing of Steve Judd, the death of the hero here is meaningless, leaving us cold. It is as if Lyle Gorch had stepped out of *The Wild Bunch* with Angel's head intent on making a killing, but a Lyle without a brother, a leader or a clue – only the detritus of the dream.

Although much of his other work outside the Western was distinctive, to survey those productions, and the later films in particular, measuring the disparity between the enormous effort and the modest achievement, is to appreciate how much the Western mattered. Divorced from the romance and epic sweep of the form, Peckinpah's characters often seem to undergo a *reductio ad absurdum*, the gestures that would carry dramatic weight in ritualistic and mythic contexts appearing affectations in modern dress. Without the historical frame of the frontier and its tragic hero motif that was Peckinpah's personal narrative paradigm, the problem the director faced was that the absurdist dilemma of his characters – trying to live out a heroic code in an unheroic, indeed post-modern world – always threatened to engulf the whole work in incongruity and inauthenticity, the theme overwhelming the material.

For a time, however, Peckinpah's great good fortune was to find his home as an action director within the greatest of action genres, the Western, within the most sophisticated and dominant of action cinemas, the American. The result was original and ground-breaking work that touched the very pinnacle of cinema. A consummate creature of the film medium, the director's great strengths were his inspired mastery of visual signs and forms, his gift for iconic representation on the one hand, and his impeccable dialectical instincts for challenging, often Brechtian, montage on the other. In my view, it was this command of the cinema's codes and modalities that allowed Peckinpah to inflect the Western genre with the force of an oppositional artist in his critique of American myths and ideologies. Ironically, in a final exchange of myth and reality, the effect of Peckinpah's critical reinvention of the genre, pushing the envelope to address a new era and audience, was to spearhead a revisionist excavation of the Western that contributed in no small measure to its virtual disappearance in the 1980s, the director finally, irrevocably, living out the tragic myth of his gunfighter-heroes whose acts help to close the door on their own freedom.

Paul Seydor would have us believe that the genre was incidental to Peckinpah's success, that the films are closer to psychological novels, the director a creative genius, his brethren Shakespeare, Melville and Mailer. We are to understand that Peckinpah is not a genre director, and his films are not Westerns 'in the generic sense than in the sense of their being set in the West and in the Western past and of their being concerned with the subjects traditionally associated with the West'. Apart from presumably validating Peckinpah as the totally original creative artist, this circumloquacious sophistry sets up the claim that the movies could be also classified and studied in other ways – 'say, between his so-called "violent" and "gentle" films'. However, in a conveniently half-baked auteurism, Seydor wisely sticks to the Westerns, and fails to confront the decline in Peckinpah's work after *Pat Garrett*.[15]

In my view, it is foolhardy to deny Peckinpah the sustaining creative tradition of the Western, the symbolic and allegorical dimensions of which were so valuable to the director. Clearly, a dialectical relationship obtained, the director taking as much as he gave. Peckinpah produced landmark works, an immense contribution, the collective impact of his work, and especially *The Wild Bunch*, bringing the form to a paroxysm, decisively mapping the genre's future. At the same time, it seems to me undeniable that the language of the Western in its turn brought Peckinpah alive, supplied his canvas, shielded him somewhat from his own toxic elements, and provided him with focus and direction.

For me, one image from *Pat Garrett* sums up Peckinpah's qualities and achievement. It comes after Billy has broken out of Lincoln's jail and ridden out into open country. As twilight falls, in a shot composed wholly in black and white but for a thin orange streak where the sun has just set, Billy makes his way along the horizon, a dark reflection of the rider materialising in the water below as he descends by a small pond and a stand of trees dark against the skyline, pausing there to doff his poncho. Oddly accented in the film, nearly forgotten in Lincoln, then donned by Billy against the heat on the trail, the poncho is a minor icon that inevitably recalls Clint Eastwood's Man With No Name. In Leone's *A Fistful of Dollars*, however, the cloak had been a source of mystery and invulnerability (a protective shield underneath), suggesting a hero who, unlike our Kid, still retained traces of a messianic function. Given that lineage, it is appropriate that this snapshot frames Bonney's removal of the garment.

At first glance, this striking image – dark rider and landscape reflected in the water – may seem simply a stock genre vista, a pretty example of Peckinpah's self-consciously painterly style. There is no dramatic weight, no brackets around it signifying 'Tragic Hero', as with the shot of Pike riding across the dunes in pain and shame after falling from his horse in *The Wild Bunch*. There is, however, a haunting quality here that grows as the travelling shot pauses, the Kid stilling his horse to remove the poncho – the pause seeming to invite our own pause and reflection, nudging us to contemplate this reflected Billy, while the 'real' Billy above remains completely hidden in shadows, visible only in the reflected image, the shadow rider and the dark leafless trees heavy in the water beyond him. The pause encourages us perhaps to understand that this is our reflection, too, America in the dark and dead in the water, asking us to turn the cowboy over in our mind, and to discover that, as always, Peckinpah is exposing the negative of the myth and its classical iconography. Employing his masterful compositional effects, Peckinpah here creates a magisterial visual design that both evokes and subverts, constructs and critiques, the image that is the very bedrock of the grand tradition of the Western, the silhouette of the lone cowboy against the sky. But here it is *reversed*, Billy revealed to us as an inverted Ford icon, a shadow reflected upside down in the water, the cowboy a dark figure in the dark, visible only as a double or dead ringer.

Both the spontaneity and the calculation of the Peckinpah style, the invitation to contemplate the past as a mirror to our own era, the complexity of the relationships with both heroes and genre, the love for what the Western was and the necessity of seeing it

Pat Garrett and Billy the Kid: turning the Western upside down

anew, of turning it all upside down, the classicism and the modernity, the loyalty and the betrayal – everything is there, crystallised in a post-modern emblem for the genre. Peck-inpah holds the shot well after Billy has left, brooding on the dark landscape of the West reflected in the still water, the mirror image of America's golden dream in its twilight.

Apart from the spaghetti Western, Peckinpah explicitly refers to two other classics of the form in *Pat Garrett* – *High Noon*, with Jurado and her judgment on the unworthiness of the new order, and *Shane*, the boy casting the stones at Garrett as he rides away from Bonney's corpse at the end. However, Peckinpah's indebtedness to the collective tradition of the Western is everywhere apparent, and I like to think it is partly repaid here, in this supreme image that defines his core as an artist, this self-referential sign so evocative of the Western myth and of Ford, the earlier master of Western horizons, whom he had succeeded.

Notes

1. Paul Schrader, 'Sam Peckinpah Going to Mexico', *Cinema* vol. 5 no. 3 (1969), p. 25; reprinted in Kevin Jackson (ed.), *Schrader on Schrader* (London: Faber & Faber, 1990), p. 75.

2. Paul Seydor, *Peckinpah: The Western Films* (Chicago: University of Illinois Press, 1980). An expanded second edition, *Peckinpah: The Western Films – A Reconsideration* (Urbana: University of Illinois Press), was published in 1997.

3. See Bill Mesce, *Peckinpah's Women: A Reappraisal of the Portrayal of Women in the Period Westerns of Sam Peckinpah* (Lanham, MD: Scarecrow Press, 2001), p. 125.

4. A fragment of the end of this scene survives in most prints.

5. Adonis Kyrou, *Luis Buñuel* (New York: Simon & Schuster, 1962), p. 111.

6. Seydor, *Peckinpah* (1980), p. 196. Seydor's voluminous scholarship positions him as a leading Peckinpah scholar. However, Seydor's roots are in literary and belles-lettres traditions, and his project is to appropriate Peckinpah for a privileged pantheon of American writers (although Shakespeare is prominent, too), from Emerson and Twain to Hemingway and Mailer, who represent a tradition, innocent of ideology, centred on 'the masculine principle'.

   Seydor constructs the films as a kind of dense visual literature, and treats their heroes as complex psychological characters rather than signs or types, who learn (and thus can teach us) how to 'face reality and its imperatives unflinchingly' (1980, p. 226). Empathic with the heroic artist, the critic is authorised to become a creative partner in the 'writing' of Peckinpah's text. Thus Seydor's account of the film as Pat Garrett's tragedy rests in large measure on seeing the main body of the work as subjective, a record of events from Pat's point of view, despite the fact that he is off-stage during half the film's action and the absence of any cues in the text that invite or endorse such an interpretation.

   > But, of course, Garrett hasn't figured it out, and it won't be over for the better part of three decades. Even then, after years of turning it over and around and upside down, he still can't figure it out, still can't make it come any clearer or better or straighter. And when it passes before him for one last time as the bullets tear through his body, the most that he achieves is a dim, tragic recollection that he was a link in the chain of causality which has brought his life to this dying fall. (1980, p. 209)

7. Quoted by Jan Aghed, '*Pat Garrett and Billy the Kid*', *Sight and Sound* (Spring 1973), pp. 65–9. Peckinpah's interest in the legend was long-standing, his first feature script in 1957 having been based on Charles Neider's *The Authentic Death of Hendry Jones*, which in turn had been based on Garrett's memoir, *The Authentic Life of Billy the Kid*, and which became Marlon Brando's *One-Eyed Jacks*, although largely transformed and long after Peckinpah and numerous others, including director Stanley Kubrick, had moved on.

8. Seydor, *Peckinpah – A Reconsideration* (1997). The second edition usefully includes a detailed record of the different versions of *Pat Garrett* (p. 298).

9. Jim Kitses, 'The Rise and Fall of the American West: Borden Chase Interviewed', *Film Comment* vol. 6 no. 4 (Winter 1970–1), p. 17.

10. Brad Stevens, '*Pat Garrett and Billy the Kid*', in Ian Cameron and Douglas Pye (eds), *The Book of Westerns* (New York: Continuum, 1996), pp. 269–76.

11. Seydor, *Peckinpah* (1980), p. 196.

12. Of course, ambitious producers who were in charge of the bucks could also seize on the concept. As Charles B. FitzSimons put it apropos the production of *The Deadly Companions*: 'Sam shot an ending for the picture I couldn't use ... that was the Peckinpah version ... But you have to understand ... I am a great believer in the auteur theory as it applies to a producer.' Quoted in Garner Simmons, *Peckinpah: A Portrait in Montage* (Austin: University of Texas Press, 1982), pp. 38–9.

13. Jim Kitses, *Horizons West* (London: Thames and Hudson/BFI, 1969), p. 169.

14. See Lawrence Shaffer, 'The *Wild Bunch* versus *Straw Dogs*', *Sight and Sound* vol. 41 no. 3 (Summer 1972), pp. 132–3, for a sustained analysis of the film's 'smell of intentionality'.

15. Seydor, *Peckinpah* (1980), pp. xvi, xvii. In his *Reconsideration*, Seydor drops the quoted equivocations about the genre, and concedes of the non-Westerns that 'it is doubtful they can be grouped together as cogently or coherently as the Westerns' (p. xxiv).

More than any other American film-maker in the post-war period, Peckinpah has generated big books, large claims, voluminous research, exhaustive analyses, a Boswell-like devotion, aptly epic undertakings. Apart from Seydor (whose *Reconsideration* runs to nearly 400 pages), there is Simmons's *Peckinpah: A Portrait in Montage* (260 pages) and David Weddle's *If They Move ... Kill 'Em* (New York: Grove Press, 1994, 586 pages), among others. Although one is grateful for the detailed research into the various versions of the films (Seydor), the extensive production histories (Simmons) and the blow-by-blow account of the director's bouts with studios, wives and addictions (Weddle), reading these studies, it is difficult to escape the impression of a collective idolatry. Peckinpah's career and films often suggest that he had heavily invested his persona in the cults of personality, masculinity and the artist. It was perhaps inevitable that he would find collaborators in his romantic myth of the 'indomitable', tortured genius, critics and journalists who heroically rescue the films from a non-existent neglect and promote them as among the supreme achievements of the 20th century.

6

Sergio Leone: A Fistful of Westerns

I don't want to be a hero – I just want the money.

The phenomenon of the Italian Western – the spaghetti Western – and the saga of Sergio Leone are now well documented. Some two dozen Italian oaters had preceded Leone's *A Fistful of Dollars*, and hundreds more were to follow, but it was Leone's five Westerns that achieved international success and decisively broke the hold of American film-makers on America's oldest and most traditional of genres. No wonder US critics and reviewers looked down on the director's debut when it was finally made available to the American audience in 1967 after copyright problems had been resolved. Like jazz and baseball, the Western was home-grown, as American as apple pie, the form that celebrated our pioneer and immigrant roots. Was John Ford not the Western? American critics, who themselves had often treated Hollywood efforts dismissively, saw only disrespect in Leone.

The subsequent US releases of *For a Few Dollars More* (1965) and *The Good, the Bad and the Ugly* (1966), six months and a year after *Fistful* respectively, appeared to confirm for many reviewers that these European productions were poor imitations that neither looked nor sounded like *the* Western. As is often the case, the audience and artist were ahead of the critics. Like moviegoers in Italy, France and Japan, US audiences responded enthusiastically to Leone and his key collaborator, newly crowned international star Clint Eastwood. Thus the *Dollars* trilogy, whose narratives some have seen as marked by a critique of capitalism, were to earn million-dollar grosses worldwide. Such ironies and paradoxes inform the production of these films at every stage. 'Fairy tales for grown-ups', as Leone described them, they played out their own fairy-tale success, not least for Leone himself. The son of a silent-film director father and film actress mother, Leone was an industry veteran whose long apprenticeship as assistant director, beginning in 1947, would stretch over eleven years with both Italian and American film-makers, including Mervyn LeRoy, Robert Wise, Raoul Walsh, Fred Zinnemann and William Wyler. Moving on to writing, Leone contributed to screenplays for a half-dozen pepla, the enormously successful costume-drama cycle featuring mythological narratives and muscleman heroes like Steve Reeves that blossomed during this period.

It was in this arena that Leone finally directed his own first feature, *The Colossus of Rhodes* in 1960, having taken over the reins on the previous year's *The Last Days of*

The Good, the Bad and the Ugly: iconic theatre

Pompeii (1959) when its director had fallen ill after pre-production. Working on these epics allowed Leone to begin to explore the stylistics that would mark his mature work, a fastidious concern with realistic detail and a parallel passion for spectacle and large-scale action. But working on the peplum, Leone was dreaming of the Western. Harbouring a fascination from childhood days, Leone had made an exhaustive study of the genre, and had wasted little time in quizzing Walsh (*Pursued* [1947] and *Colorado Territory* [1949]) and Zinnemann (*High Noon*), Wyler (*The Big Country* [1958]) and Robert Aldrich (*Apache* [1954] and *Vera Cruz* [1954]), who had asked Leone to shoot second unit on his *Sodom and Gomorrah* in 1961.

Biding his time, Leone was eventually to have extraordinary luck in the crucial areas of script, star and music when he finally pulled the trigger on his first Western. The films of Akira Kurosawa had always held interest for Leone. A great film and the model of the kind of cinema he aspired to, *Seven Samurai* (1954) had translated with great commercial success into the John Sturges-directed *The Magnificent Seven*. Was the hope already alive when Leone went to see *Yojimbo* (1961)? In any case, he would seize on it as the perfect fit for his low-budget Western, and the result would launch its struggling director on a spectacular journey that would enrich him and ultimately install him as a master of the form. But *Yojimbo* – which itself came out of an early example of the American hard-boiled thriller, Dashiell Hammett's *Red Harvest* – by no means simply inspired Leone's film, as some accounts have it. Despite minor adjustments and added material, the screenplay developed by Leone took from *Yojimbo* a scene-by-scene blueprint for the action, tone and texture of the film. Although Leone would grudgingly acknowledge only borrowing the basic structure of the Kurosawa, in fact that structure and its black comedy provided the foundation for all of the trilogy's films.

Contributing to the character of *Yojimbo* was a distinctive soundtrack that often seemed to comment ironically on narrative developments. Remarkably, although its musical conventions were Japanese rather than Italian or electronic, the effect at times was close to an embryonic expression of the philosophy and practice that Leone was to develop in his work with Ennio Morricone, who would be his perennial collaborator. These two found a true meeting of the minds in the conviction that the traditional Hollywood Western score should be avoided, and that all sound, music and silence had to be as motivated as the dialogue. In fact, the traditional notion of a soundtrack as an accompaniment and support for the images is inadequate to describe a creative process where the music was composed and recorded during pre-production, and actually played on set *while* the film was being performed and shot. The Italian system of the post-production synchronising of all performances and effects – so important to multilingual co-productions like *Fistful*, which had a polyglot cast and Italian, Spanish and German backers – furthered this independent approach to sound design. Leone was often accused of being mean in sharing credit: he and Eastwood bickered for years over who contributed the poncho, or whose idea it was to jettison dialogue. But experiencing these films, no one could possibly deny Morricone's contribution, the extraordinary effect of his auditory images.

Whoever contributed what, Eastwood was to be another crucial collaborator, indispensable as 'The Magnificent Stranger'. Leone's original title was a hopeful play off the earlier Kurosawa adaptation, but 'A Fistful of Dollars' was sharper and instantly visual, in keeping with the film's iconic character. The Stranger, briefly referred to as Joe, Monco and Blondie in the three films (in that order), in any case would retroactively be christened The Man With No Name two-and-a-half years later in a clever United Artists marketing campaign for the release of the films in the USA. *Was* Eastwood indispensable? Aiming high, Leone had tried for Henry Fonda, and had also offered the role to both James Coburn and Charles Bronson. Not surprisingly, none of these was enthusiastic about a low-budget European co-production to be shot in Spain by an unknown Italian. All three would accept later invitations – Fonda and Bronson to star in *Once Upon a Time in the West* (1968) and Coburn for *A Fistful of Dynamite* (1971) – and all would produce their own taciturn No Name style. But to be fair to Eastwood, after six seasons in his supporting role as Rowdy, the cattle drive's ramrod on *Rawhide*, one of television's most successful shows, the actor was nothing if not ready to anchor a Western. Both in appearance and temperament, he was a natural for the laconic, mask-like, minimalist character who would be No Name.

As Eastwood soon discovered on extending his partnership with Leone, however, The Man With No Name was only the rock upon which the ambitious director was aiming to build his church. In the trilogy and for the most part in his overall career, with each film Leone would shoot higher, increasing the number of dramatis personae and enlarging his running time and budget:

A Fistful of Dollars (1964)

No Name enters a town ruled by two bosses, and manipulates them to his profit. He foments warfare between the clans, aids an abused family and recovers from a vicious beating. Duping the arch-villain, Ramón (Gian Maria Volonté), by wearing a shield to ward off shots to the heart, he kills him and moves on. Italian running time: 100 min. US running time: 96 min. Budget: $200,000. Italian gross: $4.6m; US gross: $3.5m.

For a Few Dollars More (1965)

Monco (Eastwood) and Colonel Mortimer (Lee Van Cleef) are bounty hunters who form an uneasy alliance to take down the murderous Indio (Gian Maria Volonté) and his gang. After stealing the booty from a bank robbery, they eliminate the gang and Monco intervenes to ensure a fair duel between the colonel and Indio. The colonel avenges his sister, whom Indio had raped, and leaves Monco counting bodies and reward money. Italian running time: 130 min. US running time: 128 min. Budget: $600,000. Italian gross: $5m; US gross $5m.

The Good, the Bad and the Ugly (1967)

With the Civil War as a backdrop, Eastwood's Blondie, Van Cleef's Angel Eyes and Eli Wallach's Tuco scheme to find a hidden fortune. Drawn into the war, they arrive at the cemetery where the treasure is buried. Blondie kills Angel Eyes and rides out with half the wealth, leaving Tuco with a noose round his neck. On the point of hanging, Blondie's shot cuts the rope and leaves Tuco furious, but with half the booty. Italian running time: 180 min. US running time: 161 min. Budget: $1.3m. Italian gross: $4.3; US gross: $6m.

Once Upon a Time in the West (1968)

Jill (Claudia Cardinale) arrives from New Orleans to find her new husband and family murdered by Frank (Henry Fonda), hired gun of the railroad magnate, Morton (Gabriele Ferzetti). Harmonica (Charles Bronson) and Cheyenne (Jason Robards) help her retain the land that lies in the path of the coming railroad. Avenging the death of his brother, Harmonica kills Frank and rides away with the body of Cheyenne, who had been mortally wounded by Morton. Jill goes out with water for the railroad's labourers, who have reached her farm. Italian running time: 168 min. US running time: 144 min. Budget: $3m. Italian gross: $3.8m; US gross: $1m.

A Fistful of Dynamite/Duck, You Sucker/Before the Revolution (1971)

An amoral Mexican peasant bandit, Juan (Rod Steiger), tries to persuade a professional Irish revolutionary and explosives expert, Sean (James Coburn), to rob a bank. Haunted by his IRA past, Sean tricks Juan into political action that results in the loss of Juan's six children. Juan becomes increasingly involved in the Revolution, while Sean questions his beliefs. Sean dies, leaving Juan to carry on alone. Italian running time: 154 min. US running time: 138 min.[1]

The overall pattern of increasing size and complexity is clear. With *A Fistful of Dollars*, Leone had a stripped-down, existential narrative worthy of Budd Boetticher's small movies.[2] The focus is on a lone individual employing his expertise and guile to out-wit his opponents in a world bereft of law or morality. The isolation of the character, the schematic conflicts and the iconic style give the film a pronounced abstract flavour.

Doubling the heroes in *For a Few Dollars More*, Leone introduces a complicated relationship into the mix that involves both competition and friendship, as well as the psychological intensity of flashbacks evoking Mortimer's personal stake in pursuing Indio. This fleshing out and thickening continues with *The Good, the Bad and the Ugly*. The increase to three principals allows complex variations on relationships involving nicely nuanced characters, one of whom – Tuco – is again privileged with a past. Intro-ducing the epic conflict of the Civil War as a setting decisively enlarges the canvas, and allows Leone to emphasise the individual and existential nature of his heroes' violence set against the collective and socially sanctioned slaughter of warfare.

The consistency of Leone's growth and achievement in the trilogy was remarkable, but the sustained increases in both budget and running times should have been worry-ing. At a certain point, the logic dictated that returns would inevitably diminish. Ironically, Leone's watershed would come with the extraordinary *Once Upon a Time in the West*, his finest film and a milestone in the genre. Leaving the existential and savage world of his first three films behind, the director embraced the historical Western and the epic Fordian theme of the birth of the nation. Leone's cut of *The Good, the Bad and the Ugly* had lost nineteen minutes in the American version distributed by United Artists – additional time for buying popcorn, Leone had cracked. More seriously, twenty min-utes would be cut by Paramount for the US release of *Once Upon a Time in the West* that seriously damaged the experience of the film and did nothing for its box office. A suc-cess in Europe – it would play continuously for six years in Paris – it would nevertheless be the site of Leone's first major setback. Henceforth, the director would be caught up in a constant struggle with producers – the same conflict that bedevilled Peckinpah – to salvage his vision against charges that he was overly taxing the audience's capacities and risking commercial disaster.

With *A Fistful of Dynamite*, Leone was again extending himself as well as the genre in a 'post-Western' set in the 1910s in revolutionary Mexico. A project that Leone originally planned only to produce, it is nevertheless marked throughout with the director's style and interests, although in many ways resembling a war movie more than a Western. Again the film was received well in Europe but suffered in the USA, hampered by its weird original title – *Duck, You Sucker* – which the director had been adamant was an Americanism (perhaps like 'make my day'). Once again, cuts of some sixteen minutes impaired the film's design and meaning.

This pattern of a doomed outsize directorial ambition would continue. After an extended hiatus of some thirteen years during which he functioned primarily as a producer, Leone would finally return to the world stage with his last film, the gangster epic, *Once Upon a Time in America*. Contracted to be a film of 165 minutes, the director's cut of 229 minutes was re-edited and released at 139 minutes. With a budget in excess of $30 million, it would barely make $2.5 million in the USA. When he died in 1989, Leone was preparing *900 Days*, a $70-million epic on the siege of Leningrad.

Style

Much has been made of the amoral world Leone depicts, but it is the director's style that gives his work its radical edge. Comic-book-like, exhibitionist and narcissistic, Leone's films celebrate, critique and ultimately transform the Western. The style keeps the audience off balance, making the familiar genre strange. This 'making strange' creates the distance, the Brechtian rupture or space that invites contemplation of the film's ideological operation, its interrogation of Hollywood's West and the genre's heroic stereotypes, conventions and ideology. Leone biographer Christopher Frayling has characterised his films as 'critical cinema', a formulation Leone himself is ill at ease with. In any case, it is obvious that his work is at once a loving homage and a correction to the American Western.[3]

Growing up with the genre, Leone also studied it systematically in great depth. His films bear the marks of both a childlike exhilaration in enacting rituals of the form and an extreme sophistication in citing, parodying and reworking specific films. Another key factor is Leone's post-modern tendency to fuse diverse modes, forms and influences with the Western's conventions. Although comedy is basic, with a range extending from satire to slapstick, Leone also readily modulates into extreme melodrama, which together with the effects of the score and pacing at peak moments give his films their characteristic operatic tone. Numerous writers have suggested that both Italian puppet theatre and the *commedia dell'arte* are also relevant to an appreciation of Leone's characters and effects.[4] Certainly, at their most transcendent, the films also achieve liturgical overtones that further their foreignness, an Italian and Catholic invocation rather than the genre's traditional odes to Manifest Destiny.

Basic to the style is the extreme close-up, a trademark technique. The fragmenting and abstracting effect of the close-up is crucial to the transformation of character into iconic sign in Leone's expressionistic approach. Huge close-ups of secondary characters

Once Upon a Time in the West: dream-like ritual

chosen principally for their bizarre looks create a grotesque, predatory and unbalanced world of masks. Close-ups also are crucial as suspense escalates in the set piece confrontations, and to cue flashbacks. Their use in concert with other characteristic techniques, such as extreme long shots and composition in depth, intensifies the impact of the close-up. All of these, together with highly self-conscious framing, contribute to the distancing and self-reflexive charge Leone's films can carry. These effects reach their zenith in the shockingly elaborate and protracted final showdowns that stretch on and on, Leone staging them with dynamic spatial strategies generated by the circular bull-ring-like setting within which the pay-off comes.

The impact of sound and of Morricone's scores cannot be overemphasised. Transcendent moments in *Once Upon a Time in the West*, as when Timmy McBain comes rushing out to discover his assassinated family, or when Jill leaves the train station to plunge into the sprawling life of Flagstone, achieve peaks of extraordinary, spectacular expressivity buoyed by the music. In such rapturous passages, a full symphonic orchestra and choir are employed, but equally characteristic is the isolated sound of a single instrument – a piccolo, harmonica or flute – or the eerie effect of the human voice or of whistling employed as instruments. Both trumpets and the guitar often contribute to peak moments, as do especially chimes. Silence is also a crucial sound, integral to the design of the score. Often expressionistic, the music can reach ecclesiastical crescendos one moment, only to have silence reign followed by a piccolo's caricaturing punctuation of the action, as in the holstering of a six-gun after a killing. Main-title music can combine a choral 'thundering herd' motif with gunshots, whipping and horses' hoofbeats, aural icons adding up to an expressionist announcement: '*The Western*'. Morricone and Leone were also interested in using natural sound and noises (the wind, a creaking sign, etc.) together with silence to compose unnatural 'music' to underline menace, as in the openings of both *The Good, the Bad and the Ugly* and *Once Upon a Time in the West*. Pacing the performances to the music played on set adds to the overall effect of a choreographed and ritualistic theatre.

Reception of *A Fistful* and its two successors – *the* spaghettis for most audiences who would probably never encounter another Italian Western – often fastened on their 'realistic' nature, surprisingly enough. Undoubtedly, this speaks to the popular notion of the genre as an unhistorical fantasy of male power, the Leone films seen as neo-realist critiques and satires that bring a correcting vision. But such a response is still difficult to understand, given Leone's already emerging post-modern instincts and the films' extreme theatrical flavour, the self-reflexive and Brechtian distancing. In particular, the disorientingly extreme, dreamlike contrasts that Leone indulges are striking – the silence of No Name as opposed to the manic hysteria of the gargoyle villains, the giant fragmenting close-ups of detail and the vast panoramas, the quick cutting and glacially slow set pieces.

Perhaps another reason for such a perception is the film's violence, considering Hollywood conventions in place at the time. Eastwood has remarked that Leone's ignorance of industry taboos against framing shooter and victim together allowed him to achieve a more realistic effect.[5] Without doubt, although modest in comparison, Leone's over-the-top shoot-outs and high body counts paved the way for Peckinpah's bloodier, ultra-violent action in *The Wild Bunch* a few years later. But as *A Fistful*'s Silvanito observes at one point, 'It's like playing cowboys and Indians.' Even in the very first of the cycle, the self-consciousness is implausibly extreme in scenes such as the prolonged beating administered to No Name, the single-handed slaughter of the military at the river by Ramón and the endless shooting, astronomical body count and prolonged burn time when the Baxters are exterminated as they exit their torched headquarters to the insane glee of the Rojos. For all the 'realism', the self-conscious stylisation and sense of an authorial presence interposed between the audience and action are overwhelming. The iconic style, the musical commentary and heightened sound, the garish lighting and theatrical framing, these create an apt expressionist spectacle for Leone's archetypal and absurdist characters.

Heroes and Villain

'I don't want to be a hero – I just want the money': Rod Steiger's Juan in *A Fistful of Dynamite* speaks for most of Leone's people. There are no cowboys in Leone's West, only bounty hunters, bandits and drifters. As the films escalated in size, so too did the monetary stakes in their elaborate games. In the first *Dollars* film, No Name goes back and forth clipping hundreds from the gangs; the bounty killers in the second deal in thousands; the buried treasure of the third is in the hundreds of thousands. In the last two Westerns, the wealth becomes emblematic of national destinies – the land with its precious water in *Once Upon a Time in the West* is the ground of the American dream, the untold wealth of Juan's bank in *A Fistful of Dynamite* is revealed as its imprisoned Mexican revolutionaries.

But in the land of the blind, the one-eyed man is king. In a landscape peopled by the morally blinkered, a modicum of virtue qualifies one for an incipient heroism.

Eastwood's hero is only rarely disinterested in his motives. But where all coexist in the same grey world, actions that suggest a morally positive outcome stand out, even if taken for personal reasons rather than in defence of community. Implicit in the first two *Dollars* films, the rejection of traditional Western stereotypes is a major focus in *The Good, the Bad and the Ugly*, where the simplistic labelling of the title is ironic, to be undercut by the nuanced characterisations. But the struggle is not between the civilised and the savage: Leone's frontier is one where everyone appears corrupt, but where fine distinctions can still be made. The one saving value of Leone's dark West is friendship, the interrogated value – ambiguous, expedient, comically unstable – that runs through the films and brightens its principals.

Leone's West is often generalised as a Boschian hell, a brutalised medieval world of immorality. In part, this perception arises from the blackness of his gothic villains, typically coded as satanic in the unbalanced heavies played by Volonté in the first two films. As leader of the Rojo clan, Ramón becomes feverish as he machine-guns an army. *For a Few Dollars More* features a diabolical Indio who raped the colonel's sister, and betrays and kills his own men. Escaping jail, he bids his cellmate 'Hasta luego – *Amigo*', as he kills him. Smoking marijuana, he often seems transfixed by memories of his own evil. Indio typically empties his gun into his victim, a sign of his psychotic uncontrollability. After he slaughters a man's wife and baby, Indio offers the husband a straightforward duel, reflecting his certainty that he is the superior gunman. In the film's finale, no such offer is made to Mortimer, whose weapon lies on the ground: 'Just try', says the fiendish Indio as his hand hovers over his weapon.

The myth's signifiers of a savage threat to civilisation, Indians are completely missing. In Leone, the wilderness and its brutishness have invaded the community itself. The thrust is to see all in savage dress, a West defined without progress. Death rules: the logic of the action and imagery of the films is to see the frontier as a vast cemetery.

Community

The absence of women is the most telling comment on the world depicted in the *Dollars* trilogy. Leone's avowed interest was in an epic cinema, the province of which 'by definition, is a masculine universe'.[6] Paradoxically, his one true epic in fact features Claudia Cardinale's Jill as Woman and earth mother, the supreme signifier of the coming civilisation. Like both Peckinpah and Eastwood, Leone was often criticised for having his women endure rapes – as in *Once Upon a Time in the West* and *A Fistful of Dynamite*. But Jill's coerced sex with Frank is less the violation of a helpless woman than a case of epic transcendence. It is only sex, after all; she will live to fight – and triumph – another day. Dramatically, the moment further defines the same character who gets off the train, only to discover that no one is there to meet her. Girding her loins, she marches to the train station, then through it onto the busy main street of Flagstone, Leone's camera and the reverential Morricone score swooping up in awe above the building to celebrate her arrival on the stage of the emerging America.

Law in Leone is also largely non-existent. Sheriffs are rare, generally corrupt or ineffectual. In *A Fistful of Dollars*, one of the Baxters sporting a badge accuses No Name of having murdered the bullies who had insulted his mule; No Name suggests he bury them. In *For a Few Dollars More*, he goes further, stripping the lawman who had alerted

Red's friends to his badge. With tongue firmly in cheek, No Name (and Leone) reminds us of the classical Western: 'Isn't the sheriff supposed to be courageous, loyal and above all honest?' In *Once Upon a Time in the West*, Keenan Wynn's marshal impotently conducts the auction that threatens to cheat Jill of her American dream.

As with the law, so with the church. Leone frequently employs religious iconography ironically, to underline the absence of spiritual values. In *For a Few Dollars More*, Mortimer is introduced reading a bible and mistaken for a clergyman until his fellow traveller spots the guns. Indio holes up in a church, from whose pulpit he delivers his 'parable of the carpenter' concerning the El Paso bank's disguised vault. In *The Good, the Bad and the Ugly*, Tuco attacks his judgmental brother for escaping into the clergy and leaving him to cope with their family. In *Dynamite*, Juan maintains a small altar to the bank at Mesa Verde he plans to rob, but also wears a cross that he bitterly abandons when his children are killed. The towns in the *Dollars* films evidence no communal life, rituals or rites that affirm the progress of a civilised world. The absence of women, law, religion and culture make for a wilderness where savagery and greed can flower. Ordinary people exist as nervous, powerless bystanders.

As in Ford, the family is a central value in Leone, but it is a value lost, corrupted or destroyed, a structuring absence.[7] *A Fistful of Dollars* presents San Miguel as divided between two murderous family clans, with Marisol's holy family helpless in the middle. All of the films feature the slaughter of idealised Leone families; in *Dynamite*, it is Juan's children who die. Both *For a Few Dollars More* and *Once Upon a Time in the West* are driven by the obsession to avenge the past violation of the family, the narratives structured round the intensifying hallucinatory re-enactment of the event. None of the films actually represent the formation of a new family. But *Once Upon a Time*, if unable to pair the ripe Jill with either a dying Cheyenne or exhausted Harmonica, ends with a promise of the matriarch-to-be offering water to the new America.

Friendship remains the one communal value that prevails, however ambiguously. A primary source of the films' dramatic appeal, the bond is interrogated by Leone as the site of tricks and betrayals, in a parody of the treachery of the villains of the piece. The bond is typically of the moment, a product of need rather than commitment. The rapport and bonhomie that grows between Colonel Mortimer and Monco, suggesting a mellow surrogate father and son relationship, brightens *For a Few Dollars More* considerably, but nevertheless ends with a business-like parting of the ways.

Landscape

For a Few Dollars More opens with an extreme long shot of a wide vista – a broad, flat sandy plain with foothills and misty mountains beyond. It is a neutral image, without particular beauty or cruelty, functioning primarily as a vast stage on which a small exemplary vignette is played out almost immediately: the ambush of an unsuspecting rider in the far distance. This, we are to understand, is the way of the world.

In the first two films, relatively little action is set in open country. At the outset, the heroes are framed riding out of the desert and into the community, where the action plays out. In *Fistful*, San Miguel is the main location but for the ambush at the river, a Brechtian mock battle staged in a cemetery, and the removal of Marisol to the Rojo's outlying small house. The latter action opens the film up briefly, with No Name riding out to dispatch her numerous captors, effect the family's escape and then elude the gang in the surrounding ravines and foothills. Although action moves frequently in *For a Few Dollars More*, the settings shift from Tucumari to White Rocks to El Paso to Santa Cruz to Agua Caliente, with little time spent in transit and correspondingly little action in the wilderness. In both *The Good, the Bad and the Ugly* and *A Fistful of Dynamite*, the openness of the West is stressed far more, but less as an image of freedom than as a setting for war.

In general, Leone's landscape is dry, dusty and dirty, the riders throwing up clouds behind them as they navigate parched riverbeds, rocky ravines and scruffy prairie empty of everything but sand and sagebrush. Some critics see the landscape in traditional generic terms as a hostile environment that accounts for the brutalised and violent inhabitants. Although plausible, this analysis obscures the fact that Leone's landscape is not especially bleak or threatening compared to the classic American examples of Boetticher or Mann. Rather, it is a case of vacancy, of absent positives, of landscape *sans* the potential for the sublime and monumental, the uplifting signifier of pioneer nobility. Thus the spectacular quotations of Ford's revered Monument Valley in *Once Upon a Time* provide a radical contrast to his normal uninspiring terrain. Green pastoral sites are rare, although the end of *The Good, the Bad and the Ugly* hints at vegetation, as if to celebrate Blondie's good fortune. Farms or pioneer homesteads are few. The McBains' farm is one such Edenic garden, the ironic site of their slaughter at the outset of Leone's epic. Generally, landscape is rarely even picturesque. The Spanish mountains and prairies of Almeria contribute to the strangeness of the Italian Western's frontier, a vacant environment for characters who are equally empty.

A Fistful of Dollars (1964)

Leone's debut is a case study in iconic purity. The style is immediately defined in the credits' aggressive pop art montage of graphics and sound – a musical chairs of death, with the vibrant silhouettes of the riders shooting and then being shot, the echoing gunfire and beat of horses' hooves, the lonely whistle and choir. Life as a cycle of combat, killing, death. Yet the film opens on signs of spirituality and life. There is a close shot on a donkey's hooves, as the lone rider enters the town like Christ, going to the well for water. There, No Name is introduced in a defining moment. He witnesses the brutal melodrama played out, the holy family abused, little Jesus running from the gunshots, the enslaved mother, Marisol (Marianne Koch), the helpless husband humiliated by the mountainous Chico. The scene is an exemplary little vignette of life's injustice, with the child's plaintive cries playing as if in quotation marks ('Mama!'), a crying out for heroic intervention. But our not-so-noble hero turns away when Chico stares, then catches Marisol's eye and begins to smile until she slams her window shutters closed.

The stranger's passive spectatorship here emphasises the film's style of iconic theatre, an effect that is heightened by the denuded streets, a stage on which the signs of an inhospitable world multiply and darken. No Name passes a noose that hangs from a leafless tree (in *Yojimbo*, the samurai's path was crossed by a dog, its jaws clamped on a human hand), and then watches as a blind horseman, a sign pinned to his back bidding 'Adios Amigo', rides on past. Next comes the town's chattering bell-ringer to define San Miguel further as a town of funerals where one is either wealthy or dead. Like a manic jester, the morbid figure gleefully scampers about as he asks if the rider has come to 'sell lead in exchange for gold'.

Such signs and references, together with the desolate streets (an effect undoubtedly encouraged by the low budget), create an air ripe for the growth of metaphor – town as Death, a gothic construction. As No Name rides by, we catch glimpses of ordinary folks huddling indoors shrouded in shadows. Meanwhile, more bullies loll about waiting for the stranger to approach so they can terrorise him too, his mule stampeded by their gunshots. No Name is left hanging from a sign, crucified, as the burro rides out from under him, and he finally speaks, greeting Silvanito (José Calvo), the cantina owner: 'Hello'. Another talker whose chatter highlights the stranger's laconic style, this sympathetic character querulously extends some charity in the form of food, drink and advice ('*Go!*'), and adds to the gloom. The town is full of widows and the only work is the undertaker's, he informs us, pulling the shutters open like a theatre curtain to reveal the grizzled Piripero (Joseph Egger) happily building his coffins out in the warm sunlight, the window frame setting off the image like a medieval painting celebrating Death.

Images like these point to Leone's achievement in appropriating the genre and de-familiarising it. Leone's visual sensibility was crucial in this process, vivid in the casting decisions based on iconic features and body language. A case in point is the director's pursuit of Marianne Koch, an established German star who had also worked in Hollywood. As the fair Marisol, Koch has virtually no dialogue, belying her crucial role in the iconic design and the character's symbolic weight. Koch's face is quietly effective, her stoic mask and silence curiously in tune with the stranger's.

Other characters also chosen for type and physiognomy contribute further to a theatre of signs: the coffin-maker's classic cowboy geezer face, à la Gabby Hayes; Chico's bullish girth; the spear-carriers of both corrupt families, essences of avarice and brutishness. Leone's system reaches its highest pitch in theatrical set pieces, like the swap that is organised to return Marisol to Ramón in return for one of the Baxter sons, interrupted by the inconsolable child's clutching of his mother and their enforced separation. Staged and scored with the ceremony and brio that characterise Leone's operatic gunfights, the action is epic and symbolic, an exemplary melodrama of signs and meanings, an allegory of motherhood, injustice, fate.

Leone's Western is detached from America and history, its conventions inflected by a European, Italian and Catholic sensibility. This is especially visible in *Fistful* in the handling of the hero's saviour function. Always implicit in the basic formula of the embattled community, so beloved of Ford, the scenario here strips the character of traditional heroic associations by insisting on his rascally and mercenary motives. Thus much is made of No Name's going back and forth between the Rojos and the Baxters, hiring on as gunfighter for both and mockingly betraying both, apt payback in a town that is defined by deceit and greed.

Yet the action complicates this amorality by having the character re-enact extended biblical vignettes. Thus he rescues the embryonic community by effecting the escape of the holy family, and consequently endures a Christ-like suffering. Viciously beaten, No Name crawls agonisingly out of the Rojo stronghold in an extended Calvary, and leaves the compound in a coffin. Receiving word that Silvanito is enduring torture rather than betray him, the character leaves the cave where he has been recovering and prepares to face Ramón. The resurrection is completed symbolically when No Name emerges from the smoke of the exploding Rojo stronghold to defeat Ramón through a mysterious invincibility. Ramón is constructed as an anti-Christ who delivers false sermons. No Name turns this use of performance against Ramón by resurrecting and posing dead soldiers in the cemetery and suggesting that they witnessed his perfidy. This theatrical set peopled by corpses is an inspired conceit (a scene not in *Yojimbo*), in which both families jockey to reach the two men, and Ramón finally wins by killing them (again).

The enemy of love, Ramón has made Marisol his concubine, and target-practises on armour that he shoots in the heart. It is his insistence that he can kill No Name in a duel with such shots that is his undoing. To gain advantage by unnerving Ramón with another bit of theatre, the stranger has installed his own armour beneath his poncho. Absorbing Ramón's increasingly desperate gunfire, he dies and rises a half-dozen times, additional Messianic coding. Finally revealing the ruse, he offers a duel to test whether his six-gun or Ramón's rifle can be loaded and fired first. This scene has its source in one of Leone's favourite films, Howard Hawks's *Rio Bravo*, where John Wayne explains to Ricky Nelson's slick young gunfighter that he carries a rifle because 'some were faster than me with a short gun'. Like Wayne, Ramón had earlier killed a distant retreating rider with a crack rifle shot, but against No Name he stands no chance. As in the traditional Western, superior expertise serves ethical behaviour, however attenuated the latter may be.

Despite No Name's biblical aura, Leone's achievement is to create a community largely without positives. Ironically, the only 'intimate' gesture occurs when Ramón forces a kiss on Marisol to assert ownership of the woman in the eyes of 'the Americano' who has joined his gang. Later, an irritated No Name explains why he is helping Marisol: 'I knew someone like you once – and there was no one to help.' Rescuing the family and finding himself in the debt of the meek – Silvanito and Piripero – No Name acts in defence of the community. He is on the side of the angels, if reluctantly. Yet honour is a side effect rather than a principle; action is personal, gratuitous, existential.

For a Few Dollars More (1965)

Paradoxically, although he goes from being a nomadic Westerner in the first film to a bounty killer in the second, the humanising of The Man With No Name increases in *For a Few Dollars More*. Leone and screenwriter Luciano Vincenzoni, who would work with the director on all of his remaining Westerns, generated a scenario for the follow-up to his successful debut that took no chances. The Eastwood hero – Monco here – would now have a partner, a second hero with stature and expertise. The games and deceptions played out with villains, the tricks and insults, could now be doubled internally between sidekicks. To balance Eastwood, Leone found Lee Van Cleef, veteran Western character actor whose hawk-like visage he thought ideal for the righteous Colonel Mortimer. As with Eastwood, Van Cleef would enjoy a fairy-tale success, jump-starting a stalled career to become a European star.

Whistling, the striking of a match, then a rifle shot. These are the sound effects for the little show, the killing of the tiny rider in the far distance, which opens the film. The figure falls, the horse shying away. The vignette is neither explained nor connected to the narrative that will unfold: it is there as a defining sign of the film's murderous world. The

José Calvo and Eastwood in *A Fistful of Dollars*: friendship the one communal value

sounds we hear amount to the signature of No Name, implicating him as the killer who ambushes casually and cold-bloodedly from a safe distance. The text declares: 'Where life had no value, death, sometimes, had its price. That is why the bounty killers appeared.'

Announcing a rhyming strategy that will dominate the film, Leone introduces his heroic pair in tandem scenes that stress their equality from the outset. In back-to-back sequences, they both coerce information about their prey, kill a wanted man and collect their bounty from the law. The two are an amusing study in contrasts. Dressed formally in a black suit with caped coat and hat, the comfortable, stylish Mortimer reads a bible on the train that he forces to stop at Tucumari. An older, bemused figure with the air of a Southern gentleman, he apologises to a naked lady in the bath as he pursues his quarry. Constructed as a military man, the colonel has an arsenal from which he chooses appropriate weapons to shoot the fleeing man's horse out from under him, and then kill him while safely out of his opponent's range.

Cutting to Eastwood, who is thus assigned a secondary status, the film ushers in Monco as he enters White Rocks in a rainstorm. We see the defining signs of No Name: the wet, scruffy, unshaven mask, the poncho and cheroot. Despite pronounced differences of appearance and approach, the same playfulness is evident in Monco's attitude. Interrupting his man's poker game, he wordlessly deals them both a hand that he wins, the stakes 'your life'. Red Cavanaugh tries to draw but is beaten into submission. Three comrades who now materialise demanding that the stranger give up are immediately killed, as is Red with a casual snap shot. Ever ready to repeat success, Leone was replaying the killings from the beginning of *A Fistful of Dollars*.

In both the game-playing with Mortimer's weapons and Monco's poker, there is a sardonic comment on the inferiority of the competition. This lethal competency unites the two, although No Name's style is the more physical. In any case, the parallel scenes and their promise of competition are reinforced with the escape of Indio (Gian Maria Volonté) from jail, and the appearance of a wanted poster, the likeness of the bandit in a characteristic manic laugh. Once the poster is up, we see No Name, cheroot in mouth, taking it in and looking up to the reward amount ($10,000), followed by Mortimer puffing on his pipe, whose gaze in turn looks down to 'Dead or alive'. As gunfire explodes, the editing crosscuts at high speed in rhythm with the echoing shots between the poster and Mortimer in giant close-ups of face, and eventually just eyes. A small tour de force of great punch, Leone's montage links the three principals and suggests an obsessive tie between Mortimer and Indio.

The isolation of No Name as a hero in the original had made for a more schematic orchestration of events. Here the doubling of heroes fills in Leone's canvas, and the balance shifts from cynicism towards a more benign world. Despite the sign of ambush that opens the drama, the rape that is replayed in flashbacks and the demented laughter of its disturbed villain, the comical edginess of the film's central relationship recalls Hawks, one of the classicists Leone most admired. Although driven more by revenge and profit than the tacit code of honour that animates the characters of *Rio Bravo* and *El Dorado* (1966), the odd couple here are similarly refreshing in their professionalism and bemused rivalry.

But it is certainly understandable why Eastwood and Leone finally parted company. From carrying the picture in *A Fistful of Dollars*, the actor was stepping aside to make room for a co-star in the sequel. With the addition of an established star in Eli Wallach for *The Good, the Bad and the Ugly*, both Eastwood and Van Cleef would find themselves elbowed into the shadows by his clownish and more sympathetic character. It followed that Eastwood would not be ready to join a quartet of stars for a fourth Leone Western.

Be that as it may, by having Monco share the stage with the colonel, Leone found his theme and the film's spine, and achieved a nice dramatic density in a relationship involving respect and suspicion, commitment and double-dealing. The burning question, as they scheme against both Indio and each other, is whether they are ultimately complementary or at war. Are they a team or opposed? But for the audience the differences of style and strategy may seem a function of age rather than value: 'Boy' and 'Old Man', cheroots and a pipe (as opposed to Indio's pot), arrogant confidence and quiet certainty, quick action versus careful planning.

The competition comes into focus when the pair arrives in El Paso, site of the West's mega-bank. Recalling the Rojos and the Baxters, who had faced each other from opposite ends of town, the two discover themselves ensconced in hotels on opposite sides of the main drag, both spying on the bank below. Leone develops the contrasts further when Monco tries to bully Mortimer into leaving town. After besmirching each other's boots, Monco shows off his expertise by repeatedly shooting the colonel's hat further and further into the distance. Symbolically, he is shooting the colonel out of town, but practically speaking, he is only shooting himself out of range and bullets. Finally, the colonel draws his weapon and balances the books by now shooting the other's hat high into the air, where he keeps it aloft with his long-barrelled weapon.

As befits his grey hairs, Mortimer takes the lead in suggesting a partnership in their pursuit of Indio. They toast their alliance with a bemused air – 'No tricks'. Teasing the colonel, Monco asks, 'Were you ever young?' To which Mortimer replies: 'Yup, and just as reckless as you.' But fingering his pocket watch, he recalls something that had happened to make him realise how precious life is. Monco enquires further, but backs off: 'Or is the question indiscreet?' Leone enjoys presenting such diplomatic and rational killers against the emotional and psychological mess that is Indio, all drug-induced trances, haunting memories and compulsive violence.

The contrast between controlled and uncontrolled behaviour is especially prominent when Mortimer delivers a stunningly gratuitous insult to Indio's hunchbacked henchman, Klaus Kinski's Wild, by striking a match off his unshaven cheek to light his pipe, then plucking the hunchback's cigar away to finish the job, as the latter twitches violently. The business of smoking, of giving and getting a light, also a Hawks motif, runs through the film, often involving enemies uneasily leaning close. But Leone takes it to an inspired level with this grotesque provocation that nevertheless fails, confirming that the gang's agenda in El Paso must be too important to risk public killing.

The jockeying of the two bounty killers develops further with more scheming and badinage, undercover work ('You on the outside, me on the inside?') and double-crossing. This intricate play of moves and counter-moves, of pacts and cheating, constitutes the fabric of the film's society. Finishing Wild, who had sought satisfaction for his disgrace, Mortimer joins Indio's band by opening the bank's strongbox. All alignments are brief: Monco breaks into the room where the money is hidden to find Mortimer there already. While both are attempting to deceive Indio, they are also trying to one-up each other. The parallelism continues when both are caught and beaten simultaneously by the gang, a typically protracted scene of violence that Leone choreographs in a punch-for-punch rhyme on the pair, accompanied by giant close-ups of the demented laughter of the gang members. More treachery follows when Indio kills off associates and then frees the bounty hunters to eliminate the remaining gang members, whom he orders to pursue them. In the land of the double-cross, Indio is king.

Insisting on the equality of his heroes as the denouement plays out, Leone has Monco and Mortimer prowling opposite sides of a street, jumpy at a cat's false alarm, more familiar Hawks business. Moments later, they both dispatch a gang member at their back, and each then take out two more, employing typically guileful methods. Mortimer dislodges a wagon with a crack shot that rolls into a barn expelling a pair, whom he guns down. Monco enters a building, followed seconds later by baddies, who fire gleefully at his poncho, only to have him craftily blaze away from a rotating desk chair.

As with *A Fistful*'s Ramón, Indio is coded ironically in terms of Christian iconography, using a church as a blasphemous site for unholy sermons and the massacre of another of the director's helpless families. Leone poses them like a religious painting, a madonna and child whose execution Indio orders. There then follows a duel with the husband, in which the cessation of a pocket watch's chimes is the signal to fire, the first of the classic Leone operas. The music begins over the chimes and builds to a full crescendo, followed by sudden silence as the chimes slowly wind down. The visual orchestration matches the music's intensity, cutting repeatedly between giant close-ups of the duellists and the feverish faces of Indio's gang members on the sidelines. With the chimes silent and his opponent dead, Indio urgently inhales a marijuana cigarette, as if desperate to lose himself after his cruelties.

Paradoxically, however, the drug only activates memories of the event that damaged Indio psychically, and that he obsessively rehearses. To a strained, discordant, high-tension score and heavy breathing, we see Indio's face spying through a window streaming with rain on a young couple reclining on a bed; an intimate setting, but they are chaste sweethearts. They look at a matched set of pocket watches containing cameo photo inserts. Indio enters, shoots the youth, then strips the girl of her nightgown. It is the first of the flashbacks in the film that will successively provide more information about the past events, creating mystery and anchoring the audience more deeply in the film. With its further use in both *Once Upon a Time in the West* and *Dynamite*, the device would become a Leone trademark. Providing a Freudian spin, the flashbacks give the narrative psychological depth and establish key objects and cues. Here the watch and chimes are the signifiers of the past and the primal trauma that haunts both men. The final flashback reveals to us the ultimate outcome of Indio's violation of the girl, her suicide.

With the past laid bare, the final duel begins, but a distracted Mortimer loses his weapon. Indio offers his mockery of a duel, and the chimes run down as Mortimer eyes his gun on the ground. But the partnership is not over. A second watch begins to chime as Monco appears to rearm the colonel and take a seat to watch the show: 'Now we start.' The circular arena, so reminiscent of Boetticher's bullrings, emphasises the formality of

The colonel (Lee Van Cleef) and Indio (Gia Maria Volonte): 'Who are you?'

the proceedings. Echoing the duel in the church, Leone and Morricone deliberately build another operatic crescendo, the triangular cutting alternating between long shots within the circle and extreme close-ups on the faces of the three men. The chimes peter out, the moment of truth comes and Indio dies. 'Bravo', pronounces Monco.

One of the pleasures of this extremely satisfying sequel is the small growth we may discern in The Man With No Name. Monco cannot know that the colonel will renounce any reward monies, that he has not lost booty in helping to provide a level playing field. This suggests a regard for his partner that eclipses self-interest. But in any case, the colonel informs him: 'My boy, you become rich.' Monco happily commences to load dead bodies and count up his profit. Mortimer rides off alone, chuckling at his partner's maths problems, having to kill a final baddie to correct his sums. Leone's camera cranes up to frame the wagon of corpses pulling out towards the desert. The partnership is over – 'Maybe next time,' says the colonel.

That Monco and Mortimer make a team in a world defined by betrayal gives this *Dollars* film a more pronounced optimism – despite the corpses and cash – than most Leone critics grant. Amid grotesque surroundings, there is the residual promise of a civilised world where qualities such as honour, duty and loyalty are not wholly impossible. It is unquestionably Mortimer's world: *For a Few Dollars More* begins and ends with the colonel; Monco is the enabler, but it is Mortimer who rights the wrongs. Monco is finally the audience, as his ironic 'Bravo' underlines. Earlier, he had watched in disbelief as Mortimer had struck his match on Wild's cheek and later had beaten him to the draw with a typically crafty 'contraption', as Monco called the lethal toys, a quick-release derringer hidden up the sleeve. Thereafter, the mysterious colonel and the curious Indio had sat opposite each other, the latter asking, 'Who are you?' In Leone's second spaghetti, it had been Colonel Mortimer – the man *with* the name – who had been the magnificent stranger.

The Good, the Bad and the Ugly (1966)

It is Tuco who pre-empts the show in the third film. With Eli Wallach, who had appeared in prestige pictures such as Elia Kazan's *Baby Doll* (1962) and John Huston's *The Misfits* (1966), as well as genre films like *The Magnificent Seven*, Leone had landed an established and substantial star. Once again, his Tuco rather than No Name would open the film and end it, providing a key source of its energy and humour. Leone was explicit in defining his aim to interrogate stereotypes:

> what interested me was on the one hand to demystify the adjectives, on the other to show the absurdity of war. What do 'good', 'bad' and 'ugly' really mean? We all have some bad in us, some ugliness, some good ... As for the Civil War which the characters encounter, in my vision it is useless, stupid: it does not involve a 'good cause' ...[8]

Reflecting his increasing mastery and expanding narrative approach, Leone opens the film with three vignettes introducing the archetypes of the title. Tuco's is a small prose poem – no more than three minutes – of giant close-ups on hard faces intercut with extreme long shots as three killers approach to a tune of whistling winds, howling coyote, trudging footsteps and a mindlessly banging sign. Reaching their goal, they crowd through a doorway with guns drawn, whereupon shots ring out and Wallach crashes through a storefront window with a gun in one hand and a chicken leg in the other. The frame freezes and the title in cursive appears – '*il brutto*', or the Ugly, evidently a creature of violent appetites.

Working backwards, Leone next introduces the Bad with an ironic recycling of the beginning of *Shane*, a favourite film. Looking up from his chores, a farm boy spots the dark silhouette of a rider in the far distance, the shot holding as he rides into the yard and dismounts almost as slowly as had the classic's killer, Jack Palance. The distant silhouette will recur in the doorway of the house, which is framed by two arched entrances to connecting rooms leading to the kitchen where his quarry sits. The extreme deep-focus shots, the sharp black-on-white, the silence and deliberate pace (this vignette runs for ten minutes) all provide a vivid contrast to Tuco's explosive entrance.

Lee Van Cleef here is the sinister professional, villainously signifying 'bad' when he sneers an effective threat – 'Nice family'. With the same professional aplomb that Mortimer had displayed, he extorts the name he seeks, kills the farmer to fulfil his contract, pockets the thousand dollars the farmer had offered and then kills the son who appears. Leone then has the killer return to his employer, whom he also murders – had he not implicitly accepted another contract with the farmer's thousand? It appears that Angel Eyes is a corporate professional, all business. Bad, yes, but we cannot but approve of the second killing, which offers a nice poetic justice – he who orders murder at long distance is murdered in his bed. Another frame freezes – '*il cattivo*', the Bad.

The last vignette introduces the Good, who will be called Blondie but whom we will identify – as the match flares and the cheroot is lit – as the hero of the earlier spaghettis. As in *For a Few Dollars More*, however, the character is again not the lonely hero, as Tuco immediately joins him to co-star in this vignette of twelve minutes. The alignment suggests that the peasant possesses a modicum of goodness too, just as Blondie will shortly reveal an ugly side, such complications and layering clearly Leone's design.

Three gunmen bent on collecting the $2,000 reward for the bandit have Tuco surrounded. If it is not broken, why fix it? Eastwood's character is once again introduced in a display of magical skill and numerous deaths. The bounty hunter takes the noisy, buffoonish Tuco in to face justice, but we shortly discover the con. As endless charges are read in front of Tuco, who sits astride a horse, a noose around his neck, Blondie takes aim and cuts the rope. Tuco will live to see more arrests and rewards. Although it is the Good's chapter, we learn much more about the Ugly. He is the father of all criminals, guilty of every crime from murder to 'raping a virgin of the white race' to cheating at cards. He also has a peasant's taste for aphorisms. There are two kinds of people, he tells Blondie, those who put on the noose and those who do the cutting; he wants a bigger share for risking the noose. He flaunts a crazy edge, actually eating an offered cheroot as punctuation to his venomous promise to pursue double-crossers. After a second try at the scam, during which he needs three shots to slice the hanging rope, Blondie is tired of the complaining and rides off with the bounty, leaving his bound ex-partner deep in the desert minus water or weapon. How good is this Good – '*il buono*'? The shot of him receding into the distance to the tune of Tuco's curses is held to punctuate the end of the overture. Having introduced its heroes, rogues all, the film proper now begins.

The motifs that have been introduced – greed, killing, rascally cruelty – are interwoven throughout. Angel Eyes is brutal, casually slapping a whore until she reveals where Bill Carson, who knows the whereabouts of a missing strongbox, has gone. Meanwhile, Tuco has staggered out of the desert into a gun shop, where he terrorises the timid entrepreneur, jamming the shop's 'closed' sign into his mouth as he leaves. Such small cruelties are nothing, however, compared to the punishment doled out to Blondie shortly – a forced march into the desert with Eastwood hatless and staggering behind the vengeful Tuco, who comfortably rides a high-stepping mount under a fringed parasol.

However, this is a picaresque West, a whimsical frontier of chance encounters, perverse timing and painful reversals. The events as they play out suggest an almost diabolical conspiracy to defeat greedy Tuco. Earlier, a footstep fortuitously heard after the Confederate ordinance outside had passed had saved Blondie from ambush. Thereafter, Tuco's attempt to hang him had been thwarted when a cannonade had brought down the building around them. Now, as Tuco draws his gun to finish off his exhausted opponent, a runaway stagecoach materialises in the distance. Stopped, it reveals numerous Confederate bodies and one dying Bill Carson, who with his next-to-last breath tells Tuco the name of the cemetery where $200,000 is buried and – when the former rushes off for water – gives Blondie the name on the grave.

The partnership is back on. After nearly killing Blondie in the wilderness, Tuco must now resurrect him. Shortly thereafter, the two rogues suffer another of fate's pendulum swings. Decked out in Confederate uniforms, they are arrested by Union troops and find themselves under Angel Eyes, who runs the stockade. Now it is Tuco's turn to suffer, viciously beaten by Angel Eyes to reveal the name of the cemetery. Befitting the film's cynical musical chairs, Angel Eyes then establishes his own partnership with Blondie, who he knows will not give up the name on the grave.

The remaining plot plays out further variations on the themes of partnership and competition, loyalty and betrayal. When Blondie finds himself travelling with Angel Eyes and four henchmen, he searches out Tuco to better the odds. The gang killed off and Angel Eyes having vanished, they are 'together again', as Tuco puts it. This final partnership will hold as they make their way through the war-torn countryside, pausing to succour a dying Union officer whose dream is to blow up a bridge. Working as a team, the pair undertakes the task in part to clear their path. Tuco suggests a trade, his name of the cemetery for Blondie's name on the grave. The swap is made, whereupon at the first opportunity Tuco leaps on a horse and belts off. End of alliance.

Wallach's antic Tuco presides comfortably over a world of deceit and cheating. Leone's West replaces the traditional genre's code of honour with a counter-ideology characterised by double-dealing, game-playing and self-interest. The picaresque form, with its ups and downs, journeys and pauses, pacts and betrayals, provides the perfect ground for this world and its exemplar, the devious peasant bandit ruled by greed. Tuco is a figure of irony, a marionette that life is always cheating. By making him the centre of events and the motor force of his epic, Leone was installing him as the embodiment of the anarchic, two-faced spirit that rules events. He who lives by the con dies by the con, and Tuco dies many deaths – in the play-acting for the bounty but also in the high hopes that are invariably dashed for the big score. After ensuring that Blondie was being cared for in the monastery, Tuco had paused before an icon to pray surreptitiously, nervous that a monk might catch him at it. Investigating the stagecoach's load of dead bodies, he had repeatedly made the cross as he scavenged the bodies; moments later he is bullying the dying Carson for the name on the grave. With Carson dead, he takes his name and borrows his eye-patch, an apt signifier of piracy.

The backdrop of the Civil War allowed Leone to enlarge on his theme of shifting loyalties. This is raised to epic levels when the pair leave the monastery to greet an oncoming troop with Confederate whoops of solidarity, soon chagrined to discover Union soldiers whose blues are covered with dust. Do familial ties go any deeper? The stop at the monastery had featured a bitter reunion between Tuco and his brother, Pablo (Luigi Pistilli), a priest. Quarrelling over who had betrayed whom, the two had come to blows and Tuco had made a silent exit. As with Colonel Mortimer in the earlier film, the scene opens a window on the character's history, helping us to make sense of his needy and suspicious nature. Just how deprived he remains is evident as he and Blondie drive away and he lies, bragging – 'My brother, he's crazy about me.' Having eavesdropped on the painful exchange, Blondie opines that 'after a meal there's nothing like a good cigar', and offers his half-smoked cheroot.

In *Fistful*, Silvanito had proved a stand-up guy, giving No Name a hand and coming forward with a shotgun when the Rojos had threatened to kill Marisol's husband. The beatings Silvanito had taken had triggered the stranger's return and the end of the town's bosses. With *For a Few Dollars More*, Leone had foregrounded the theme of friendship in a West again defined by mercenary and savage impulses. The working out of that relationship, the various attempts both to betray and honour it, gives the film its warmth and pleasure. Monco's final act, intervening to ensure a fair fight between Indio and the Colonel, was that of a friend.

Are Blondie and Tuco friends? Originally partners in crime, thereafter the two had joined in a rascally exchange, each abandoning the other in the desert. They had ended up in the monastery, with Tuco shedding crocodile tears at Blondie's bedside: 'We're all alone in the world.' Friendship on Leone's frontier is as unstable a relationship as other forms of alliance. In this, it appears a more flexible and complex bond, more 'realistic' than conventional notions allow, in that it can accommodate both respect and warmth, however unspoken, as well as lies and betrayals. There is a kind of reverse romanticising here, an inverse macho sentimentality. Leone seems to suggest that tricks and treachery in the service of self are a signifier of a more honest maturity, as well as a source of energy and amusing competition that helps to make life tolerable. It is evident in the scene where Tuco looks down the road with relish as they ride their buckboard away from the monastery, coming alive at the prospect of whatever lies ahead. What are brothers for if not to betray you? We are close here to Peckinpah's idealisation of the whore as the most honest representative of humanity.

Fundamental to these relationships, and to Leone's films generally, is the idea of life as game. This notion is perhaps logical in a barren wilderness society where competition is an ongoing affair. In an existential landscape the ultimate gamble is for survival. About to eat at Angel Eyes' table at the POW camp, Tuco suddenly pauses, and Angel Eyes smiles and eats a spoonful off the other's plate. A man cannot be too careful in Leone's West, where even treachery à la the Borgias is possible. Later, when Tuco is having a bath and the killer (Al Mulloch) – whose gargoyle's mask in extreme close-up opens the film – reappears to crow over finally catching up with him after eight years, Tuco promptly shoots him with a gun hidden in the suds. The scam for collecting the bounty and then rescuing the wanted man to repeat the process is another game, albeit a dangerous one, as his replacement finds out when Tuco interrupts Blondie about to cut the rope. 'Sorry, Shorty,' drawls Blondie.

In Leone's terms, war is also a kind of game. With its episodic structure and merce-nary tricksters as heroes, Leone's inspired conceit was to employ the Civil War as the setting through which the two picaros must make their way. Blundering into it, our heroes find the conflict to be variously an irrelevance, a nuisance, a spectacle and a tragic affair. The first hint of war's shocking costs is provided by the soldier whose lower half has been amputated, who works Angel Eyes for coins in exchange for information, before vaulting himself forward into a saloon, like a fugitive from a Buñuel film. But for our 'two magnificent tramps', as the project was originally titled, their first encounter – apart from the grisly stagecoach in the desert – comes with the visit to the monastery, parts of which have been turned into a field hospital. Leone employs the same sad bal-lad over all the war scenes, introducing it here, where even Tuco expresses awe at the rows of wounded on both sides of the dark rooms through which they pass. At Ander-sonville, the Union's infamous POW camp, Leone emphasises the madness of war by including a scene in which the camp orchestra is ordered to play the theme 'with feel-ing' to cover the sounds of firing squads and torture.

Leone has said that the Civil War did not involve 'a good cause'; slavery's subjects might have insisted on a different perspective, but not a single black face is in evidence. Dramatising the Civil War at such length and dismissing it as a site of wasted lives, as Blondie does, without addressing its politics, is an approach perhaps available only to a foreign director. On the other hand, American film-makers for the most part have also ignored the event. Traditionally, the Western is staged in the three decades *after* the Civil War. An ideological perspective might argue the omission as another form of America's institutionalised racism, a fear of projects that occur at the intersection of history, regional loyalties, politics and box office. The Civil War united America and in so doing divided it, a seismic event that drove fault lines deep into the nation, an operation that left scars still unhealed today. But for Leone, it is a defining moment of life's absurdity. Evidencing this cynicism, Leone here exercises his extraordinary visual imagination to mount the conflict on a spectacular scale precisely to suggest its futility and tragic devastation.

As in John Ford's one direct foray into the Civil War, *The Horse Soldiers*, Leone has his Union officers posing for a photographer. For Ford, it is an opportunity to record their awareness of a historic moment in the nation's progress, but Leone, the inveterate ironist, captures them memorialising a disaster. As with Ford's rendering of a specific mission behind enemy lines, Leone's bloody battle is exemplary, standing in for the larger conflict. Yet Leone was not making a Civil War film so much as an anti-Civil War film. He was out to correct myths – that the South had been the more brutal, and that the war was a glorious victory for a united America: 'I wanted to show human imbecil-ity in a picaresque film where I would also show the reality of war.' The nation had been founded on violence that 'neither literature nor the cinema had ever properly shown'.[9]

If Tuco is an imbecile, Leone suggests that the bandit is protected by his peasant dog-eat-dog philosophy from the collective insanity of war – the slaughter of far greater 'imbeciles' who follow codes of patriotism, loyalty and duty. Correcting Ford, Leone catalogues disillusioned officers, maimed soldiers, field after field strewn with bodies, endless cannonades. The last image is of a beautiful dying youth, a victim that even the hardened Blondie responds to by covering him with his coat and sharing his cheroot. Leone's iconic instincts raise the boy to a signifier of the death of American innocence. Leaving, Blondie dons a poncho that formally marks the return of the mysterious stranger of the previous films for the saga's last act.

When the grand finale comes and the Good, the Bad and the Ugly take up their tri-angular design within the fateful circle at film's end, Tuco's gun is revealed to be empty. Is Blondie's act here – like Monco's in the earlier film – that of a friend? Who was Blondie protecting? Himself first – since he could now concentrate on eliminating Angel Eyes as all three draw – but surely also Tuco, who was being shielded by being sidelined. Yet as if to prevent any sentimental notions, with Angel Eyes dead, Blondie rides off leaving Tuco balanced precariously on an unstable cross with the inevitable noose round his neck. His share of the booty awaits if the thief can survive. After an eternity a shot rings out, saving Tuco. The film ends as it began, marked by death, greedy appetites and a ras-cally cruelty. As if to correct John Ford, Leone's characters, images and action all seem to assert, 'this is what the world is really like'.

Once Upon a Time in the West (1968)

The theme of death had been everywhere in the *Dollars* films. In the first, a noose marks the trail into the town whose most cheerful citizen is its undertaker. *For a Few Dollars More* features the bounty killers in a landscape 'where life had no value'. In *The Good, the Bad and the Ugly*, the theme receives epic treatment in the Civil War slaughter and the final setting's huge cemetery. With *Once Upon a Time in the West*, he was embracing Ford's central subject of the coming of civilisation, but the mordant Leone inevitably installs death as the foundation upon which the new America rises, the subtext that gives this extraordinary film its unique character.

Leone's original version runs for two hours and forty-eight minutes, but to many audiences feels much longer. Intensifying the effect of his excruciatingly long con-frontations, the director's design here involves a slow overall pace set by an 'ancient race' of exhausted, deliberate heroes reluctantly making way for the coming modern world. In effect, they are all dead men walking. The all too mortal Morton – 'Mr Choo Choo', as Cheyenne calls him – is the diseased railroad magnate who is rotting on his feet and will not live to realise his dream of seeing the ocean.

For Frank, the crippled capitalist's henchman, Leone had finally achieved his long-standing wish to snare Henry Fonda, icon of America, here to incarnate death itself. For shocks in the popular cinema, few match up to the moment when the camera slowly tracks around the leader of the McBain family's killers who have emerged from the desert like ghosts, to reveal Fonda. Deliberately, he smiles with gentle, sadistic pleasure as he shoots freckle-faced Timmy, the youngest McBain, who stands transfixed by his family's slaughter, the little boy's constant running decisively arrested. The gunshot segues into the whistle of the incoming train that brings Mrs McBain, the sound cut revealing the ultimate source of the violence.

The killing of Timmy that introduces Frank looks forward to a final reprise, before the killer's own death, of earlier devastations of the young, of Harmonica (Charles Bronson) and his long-dead brother. Frank has left his own trail of dead men that Harmonica recites whenever Frank asks who he is. At the end Jill (Claudia Cardinale) will hope for a future with her saviour, but Cheyenne (Jason Robards, Jr) will gently put her in the picture: men like Harmonica have inside them 'something to do with death'. The litany of dead men that Harmonica recites describes his own trail as well as Frank's, a bloody path that he has tracked consumed by the memory of his dead sibling. It was a death in which, with exquisite torture, the killer had made Harmonica an unwilling accomplice. He and Frank are unholy partners in death.

Finally, we have Cheyenne, the charming desperado who comes into the action handcuffed after killing a number of jailers off-stage. He will assist Harmonica in foiling Frank, and he and his men will build the station to receive the train on its arrival. If Frank is a quieter version of Liberty Valance, Ford's most flamboyant villain, Harmonica and Cheyenne are heirs to that director's tradition of sacrificial figures whose efforts help to seal their fate. The logic of the equation works itself out in Morton's mortal wounding of Cheyenne, who gives no sign of his approaching death as he pays a last visit to Jill. She must bring water to the men, he tells her, and having waited out Harmonica's duel with Frank, he wearily makes his goodbye. Moments later he expires in a dusty gully and, as Jill goes out to the railroad workers, Harmonica rides off with his body. As Morricone's score swoops up in a triumphant celebration of American progress, the shot pans away from Jill amid the thirsty labourers to settle on the figures vanishing in the far distance, the shell of a man and the dead body. Inevitably, Leone's vision of the birth of America is ambivalent, a struggle played out between progress and paralysis.

The logic of Leone's structure is nevertheless clear. In the ex-prostitute who came west to help settle it, Jill's character collapses *My Darling Clementine*'s icons, the nurse-turned-schoolmarm of the title and the saloon gal Chihuahua. Positioned as the central figure in the saga, the only woman of substance in Leone's Westerns, Jill is the earth mother, she who brings the water, the fount for the civilisation to come. Audaciously setting the action in Monument Valley, self-consciously entering Ford country, Leone employs his operatic style at full stretch to celebrate, however ambiguously, the historical base of his adopted genre.

Leone was dispensing with the existential heroes of the trilogy. He had originally hoped to signal this directly by having Harmonica dispatch the good, bad and ugly characters before the credits to underline the shift to heroes who are agents of history. However, by this point relations between director and star had deteriorated, and although Van Cleef and Wallach agreed to the cameos, Eastwood would not. The actor was hardly ready to bury The Man With No Name. Leone was forced to fall back on Western icons Jack Elam and Woody Strode, plus Canadian actor Al Mulloch as Knuckles.

These worthies are ushered in with another of the patented elaborate Leone/Morricone image-and-sound constructions, the three materialising as silhouettes framed in extreme deep focus as they invade and occupy the train station to the tune of a creaking windmill, the buzz of a fly, a water's drip and knuckles being cracked. The conceit of building a scene with minimal narrative content – *High Noon*'s three baddies awaiting the train – in such a slow, weighty and self-conscious style, providing each principal

Claudia Cardinale's Jill, the matriarch-to-be, brings the water

with their own defining, comical idiosyncrasy, is a model of post-modern excess. Although his films contain numerous scenes of more conventional style and content, it is passages like these where invention is at its peak that tend to colour Leone's films and to install the outrageous as their norm.

Water is the key motif that runs through the film, Woody Strode's capturing of drops from the station's roof in his hat introducing it in comic fashion. Sweetwater is the name that McBain had chosen for his farm – McBain, 'that loony', as Sam calls him, driving Jill out there 'in the middle of nowhere'. McBain will be at the farm's well – the crux of the matter – when the shots ring out that kill his daughter. On breaking her journey, Jill's first request to the leering way station's bartender (Lionel Stander) is for water, and later Harmonica will also force her to make her own trip to the well, to tempt Frank's men into their attack. The ocean obsesses the disabled Morton, who worships at a painting of its waves. As Leone's saga comes to its end, Jill distributes the precious water, classic symbol of life, purity, rebirth, to the men building the new nation.

The death of the three gunmen waiting at the station – Leone's trademark opening – appears initially to be matched by the death of Harmonica. However, as the title makes clear, this is Leone's fairy tale, and the mysterious stranger must be resurrected to rescue the damsel, destroy the villain and preserve the Holy Grail. Returning to the iconic theatre of *A Fistful of Dollars*, but with full-blooded characterisations that film lacked, Leone presents the action at once as a saga of American destiny and a drama of signs and archetypes. Like his prototype Shane, Harmonica is endowed with almost supernatural powers, gliding mysteriously into frame, discovered in silhouette in a dark corner or high atop a barn, inevitably to the strains of his music. Like the pocket watch and chimes of *For a Few Dollars More*, the instrument is a haunting aural signifier of the ancient pain that awaits vengeance, if not healing. As with the earlier film, three flashbacks each take us deeper inside Harmonica and the site of the bond between him and Frank.

The first of these comes when Frank has captured Harmonica on the doorstep of Morton's private coach as the train begins to slow. Briefly, we see a figure advancing towards us, indistinct, out of focus. The second flashback comes after the auction for the McBain farm, when Frank offers a dollar more than the $5,000 that Harmonica had bid, earned by turning Cheyenne in for reward. Now in the middle distance, the figure is beginning to come into sharper focus, although still unrecognisable. The final flashback occurs as the two men face each other in their showdown in the circular space behind the McBain farmhouse. His face frozen in a scowl, Frank deliberately circles to find a position where the sun will not be a factor. Harmonica's face – a marble mask – relaxes in a smile as he comes forward to stand opposite. The shot slowly zooms in to Harmonica, to his eyes in extreme close-up. Now the past's mystery comes into full focus, the figure moving closer, a young Frank, bearded, grinning, a sadistic devil. There are two distinct climaxes in this final resolution of the film's action. Harmonica's agonised recall of the past – the harmonica being pushed into his mouth as he struggles to balance the older brother on his shoulders whose head is in a noose – culminates in the remembered failure, as he fell forward into the dust. After a beat we cut to present time, the guns booming, Frank turning his back in shock at the mortal wound he has received.

Now the second act is played out, Frank staggering, literally a dead man walking now, asking again – 'Who are you?' Harmonica snaps the instrument from around his neck, kneels and slowly repeats Frank's act of the past. In his mind's eye, Frank sees the young boy falling, the harmonica dropping from his mouth, as he now himself falls, the harmonica coming free. In a perfect rhyme to the original cruelty, Harmonica delivers an exquisite revenge.

The dynamic charge delivered is Leone at his most expressive. There is the typically extreme melodrama, the fiendish Frank grinning, looking upwards, then pushing the harmonica further forward – 'Keep your loving brother happy' – into the tearful face of the young boy trapped by evil genius as a prop in the slaying of his own brother. Such extremes of action and detailing give the events the aura of ritual theatre, a quality suggested by the strange setting of a ruined stone arch in the middle of a vast open space, the buttes of Monument Valley in the distance, as well as by the audience of gang members. At the same time, the intensity of Leone's close-ups, the sense of the camera's gaze boring in on the two men, insists on psychological action, the interior drama of memory, guilt and pain that the two share. Releasing the long-buried secret kept from both Frank and the audience in slow, deliberate fashion, releasing Harmonica from his tortured memory and mythic quest, Leone's editing bridges past and present, the death of the boy long ago and the arch-villain now.

The suggestion of demigods at war – divine and diabolical – is sustained by Leone's iconic treatment of his other characters. He had chosen the tired stereotypes of the Western: the revenge hero, the good-hearted bandit, the villainous hired gun, the whore and the capitalist. But like Ford, Leone had detailed and humanised them. The crippled Morton, yearning to see the water, is trapped with Frank, who dreams of a businessman's status, as his craving for Morton's cigars testifies. 'A remarkable woman', as both

Harmonica and Cheyenne term her, Jill had escaped an elegant whorehouse on Bourbon Street to find her new family's bodies awaiting burial, and had risen to the occasion. In some ways the most detailed of the characters, the romantic Cheyenne is reminded of his own harlot mother by Jill's tough style, and is immediately in rapport with the mysterious nomadic harmonica-player, and at war with 'Mr Choo Choo'.

However, Leone's strategy was also to raise them to mythic levels, constructing them ultimately as 'frozen archetypes', in Umberto Eco's phrase.[10] In the last appearance of a No Name in Leone, although finally humanised by the flashbacks, Harmonica was also the most abstract of the characters. Leone had spoken of how pleased he was with Bronson's chiselled visage as an embodiment of 'Destiny'. Paralleling the struggle of the latter's saviour and Fonda's anti-Christ was the conflict of Cheyenne and Morton, life force and paralysis, the romance of the West and its destruction. Cardinale had recently served as Federico Fellini's spirit of purity and renewal in his *8½* (1960), preparing her for Leone's earth mother. The slowly unfolding narrative's 'chess-like moves', in Frayling's phrase, were being made deliberately by supreme archetypes, figures in repose, each patiently inching towards their moment of truth, action and history.

Jill's heroic character transcends the brutalising effects of the frontier, her progress symbolic of the feminising of the West, the domestication that Ford saw as its civilising. Her arrival clearly codes her as central to the new world, as she marches to the train station, the black children with her luggage behind, and then through to Flagstone's main street, the camera craning up over the building as the music builds to a shivery crescendo, to reveal the sprawling, awesome humanity below, the America-to-be that Jill is now joining.

'Frozen archetypes': Destiny and Death

Some critics have seen her as a passive victim of rape at the hands of Frank. Yet that scene has something of the same quality as her determined entrance. Beginning with an extreme vertical close-up of Frank and Jill nose-to-nose, the shot slowly retreats and simultaneously tilts horizontally to reveal the couple in bed, Frank atop the woman, who lies helpless below him. The bravura shot has a disorienting effect, suggesting a world out of whack. Yet Frank is making love to Jill, who responds, helping him strip her; he marvels at how vital and responsive she is. He is in awe that she will do anything to stay alive: 'What a little tramp.' Jill shows no self-pity or shame, fear or disgust. Even in the face of an implied threat of death, she turns and rises above him. She is less the victim than an expression of feminine spirituality and power in the most squalid of circumstances. She is not Vienna of the delirious, gothic *Johnny Guitar* (1954), strapping on six-guns herself. But ultimately her honesty and determination prevail; at the end, a figure of purity, she goes out to give water to the workers, the matriarch who symbolises the settling of the new nation.

Leone's earlier films had all communicated a high degree of self-consciousness, reworking the American Western, sometimes quoting ironically. They had been called revisionist Westerns, anti-Westerns, reinventions of the genre as the 'dirty Western'. But with *Once Upon a Time in the West* Leone was escalating the self-consciousness, the slow, rhetorical pace communicating the sense of a pre-existing language, the presence less of an author than of a series of citations and models, of pastiche and recycling. Literate cinemagoers could not but recognise the opening borrowed from *High Noon*, the setting and events of the McBain farm referencing both *Shane* and *The Searchers*, Jill's situation modelled on *Johnny Guitar*, the coming of the railroad recalling *The Iron Horse*, *Union Pacific* and *The Man Who Shot Liberty Valance*. And so on.

Above all, there was Ford, the architect of the genre, whose massive contribution provided another subtext for Leone. The Western was the most iconographic of genres, and Leone the most iconographic of film-makers. How could he not include a trip through Monument Valley's sacred terrain as Jill made her pilgrimage into the West? A journey through Ford's personal landscape had always been an essential component in the story brainstorming sessions that Leone had conducted with Dario Argento and Bernardo Bertolucci for some months before turning to one of his regular writers, Sergio Donati, for the script. That moment in the film is one of its richest, the sense of quotation overwhelming. The music is reverential as the camera slowly pans with the buggy carrying Jill, to discover the classic topography of monumental mesas and sandstone formations, the icons of America that Ford had shaped and celebrated in the series of outstanding films that had been launched with the legendary *Stagecoach*.

No less an authority than French philosopher Jean Baudrillard had proclaimed Leone 'the first postmodernist director'.[11] It is impossible to quarrel with such a view. As Adrien Martin has suggested, more than anyone else Leone could be said to have generated 'a global tradition' variously described as 'mannerist, baroque, spectacular, exhibitionist, performative, carnivalesque, "pop formalist" – a cinema of "effects" rather than meanings, of playful excess rather than classical expressivity'.[12] Leone fused all manner of sources and influences to produce a ritual theatre of masks, a *commedia dell'arte* out West. The almost glacial pace, the recycling and citations, the ironic inversions and parodies – these were Leone's Brechtian strategy that was too successful in alienating some audiences. The *Dollars* films had been too irreverent and nihilistic for many American critics; now his epic was too slow and portentous. Nevertheless, a more traditional Western than the trilogy – hardly a spaghetti at all, given its optimism, however restrained – *Once Upon a Time in the West* was Leone's own monument to the genre.

A Fistful of Dynamite (1972)

A Fistful of Dynamite opens with an echo of *The Wild Bunch*'s children playfully torturing killer ants and a scorpion: someone is urinating on an anthill. Sam Peckinpah had been offered the film, which Leone had originally planned only to produce. Leone was ecstatic at the idea of a film with both their names on it, although it is impossible to conceive of two such controlling personalities sustaining a collaboration. In any case, Peckinpah had passed, although Leone had thought they had an agreement. With his hero pissing on ants, was Leone now sending the American a message? Two years later, in *My Name is Nobody* (Tonino Valerii, 1973), a film that Leone would produce and some scenes of which he would direct, the hero comes across a gravestone marked 'Peckinpah'; Leone had buried his rival.

In any case, *A Fistful of Dynamite*'s opening scene is an aptly earthy introduction to Rod Steiger's Juan, a barefoot peasant who will shortly metamorphose into a bandit. Unzipping himself again, he compels a highborn lady to inspect his manhood ('Pretty good, eh?') before forcing himself on her. This scene is a good example of why women have problems with Leone. Maria Monti's is the only woman's name in the long list of credits for a film that ran for 160 minutes in Leone's cut, and her character is humiliated and raped in the first quarter of an hour after minimal and egregious detailing suggesting that she both deserves and craves violation. Understandably, much of the scene would disappear in the truncated US release.

However, initially we are lulled into seeing Juan as a rather more humble character, as does the party of travellers he joins. Wealthy and aristocratic types travelling in a luxurious coach, they heap scorn on the barefoot Mexican peasant ('Do you know who your father was?'), and generalise in bigoted fashion about the 'animals' of his class. Resorting early to expressionist attack, Leone cuts back and forth in extreme close-up on the cardinal, the American businessman, the lawyer and the upper-class couple, as they eat and spew venomous comments, the pace of the montage quickening and closing in on the faces, the eyes and finally just the masticating mouths. Leone's strategy of extreme exaggeration creates the group as grotesques who absolutely deserve their comeuppance when Juan's family and followers ambush the stage. Moreover, the attack on these effete and decadent characters seems to relate directly to the prefatory text that opens the film:

THE REVOLUTION
IS NOT A SOCIAL DINNER,
A LITERARY EVENT,
A DRAWING OR AN EMBROIDERY;
IT CANNOT BE DONE WITH
ELEGANCE AND COURTESY,
THE REVOLUTION IS AN ACT OF VIOLENCE

However, the behaviour of Juan and his gang – in effect, raping and pillaging – readily makes clear their status as bandits. Stripping the men naked and the lady of her jewellery and black hat, Juan consigns the group to a handy dung heap, bowing and delivering a sarcastic 'Thank you for *everything*'. Meanwhile, explosions have been going off, and now their source enters through a cloud of smoke and dust, putt-putting his way towards the group on a motorbike. The vehicle confirms what references in the coach to Huerta and Madero had suggested, that the scene is revolutionary Mexico in the second decade of the 20th century, a much later era than the traditional Western's time frame.

The driver is James Coburn's Sean Mallory, former IRA revolutionary and explosives expert, whose progress is halted by a gunshot from Juan that flattens a tyre. Unbeknown to the peon bandit, he has fired an opening salvo in what rapidly becomes a battle waged via and against conveyances. In retaliation, Sean blows a hole in the roof of the confiscated coach, and when threatened reveals his duster hides explosives enough to blow them and 'half the country' away. This discovery convinces the bandit that destiny has brought them together to realise his dream, robbery of the bank at Mesa Verde. The certainty, so strong that in another example of Leone expressionist whimsy, Juan literally sees a halo above Sean's head spelling out the bank in bright lights, grows with the knowledge that their names suggest a team – Juan and Sean, Johnny and Johnny. 'The firecracker', as Juan calls him, is still bent on leaving to continue working for the Germans setting charges to find silver, so Juan shoots his bike once again, whereupon Sean ups the ante ('Duck, you sucker!') by blowing up their whole coach.

Vintage Leone, the action has this quirky odd couple scheming and jockeying, albeit with darker outcomes than in the spaghettis. Minus No Name's look or trademarks, Sean has the character's competency and reticence, the latter in contrast to Juan's excitable nature. He also recalls Mortimer for his specialised weapons and professionalism. Juan, on the other hand, vividly evokes the Ugly Tuco in his peasant origins, suspicious nature and self-interest. Inevitably, reversal follows reversal. When a robbery is pulled off, Juan opens the vaults to find not cash but prisoners of the revolutionary struggle. Freeing them, he is hoisted aloft, an instant revolutionary hero who insists to Sean that he only wants the money as he is carried off in triumph, like Chaplin in *Modern Times* (1936). But soon enough he will become the militant, while Sean will take up his cynicism.

Sean also recalls both Mortimer and Harmonica in being haunted by memories, in Leone's typical progressive flashback structure. However, the past for Mallory is not the site of family dishonour defining him as a revenge hero. Rather, he is driven by guilt, fleeing himself rather than pursuing satisfaction. Adrift in Mexico, his meeting with Juan will be as pivotal for him as for the bandit, a discovery of his true nature. His first reverie comes when Juan excitedly discovers their common names and speaks of destiny. We see a handsome young man driving an open car, the camera retreating to reveal Sean and a beautiful girl, who in slow motion embrace and kiss as they travel through a wood dappled with bright sunshine. Recalling the idyllic romantic Ireland of Ford's *The Quiet Man*, it is also evocative of Francois Truffaut's *Jules et Jim* (1962) for its suggestion of close friends competing for an idealised woman.

The second flashback occurs when the two have reunited in a Mesa Verde café, Juan

Leone recycles Chaplin's reluctant revolutionary

complaining of the soldiers everywhere, Sean commenting that it is an agreeable situation: 'If it's revolution, it's confusion.' We now see Sean entering a pub to find his IRA activist friend passing out a newspaper, *Freedom*, to perhaps a dozen men. Sean looks on speculatively. The third flashback comes when Sean witnesses the bloodied Dr Villega (Romolo Valli), a leader of the revolution, betraying followers for a firing-squad. The past has a similar scenario, police entering the pub with the badly beaten friend who points out individuals, who are taken out. His back turned to the door, Sean views the events steadily in a mirror, turning to fire a concealed weapon when he is also implicated.

This flashback is taken up again when Sean is on the locomotive with Villega on a collision course with an army train carrying a thousand troops. In ironic payback for his disloyalty, Sean has chosen the traitor to help fire the engine. Villega argues that torture will turn anyone, and that he has not changed and can still 'serve the cause'. Sean stares at him and sees the bloody face of his friend and his ancient act, killing the two officers and, after a long pause, his friend. Back to the present: Sean tells Villega he used to have ideals but that now he does not judge – 'I only did that once in my life.' Executing his friend, he had scarred himself.

More a dream than a flashback, Sean's last vision comes just before he blows himself up. The Irishman has taken three bullets in the back in the battle that raged after the trains crashed. If he dies, 'What's gonna happen to me?' Juan wants to know. Sean asks for a light, and Juan then goes off for help. Inhaling deliberately, he smiles as he sees in his mind's eye another sun-drenched, carefree scene in slow motion, as the girl is pursued by Sean and his friend, coming to rest as Sean approaches and kisses her, the friend also leaning forward. The cigarette explodes.

The memories illuminate Sean's conflict with Juan. A paradox of their struggle is that the peasant's attempts to manipulate him into banditry finally result in the Irishman's return to revolutionary activity. The need for such action is evident in Mesa Verde, which is presided over by numerous posters of its smug governor. Standing and admiring its bank, Juan has an escaping prisoner die in his arms. Its streets are so crowded with troops and firing squads that Juan is disbelieving: 'Hey God, are you sure this is Mesa Verde?'

Looking at his new friend, Sean sees the old. However much he fights it, his destiny appears to be to rob the bank, a prison full of political prisoners, as if in compensation for the past. But he is clearly a half-hearted rebel, as his debate with Juan reveals. At the outset, the latter disavows larger allegiances: his country is 'me and my family'. He knows about revolution, where 'the people who read the books' get the poor, who end up dead, to do their bidding. Sean has no rejoinder to this perspective from the peasant class, and acknowledges defeat by discarding a radical text by the Russian theorist Bakunin that he has been reading. Eschewing ideology, Sean henceforth operates out of personal and semi-suicidal instincts, as when he volunteers single-handedly to attack an oncoming armoured army unit and blow up a bridge.

Tragically, the film turns on the death of another Leone family, this time the protagonist's own. Deciding to stay and help Sean at the bridge, Juan had posed self-importantly to his kids: 'If your father doesn't come back ...'. But the mission had been a success, the friends bonding joyously in their rout of the army and the liberating detonation of the bridge. Rather than his own life it is his family ('Six – I never counted them before') that he loses. So the cynical bandit becomes the militant, and in turn Sean's disillusionment grows.

The exchange of positions is ironic. 'I gave you a royal screwing,' Sean tells Juan as he is dying, holding out the cross that Juan had torn from his neck on discovering his dead kids. Juan disagrees, but at the end he is left without friend or family, role or ideals. The truncated release version ends with an extreme close-up on Juan, looking directly at us and poignantly asking: 'What about me?' For Leone, the fate of Juan was evidently a case study in the futility of politics. The success of the spaghettis had stimulated the Italian film industry, and especially the Italian Western. Hundreds had been made, many of them political, unsurprising in the context of the turbulent 1960s. An anarchist by inclination, Leone also described himself as a failed socialist. Had he felt marginalised by the new vogue in the genre he had resurrected? At any rate, the end result of the two heroes' reversals is clearly an argument for inaction, a cancelling out of commitment. His film at one point had been titled *Giu la testa* or *Keep Your Head Down*, an apt title for a remarkably quietist and solipsistic contribution to the political debate.

Never less than interesting, *A Fistful of Dynamite* suffers dramatically as a result of the extended emphasis on military combat and logistics. The relationship between Juan and Sean in the foreground is focused nicely in terms of their mutual competition, manipulation and betrayals. The stylish Coburn and hammy Steiger provide a vivid contrast, reinforced by their different acting styles: Coburn's behaviourist approach versus Steiger's method. But apart from the two principals, few characters are developed. Villega, the failed intellectual, serves to incarnate the theme of betrayal and the perfidy of those who read books. Colonel Gunther Reza (Jean Michel Antoine), the Nazi-coded army commander who ends up with the Bakunin text and shoots Sean, sucks on a raw egg in early morning sunshine. Most seriously, Juan's children – despite significant screen time – are never realised in sufficient depth.

The effect of this narrow focus is intensified by the large-scale combat and impersonal violence of the film's later period. As if to compensate, much of the action is composed by Leone to reference larger conflicts to add depth and enrich his canvas. Thus the scene of Villega fingering activists who line up for his inspection in the light of truck headlamps is evocative of Goya and Spain's own revolutionary struggle.[13] In the same way, the epic scenes of mass murder in trenches strongly recall World War II concentration camps.

As with the earlier films, the star-crossed partners and ill-matched friends provide Leone with a strong foundation on which to ground action and spectacle. The flashbacks are characteristically haunting, the slow motion and idealisation foregrounding the dynamics of time and change. Morricone's score also contributes its self-conscious edge with the 'Sean, Sean' theme that accompanies the manoeuvres and reversals of the two principals. But the shift in emphasis dictated by what has been called the post-Western is crucial: absent are classic conventions to rehearse and push against. Collective struggles replace traditional individualised rituals and iconographic encounters. Instead of 'He can shoot, too' – Cheyenne's praise for Harmonica – we have Sean's refrain, 'Duck, you sucker', and the dynamiting of mountains, coaches, buildings, banks, bridges, troops and trains. With his last Western, the prescient Leone was moving in the direction of the action film, the form that would dominate popular cinema in the last decades of the 20th century.

Leone's own immediate future would be problematic, as he entered a period devoted primarily to producing and filming commercials that would last thirteen years. The one film from this period bearing the marks of his themes and style was the Western, *My Name is Nobody*. Directed by Tonino Valerii, who had served as assistant director on *For a Few Dollars More* and had behind him some six Westerns of his own, the film is a weird conjunction of the American and Italian traditions.

Based on an idea by Leone from Homer's *Odyssey*, the film features Henry Fonda as Jack Beauregard, a legendary, ageing gunfighter seeking retirement and trying to avoid a confrontation with an aspiring young contender. This is Nobody, enacted by Terence

Terence Hill/Mario Girotti and Henry Fonda in *My Name is Nobody*: burying the American Western

Hill (formerly Mario Girotti), a blue-eyed blonde Italian actor who had worked with Luchino Visconti in *The Leopard* (1963) and starred in a string of successful Westerns. The two stage a duel that allows Beauregard to fade away, and Nobody to become a somebody, the man who shot Jack Beauregard. A schizoid film, it juxtaposes the deliberate Fonda with the slapstick hijinks of Hill. Satirising the expertise of the gunfighter, the film has Nobody deliver multiple slaps to an opponent's face with such speed that a saddle he holds over his shoulder with the same hand never drops.

Leone closely supervised the production and actually shot some scenes. In *Once Upon a Time in the West*, he had enjoyed blackening Fonda, revealing the icon of Western heroism and American idealism as the grand villain. Here his casting of the actor bequeathing the heroic mantle (aptly enough in his last Western) to a brash young Italian nobody was all of a piece with Peckinpah's tombstone planted in a frontier cemetery: Leone had usurped and mastered the American myth. But in truth, he and Peckinpah had both made outstanding contributions. In some respects they were a matched set, both anti-Fords, deconstructionists, painters of a debased macho frontier of broken traditions, dishonoured codes and an embattled feminine.

American audiences may see Peckinpah as the more profound in his engagement with fundamental themes of national identity, his tragic vision of a soulless American pragmatism expiring in a suicidal ballet. Yet it is impossible to deny that Leone had captured the moral and cultural climate of the era, Europeanising and globalising the genre, 'operacising it' in Eastwood's phrase.[14] He had galvanised the Western, decisively shaping its vision for the troubled audiences and cultures of the 1960s. Few other examples of the genre match the enormous popularity his films continue to enjoy. The mark he left is also visible in the countless clones of The Man With No Name, and the widespread borrowings of his unique style.

Yet Leone's last hurrah was not to be a Western, but the project he had been developing for some sixteen years, the gangster film, *Once Upon a Time in America*. Having turned down *The Godfather* before it was offered to Francis Coppola, Leone had developed his trademark narrative structure of two men marked by betrayal into a tragic study of America. A noir epic, the film follows the rise of young Jewish gangsters and their different destinies – Robert De Niro's Noodles and James Woods's Max. Shot in his expressionistic style, the film in its original uncut form provides evidence that Leone's ambivalent love affair with America could be richly productive outside the Western as well.

Some critics have suggested that Leone's work and especially the spaghettis provide clear evidence of his anti-Americanism. The Yanks had defeated Italy and occupied it after World War II. Now revenge was being had, the Italians invading Hollywood and making foreign its most classical of genres, the national epic. If Leone is ultimately defined by the Western, however, his affectionate critique of the genre hardly suggests anti-Americanism. Pushing against the classical, Leone's post-modernism and formalism radically refashioned America's frontier mythology, allowing his cynicism and black comedy to flower, his themes of a mercenary world and compromised friendship to find a comfortable fit.

Without America to correct what does Leone stand for? Without the Western, where would Leone have gone? Leone's anarchic instincts may have naturally predisposed him towards a left-wing critique of the USA, but like his characters, he was corrupt, the evidence of his love for things American everywhere. He had found a home in the genre. As with Peckinpah, his huge debt and gift to it were undeniable: it had been the Western that had first brought Leone alive and that he had mastered, creating a distinctive body of work the likes of which no one could possibly have predicted.

Notes

1. I am indebted to Christopher Frayling's indispensable critical biography, *Sergio Leone: Something to Do with Death* (London: Faber & Faber, 2000), pp. 532–7, for all running times and box-office grosses. Figures for *A Fistful of Dynamite*, which played well in Europe but failed in the US, are not included.

2. When Leone met the American director Budd Boetticher at a film festival in Milan, he shouted, 'Budd, dear Budd, I stole *everything* from you!' Quoted in Frayling, *Sergio Leone*, p. 182.

3. Christopher Frayling, *Spaghetti Westerns: Cowboys and Europeans from Karl May to Sergio Leone* (London: Routledge & Kegan Paul, 1981), p. 40.

4. Ibid., p. 131. See also Marcia Landy, 'He Went Thataway: The Form and Style of Leone's Italian Westerns', *Boundary* vol. 2 no. 23; reprinted in Jim Kitses and Gregg Rickman (eds), *The Western Reader* (New York: Limelight Editions, 1998), pp. 213–22.

5. Patrick McGilligan, 'Clint Eastwood', in Robert Kapsis and Kathie Coblentz (eds), *Clint Eastwood: Interviews* (Jackson: University of Mississippi Press, 1999), p. 27.

6. Frayling, *Sergio Leone*, p. 449.

7. I cannot agree with Frayling that the family is 'a central, positive force' in Leone and 'a *substitute* for Nash Smith's evocation of the "garden" or "agrarian" ideal'. *Spaghetti Westerns*, pp. 181–2.

8. Ibid., p. 172.

9. Frayling, *Sergio Leone*, p. 205.

10. Ibid., p. 300. Frayling refers to Leone's 'use of iconic actors as walking pieces of mythology' (p. 438).

11. Quoted in ibid., p. 492.

12. Adrian Martin, *Once Upon a Time in America* (London: BFI, 1998), pp. 10–11.

13. Noel Simsolo asked the director how he worked with light and colour: 'I show paintings. For the execution scene in *The Revolution* I displayed some drawings by Goya on "The Disasters of War"'. 'Sergio Leone Talks', *Take One* vol. 3 no. 9 (January–February 1972), pp. 26–32.

14. Kapsis and Coblentz, *Interviews*, p. 130.

7
Clint Eastwood: Tightrope Walker

I never considered myself a cowboy.

Clint Eastwood is the last Western hero and the only active major director of the genre
to survive into the new millennium. But to see him principally as a practitioner of the
Western is impossible given a career that stretches over five decades and ranges across a
wide diversity of genres and projects. If we look at his work in the last decade of the 20th
century, for instance, we find one Western (1992's Oscar-winning *Unforgiven*), three
high-powered thrillers (*In the Line of Fire*, *Absolute Power* [1997], *True Crime* [1999]),
two upscale literary adaptations (*The Bridges of Madison County* [1995],
Midnight in the Garden of Good and Evil [1997]), a road movie/thriller (*A Perfect World*
[1993]) and an adventure/comedy (*Space Cowboys* [2000]).

Given such a perspective, it may be difficult to see why more than one critic has
argued that all of Eastwood's films either reference or are in fact essentially Westerns.[1]
Without entertaining the *reductio ad absurdum* of star-text analysis that fuels such here-
sies of genre definition, we can look at the basics of his career, and in particular at its
key moments of association with the Western. Discounting bit parts, from *A Fistful of
Dollars* in 1964 through *Blood Work* in 2002, Eastwood had appeared in some forty-five
films. He began to work as a director in 1971 with *Play Misty for Me*; *Unforgiven* was his
sixteenth directorial outing, *Mystic River* (2003) his twenty-fourth. He has acted in
eleven Westerns, and directed four. Two other films have a Western slant, the noir thriller
Coogan's Bluff (1968), and *Bronco Billy* (1980), a screwball comedy and road movie.
These numbers, perhaps abetted by the fact that it is Sergio Leone's films that fixed Eastwood's star, may explain why he has so often complained of the frontier stereotype.

But the numbers belie his actual contribution to the genre, and obscure its pivotal
role at key moments in its progress. As an actor, his first break came within the Western: playing Rowdy Yates, the ramrod of the 1950s television series *Rawhide*'s cattle
drive, would firmly establish Eastwood as a frontier type. Freeing himself of the series'
strictures against other commitments after the sixth season, he enterprisingly accepted
an offer to star in an Italian Western to be shot in Almeria, Spain, and at Rome's Cinecittà
by one Sergio Leone, a relatively unknown film-maker. In retrospect not only a radical
challenge to the American Western but also a defining moment in post-modern culture,
A Fistful of Dollars would catapult Eastwood to the centre of global attention.

The Outlaw Josey Wales: The Man with a Name

The television performer would become an icon, The Man With No Name, who would reappear, although less centrally with each film, in Leone's two follow-ups, *For a Few Dollars More* and *The Good, the Bad and the Ugly*.

From Leone, Eastwood would take the screen persona they forged together – a character of mystery and mythic power, amoral, insouciant, a redemptive force despite himself – and recycle it throughout his career. Eastwood would also borrow Leone's mythic narrative, the tests and killings, the symbolic death, the resurrection and final transcendence. With his first American feature, *Hang 'Em High* (1968), Eastwood cautiously transplanted the persona into a low-budget Western surrounded by personnel familiar from *Rawhide* days, as with director Ted Post. Opening with Eastwood's innocent cowboy being lynched, the film creates The Man With No Name as a bitter avenger who operates ambivalently within the law as a righteous hanging judge's marshal, allowing him to pursue his vendetta.

His next film, *Coogan's Bluff*, would launch another influential and productive collaboration, with director Don Siegel. Leone's outrageous style, mocking, self-referential, operatic, the key to the success of the spaghettis, was not really to Eastwood's taste. In Siegel he would find the polar opposite, a lean, economical style that the director had developed in a long apprenticeship running the montage department at Warner Bros., doing second-unit work for different studio film-makers. It was a rigorous, abstract yet physical style, ideal for the urban action thriller. Eastwood learned from working with Siegel, shot second unit for him, and cast him in *Play Misty for Me* partly as a resource if needed on his own first directorial effort.

Coogan's Bluff unceremoniously welcomed Eastwood's Arizona marshal to the modern urban world, playing on the edgy tension between the West's individualism and big-city bureaucracy. Launching Eastwood's lawman anti-hero, that film and *Dirty Harry* (1971) were parts of a work-in-progress for Siegel, whose filmography features a series of disturbing portraits of alienated neurotics for whom violence provides the only meaningful expression of self in a conformist society. Often psychopathic in tone, such extreme violence was a characteristic of both Siegel's cops (Coogan, Harry, *Madigan* [1968]) and his gangsters (*Riot in Cell Block Eleven*, *Baby Face Nelson* [1957], *The Killers* [1964]), as well as the odd soldier (*Hell is for Heroes* [1962]). The taut images that defined Harry – the receding aerial shot of him sadistically stepping down on the howling killer's wounds in foggy Kezar stadium, the finale of the bitter cop scaling his badge into the swamp – were pure Siegel.

What Leone and Siegel had in common were an outcast mentality and sympathies, a leaning towards anarchism. Both felt victims of the industry. Siegel, a prisoner of B-movies and small-scale productions, would find collaboration with Eastwood the period of his greatest freedom. Leone had perennial problems with producers; their failure to pay a fee to Akira Kurosawa for *Yojimbo*'s rights had robbed him of *A Fistful*'s profits, and held the films out of the US market until 1967. The thrust of their respective visions found a receptive response in Eastwood; Siegel would remark on the star's readiness to embrace anti-heroic roles. In fact, what had drawn the actor to the first spaghetti's script had been that hero's outrageously ignoble inaction at its outset as he observes a child being abused. A scene he had himself directed in *Dirty Harry*, where the cop infuriates a potential suicide by urging him to jump, is also relevant, the best example of the perverse point of view he shared with Siegel.

After experimenting with acting roles in several large-scale projects – *Where Eagles Dare* (1968), *Paint Your Wagon* (1969), *Kelly's Heroes* (1970) – that Eastwood has maligned as learning experiences in bad production practices, he had rejoined Siegel for *Two Mules for Sister Sara* and *The Beguiled* (1971). These two modest films are interesting for their early recasting of the dominant Eastwood persona in subsidiary and victim roles, initiating an inversion of the ultra-masculine character that would be a continuing secondary theme in Eastwood. Based on a story by Budd Boetticher – whose Randolph Scott Westerns had been one of Leone's models – and with music by Leone collaborator Ennio Morricone, the first film self-consciously evokes the spaghetti world, although No Name here is outwitted by Shirley MacLaine's whore in nun's clothes. In the darker, gothic *The Beguiled*, emasculation goes further, as Eastwood's wounded Union soldier suffers both the symbolic castration of an unnecessary leg amputation and finally death for his philandering with the Southern schoolgirls nursing him.

His debut with *Play Misty for Me* would carry on the torture of the strong male for sexual sins, the film anticipating *Fatal Attraction* (1987) in its vivid delineation of the costs of the one-night stand, Jessica Walter as an archetypal fury tearing at the hapless Carmel disc jockey. In the kind of straddling of the issue that defines Eastwood's career, he would follow this trifecta of masculine frustration and downsizing with equal time for macho empowerment as represented by *Dirty Harry*, a John Sturges-directed *Joe Kidd* (1972) and *High Plains Drifter*. The lacklustre *Joe Kidd* apart, there was here a very strong return of heroic male agency. Moreover, when he speaks of his view that it was time 'to analyze the classical Western', as he does apropos the later *Pale Rider*, there can be little doubt that reclaiming the Western hero from the nihilism of the spaghettis was an additional objective of the director's.[2]

Revenge of the Creature (1955), the first film in which the actor had had a bit part, was an apt title to launch a career that would be built on bloody vengeance and uncivil justice, a celebration of instinct over regulation, and archetypal solutions to social problems. *High Plains Drifter* is exemplary of the strategies and values that Eastwood would follow in the four Westerns he would direct, efforts that would constitute an almost single-handed attempt to resurrect the genre during a largely dormant period. Enacting a remarkable vengeance, the film's mysterious hero invades and conquers, rapes and pillages, deceives and betrays the frontier community of Lago. As in both *A Fistful of Dollars* and its source, *Yojimbo*, the town is punished for its venality and corruption – especially that of its most respected capitalists. Lago, it is suggested, has sold its soul.

Apart from these predecessors that contribute to the film's quirky tone, a very different primary source was the classical Western, *High Noon*. Infuriated by that film for making a supplicant of the Western hero, Howard Hawks had replied with the robust *Rio Bravo*. But in their own analysis, Eastwood and his screenwriter Ernest Tidyman would take as its starting point the posing of a question: what if Gary Cooper's Marshal Kane had not been 'good enough' in Hawks parlance, had in fact been whipped to death as the town looked on? Enter Eastwood as a ghost, a god or a reincarnation – in any case a superhero – to provide a cosmic justice, a shadow-figure to redeem and avenge the fallible, human martyr. Driving the narrative of *High Plains Drifter*, this dialectic of the vulnerable, fallen common man and the redemptive higher authority is a microcosm of Eastwood's typical play with the heroic and ironic modes in his Westerns and throughout his career. Although not as tidy a group (or as concentrated in time) as Boetticher's Ranown series with Randolph Scott, the kinship created here by the common structure of a mysterious revenge hero is similarly suggestive of a cycle:

High Plains Drifter (1972)

Avenging the murdered sheriff of Lago, the mysterious Stranger punishes the three killers, their capitalist employers and the townspeople who ignored his cries for help. He makes the town's dwarf, Mordecai, its mayor, rapes one woman and forces himself on another, and has the town painted red to welcome the paroled killers, whom he kills before leaving.

The Outlaw Josey Wales (1976)

Seeking revenge on the Union guerrilla redlegs (renegades) who killed his family, the hero refuses to surrender at Civil War's end, is pursued by the redlegs and becomes the head of a ragtag community, whom he leads to a settlement. There the legendary figure defeats his persecutors and retires by accepting a fictional death.

Pale Rider (1985)

In answer to a young girl's prayers, the Preacher materialises to empower her family and their oppressed mining community, whom he defends against capitalist bullies. In the process, he takes revenge against the gunfighter who had apparently killed him in the past. He inspires the community's leader, Hull, by his example, and Hull's woman by making love to her.

Unforgiven (1992)

A reformed killer comes out of retirement to earn a stake, the bounty for the two men who mutilated a whore. Reverting to type after the brutal killing of his friend by the town's sheriff, he avenges him by killing the tyrannical lawman and his deputies, and threatens to lay waste to the town if it errs in the future. An immature companion of the hero and a writer of pulp novels are both disabused of their illusions about the era's bad men and violence.

Stretching over two decades, this quartet of Westerns nicely focuses the parameters of the Eastwood persona, and highlights the typical structure and strategies he employs. As with both Boetticher and Anthony Mann, the motor drive of the films is vengeance. Although he was twenty in 1950 when *Winchester '73* launched the Mann/Stewart series, Eastwood often cites Mann, whose Westerns he remembers 'growing up with'.[3] If the latter's protagonists were invariably agonised, Eastwood's operate from a higher authority and are serene but for *Unforgiven*'s guilt-ridden killer. Still, if Sam Peckinpah can be seen as John Ford's bastard son, Eastwood seems in many ways the altogether legitimate offspring of Mann, the earlier model of archetypal and retributive action.

The films match up in pairs. As the titles suggest, *High Plains Drifter* and *Pale Rider* are supernatural Westerns featuring archetypal heroes with magical powers. Part of the appeal of these narratives is the mystery surrounding the god-like hero and his relationships with the other characters. *The Outlaw Josey Wales* and *Unforgiven* humanise their fallen heroes (the titles are again apt), men with names, men who suffer grievously, Job-like. In both films, issues of celebrity and fame, anonymity and retirement figure in their denouements, the renowned Josey faking his death to mark the end of hostilities, Munny the pig-farmer murderously reanimating his legendary persona of old. This kind of 'tinkering with the persona', as a *Pale Rider* review in the *Village Voice* was headed, was a continuing project with Eastwood. An actor before he became an icon, an icon before he became a director, Eastwood was shrewdly sensitive to the needs of the star performer to explore dramatic range and the audience's expectations. The impulse to play against type, to reveal the sheep in wolf's clothing, was his attempt to avoid classification, and to deviate from and subvert the dominant persona that had evolved. An important tool in this humanising process, Eastwood's saving grace was his sense of humour. Taking the mickey out of his superhero, Eastwood could cut his characters down to mortal size, as with the homicide detective and abandoned dad of *Tightrope* (1984) who sleeps with a huge, slobbering canine.

In discussing his Universal melodramas of the 1950s, Douglas Sirk spoke of the dangers of typecasting for stars:

> Of course, there is always the danger of petrification, of sameness, of not re-shaping your style. Because the only kind of style these actors have at their command is the one of their personality. But don't forget that petrification makes for greatness sometimes. Petrification leads to being a statue of yourself. [John] Wayne is a great actor because he has become petrified.[4]

Sirk goes on to talk of the advantage in melodrama of having a balance between 'one immovable character' against which a more interesting 'split' character can be placed. Surveying Eastwood's development, it is clear that after the spaghettis he both exploited and resisted petrification, and embraced both immovable and split characters. The iconoclastic impulse of the icon to emasculate or even kill off the icon evidenced early in *The Beguiled* and *Play Misty for Me* would continue in the 1980s with *Tightrope*. Eastwood's darkest effort humanises his superhero as a single parent cop who is fearful of women, a haunted prisoner of the same kinky noir world inhabited by the serial killer he tracks. There were also gentler, less commercial deconstructions, as with the charming *Bronco Billy*, a parody of Eastwood's cowboy star/director/producer image in the small-time impresario of a ragtag carnival's anachronistic Wild West show. In the same vein was the appealing *Honkytonk Man* (1983). A depression-era country music singer-songwriter and utter failure as a family man, the consumptive loser Red Stovall is nevertheless immortalised as the songs he recorded on the eve of his death flow over his grave at film's end.[5]

Commencing in the 1960s, Eastwood's career paralleled a growing woman's movement on the one hand, and an ideological interrogation in the American cinema of the absent father and the inadequate male on the other. The rise of feminism and the increasingly unstable state of the family in American society resulted in the social construction of masculinity as a confused and contested battleground. The question of what constitutes male heroism was increasingly posed in terms that included a greater sensitivity and honouring of fatherhood's responsibilities as true measures of manhood.

Bronco Billy: tinkering with the persona

This domesticated ideal of manliness provides a useful perspective on the super-masculinity of the Eastwood persona and the hard-body action heroes who follow him – Bruce Willis, Sylvester Stallone, Arnold Schwarzenegger. The grotesque excess of these later figures testifies further to the crisis of a troubled manhood.

Eastwood's tinkering with image showed an awareness of these developments and an effort to exploit and address them. Unlike many of Hollywood's action-film specialists, he has at least flirted with the situation of the domesticated male. Nearing the end of the trail, we even find the star yearning for the road not taken, the globetrotting photographer-hero of *Madison County* ready to forsake all the adventure and fame for true love with Meryl Streep's housewife. But, of course, the film dramatises the struggle to enter the settled life rather than the actual living of it. As Hawks argues most vividly in *His Girl Friday*, the traditional view has been that there is little adventure in diapers and galoshes. For all his interrogation of gender roles, Eastwood is finally like Rosalind Russell's Hildy, fleeing with relief back into the macho world of action. In John Ford's world, if charismatic power bequeaths independence, it can also signal anguish, isolation, exclusion. In Eastwood as in Hawks, the hero rarely seems to suffer from an absence of the social and the feminine.

However, given Eastwood's persistent interest in masculine authority's forms and practices, it is not surprising that family and fatherhood command some attention in his work. It is also relevant that Eastwood has sired seven children over the span of four decades, most recently while in his sixties. In interviews and publicity, this point tends to be obscured, while his patriarchal function is stressed in his shepherding of a quasi-family/stock company of performers, technicians and assistants under the banner of Malpaso, the production company he first formed with *Hang 'Em High*. Sheltered originally within United Artists before moving to Warner Bros., Malpaso has allowed Eastwood to operate with major studio support within a small independent structure that ensures him virtually total financial and artistic control. As the actor has regularly enjoyed an unassailable position as one of America's most popular stars since 1971, and as a director has unfailingly ridden a tight-fisted ramrod on his own efforts, this relationship has never been in danger. From this base, Eastwood has enjoyed the freedom to employ newcomers and advance the careers of relatively unappreciated collaborators, a benign but also thrifty policy.

In any case, the assembling of a makeshift family under his wing has been a prominent narrative structure within some films, as in *Josey Wales* and, four years later, *Bronco Billy*. This surrogate fatherhood also relates to other roles where the star has been on occasion a single parent, abandoned by his wife in *Tightrope* and widowed in *Unforgiven*, in both cases left with two children. As in *Dirty Harry*, the role of widower (or divorced dad) is a convenient method of bestowing the ideals of the settled without constraining the hero within them. More often than not, family, domestic life, woman – these constitute Eastwood's structuring absence. Yet *Tightrope* at least assays more in its delineation of a man torn between parenting ('Daddy, what's a hard-on?') and prostitutes. The schizoid struggle to balance quite different roles ends disastrously when the darkness invades the home, the killer menacing the children and attacking his woman. *Tightrope* explores the broken family and single parenthood, a dilemma of confused identity familiar to millions of Americans. Moreover, the film appears to resonate with a personal energy, with Eastwood's own daughter, Allison, portraying the older child scarred by the father's double life.

Over his long mega-star career, Eastwood's films have inevitably excited extreme reactions. In the 1970s the macho violence of *Dirty Harry*'s anti-hero and the zeal of his mission led some reviewers to talk of the character's fascist overtones. The other main criticism was the wooden acting and the lack of emotion – the petrification that Sirk speaks of. Perhaps piqued at Eastwood's independent success, even Leone could be unfair. Explaining that he had seen in Eastwood 'a block of marble' from which he could sculpt his hero à la Michelangelo and his Moses, he had complained that in contrast to Robert De Niro (whom he had directed in *Once Upon a Time in America*), 'Eastwood throws himself into a suit of armour and lowers the visor'.[6] But as Leone well knew, the minimalist style, the mask and the silences were in fact the basis of the Man With No Name's mystery and power. Somewhat laconic by nature, the actor had appreciated and taken to heart an early mentor's counsel: 'Don't just do something, stand there!'

A more sophisticated film culture is now more tolerant of different acting styles. A recent profile of Tilda Swinton in *The New Yorker* described 'the avante-Garbo' as 'one of the last of the great cinema objects', an actress 'seeming to do nothing at all ... the stillness of her face conveying a complex and distinctly cinematic presence informed by language and distance rather than the dramatization of emotion'. It is impossible to read such a description without thinking of Eastwood and the arch hostility of that magazine's film critics (especially Pauline Kael) towards his work over the years.[7]

Eastwood has been at the centre of global popular culture for three decades. John Wayne's heir (although he disputes that legacy), a granddaddy of the popular cinema, he has provided so much sheer entertainment value to so many audiences for so long that he has become, as he once put it, 'part of the landscape'. Many in the past may have undervalued the film-maker, but his ranking now, after Oscars and medals, retrospectives and reams of publicity, if anything seems inflated, approaching canonisation. Revered variously as a great American film artist, a feminist (despite the rapes that perennially threaten his women), a post-modernist, a radical, Eastwood is eulogised as one who has the courage to take risks, as in the films where he has played against type, and to enact a subversive revisionism.[8]

If one stands back from his whole career and registers its different projects and strategies, such perspectives are difficult to sustain. In contrast to his genuinely radical mentors, Eastwood appears above all a centrist, instinctively seeking out balance and parity. Morally and aesthetically, the style is conservative, his career finally a celebration of compromise and equal time. A juggler, a tightrope walker, a trade-off artist, an accountant, a hip classicist, an old-fashioned modernist, a gentle revisionist, Eastwood revels in contradiction and bedevilling classification. Variously and at different moments in his career, he enjoys taking risks and watching his flank, offending both the left and the right, speaking out and spin control, being the artist and the politician.

Thus the radical vigilantism of Siegel and *Dirty Harry*'s pro-victim, pro-cop original is recuperated in *Magnum Force* (1974), the first sequel where rebellious police officers' vigilantism is now critiqued as murder. Blurring the issue further, *Sudden Impact* (1983) makes the vigilantism politically correct by locating it in Sandra Locke's feminist serial killer. But balancing the books on his female characters, Eastwood provides both a trau-

'Make my day'. Eastwood's signature line in *Sudden Impact* prompted a rebuttal from Robert Townsend

matised Locke and her catatonic rape-victim sister, and a monstrous lesbian-coded gang member. Similarly, the hero briefly has a doomed black sidekick to balance the three dense brothers he wastes over a cup of coffee. That scene of a botched diner robbery is brilliantly parodied in Robert Townsend's *Hollywood Shuffle* (1987), where the director/star and his homeboy, African-American versions of Siskel and Ebert, give 'Dirty Larry' not the thumbs up but the finger – 'Do fifty bullets in yo' ass make yo' day?'

Eastwood's career generally betrays the same tendency to tack against the winds of critical opinion and audience expectations, refusing to be pinned down. He often maintains that each film is a different project, calling for a different approach and style, in contrast to Siegel's method. This compartmentalising may well contribute to the effect of being on both sides of an issue and of an ideologically high-strung consciousness. If this way of working undoubtedly inclines the director at times to experiment and produce deviations from the norm, the final overall impression is of a tasteful diversity and modest revisionism.

These are the considerable virtues of the four attractive Westerns that Eastwood would direct, returning to the form every few years, during the 1970s and 80s. It is perhaps possible to see all of Eastwood's movies as constituting an altar to his own image. Certainly when directing he has been his own favoured subject, starring in all the films but for *Breezy* (1973), *Bird* (1988), *Midnight in the Garden of Good and Evil* and *Mystic River*. However, narcissism is basic to the star system, and Eastwood's imposing physical stature and action roles simply allow him to exploit it at a more extreme level. In the Western, Eastwood's stiffly erect body provides an image of the super-masculine, the source of an authority, power and violence hardly accessible to the common man.

High Plains Drifter (1973)

If ever there was a scene built around the high and mighty entering a low-down town, the opening of *High Plains Drifter* is it. The credits evoke the Leone flavour immediately, the music eerie with moaning, funereal overtones as a figure materialises like an apparition in the distant heat waves. Coming closer, his progress becomes steeply downward, the silhouetted figure pausing briefly to gaze to the prairie floor far below and the straggling town at water's edge. Passing the cemetery, the rider, tall in the saddle, enters the town, the high crane shot framing the beginning of his parade, the cutting emphasising high-angle shots of the curious citizenry below, the tension and mystery underlined by the horse's steady shuffling culminating in the sharp crack of a whip as a wagon rumbles off. If anything is made clear in this initial scene, it is that the community is below the individual, the normal state of affairs in Eastwood.

As in *A Fistful of Dollars*, the entrance provides a tour of the one-street community and sketches some of the players, providing a trailer for the coming action. Two elements predominate. Befitting a community corrupted by greedy capitalism, signs and markers identifying businesses – store, hotel, barber, saloon, mining company – figure prominently. Further developing the spatial motif of the opening, the staging insists on the elevated status of the Stranger in a bearing and point of view that carry the force of judgment. Always implicit in genre conventions of landscape and hinted at in its title (as in Sam Peckinpah's *Ride the High Country*), the association of height with superiority is externalised in the topography of the film's action, the Stranger typically attacking his foes from above. A temporal drama, *High Noon* had been ruled by the clock, its chiming connecting all its flawed, mortal players in a fateful montage. Opening up the action in a quasi-sequel, *High Plains Drifter* had redefined the drama in terms of both space and morality – high was not the hour but where the omnipotent Stranger hailed from.

Such intimations of heavenly origins have not discouraged Robin Wood from an interesting reading of the film in terms of a fusion of Western and horror conventions, the Stranger satanic, his mission to consign the community to Hell, the red town burning at the end.[9] The coding of a devilish antagonist is standard Leone, and certainly the film evidences his strong influence everywhere: in its iconic superhero, the obsessive flashbacks, gothic touches such as painting the town, and bizarre characters like Mordecai, the dwarf. On the other hand, the moral and spiritual function of the Stranger seems less diabolical and more in keeping with an Old Testament deity, dealing out retribution and justice. The outcomes are certainly biblical, the sinners punished, the faithful rewarded.

In any case, as in the later *Pale Rider*, the intervention is coded as supernatural. At the end, the character pointedly insists that Mordecai knows his name as he rides out past the tombstone on the dead sheriff's grave. According to Eastwood, the original script identified the hero as a brother, but the film blatantly constructs him more as a ghost or a god. Upset at the film's rabble-rousing attitude towards early settlers and entrepreneurs, John Wayne had complained to Eastwood that the film was not portraying the American pioneer accurately.[10] Wayne was looking through a historical lens; Eastwood defends the film as allegory, its roots in archetype and myth. It was a fable, an early American ghost story, a morality play. Smiting the unjust, cauterising the community, his saviour allows the dead cowboy to rest in peace, as the gravestone has it, before returning to the high country.

In part a dark revenge comedy, the film's tone is set at the beginning in classic fashion with the obligatory early dispatch of three dense heavies, a signature scene that goes back through all the spaghettis to its source in Kurosawa. Menaced in the barber's chair by bullies, the Stranger introduces himself to the town by murderously gunning them down from beneath the barber's sheet before they even draw. Shortly thereafter, he rapes an aggressive town hussy, Callie Travers (Marianna Hill), scandalous behaviour presented deadpan. Immediately establishing the mastery of the Stranger over both genders, the pointedly outrageous excess and the (intended) comic, liberating effect is immediately checked by the dark moment that follows. Haunting *High Plains Drifter* as it does its hero and the townspeople, the spectacle of the marshal being whipped to death played out in the middle of the town before a fascinated, implicated audience occurs twice in flashbacks before being reprised at the end. The Stranger's remembering comes some twenty minutes into the film as he sleeps, a nightmare darkening the tone and establishing the enigma of Lago's mysterious past that links the character and the town. As in Leone, the memories are triggered by an aural cue, the whip's lash a signifier of the primal trauma. The obscene events are also rehearsed in the dwarf's memory, nudged when he takes up a hiding place beneath the town's boardwalk, the vantage point from which he had witnessed the murder. The final scenes satisfy narrative logic, with the night again echoing with the lash inflicted in a poetic justice on two of the marshal's killers in the same street, the third hung by the neck with the whip.

Balancing comic, increasingly absurdist episodes of the Stranger bullying the citizenry, the haunting flashbacks define the gravity of the stakes beyond the town's buffoonery and cowardice. The weight is partly the result of the excess, the shots of the whipping held far beyond their narrative function, the vicious, repeated crack of the whip marking the event as unholy. The sadism is emphasised, the killers all staring eyes and licking lips. The townspeople are mesmerised, watching from the shadows. A frontier noir community who by their silence 'all had a hand in it' is vividly sketched; they had supported the town's capitalists in the killing of the marshal to prevent the loss of their mine. The town's preacher is critiqued for his hypocrisy even beyond his equivocating prototype in *High Noon*, offering his beds to dispossessed lodgers at hotel rates.

Part catalyst, part conscience, the Stranger performs a spiritual function, forcing the town to face its demons. With his arrival, the repressed evil begins to return, as the town is forced to relive its infamy. 'What people fear is what's inside them,' he tells Verna Bloom's Sarah Belding, in the kind of moral-pointing line that Eastwood often employs. Wife of the hotel owner, Sarah is set apart from the outset, looking down on the Stranger from a veranda, significant staging in a film that privileges the elevated.

Mordecai's flashback exonerates Sarah, who alone was moved to intervene but was held back by her husband. Riven with pity, Mordecai is also exonerated. Under the boardwalk, the lowest of the low, he is superior to the businessmen, pillars of the community. In another interesting reading, Paul Smith suggests that in trying to recuperate the traditional 'Oedipalised' Western, the film can be seen as constructing an embryonic family made up of the Stranger, Sarah and Mordecai as child. Smith posits the film as a Hollywoodising of the spaghettis, repositioning the dirty hero as patriarch, whereas biographer Richard Schickel claims for the film a radical revisionism: 'Far more than *Dirty Harry*, it tests, redefines the nature of screen heroism.' That such opposed readings can be argued would undoubtedly please Eastwood.[11]

The Stranger and Mordecai (Billy Curtis) pillage Lago

However, Mordecai's role has more explicit functions. Most prominently, he provides a surrealist and comic jolt, a dwarf out West as the hero's sidekick who is appointed both mayor and sheriff. The butt of jokes and a despised errand boy, Mordecai's inversion of status is the Stranger's mocking comment on the town's power structure. In a film that embraces elevation as a signifier of superiority and advantage, the vertically challenged Mordecai is the film's device for qualifying the point: the size of the inner person is what counts. So Mordecai is given Grace Kelly's privileged function in *High Noon*, killing off a final threat to the Stranger. Modest Mordecai thus qualifies the virulent anti-populism that the film otherwise shares with its predecessor.

Like much Eastwood, the film appeals rousingly to the audience's desire for justice, the avenging angel punishing Sodom for its crucifixion of the law, instructing the mean-spirited in the ways of charity. Divesting them of their goods, the price of his service for the town against its own hired killers, the Stranger then abandons its citizenry. Having balanced the moral accounts with the anti-community that is Lago, he turns to the final act of its judgment day, executing the executioners.

'Forgive and forget', the cherubic sheriff tells us, is the town's amnesiac motto, but the opening images of its cemetery position Lago under the sign of the cross, site of the unspeakable act that haunts the tortured community. In *High Plains Drifter*, Eastwood exploits the genre's mythic substructure to create a crypto-Calvary fable, an allegory where revenge and resurrection meet, hero as Christ and anti-Christ. Aptly, this noir redeemer's spiritual force appears vested in a super-masculinity embodied in a supreme physical presence. Authority in various forms – spiritual, moral, legal – and in different guises – corrupted, usurped, butchered – is clearly the film's subject, but the authority of the Stranger is first and foremost a matter of superior manhood. A cigar may be only a cigar, but it also can be the sign of a male deity who will take your goods and your woman if you are evil. A town without children, without innocence, Lago is also a town without balls, as Callie puts it, complaining of her 'forcible rape in broad daylight'.

The mockery that is a prime weapon of the Stranger is also visited on Callie and Sarah, humiliated for their sexual hypocrisy. Both women are stereotyped as in denial, physically attacking the arrogant man, in effect asking for it. This hoary sexist cliché is particularly egregious in the case of Callie, who is coded as town tramp, belonging to Stacey (Geoffrey Lewis), the lead killer before he went to prison, and thereafter to one of the capitalists, but succumbing to the Stranger, and then returning for seconds as well as to set him up. The two women can be seen as offshoots of *High Noon*'s Mrs Ramirez, with Callie embodying the sexual side of the Katy Jurado character, who was likewise linked to three men, including Gary Cooper's hero and Frank, the head killer. Verna Bloom's Sarah, on the other hand, can be seen to represent her predecessor's honesty and independence, although in a typical Eastwood motif she requires the touch of the Stranger to rediscover herself, abandon her corrupt husband and – like Ramirez – leave town. These sexual dynamics confirm the body as the vessel of the Stranger's spiritual authority.

The Outlaw Josey Wales (1976)

'Josey' – a sweetly feminine name if ever there was one – is more apt for the hero we meet briefly in the pre-credit sequence, the vulnerable family man and yeoman farmer who loses his wife and son to a murderous raid by Union redlegs, than for the bitter vigilante born of that ordeal. Again harking back to Leone's practice of coding his mysterious heroes in religious terms, Eastwood's martyr buries his family and then drives a cross into the ground, his body draped across it as if on a rack, a frontier Job. Unearthing a gun from the ruins, the blood streaking his face like stigmata, he performs a tortured target practice, in the process beginning to metamorphose into the transcendent character of legend that will refuse to renounce his quest for revenge at war's end.

Collapsed into a bleached, blue-tinted montage credit sequence, the brevity of the Civil War's depiction serves nicely to underscore its failure to heal Josey's scars. Offered amnesty by his unit's commander, Fletcher (John Vernon), Josey refuses to 'come in', and thus embraces the renegade status that will result in the irony of his pursuit by Terrill (Bill McKinney), the destroyer of his family, the hunter thus being hunted by his prey. In this second Western directed by Eastwood, there is little doubt as to the satanic function of the villain, the red-headed commander who not only devastates Josey's Edenic homestead but also slaughters Josey's comrades when they accept the offer of amnesty. Thus the plot's wrinkle is to position Josey as a classic righteous revenge hero, but simultaneously to construct him as a fugitive due to his refusal to surrender. Forestalling the normal trajectory towards vengeance, this reversal softens the character, in contrast to Terrill who takes on a depraved righteousness. It is as if he is the wounded one on a personal mission. He will not only track Wales to Texas but will also ferret out others: 'Texas is full of rebels ... doing good ain't got no end.' The missionary zeal is perverted, recalling Milton's Satan of *Paradise Lost*: 'Evil, be *thou* my good.'

Walking a tightrope with his character, Eastwood emphasises the humanity of Josey both in the beginning and as his odyssey progresses, while still cloaking him in mythic dimensions. Anticipating the ambush of his comrades, he rides in to commandeer a Union machine gun and single-handedly reverse the slaughter, then mysteriously vanishes from its covered wagon site. 'Hell is where he's headed,' observes the senator pulling the strings behind the ambush.

The plot's ingenious reversal of the avenger pursued by his quarry was Philip Kaufman's idea, for which he duly received a shared screen credit with Sonia Chernus, Eastwood's story editor. Director of *The Great Northfield Minnesota Raid* (1972) and *White Dawn* (1974), Kaufman had originally been hired by Eastwood to helm the project, but had been unceremoniously removed when he pondered over a shot whose logistics seemed straightforward to the impatient actor-producer. Eastwood probably felt that what he had absorbed working with Siegel applied: 'I think if there is one thing I learned from Don Siegel, it's to know what you want to shoot and to know what you're seeing when you see it.'[12]

Positioning Josey as a fugitive, the film defers the revenge and relaxes the tone – Ford's *My Darling Clementine* comes to mind – as the hero makes his episodic journey and accumulates a scruffy band around him. Making his escape from the ambush, Josey had a young sidekick, Jamie (Sam Bottoms), who had been mortally wounded by Terrill. A surrogate son, Jamie had helped to thwart Josey's arrest by two river rats lusting for the reward on his head. Reluctantly, Josey had tied the boy's body to his horse, and sent it off as a decoy.

Enter Chief Dan George's Lone Watie, the witty Native American who becomes Josey's lieutenant. His own wife and two sons had died on 'the trail of the tears'; he and Josey, who had cried after burying his family, are empathic. The chief mourns the loss of Indian skills since he and his tribe were declared 'civilised', and joins the fugitive, burning his Lincoln get-up of stove-pipe hat and coat. Their land taken from them, they had been encouraged 'to endeavour to persevere', which also appears to be Josey's lot. In due course, a Navajo maiden, Little Moonlight (Geraldine Keams), and a mutt who Josey keeps spraying with tobacco juice, follow them. Shortly thereafter, they add the survivors of a Kansas family that includes garrulous old Granny (Paula Trueman) and Sondra Locke's waif, Laura Lee, as well as the remaining citizens of Santa Rio, the ghost town adjoining the El Dorado on which they settle.

'I don't want no one belonging to me,' says Josey, having lost everything once. As in Hawks's *Rio Bravo*, the hero both resists and needs comradeship, the point underlined by the final battle where the whole group backs Josey against the siege of Terrill's redlegs. In contrast to *High Plains Drifter*, where the corrupt town is cauterised, here the seeds of a new community are planted. Reconciliation is the theme: 'we all died a little in that damn war'. Josey's epitaph is in part for himself, the unreconstructed Southerner acknowledging the costs of the hostilities as he and Fletcher, who had been forced to play Judas to Josey's Christ, tacitly agree to let the legendary gunfighter die. It is a stratagem devised by Ten Spot (Royal Dano, the Anthony Mann veteran), who tells Texas Rangers that he witnessed Wales's death. Josey's line, a typically pointed reference by Eastwood, invites us to draw parallels between the action and the divisions of American society. *Josey Wales* can be seen, in J. Hoberman's phrase, as 'a crypto-Vietnam film'.[13]

Reaching their rural paradise, the Texas equivalent of Josey's destroyed Eden that the fiendish Terrill will also threaten, Josey and his group have re-enacted the genre's archetypal journey of pioneers to the Promised Land. Eastwood marks the spot by borrowing windows with apertures in the shape of crosses from Ford's *Rio Grande* for their new home – you can shoot up or down, from side to side, Josey explains helpfully. A Ford-like celebration is also enacted, Josey and Laura Lee dancing to 'Rose of Alabama', the dead Jaimie's tune. At one point, Granny says grace, giving thanks that Josey has changed 'from a murderous bushwhacker on the side of Satan to a better man trying to deliver us from the philistines'. The religious coordinates may not be accurate, but Josey is changing. The farm reminds him of the loss of his earlier settled life, and he walks into the woods with the virginal Laura Lee. Esssentially another revenge comedy, and mildly revisionist, the film reconstitutes the Chosen People for the most part as Native American and/or female. However, Josey's leadership and violent skills position him as the empowering patriarch, as crucial to the survival of this new multicultural nation as we may speculate that his seed, presumably deposited in Laura Lee, will also be to its future.

The trajectory of the film, the community forming under the shadow of bloodshed, describes the film's main action. The theme is further developed in the bond of peace struck between Josey and Ten Bears (Will Sampson), chief of the neighbouring Comanche that also threaten the new community. The scene is unusual for the sustained length of the Eastwood character's speech, a formal presentation that in part is designed to show respect for Ten Bears. For warriors like themselves, Wales tells the chief, dying is not hard; it is living that is the challenge. He has come to offer a choice – the word of

life or that of death. The care Eastwood takes in this scene is reflected in the choice of
Native American actor Will Sampson and the integrity of his performance as Ten Bears.
Throughout the film, representation of Native American characters and their treatment
is given similar respect. Chief Dan George's presence sets the tone, and his one-liners
help sketch a history lesson from an old Cherokee's point of view: 'The white man has
been sneaking up on us for years.' Little Moonlight is nearly raped in a trading post ('Put
her on the bill, too'), and is gratuitously slashed across the face by a Union soldier. Violence against Indians is an everyday occurrence; Indian scalps are on sale in Western
towns.

   A journey film and saga, *Josey Wales* recalls *The Searchers*, which also features an unreconstructed Confederate hero whose path takes him into the Indian nation. Invidiously
comparing the two, Schickel has critiqued Ford's film for its racist portrayal of Indians
as savage, and for suggesting that obsession can be heroic. He also finds *The Man Who
Shot Liberty Valance* wanting in affirming the lie – 'Print the legend' – whereas Josey
Wales lets the legend die. Schickel suppresses the advantage Eastwood enjoys of a later
generation's ideological awareness in his representation of the Indians. A pitfall of authorised biographies, Schickel's bias downsizes outstanding films from an earlier era that
have a radical edge to uplift a later, fine film, mellow and adventurous in its way. Schickel
is also silent about the treatment of Sondra Locke's character, the film licking its chops
over a protracted near-rape that gratuitously strips the woman top and bottom.

Eastwood and Will Sampson as Ten Bears: updating Ford's multicultural frontier

Although evidencing much less sauce, the film everywhere shows borrowings from and references to Leone's spaghettis. The slaughter of the surrendering rebels echoes Ramon's very similar treachery from *A Fistful of Dollars*, and the turncoat ferryman who expediently sings the 'Battle Hymn of the Republic' or 'Dixie' depending on his cargo is pure Leone. Bruce Surtees' lighting often recalls Leone's dark interiors, as with the scene of Little Moonlight's abuse, where the heavily shadowed trading post is not unlike Monument Valley's in *Once Upon a Time in the West*. Eastwood's villains and river rats show flashes of Leone-like bestiality. No Name's descendant here is older, bearded, but the backlit silhouette suddenly framed in the trading post's doorway is unmistakable, a virtual ideogram of The Man With No Name.

Josey Wales replaces the spaghettis' business of smoking a cheroot with the chewing and spitting of tobacco. Josey decorates with its juice the heads of various dead villains, the white suit of a carpetbagger and the family's hound, as well as handy scorpions and beetles. He risks Granny's wrath by nearly staining their new abode, but gulps and swallows instead. A sign of the character's uncivilised state, the spitting gives way finally to bleeding, evidence that it is over, the wound is open. Josey is born again at the end, leaving the nomadic life behind. Pursuing the defeated Terrill after the final battle, he corners him and bears down with revolvers in each hand, clicking off empty rounds. Is he acknowledging his readiness to forgo revenge? The bloodied, fanatical redleg draws his sabre high and the two struggle, the blade finally dispatching Terrill in a forced suicide. The film ends with the hero riding into the sun. Will he return to the community? Eastwood claims it is open-ended, but logic insists The Man With No Name has been civilised.

Pale Rider (1985)

The heroes of *High Plains Drifter* and *Josey Wales* describe a trajectory from anonymity to celebrity, both achieving mythic status. The Stranger rides off, but with his fictional death, Josey retires. This is logical enough, since although the film amply provides the typical Eastwood punch of villains dispatched by a charismatic hero, its charm comes from a balancing warmth and humanity less in evidence in the much darker *Drifter*. In part, this reflects the action of the two films as well – Josey's redemption and reconciliation as opposed to the Stranger's retribution.

At first glance, *Pale Rider* clearly offers itself as a bookend to *High Plains Drifter*, both in its debt to an earlier classic and for its super-natural hero. There are, however, significant distinctions. Elevating George Stevens and Alan Ladd's gunfighter-hero of *Shane* to biblical proportions, *Pale Rider* essentially remakes the original with modest adjustments to update the action for a contemporary audience. *High Plains Drifter*'s approach is trickier, positing a parallel universe, where on the one hand the events of *High Noon* have already transpired, albeit with catastrophic outcomes, and where those events are now rehearsed to provide redress.

Benefiting from this much freer structure, *High Plains Drifter* darkens the dead marshal's shade, positioning the Western hero as a doppelgänger, a harsh noir god who brings Lago its judgment day by all but destroying the community. Benign effects – empowering Mordecai and Sarah – are marginal to the Stranger's punitive mission. In contrast, the Preacher (the name is significant), like Shane before him, comes first to empower a faltering frontier family and community. Smite the wicked he must, but such action is secondary to the love and support he brings. *Pale Rider*'s trick is to elevate the gunfighter to divine status to punish evildoers, but yet give him a humanising face-lift that will allow the character to inspire the victimised community with a spiritual uplift. Given this perspective, the film would seem to be closer to the positive energy of *Josey Wales* than to the darker *High Plains Drifter*.

Crucial to the design and action of *Pale Rider* is the sidekick, a staple genre charac- ter. In the earlier films, Mordecai, the dwarf, and Lone Watie, the Cherokee chief, had taken the role. In each case a source of humour and warmth, they reduce the isolation of the revenge hero, a classic function, and also serve to underscore the hero's superior masculinity. This is explicitly foregrounded with the dwarf in his role as witness to the Stranger's violent and sexual prowess, which he rewards (like a Leone character) with cigars. More important structurally, Chief Dan George's character, like that of Ten Bears, works to extend reconciliation beyond the warring sides of the Civil War to include the Native American in the emerging American community. Functioning more like the genre's traditional sidekick, Lone Watie also sides Wales in a face-off with four Union soldiers, and picks one off. Comically, the ageing chief also beds Little Moonlight in a mock competition, the humour of which flows from the idea of the super-sexual white male being defeated by the old Indian geezer.

In *Pale Rider*, the relationship of hero and sidekick is far more central to the issues of masculine authority that the film debates. Hull Barret (Michael Moriarty), the prospec- tor who heads the struggling community terrorised by the mining baron, Coy Lahood (Richard Dysart), is immediately drawn to the Preacher but remains his own man. A more familiar populist American type than either the dwarf or the chief, Hull's com- mon man is the industrious prospector and yeoman settler. Above all, he is the dedicated family man, albeit ambiguously positioned, since he has failed to persuade Sarah Wheeler (Holly Hunter), abandoned by her husband with daughter Megan (Sydney Penny), to commit herself. 'You'll wait a long time if you wait for a woman to make up her mind,' opines the Preacher.

This suggestion of an uncertain masculinity is confirmed from the outset. Hull is emblematic of the frontier community's inability to protect itself against the land- hungry Lahood's hired guns. Thus the film opens with the prospectors helpless against an attack on their camp perched precariously on a hillside, followed by a scene where Hull insists on going into town alone, a foolhardy step, onlookers suggest. Sure enough, taking supplies to his wagon, he is surrounded by Lahood bullies who beat him repeat- edly with axe handles in the town's muddy street. Enter the Preacher.

Leone's trademark introduction of his mysterious stranger blowing away a gaggle of oafs is adapted here by Eastwood to a less bloody encounter. Hefting his own axe han- dle like a pike, the Preacher whacks the gang into submission, rescuing Hull with awesome efficiency. Eastwood emphasises his hero's stature by giving him an imposing top hat and dandyish greatcoat that signify a judicial authority, as well as a black kerchief around his neck that hides his parson's collar.

Grateful, the bedraggled Hull invites his saviour to stay in a spare room in the cabin he shares with Sarah and Megan. There the plight of the domesticated male is vividly demonstrated. A shrewish Sarah has assumed that a hired killer is among them, and hysterically berates Hull, only to be brought up short by the stranger with a preacher's collar around his neck, bright white in the dark interior. More evidence of Hull's henpecked situation will emerge when the Preacher disappears. Thinking they have been abandoned, Sarah criticises Hull mercilessly. To his 'I reckon I did all right by you before he came! Didn't I?' Sarah makes no reply.

How can Hull win? He is being measured against a mythical standard, a superhero's masculinity. Burying her murdered dog in a dark glade, Megan had prayed for a miracle, the image superimposed with the stranger descending snowy heights. Later Megan reads the Book of Revelation as the mysterious stranger rides into camp: 'I looked and beheld a pale horse; and his name that sat on him was Death and Hell followed with him.' Washing for dinner, the stranger looks in the mirror and then bends to reveal the scars of a half-dozen bullets in the back. 'YOU!' Stockburn (John Russell), Lahood's chief enforcer, will shout at the figure he thought dead before taking his own six bullets in the chest plus one to the forehead, the *coup de grâce*. Stockburn had not recognised his opponent until the Preacher had lifted his gaze from under the shadow of his hat. Like John Ford's young Lincoln, the Preacher has a castrating gaze that unnerves his opponents. Eastwood has described his hero variously as a supernatural being from a higher plane, an archangel, and one of the Four Horsemen of the Apocalypse.

Hull is oblivious to the fact that Sarah's hysteria (she will apologise for being 'highstrung') has been prompted by the sudden appearance in her life of this extraordinarily forceful figure, as well as by his sudden disappearance, rhyming with that of her husband. Hull is 'a good man', as everyone seems to concede in a kind of mild contempt for an emasculated male who appears to enjoy the burdens of domesticity but not its privileges. In contrast, the stranger and his remarkable mix of virtue and virility overcome both Megan and Sarah.

That manhood is the theme is further confirmed when Club (Richard Kiel), a colossus in the employ of Lahood, visits the camp to eject the newcomer and is incapacitated by the Preacher's uppercut with a sledgehammer to the loins. Such inspired violence converts the giant, and he later prevents Josh Lahood (Christopher Penn), the tycoon's young son, from shooting the Preacher in the back. Another victim of uncertain masculinity, Josh attempts to rape Megan before the Preacher materialises to interrupt the show for all the Lahood workers, putting a bullet through the boy's hand when he tries to draw.

If *Pale Rider* is ultimately less forceful than either of its predecessors, it is because it attempts to meld the fable structure of the first with the historical and pioneer focus of the second. Hull is persuasive at the community's meeting held in the shadows of a campfire. It is not the gold, he tells them, it is the American Dream they are giving up – roots, a home, community, the chance to make something of yourself and of your own. 'I ain't a brave man, but I ain't a coward either,' one of the prospectors had put it, deciding to stick rather than sell. As in *Shane*, the point is made that, ironically, such were the original motives of their oppressor as well. But now Lahood is an empire-builder at a later stage of ambition. Unregulated, his imperialism threatens the community and destroys the land through hydraulic mining. With *Pale Rider*, Eastwood was consciously attempting to resurrect the genre by relating it to contemporary issues, employing environmental sins to blacken its capitalist villains and appeal to the audience's ecological conscience. A few years later, Kevin Costner would employ the same strategy with similarly mixed results in *Dances with Wolves*.

The ecology issues in *Pale Rider* relate the characters' values and behaviours to the larger issues of power and sexuality. Spectacular high-pressure water blasting at the Lahood mine contrasts corporate power with the efforts of the 'tin pans', as the prospectors are contemptuously termed for their old-time prospecting methods. The explosive images of water discharged destructively at enormously high pressure provide an appropriately Freudian rape of the land as background for Josh's attempt on Megan. In contrast, the struggle of the miners (rather like Hull's courtship of Sarah) is a slow and tenacious effort that respects nature as a worthy adversary. Hull had picked a fight with a giant boulder (another borrowing from *Shane*), and the Preacher approves – 'I'd hate to lay odds on who's gonna win that one.' Commencing to sledgehammer the rock in tandem, their teamwork generates interest documented in a montage of other characters given pause. Once the Lahood henchman, Club, has been himself clubbed, the work goes faster as others join in, the empowerment visibly taking hold. Meanwhile, inside, Sarah and Megan check their looks in the mirror, enjoy a girlish chat about early marriage, and discuss whether preachers can wed. Both appear in an erotic daze under the impact of the Preacher's presence.

Although it comes early, the scene is the high point of the film in its vivid picture of a community coming together. However, the test of this emerging identity comes with the news that Lahood is bringing in Marshal Stockburn and his six deputies, instruments of a lethal law available to the highest bidder. At their camp meeting to consider a buyout, the Preacher warns them about Stockburn, for whom 'killing is a way of life', but it is their decision. Eastwood and Surtees shoot the scene in firelight, the faces floating in a threatening darkness as they listen to Hull's eloquent argument.

Shane recycled: a rare display of solidarity in Eastwood

Spider (Doug McGrath), the film's recycling of the Elisha Cook, Jr character who is the brutal Jack Palance's victim in the original, is similarly dispatched by Stockburn and his deputies in the town's snowy main street. The Preacher again addresses the miners, who encircle the body retrieved from town. Eastwood's antipathy to long dialogue scenes is well known, but his character is often allowed to focus themes:

> The vote you took the other night showed courage. You voted to stick together and you should. Spider made a mistake . . . A man alone is easy prey. Only by staying together are you going to be able to defeat the Lahoods of the world.

Good advice, but the notion that the settlers may control their fate is soon dismissed. Spooking Hull's horse the next morning to prevent him joining in the final confrontation, the Preacher tells him to take care of the women, defining the domesticated male's turf and leaving Hull to walk home. Refusing to accept an emasculated role, Hull materialises after the Stockburn enforcers are all dead in time to waste Lahood, who was about to deliver a shotgun blast to the Preacher's back.

Hull's action is important to the film's investment in the common man. However, despite this small dignity finally accorded him, Eastwood had actually reduced the stature *Shane* accorded the homesteader. There the chasm between miner and gunfighter was negotiable, and in a key scene the two had fought the enemy back to back. The decline in commoner status and increased gap between saviour and saved is also reflected in the casting, Van Heflin's stardom downgraded to character actor Michael Moriarty.

Eastwood was fond of characterising his audience as working stiffs who'd like to tell their bosses off. They identified with No Name and Harry, because those worthies cut through to essentials and delivered justice. Evidently the audience was like Hull, downtrodden, needful of transcendence, but reclaimable. But crucially, Hull's growth is not extended to a general empowerment of the collective, the film simply collapsing back on its superhero to install a frontier democracy. As opposed to *Josey Wales*, the focus remains fixed on the hero's magical skills, the miners left behind in the film's denouement. In keeping with its hero's adopted persona, the film cannot dramatise its theme, only preach it.

Much more than *Shane* or even *High Plains Drifter*, *Pale Rider* brought to the surface the saviour subtext of the classical Western in a biblical and supernatural form. Entering as a soft-spoken clergyman with good manners and respect for women, the hero gradually emerged as the violent super-male. Thus a classic turning point is the retrieval of the guns that had been hung up in the past that precedes the two finales, the gift of love to Sarah and the wholesale deaths of the Lahood forces at the end.

If making the defeat of villainy essentially a one-man affair weakens the film's empowering of the community, *Pale Rider*'s going beyond *Shane* in having the hero bed the good man's woman also has its problematic consequences. The teenage Megan is gently discouraged but the Preacher allows her mother knowledge of him in the biblical sense, an act of charity to repair Sarah's self-esteem and free her to marry Hull. In *High Plains Drifter*, the sexual exploits of the Stranger were in keeping with his mission of stripping the town of its hypocrisy. Above the crowd, he had no need of the women. Josey's encounter with Sondra Locke's Laura Lee, on the other hand, was a sign that the character was healing, going home.

However, in Sarah's encounter we are to understand that she is given the opportunity to find out what a real (or unreal) man is like. Hopefully, memories of this will not diminish the intimacy she shares with Hull, and what that good man does not know evidently will not hurt him (even if, as seems likely, the god will leave his seed behind). If an attempt to update the original to a sexually sophisticated era, the conquest of Sarah by Eastwood's superhero increases the already yawning gap between him and Michael Moriarty's inescapably diminished citizen.

Often accused of catering to the rednecks, Eastwood's films certainly can be said to engage populist sympathies in seeking to vicariously inspire the audience. The director often expressed his contempt for the intellectual who presumes to speak for 'the masses'. At the same time, he himself has referred impatiently to the needs of 'the eighty million popcorn eaters', and of having to supply them with a taste of power as opposed to being freer to experiment. This difficult balancing act is reflected in *Pale Rider*. Eschewing the irony and nihilist edge reminiscent of Leone in *High Plains Drifter*, *Pale Rider* also lacks the satisfying generosity of *Josey Wales*. Its ecological theme remains undeveloped, so that the struggle between the small entrepreneur and oppressive monopoly capitalism never rises above stock genre conventions. A pleasant entertainment, *Pale Rider* attempts to bring the traditional Western into a contemporary relevance that never coheres. The film remains a conservative post-modern work, a nostalgia text.

Unforgiven (1992)

As Eastwood increasingly became his own director, he showed a disinclination to put himself under the authority of other, especially established, film-makers. The fiasco of collaborating with Kaufman provided an exemplary lesson. Eastwood would disparage talk of the auteur – movies were a collaborative medium. Perhaps so, but both films and life suggested a controlling personality, preoccupied with issues of masculinity and authority. Relevant was his two-year stint (1986–8) as mayor of Carmel, his home base, undertaken in a fit of pique over a planning commission's rejection of plans to extend his restaurant, the Hog's Breath Inn.

Either way, after Don Siegel, Eastwood would only rarely work with a veteran craftsman like Ted Post (*Magnum Force*) whom he knew from *Rawhide* days and had used on *Hang 'Em High*. *City Heat* (1984), a depression comedy with Burt Reynolds, was originally to have been directed by the high-powered Blake Edwards, but after 'creative differences' with Eastwood emerged, he was replaced with a more malleable Richard Benjamin. Offered the role of Willard that Martin Sheen was to play in *Apocalypse Now*, Eastwood had declined, citing a reluctance to commit to a protracted stay in the Philippines. It is impossible to envisage the star under Francis Ford Coppola's direction. Leone and Siegel had helped to craft his persona; he was clearly loath to lend it to strong film-makers, in effect to subordinate it to another's vision.

Most frequently, Eastwood preferred debuting directors such as Michael Cimino (*Thunderbolt and Lightfoot* [1974]), James Fargo, his former assistant (*The Enforcer* [1976], *Every Which Way But Loose* [1978], *Any Which Way You Can* [1980]), and screenwriter Richard Tuggle (whose *Tightrope* Eastwood had taken over while eschewing the credit). This pattern was to continue between *Pale Rider* and *Unforgiven*, during which he made *Dirty Harry*'s swansong, *The Dead Pool* (1988), and a light-hearted road movie with Bernadette Peters, *Pink Cadillac* (1989), both directed by his former stunt coordinator, Buddy Van Horn.

His own directorial efforts included *Heartbreak Ridge* (1986), a comic portrait of a macho Marine hero, *Bird*, which starred Forrest Whitaker as jazz great Charlie Parker, and *White Hunter, Black Heart* (1990), where Eastwood portrayed a thinly disguised John Huston in Africa during his filming of *The African Queen* (1951). These latter two efforts, both of which Eastwood took to Cannes, suggested an impulse to capitalise on a rise in critical stock that less mainstream efforts such as *Bronco Billy* had helped generate. In 1983 the director had been feted with retrospectives in Paris, Munich and London; in 1988 he received a Cecil B. DeMille Lifetime Achievement Award at the Golden Globes. After a long period of condescension from the critics, Eastwood was coming in out of the cold. Despite the contrary evidence of *The Rookie* (1990), a slapdash cop film with Charlie Sheen, this ambition for prestige and status was to be confirmed with Eastwood's final return to the Western, *Unforgiven*.

The tendency to control the show is also evidenced throughout Eastwood's career by an extreme reluctance to share the stage with significant co-stars, players at his level. Most of his films, like the *Dirty Harry* series or his Westerns, after all, were solidly built around his characters. Audiences liked Clint, with whom they felt on a first-name basis, and who satisfied their needs for transcendence. Especially in Malpaso productions, why build in unnecessarily large above-the-line actor fees? In fact, claims for Eastwood's enlightened policy of advancing the careers of neglected or newcomer actresses (Jessica Walter, Tyne Daly, Sondra Locke, Genevieve Bujold) also need to be seen through the lenses of economics and control. Eastwood's one early experience of work with a major female star, the formidable Shirley MacLaine in *Two Mules for Sister Sara*, had also been instructive.

Certainly the ensemble cast of *Unforgiven* had no precedent in the director's previous efforts; the casting of heavyweights like Gene Hackman, Richard Harris and Morgan Freeman was clearly a marker indicating an unprecedented ambition. The importance of the casting cannot be overstated. In particular, Hackman's overbearing marshal solidly anchors the scene in Big Whiskey, laying the foundation for the extended parallel narrative action that develops dynamically between his violent, autocratic dealings with the miscreant cowboys and English Bob, and the journey of Will, Ned and the Schofield Kid in his direction.

The scale of the film must have called for caution. Optioned by Eastwood some six years earlier, David Webb Peoples's screenplay had been shelved until the opportune moment, in the end to be shot largely as written. Half-seriously, Eastwood entertained the notion that he was waiting to grow into the role (he was sixty-two in 1992). More to the point, the spectacular success of Costner's *Dances with Wolves* two years earlier undoubtedly played into the timing of his decision. In any case, the delay provided a space for hibernation and gestation, reflected in the extraordinary sure-footedness and deliberation the film's crafting communicates.

The epic scope of Peoples's dark canvas must have intrigued Eastwood, especially as it involved in its protagonist a further combining of the humanised hero of *Josey Wales* with the archetypal construct of his *Drifter*. *Unforgiven* offered a synthesis, far more dramatic than in the case of Josey, of farmer and legend, person and avenging angel. Domesticated by his now dead wife, Will Munny at the outset of the film is 'just a feller now', an ageing Kansas pig-farmer barely able to shoot or ride. A noir Western, *Unforgiven* reverses the humanising trajectory of *Josey Wales*, its hero taking on murderous and monstrous proportions. It is as if Josey was coming out of retirement, reclaiming his ambiguous legend and archetypal function rooted in the frontier's violent past. Will's rampage is fuelled by the wrath of the fallen convert, the unborn-again.

The historical framework sketched by *Unforgiven* gives the film a reach and depth unprecedented in Eastwood. After five decades of sustained success in popular cinema, Eastwood is routinely referred to as an American icon, but it is debatable whether the actor has the national resonance of a Wayne, Fonda or Stewart. An earlier generation, veterans of work with giants like John Ford and Frank Capra, they seemed wrapped in national values, products of the American experiment, exemplars of a historical energy and will. Eastwood's ultimate iconic meaning generally has to do with an image of masculinity rather than a national ethos, with a fusion of the dirty Westerner and Dirty Harry, figures in an existential landscape.[14]

However, William Munny was a novel hero for Eastwood because of the epic scale of the history – his and America's – that was brought into focus. As Will and Ned ride with the Schofield Kid towards their rendezvous with the two cowboys who had cut a whore's face, a discourse arises that has to do with the morality of the frontier experience. As Will talks of his nightmares of the bloody past and feverishly raves on about his demons, the confessions by firelight paint a tarnished image of the Old West. Parallel to and synchronised with these morbid reveries is the encounter of English Bob (Richard Harris) and his biographer, Beauchamp (Saul Rubinek), with Sheriff Little Bill Daggett (Gene Hackman). The resulting critique of the writer's dime novel featuring the exploits of English Bob brings to bear an analysis of myth's role as historical construct. Bill's wilful correction of the novel's title – *Duck of Death* rather than *Duke of Death* – nicely replaces nobility with cowardice as a defining focus.

The result of this self-conscious, critical structure is a film that inevitably recalls John Ford's *The Man Who Shot Liberty Valance* in its interrogation of American identity and its critique of historiography. However, in a surprisingly sentimental touch, Eastwood had dedicated *Unforgiven* to Leone and Siegel, his two mentors, and thought that the latter, in particular, would have liked the film, presumably for its anti-hero. It seems certain that Leone would have also applauded No Name's last hurrah as the Grim Reaper in what can be seen as Eastwood's own version of 'Once Upon a Time in the West'.

The two characters who are structurally central to this revisionism are the Kid (Jaimz Woolvett) and Beauchamp, the student and the writer. Both are seen as deluded, the boy blind and the author possessed. The appeal of legend, its intrinsic exaggeration, is demonstrated in the embroidered accounts of the mutilated prostitute, first by the Kid, who describes her eyes being cut, and then by Will, who reports wounds to 'everything but her cunny, I guess'. Victims of romance, the boy aspires to live in its rarefied air, and the writer aims at a 'certain poetry'. Education is a stock motif of the genre, traditionally involving lessons in the character and skills needed for survival. But the process here disabuses us of illusions. The heroic fictionalised history is corrected by Little Bill's testimony, which paints a world of incompetence and dishonour. Meanwhile, the Schofield Kid painfully learns the mortal costs of adventure: 'I ain't like you, Will,' he finally concedes. He is ready to forgo the reward, but Munny insists on the split and sends the Kid off to 'get those spectacles'.

The film opens under the sign of the 'teensy little pecker' and the cut whore, masculinity and its discontents. The violence that defines the West is an expression of disturbed men: 'I was drunk most of the time.' Munny carries guilt for indiscriminate murder of the innocent, of women and children. The law is equally unbalanced, a tyrannical and brutal justice ('Innocent of what?') that is personally administered with a sadistic pleasure. As in Leone's West, savagery has invaded the community. *Unforgiven* offers a Freudian account of American's past where the gun stands in for the penis, as well as embodying the phallus. According to Little Bill, English Bob's victim, Two-gun Corrigan, had been so called not because he carried two guns, but because of his outsize member, longer than the barrel of his weapon. The sheriff clarifies the power of the six-gun, correcting misconceptions. It is not speed that produces success but the authority with which it is employed. 'Hot, ain't it?' laughs Bill as he takes the gun back from Beauchamp.

Women have no access to such power. As Strawberry Alice (Frances Fisher), the leader, points out, 'Just because we let 'em ride us doesn't mean we're horses – we're whores, not horses!' Women as '*prop*-erty', a bemused Daggett remarks, recognising the claim that a disfigured prostitute is damaged goods. Eastwood has been praised for giving the plight of women a centrality that sets in motion the bloody saga, and for representing a Western hero who, like Ford's characters, honours the memory of his wife. But a catalyst they remain, the dead Claudia and the women relegated to the sidelines. In its overview of the frontier, *Unforgiven* constructs a community at the grassroots level of civilisation, a primitive 1880 represented by macho dynamics where women are marginalised, and their civilising function is absent, or put in question: 'Why do women marry men of notoriously vicious and intemperate disposition?' The mystery of Claudia's choice of Munny, posed at the outset, remains in the film's last statement.

Seeing Strawberry Alice's act in leading the whores to seek redress as evidence of a praiseworthy independence and nascent feminism is to overlook its consequences. It is Alice's thirst for blood that triggers the cycle of violence, the expanding arc of savagery and death that structures the film's action – the brutal beatings and messy executions finally culminating in the whipping of Ned and the finale's slaughter. 'We all got it coming': the design of the film is to show how violence begets violence, how the appetite for blood grows.

A key moment that focuses these issues is the return of the errant cowboys with their horses for Skinny Dubois (Anthony James), payment for disfiguring Delilah (Anna Thomson). The best of the lot is held back by the young Davey (Rob Campbell), who instead extends it to the cut whore in a transparently sincere offer of penance. 'A *pony*?' Alice is aghast that such is being volunteered to compensate for the devastated face. How much might such a fine animal be worth towards a new life for Delilah? The question does not arise in the context of the thousand dollars the women have amassed as a reward to induce candidates for the job of killing the two men. Alice's mission is less the recovery of Delilah and more the advancement of rights for the most despised of women, whore's rights; it is less humanitarian than political.

From this point of view, Alice qualifies as a frontier femme fatale whose crucial role ultimately triggers the emergence of Will Munny's classic noir hero as purveyor of a monstrous justice. The beckoning reward draws the characters to Big Whiskey's dark frontier: English Bob, who will be expelled, damaged in body and soul; the Kid, who will escape broken in spirit; Ned, who will die of torture; Will, who will regress into a black creature of the night. In the best tradition of noir protagonists, Munny finds himself being overtaken by a previous identity, feelings and actions out of the past. Signs of this eruption flare in the dark around the campfire as a classic storm rattles overhead and Will is tortured by his memories. In fact, the film features three dark storms, its last cataclysmic, which contribute to the film's cosmic, metaphysical edge.

Hero as executioner

Over and over again, protesting too much, the man tells us he's 'no longer like that'. Yet the noir coding of darkness, shadows and rain on the trail testify to a journey back to the future, as does the sign of the grave that frames and hovers over the narrative. Like the unstable, lost and amnesiac characters of classic noir, Will's grip on his identity is uncertain, shifting back and forth from born again to dead again. Indeed, his monstrous manifestation as an Angel of Death at the end represents an inglorious escalation of the classic noir hero's walk of the dead man as the ultimate incarnation of the retribution the film contemplates. He is a dead man walking, the condemned, but as executioner rather than victim.

It is possible to read *Unforgiven*'s noir trajectory in relation to an American society in which an appetite for such bloody justice persists. Indeed, the decade after the film's release saw a continued defence of capital punishment in an attempt to silence the insistent raising of voices against the death penalty. To the dismay of many of its citizens, the USA remains one of the few Western democracies to retain execution as punishment. In the words of the Supreme Court in ruling it constitutional, 'certain crimes are themselves so grievous an affront to humanity that the only adequate response may be the penalty of death'. Against this, however, are the questions that have come increasingly into focus concerning the administration of the death penalty, and the growing conviction that, like Will Munny, the state is a killer of innocents, women and children. The emergence of DNA testing has seen the exoneration and release of a growing number of the imprisoned, often from the nation's death rows. Questions surrounding forced confessions and the possibilities of a miscarriage of justice have led a number of states to declare a moratorium on executions. In 2003, Illinois went further, pardoning four wrongly convicted inmates and commuting the death sentences of some 160, rescuing them from 'society's ultimate weapon'. The debate is especially fuelled by the numerous executions in Texas – the Big Whiskey of our day – including minorities in disproportionate numbers, the young and retarded, as well as the occasional woman. In its study of the prosecution of a murder case in Houston, Errol Morris's distinguished 1988 documentary *The Thin Blue Line* penetrates to the heart of the matter. It describes vividly the bloodthirstiness that is aroused by events that can finally override questions of guilt and innocence, and the politics that invariably play into whether individuals are executed, pardoned or paroled.

Unforgiven insists on the construction of its drunken killer as cowboy, Western hero, America. But although the film allows for a reading of its bloodthirsty frontier justice as a historical perspective on the nation's troubled policies of capital punishment, it nowhere highlights or, indeed, even seems aware of such parallels. *True Crime*, which Eastwood produced, directed and starred in six years later, is relevant. Screwing the suspense tight, the film has Eastwood's burnt-out alcoholic journalist racing to pull off a last-minute rescue of an innocent man. However, while effectively dramatising a potentially tragic miscarriage, capital punishment is less the subject than a context. Instead, the focus is on the paradox, reminiscent of Ford's heroes, of a damaged man incapable of sustaining a family role saving an African-American who, with his wife and child, are coded spiritually (it is Christmas) as a holy family, exemplars of the domestic ideal. A typical Eastwood reverse, the Christ figure saved by the flawed mortal.

However, that *Unforgiven*'s project is to explore violent justice as an American affair becomes clear with the film's vignette of English Bob's arrival as the first aspiring bounty hunter on Independence Day. Beaten brutally, Bob is punished in part for the suggestion that British royalty is a superior system immune from violent attacks such as the assassination of President Garfield. Making such scurrilous statements in a town decorated with Old Glory calls for a lesson by the sheriff, who evidently fancies himself the protector of the nation's honour. However, as the leaky house Little Bill is building signals, his claim to the settled life is shaky. Daggett dispenses a savage public injustice personally, entertaining a shamed community with his brutality. As in *High Plains Drifter*, whipping is the ultimate violence, a sadistic spectacle of one-upmanship disguised as legal authority. In the noir frontier that is the film's subject, retribution is always inequitable; everyone gets unjust deserts.

Unforgiven's revisionist agenda is obvious. Putting three bullets from his big gun into the man who sits helplessly on an outhouse toilet, the Kid discovers killing's impact on the soul. In a strange, static scene in an open bleak landscape ominous with dread, the boy guzzles from a bottle desperate to drown the memory ('I blazed away'), as Munny looks off to the far distance where one of the whores is coming with their reward: 'Take a drink, Kid.' But it is Will who takes the bottle when he hears of Ned's fate, the drink animating the ghost of his past. Like earlier versions of The Man With No Name, Munny had suffered a ritual beating and symbolic death at the hands of Daggett. Now whiskey's unholy sacrament seals the process, the killer resurrected. Similarly, the writer is introduced to death at first hand as Will shoots down Skinny Dubois for 'decorating his saloon with my friend', along with the sheriff and a half-dozen deputies. His attempt to perform a ghoulish on-site interview about the order in which the victims having irked the killer, he scuttles away to huddle in the rain as the murderous apparition rides out.

Death is unheroic, ignominious. The killing of the cowboys is a messy business, 'Davey boy' crawling desperately away, Ned unable to pull the trigger, Will firing, missing, firing – 'I'm dyin', boys.' A lonely, cruel death, it is matched by the ignominious outhouse killing. The film also pauses over Little Bill's end, emphasising that death and justice (as he should know) are not related: ' "Deserves" got nothing to do with it.' The intimate nature of killing, the personal violation of the person, is insisted upon, Eastwood cutting between the squinting man above deliberately aiming the weapon and the victim helpless below.

Like *The Man Who Shot Liberty Valance*, the film would appear to critique Hollywood's treatment of the West, the classical myth and its conventional representations of violence. Will Munny, the Western, America itself – all are unforgiven, guilty of the original sins of violence and vigilantism, as well as their denial. As with Ford, the film can be seen as a critical look back at the work its maker had himself produced in the past, an apologia acknowledging the exploitation of violence. Eastwood has vehemently rejected such an interpretation. What drove him were attitudes towards violence in American society:

> I'm not doing penance for all the characters in action films I've portrayed up till now. But I've reached a stage of my life, and we've reached a stage of our history, where I said to myself that violence shouldn't be a source of humor or attraction ... We had a chance here to deal with the moral implications of violence.[15]

It is difficult to understand how the director can hold such views, given the film he has made. The massacre executed by a Munny of mythic proportions is vastly fulfilling and entertaining, a spectacle that is both 'source of humor' and 'attraction', effectively blurring the film's argument that violence is the property of an unhinged masculinity. Having Munny become the tool of a lethal and transcendent retribution that culminates the film's action and supposedly resolves its issues in fact implicates the film in the violence it is critiquing. Apart from the deadly moment shared by Will and Little Bill, the killings at the end register only for their competency, the deputies sketches rather than characters. In fact, in staging much of the violence, *Unforgiven* subscribes to the genre's most conventional methods of representation. A classicist and conservative both aesthetically and financially, Eastwood's revisionism is inevitably compromised as well by his extreme individualist ideology and fascination with archetypal drama. No Brechtian, his aesthetic requires the audience to identify with and invest in the action. *The Outlaw Josey Wales* ends with Josey riding into the sun. Is he returning to the commune? 'The audience is willing him to go back. That's their participation.'[16]

There is no attempt, as in Peckinpah, to implicate the audience in an edgy awareness of the guilty visual and kinetic pleasures that the violence affords; nor is the scale of the violence such as to upset the appetite. Ambitious, compelling, but finally flawed, Eastwood's critique of the Western as a genre sustained by masculine codes of violence is itself all too satisfyingly sustained by that same violence. Turning back on itself, having it both ways, *Unforgiven* offers further evidence of a career that has been artfully balanced between risk and safety.

Transcendence

> I was never John Wayne's heir.

Capitalising on his enhanced stature arising from *Unforgiven*'s Oscars for best picture and director, Eastwood's work thereafter exhibited a pronounced ambition, increased budgets and a shift away from cop movies. Although he portrayed a Texas Ranger in *A Perfect World*, it was really Kevin Costner's film in a role a younger Eastwood would have relished as a charming sociopath on the run, surrogate father to a young hostage. Two thrillers featured complex characters in rarefied presidential territory. Recovering from the rigours of *Unforgiven*, Eastwood had embraced the role of a secret service agent in Wolfgang Peterson's *In the Line of Fire*. Stricken with guilt over his failure to save President Kennedy, the agent was threatened with a replay of the past by John Malkovich's psychopath. Four years later in *Absolute Power*, he would be a master burglar whose witnessing of the president's killing of a mistress traps him and an estranged daughter in the inevitable cover-up. Like bookends, the titles pointed to the familiar poles of Eastwood's universe, the dualities of victim and higher authority, but with the actor in the underdog alignment now.

A departure would be *The Bridges of Madison County*, adapted from the hugely successful but critically disparaged bestseller, which offered the unusual challenge of sharing a small romantic stage with a major female star, Meryl Streep. In earlier films Eastwood had portrayed the charismatic hero empowering a humble woman with his touch. Doing penance for the condescension, Eastwood's Kincaid would suffer ironic reversal, the brief encounter with a Kansas housewife opening the door to a consuming regret.

Space Cowboys had Eastwood sedately married and a retired aerospace engineer, albeit soon required to save the world from an incoming nuclear-armed spaceship. Another ensemble piece with heavyweight co-stars and a macho comedy, it features Tommy Lee Jones, James Garner and Donald Sutherland as senior-citizen sidekicks. Some critics praise Eastwood for his readiness to take on old geezer roles – as in his reedy-voiced heart-transplant hero of *Blood Work* (2002). But as actresses have often bitterly observed, men are allowed to age visibly by both our culture and the film business; Eastwood now enjoys the freedom to address an audience that continues to follow him in his eighth decade. Such projects obviously allow him to ring further changes on the vulnerability/tran-scendence dialectic so central to his image and career. He began by incarnating the superhero who stooped to conquer and to lift up a fallen humanity; he is ending by play-ing ageing and vulnerable mortals. His other main strategy is increasingly to seize on contemporary upmarket bestsellers where he stays in the director's chair, as with *Mid-night in the Garden of Good and Evil* and *Mystic River*, and where he again employs impressive casts with front-rank performers such as Kevin Spacey and Sean Penn.

In particular, *Mystic River*, Eastwood's adaptation of prestigious crime fiction author Dennis Lehane's noir novel, demands attention, given that it provides another ambitious capstone to a career built on vigilante justice. In this it is a strong match for *Unforgiven*, as in its excellent ensemble playing, masterful direction and central theme of America's cyclical violence. However, less satisfactory parallels are also in evidence. There was again a rapturous reception and a number of industry awards, but also inflated critical claims: *Mystic River* was 'great art', going far beyond merely generic noir-and melodramas of the past. As with *Unforgiven*, such views depend on ignoring a disturbing denouement that complicates a reading of the film as a tragic critique of American appetites for violence. *Mystic River*'s ambiguous impact is in fact the result of its unsettling endorsement of a misfiring vigilante justice. Penn's Jimmy literally gets away with the murder of Tim Robbins's innocent and abused soul, an act endorsed by his wife, his friends and by implication the patriotic community that joins him in celebrating a parade's passing at the film's end.

A noir journey back to the future

It is amazing that Eastwood produces blockbusting crowd-pleasers that live so successfully on the knife's edge of ambiguity, embraced by influential critics as profound indictments of violence while absolutely living off the same. It could be argued that John Ford, the Western's grand master, also made a career out of straddling the issues; but despite compromises and duplicities, no one could ever deny the deep faith and sincerity of his work. *Mystic River's* enormous critical success, like that of *Unforgiven*, testifies to its director's extraordinary ability to walk the line and play to the prevailing mood. The conjunction of a film that insists immoderation and collateral damage are no sins in the pursuit of retribution and of a wartime America reveals Eastwood at the top of his game.

His increasingly ambitious output since *Unforgiven* testifies to how decisive its success was in spurring Eastwood to embrace new challenges. It is both fitting and ironic that to the genre the actor-director now owes not only his first breakthrough as a performer in his *Rawhide* days and his ascension to global stardom in the spaghetti Western, but also his final promotion to the ranks of 'serious artist' as well. Like the classics *High Noon* and *Shane* that he had reworked, *Unforgiven* had been packaged and received as something more than a Western, a film that transcended its genre. It is ironic that in order to achieve such ultimate recognition, Eastwood had to embrace this ancient insult to the tradition from which he had sprung, the Western seen once again as a form that is only rarely transfigured into art. The notion that Eastwood lifted up the lowly genre, stooping to conquer, of course agrees with the transcendental dynamic of his image. But if such a spin looks down on the cowboy world that had provided the foundation for his career both as star and director, the facts are indisputable: no film-maker owes their identity to the Western more than Clint Eastwood.

Notes

1. Shari Roberts, 'Western Meets Eastwood', in Steve Cohan and Ina Rae Hark (eds), *The Road Movie Book* (London and New York: Routledge, 1997), pp. 45–57; Gerald Mast and Bruce Kawin, *A Short History of the Movies* (Needham Heights, MA: Simon & Schuster, 1996). From the latter: 'Whether they are set in the wide open spaces or the violent streets of modern cities, the films of Clint Eastwood are Westerns' (p. 487).
2. *Rolling Stone*, 4 July 1985, pp. 18–23; reprinted in Robert Kapsis and Kathie Coblentz (eds), *Clint Eastwood: Interviews* (Jackson: University of Mississippi Press, 1999), p. 127.
3. Kenneth Turan, 'A Fistful of Memories', *Los Angeles Times* (2 August 1992).
4. Jon Halliday, *Sirk on Sirk* (New York: Viking Press, 1972), pp. 71–2.
5. This scene may owe its inspiration to Anthony Mann's *Glenn Miller Story*, which has a similar climax of musical transcendence.
6. Richard Schickel, *Clint Eastwood: A Biography* (New York: Knopf, 1998), p. 149. 'Bobby, first of all, is an actor. Clint, first of all, is a star. Bobby suffers. Clint yawns.'
7. Hilton Als, 'Tilda Moments', *The New Yorker* (18 March 2002), p. 97.
8. See, for instance, Tom Stempel, 'Let's Hear it for Eastwood's "Strong" Women', *Los Angeles Times* Calendar (11 March 1984); Gail Jardine, 'Clint: Cultural Critic, Cowboy of Cathartic Change', *Art Journal* vol. 53 no. 3 (Autumn 1994), pp. 74–5.

9. Robin Wood, 'An Introduction to the American Horror Film', in Bill Nichols (ed.), *Movies and Methods* vol. 2 (Berkeley: University of California Press, 1985), p. 208.

10. Peter Biskend, 'Any Which Way He Can', in Kapsis and Coblentz (eds), *Interviews*, p. 202.

11. Paul Smith, *Clint Eastwood: A Cultural Production* (Minneapolis: University of Minnesota Press, 1993), pp. 39–42; Schickel, *Clint Eastwood*, p. 293.

12. Don Siegel, *A Siegel Film: An Autobiography* (London: Faber & Faber, 1993), p. x.

13. J. Hoberman, 'How the Western Was Lost', *Village Voice* (27 August 1991); reprinted in Jim Kitses and Gregg Rickman (eds), *The Western Reader* (New York: Limelight Editions, 1998), p. 89.

14. For an opposing view that sees Eastwood's work and persona 'as intimately involved with his national culture', see Edward Gallafent's *Clint Eastwood: Filmmaker and Star* (New York: Continuum, 1994), pp. 8–9. Eastwood's work is defined as continuous with 'the America expressed in the vision of a Mark Twain or Henry David Thoreau'.

15. Kapsis and Coblentz (eds), *Interviews*, p. 189.

16. Ibid., p. 60.

Select Filmography

Complete filmographies are available either in biographical studies or on the Internet. Listings below provide producer and script credits for films discussed.

John Ford
Straight Shooting (Butterfly-Universal, 1917)
Script: George Hively; 68 mins

Marked Men (Universal Special, 1919)
Producer: P.A. Powers; **Script:** H. Tipton Steck, from Peter B. Kyne's story 'The Three Godfathers'

The Iron Horse (Fox, 1924)
Script: Charles Kenyon, from story by Kenyon and John Russell; 119 mins

3 Bad Men (Fox, 1926)
Script: Ford and John Stone, from Herman Whitaker's novel *Over the Border*

Stagecoach (Walter Wanger/United Artists, 1939)
Producer: Ford; **Executive Producer:** Walter Wanger; **Script:** Dudley Nichols, from the story 'Stage to Lordsburg' by Ernest Haycox; 95 mins

Drums Along the Mohawk (20th Century-Fox, 1939)
Producer: Raymond Griffith; **Executive Producer:** Darryl F. Zanuck; **Script:** Lamar Trotti and Sonya Levien, from Walter D. Edmonds' novel; 103 mins

My Darling Clementine (20th Century-Fox, 1946)
Producer: Samuel G. Engel; **Script:** Engel and Winston Miller, from a story by Sam Hellman based on Stuart N. Lake's book *Wyatt Earp: Frontier Marshal*; 97 mins

Fort Apache (Argosy Pictures/RKO, 1948)
Producers: Ford and Merian C. Cooper; **Script:** Frank S. Nugent, from James Warner Bellah's story 'Massacre'; 127 mins

3 Godfathers (Argosy Pictures/M.G.M., 1948)
Producers: Ford and Merian C. Cooper; **Script:** Laurence Stallings and Frank S. Nugent, from Peter B. Kyne's story 'The Three Godfathers'; 106 mins

She Wore a Yellow Ribbon (Argosy Pictures/RKO, 1949)
Producers: Ford and Merian C. Cooper; **Script:** Frank S. Nugent and Laurence Stallings from the stories 'War Party' and 'The Big Hunt' by James Warner Bellah; 103 mins

Wagon Master (Argosy Pictures/RKO, 1950)
Producers: Ford and Merian C. Cooper; **Script:** Frank S. Nugent and Patrick Ford; 86 mins

Rio Grande (Argosy Pictures-Republic, 1950)
Producers: Ford and Merian C. Cooper; **Script:** James Kevin McGuiness, from James Warner Bellah's story, 'Mission with No Record'; 105 mins

The Searchers (C.V. Whitney Pictures/Warner Bros., 1956)
Producers: Merian C. Cooper and C.V. Whitney; **Script:** Frank S. Nugent, from Alan LeMay's novel; 119 mins

The Horse Soldiers (Mirisch Company/United Artists, 1959)
Producers/Script: John Lee Mahin and Martin Rackin, from Harold Sinclair's novel; 119 mins

Sergeant Rutledge (Ford Productions/Warner Bros., 1960)
Producers: Patrick Ford and Willis Goldbeck; **Script:** Willis Goldbeck and James Warner Bellah; 111 mins

Two Rode Together (Ford-Sheptner Productions/Columbia, 1961)
Producer: John Ford; **Script:** Frank Nugent from Will Cook's novel *Comanche Captives*; 109 mins

The Man Who Shot Liberty Valance (Ford Productions/Paramount, 1962)
Producers: Ford and Willis Goldbeck; **Script:** Willis Goldbeck and James Warner Bellah, from Dorothy M. Johnson's story; 122 mins

How the West Was Won (Cinerama/M.G.M., 1962)
Producer: Bernard Smith; **Script:** James R. Webb, suggested by a series in *Life* magazine; 25 mins

Cheyenne Autumn (Ford-Smith Productions/Warner Bros., 1964)
Producers: Ford and Bernard Smith; **Script:** James R. Webb, from Mari Sandoz's book and Howard Fast's novel *The Last Frontier*; 159 mins

Anthony Mann

Devil's Doorway (Universal-International, 1950)
Producer: Aaron Rosenberg; **Script:** Robert L. Richards and Borden Chase, from a story by Stuart N. Lake; 83 mins

Winchester '73 (Universal-International, 1950)
Producer: Aaron Rosenberg; **Script:** Robert L. Richards and Borden Chase, from Stuart N. Lake's story; 92 mins

The Furies (Paramount, 1950)
Producer: Hal B. Wallis; **Script:** Charles Schnee, from the novel by Niven Busch; 109 mins

Bend of the River (Universal-International (1952)
Producer: Aaron Rosenberg; **Script:** Borden Chase; 91 mins

The Naked Spur (M.G.M., 1952)
Producer: William H. Wright; **Script:** Sam Rolfe and Harold Jack Bloom; 91 mins

The Far Country (Universal-International, 1954)
Producer: Aaron Rosenberg; **Script:** Borden Chase; 96 mins

The Man from Laramie (Columbia, 1955)
Producer: William Goetz; **Script:** Philip Yordan and Frank Burt, from a *Saturday Evening Post* story by Thomas T. Flynn; 101 mins

The Last Frontier (Columbia, 1955)
Producer: William Fadiman; **Script:** Philip Yordan and Russell S. Hughes, based on a novel by Richard Emery Roberts; 97 mins

The Tin Star (Paramount, 1957)
Producers: William Perlberg, George Seaton; **Script:** Dudley Nichols. Story: Barney Slater, Joel Kane; 93 mins

Man of the West (United Artists/Ashton, 1958)
Producer: Walter M. Mirisch; **Script:** Reginald Rose, from a novel by Will C. Brown; 95 mins

Cimarron (M.G.M., 1960)
Producer: Edmund Grainger; **Script:** Arnold Schulman, based on Edna Ferber's novel; 135 mins

Budd Boetticher

Seven Men from Now (Batjac, 1956)
Producers: Andrew V. McLaglen, Robert E. Morrison; **Script:** Burt Kennedy; 77 mins

The Tall T (Scott-Brown Productions, 1957)
Producer: Harry Joe Brown; **Script:** Burt Kennedy, based on a story by Elmore Leonard; 77 mins

Decision at Sundown (Scott-Brown Productions, 1957)
Producer: Harry Joe Brown; **Script:** Charles Lang, Jnr, from a story by Vernon L. Fluharty; 77 mins

Buchanan Rides Alone (Scott-Brown Productions, 1958)
Producer: Harry Joe Brown; **Script:** Charles Lang, from the novel *The Name's Buchanan*, by Jonas Ward; 77 mins

Ride Lonesome (Ranown/Columbia, 1959)
Executive Producer: Harry Joe Brown; **Script:** Burt Kennedy; 73 mins

Westbound (Warner Brothers, 1959)
Producer: Henry Blanke; **Script:** Berne Giler, Albert Shelby Le Vino; 69 mins

Comanche Station (Ranown, 1960)
Executive Producer: Harry Joe Brown; **Script:** Burt Kennedy; 73 mins

A Time For Dying (Fipco, 1969)
Producer: Audie Murphy; **Script:** Budd Boetticher; 90 mins

Sam Peckinpah

The Deadly Companions (Pathé-America-Carousel, 1961)
Producer: Charles B. FitzSimons; **Script:** A.S. Fleischman, based on his own novel; 90 mins

Ride the High Country (M.G.M., 1961)
Producer: Richard E. Lyons; **Script:** N.B. Stone, Jnr; British title: *Guns in the Afternoon*; 93 mins

Major Dundee (Jerry Bresler Productions, 1964)
Producer: Jerry Bresler; **Script:** Harry Julian Fink, Oscar Saul, Sam Peckinpah, from a story by Harry Julian Fink; 134 mins

The Wild Bunch (Warner Brothers-Seven Arts, 1969)
Producer: Phil Feldman; **Script:** Walon Green and Sam Peckinpah, from a story by Walon Green and Roy N. Sickner; 145 mins

The Ballad of Cable Hogue (Phil Feldman Productions-Warner Bros., 1970)
Executive Producer: Phil Feldman; **Script:** John Crawford; 121 mins

Pat Garrett and Billy the Kid (M.G.M., 1973)
Producer: Gordon Carroll; **Script:** Rudolph Wurlitzer; 122 mins

Sergio Leone

A Fistful of Dollars/Per un pugno di dollari (Jolly, 1964)
Producers: Arrigo Colombo, Giorgio Papi; **Script:** Sergio Leone, Duccio Tessari; 96 mins

For a Few Dollars More/Per qualche dollaro in piu (PEA, 1965)
Producer: Alberto Grimaldi; **Script:** Sergio Leone, Vincenzoni; **Story:** Sergio Leone, Fulvio Morsella; 130 mins

The Good, the Bad and the Ugly/Il buono, Il brutto, Il cattivo (PEA, 1966)
Producer: Alberto Grimaldi; **Script:** Age Scarpelli, Luciano Vincenzoni, Sergio Leone; 161 mins

Once Upon a Time in the West/C'era una volta il West (Ranfran-San Marco, 1968)
Producer: Fulvio Morsella; **Script:** Sergio Donati, Sergio Leone; **Story:** Dario Argento, Bernardo Bertollucci, Sergio Leone; 165 mins

A Fistful of Dynamite/Duck, You Sucker/Giu la testa (Ranfran-United Artists, 1971)
Producer: Fulvio Morsella; **Script:** Luciano Vincenzoni, Sergio Donati, Sergio Leone; **Story:** Sergio Leone, Sergio Donati; 138 mins

My Name is Nobody/Il mio nome e Nessuno (Ranfran, Leitienne, Alcinter, Rialto, 1973)
Supervised by Sergio Leone; **Director:** Tonino Valerii; **Producer:** Claudio Mancini; **Script:** Ernesto Gastaldi; **Story:** Fulvio Morsella, Ernesto Gastaldi, from an idea by Sergio Leone; 115 mins

Clint Eastwood

As actor:
See Sergio Leone's credits above for *Fistful of Dollars*, *For a Few Dollars More* and *The Good, the Bad and the Ugly.*

Hang 'em High (United Artists/Malpaso, 1968)
Producer: Leonard Freeman; **Director:** Ted Post; **Script:** Leonard Freeman, Mel Goldberg; 114 mins

Two Mules for Sister Sara (Universal Malpaso, 1970)
Producer: Martin Rackin; **Director:** Donald Siegel; **Script:** Albert Maltz; **Story:** Budd Boetticher; 106 mins

Joe Kidd (Universal/Malpaso, 1972)
Producer: Robert Daley; **Director:** John Sturges; **Script:** Elmore Leonard; 88 mins

As director:
High Plains Drifter (Universal/Malpaso, 1973)
Producer: Robert Daley; **Script:** Ernest Tidyman; 105 mins

The Outlaw Josey Wales (Warner Bros./Malpaso, 1976)
Producer: Robert Daley; **Script:** Philip Kaufman, Sonia Chernus, from Forrest Carter's novel; 135 mins

Pale Rider (Warner Bros./Malpaso, 1985)
Executive Producer: Fritz Manes; **Producer:** Clint Eastwood; **Script:** Michael Butler; 116 mins

Unforgiven (Warner Bros./Malpaso, 1992)
Executive Producer: David Valdes; **Producer:** Clint Eastwood; **Script:** David Webb Peoples; 127 mins

Select Bibliography

Aghed, Jan. '*Pat Garrett and Billy the Kid*', *Sight and Sound* (Spring 1973), pp. 65–9.

Als, Hilton. 'Tilda Moments', *The New Yorker* (18 March 2002), p. 97.

Altman, Rick. *Film/Genre* (London: BFI, 1999).

Anderson, Lindsay. 'The Director's Cinema?' *Sequence* no. 12 (Autumn 1950), p. 8.

———. *About John Ford* (New York: McGraw-Hill, 1981).

Barkun, Michael. 'Notes on the Art of John Ford', *Film Culture* no. 25 (Summer 1962), pp. 9–15.

Basinger, Jeanine. *Anthony Mann* (Boston: Twayne, 1979).

Baxter, John. *The Cinema of John Ford* (New York: A. S. Barnes, 1971).

Bazin, André. 'The Evolution of the Western', in Hugh Gray (ed.), *What is Cinema?* vol. 2 (Berkeley: University of California Press, 1971), pp. 140–8.

———. '*Seven Men from Now*: An Exemplary Western', *Cahiers du Cinéma* no. 174 (August–September 1957); reprinted in Jim Hillier (ed.), *Cahiers du Cinéma: The 1950s: Neo-Realism, Hollywood, New Wave* (Cambridge, MA: Harvard University Press, 1985), pp. 169–72.

Berg, Charles Ramirez. 'The Margin as Center', in Gaylyn Studlar and Matthew Bernstein (eds), *John Ford Made Westerns* (Bloomington and Indianapolis: Indiana University Press, 2001), pp. 75–101.

Bingham, Dennis. *Acting Male* (New Brunswick, NJ: 1994).

Biskend, Peter. 'Any Which Way He Can', in Robert Kapsis and Kathie Coblentz (eds), *Clint Eastwood: Interviews* (Jackson: University of Mississippi Press, 1999), p. 202.

Bliss, Michael (ed.), *Doing it Right: The Best Criticism on Sam Peckinpah's The Wild Bunch* (Carbondale and Edwardsville: Southern Illinois University Press, 1994).

———. *Justified Lives* (Carbondale and Edwardsville: Southern Illinois University Press, 1993).

Bluestone, George. 'Recalling a 1955 Interview with John Ford', in Gerald Peary (ed.), *John Ford Interviews* (Jackson: University of Mississippi Press, 2001), pp. 34–7.

Bogdanovich, Peter. *John Ford* (Berkeley: University of California Press, 1967).

Brown, Dee. *Bury My Heart at Wounded Knee: An Indian History of the American West* (New York: Bantam Books, 1972).

Budd, Michael. 'A Home in the Wilderness: Visual Imagery in John Ford's Westerns', *Cinema Journal* vol. 16 no. 1 (Autumn 1976), pp. 62–75.

Buscombe, Edward. 'The Idea of Genre in the American Cinema', *Screen* vol. 11 no. 12 (1970), pp. 33–45.

———. *The BFI Companion to the Western* (New York: Atheneum, 1988).

———. 'Painting the Legend: Frederic Remington and the Western', *Cinema Journal* vol. 23 no. 4 (Summer 1984), pp. 12–27.

——. *Stagecoach* (London: BFI, 1992).

——. 'Inventing Monument Valley: Nineteenth-Century Landscape Photography and the Western Film', in Patrice Petro (ed.), *Fugitive Images: From Photography to Video* (Bloomington: Indiana University Press, 1995), pp. 87–108.

—— and Roberta E. Pearson (eds), *Back in the Saddle Again: New Essays on the Western* (London: BFI, 1998).

——. *The Searchers* (London: BFI, 2000).

Butler, Terence. *Crucified Heroes: The Films of Sam Peckinpah* (London: Fraser, 1979).

Byron, Stuart. '*The Searchers*: Cult Movie of the New Hollywood', *New York* (5 March 1979), pp. 45–8.

Cahiers du Cinéma, editors, 'John Ford's *Young Mr Lincoln*', *Cahiers du Cinéma* no. 223 (August 1970); reprinted in Bill Nichols (ed.), *Movies and Methods* (Berkeley: University of California Press, 1976), pp. 493–529.

Cameron, Ian and Douglas Pye (eds). *The Book of Westerns* (New York: Continuum, 1996).

Campbell, Russell (ed.). 'John Ford', *Velvet Light Trap* no. 2, special John Ford issue (1971).

Carey, Jr, Harry. *My Life as an Actor in the John Ford Stock Company* (Metuchen, NJ: Scarecrow Press, 1994).

Cawelti, John G. *The Six-Gun Mystique* (Bowling Green, OH: Bowling Green University Popular Press, 1970).

Cohan, Steve and Ina Rae Hark (eds). *The Road Movie Book* (London and New York: Routledge, 1997).

Collins, Jim. *Architectures of Excess: Cultural Life in the Information Age* (New York: Routledge, 1995).

Combs, Richard. 'At Play in the Fields of John Ford', *Sight and Sound* vol. 51 no. 2 (Spring 1982), pp. 124–9.

Corliss, Richard (ed.). *The Hollywood Screenwriters* (New York: Avon Books, 1972).

Coyne, Michael. *The Crowded Prairie: American National Identity in the Hollywood Western* (London: I. B. Tauris, 1997).

Dibb, Mike. 'A Time and a Place: Budd Boetticher and the Western', in Ian Cameron and Douglas Pye (eds), *The Movie Book of Westerns* (New York: Continuum, 1996), pp. 161–6.

Durgnat, Raymond and Scott Simmon. 'Six Creeds That Won the Western', *Film Comment* vol. 16 no. 5 (September–October 1980), pp. 69–83.

Eyman, Scott. *Print the Legend: The Life and Times of John Ford* (New York: Simon & Schuster, 1999).

Fiedler, Leslie A. *Love and Death in the American Novel* (New York: Dell Publishing, 1969).

Ford, Dan. *Pappy: The Life of John Ford* (Englewood Cliffs, NJ: Prentice-Hall, 1979).

Frayling, Christopher. *Spaghetti Westerns: Cowboys and Europeans from Karl May to Sergio Leone* (London: Routledge & Kegan Paul, 1981).

——. *Clint Eastwood* (London: Virgin Books, 1992).

——. *Sergio Leone: Something to Do with Death* (London: Faber & Faber, 2000).

French, Philip. *Westerns* (London: Secker and Warburg, 1973).

Fry, Northrup. *Anatomy of Criticism* (Princeton, NJ: Princeton University Press, 1957).

Gallafent, Edward. *Clint Eastwood: Filmmaker and Star* (New York: Continuum, 1994).

Gallagher, Tag. *John Ford: The Man and His Films* (Berkeley: University of California Press, 1986).

——. 'John Ford's Indians', *Film Comment* vol. 29 no. 5 (September–October 1993), pp. 68–72.

Gillam, Barry. 'Budd Boetticher', in Jean-Pierre Coursodon (ed.), with Pierre Sauvage, *American Directors* vol. II (New York: McGraw-Hill, 1983), pp. 40–8.

Gomery, Douglas. 'Mise-en-scene in John Ford's *My Darling Clementine*', *Wide Angle* vol. 2 no. 4, special John Ford issue (1978), pp. 14–19.

Hall, Stuart and Paddy Whannel. *The Popular Arts* (London: Hutchinson, 1964).

Halliday, Jon. *Sirk on Sirk* (New York: Viking Press, 1972).

Hardy, Phil. *The Film Encyclopedia: The Western* (London: Aurum Press, 1991).

Henderson, Brian. '*The Searchers*: An American Dilemma', *Film Quarterly* vol. 34 no. 2 (Winter 1980–1), pp. 9–23.

Hoberman, J. 'How the Western Was Lost', *Village Voice* (27 August 1991).

Holmlund, Chris. *Impossible Bodies: Femininity and Masculinity at the Movies* (London and New York: Routledge, 2002).

Jacobs, Lewis. *The Rise of the American Film* (New York: Teachers College Press, 1939).

Jardine, Gail. 'Clint: Cultural Critic, Cowboy of Cathartic Change', *Art Journal* vol. 53 no. 3 (Autumn 1994), pp. 74–5.

Kael, Pauline. *I Lost it at the Movies* (Boston: Little, Brown and Company/Bantam, 1969).

Kaminsky, Stuart. 'The Grotesque West of Sergio Leone', *Take One* no. 3 (January–February 1972), pp. 26–32.

Kaplan, E. Ann. *Women in Film Noir* (London: BFI, 1998); rev. edn.

Kapsis, Robert and Kathie Coblentz (eds). *Clint Eastwood: Interviews* (Jackson: University of Mississippi Press, 1999).

Kazan, Elia. *A Life* (New York: Knopf, 1988).

Kennedy, Burt. *Hollywood Trail Boss: Behind the Scenes of the Wild, Wild Western* (New York: Boulevard Books, 1997).

Kitses, Jim. *Horizons West: Anthony Mann, Budd Boetticher, Sam Peckinpah; Studies of Authorship within the Western* (Bloomington: Indiana University Press, 1969).

——. 'The Rise and Fall of the American West: Borden Chase Interviewed', *Film Comment* vol. 6 no. 4 (Winter 1970–1), p. 17.

——, and Gregg Rickman (eds). *The Western Reader* (New York: Limelight Editions, 1998), pp. 213–22.

Knight, Arthur. *The Liveliest Art* (New York and Toronto: New American Library, 1957).

Lahr, John. 'Walking Alone', *The New Yorker* (1 July 2002), p. 82.

Landy, Marcia. 'He Went Thataway: The Form and Style of Leone's Italian Westerns', *Boundary* vol. 2 no. 23; reprinted in Jim Kitses and Gregg Rickman (eds), *The Western Reader* (New York: Limelight Editions, 1998), pp. 213–22.

Lenihan, John H. *Showdown: Confronting Modern America in the Western Film* (Urbana: University of Illinois Press, 1980).

Leonard, Elmore. 'The Captives', in *The Tonto Woman* (New York: Delacorte Press, 1998), pp. 16–53.

Limerick, Patricia Nelson. *The Legacy of Conquest: The Unbroken Past of the American West* (New York: Norton, 1987).

——, Clyde A. Milner II and Charles E. Rankin (eds). *Trails: Toward a New Western History* (Lawrence: University Press of Kansas, 1991).

Lovell, Alan. 'The Western', in Bill Nichols (ed.), *Movies and Methods* (Berkeley: University of California Press, 1976), pp. 164–75.

Lusted, David. *The Western* (Harlow, Essex: Pearson Education Limited, 2003).

Lyons, Robert (ed.). *My Darling Clementine* (New Brunswick, NJ: Rutgers University Press, 1984).

Maltby, Richard. 'A Better Sense of History', in Ian Cameron and Douglas Pye (eds). *The Book of Westerns* (New York: Continuum, 1996), pp. 34–49.

Martin, Adrian. *Once Upon a Time in America* (London: BFI, 1998).

McBride, Joseph. *Searching for John Ford: A Life* (New York: St Martin's Press, 2001).

—— and Michael Wilmington. *John Ford* (New York: Da Capo Press, 1975).

Mesce, Bill. *Peckinpah's Women: A Reappraisal of the Portrayal of Women in the Period Westerns of Sam Peckinpah* (Lanham, MD: Scarecrow Press, 2001).

Milne, Tom (ed.). *Godard on Godard* (New York: Viking Press, 1972).

Mitchell, Lee Clark. *Westerns: Making the Man in Fiction and Film* (Chicago: University of Chicago Press, 1996).

Mitry, Jean. 'John Ford', *Cahiers du Cinéma* no. 45 (March 1955); reprinted in Andrew Sarris (ed.), *Interviews with Film Directors* (New York: Avon Books, 1967), p. 197.

Mulvey, Laura. *Visual and Other Pleasures* (Bloomington: Indiana University Press, 1989).

——. 'Afterthoughts on "Visual Pleasure and Narrative" inspired by King Vidor's *Duel in the Sun* (1946)', *Framework*; reprinted in Mulvey, *Visual and Other Pleasures* (Bloomington: Indiana University Press, 1989), pp. 29–38.

Myres, Sandra L. *Westering Women and the Frontier Experience, 1800–1915* (Albuquerque: University Press of New Mexico, 1982).

Nachbar, Jack (ed.). *Focus on the Western* (Englewood Cliffs, NJ: Prentice-Hall, 1974), pp. 64–72.

Neale, Steve. *Genre* (London: BFI, 1980).

——. 'Masculinity as Spectacle: Reflections on Men and Mainstream Cinema', in Steve Cohan and Ina Rae Hark (eds), *Screening the Male: Exploring Masculinities in Hollywood Cinema* (London: Routledge, 1993), pp. 9–20.

——. *Genre and Hollywood* (London and New York: Routledge, 2000).

Nichols, Bill. 'Style, Grammar and the Movies', in Nichols (ed.), *Movies and Methods* (Berkeley: University of California Press, 1976), pp. 607–28.

Perez, Gilberto. *The Material Ghost: Films and Their Medium* (Baltimore, MD: Johns Hopkins University Press, 1998).

Place, J. A. *The Western Films of John Ford* (Secaucus, NJ: Citadel Press, 1974).

'Playboy Interview: Sam Peckinpah', *Playboy* vol. 19 no. 8 (August 1972), pp. 65–74.

Poague, Leland. ' "All I Can See is the Flags": *Fort Apache* and the Visibility of History', *Cinema Journal* vol. 27 no. 2 (Winter 1988), pp. 8–26.

Prince, Stephen. *Savage Cinema: Sam Peckinpah and the Rise of Ultraviolent Movies* (Austin: University of Texas Press, 1998).

Pye, Douglas. 'Genre and History: *Fort Apache* and *The Man Who Shot Liberty Valance*', *Movie* vol. 25 no. 1 (Spring 1976), pp. 9–16.

Ray, Robert B. *A Certain Tendency of the Hollywood Cinema 1930–80* (Princeton, NJ: Princeton University Press, 1985).

Rollins, Peter C. and John E. O'Connor (eds). *Hollywood's Indian: The Portrayal of the Native American in Film* (Lexington: University Press of Kentucky, 1998).

Sarris, Andrew. 'Cactus Rose or *The Man Who Shot Liberty Valance*', *Film Culture* no. 25 (Summer 1962), pp. 13–15.

——. (ed.). *Interviews with Film Directors* (New York: Avon Books, 1967).

——. *American Cinema: Directors and Directions 1929–1968* (New York: E. P. Dutton, 1968), p. 98.

——. *The John Ford Movie Mystery* (Bloomington: Indiana University Press, 1975).

Saunders, John. *The Western Genre: From Lordsburg to Big Whiskey* (London: Wallflower Press, 2001).

Schatz, Thomas. *Hollywood Genres: Formulas, Filmmaking, and the Studio System* (New York: Random House, 1981).

Schickel, Richard. *Clint Eastwood: A Biography* (New York: Knopf, 1998).

Schrader, Paul. 'Budd Boetticher', *Cinema* vol. 6 no. 2 (1971), pp. 23–9.

——. 'Sam Peckinpah Going to Mexico', in Kevin Jackson (ed.), *Schrader on Schrader* (London: Faber & Faber, 1990), p. 75.

Seydor, Paul. *Peckinpah: The Western Films* (Chicago: University of Illinois Press, 1980).

——. *Peckinpah: The Western Films – A Reconsideration* (Urbana: University of Illinois Press, 1997).

Shaffer, Lawrence. '*The Wild Bunch* versus *Straw Dogs*', *Sight and Sound* vol. 41 no. 3 (Summer 1972), pp. 132–3.

Sherman, Eric and Martin Rubin (eds). *The Director's Event* (New York: Atheneum, 1970).

Simmon, Scott. 'Concerning the Weary Legs of Wyatt Earp: The Classic Western According to Shakespeare', *Literature/Film Quarterly* vol. 24 no. 2 (April 1996), pp. 114–27.

——. *The Invention of the Western Film: A Cultural History of the Genre's First Half-Century* (Cambridge: Cambridge University Press, 2003).

Simmons, Garner. *Peckinpah: A Portrait in Montage* (Austin: University of Texas Press, 1982).

Simsolo, Noel. 'Sergio Leone Talks', *Take One* 3 no. 9 (January–February 1972), pp. 26–32.

Sinclair, Andrew. *John Ford: A Biography* (New York: Dial Press, 1979).

Slotkin, Richard. *Regeneration through Violence: The Mythology of the American Frontier, 1600–1860* (Middletown, CT: Wesleyan University Press, 1973).

——. *Gunfighter Nation: The Myth of the Frontier in Twentieth-Century America* (New York: Atheneum, 1992), pp. 9–16.

Smith, Henry Nash. *Virgin Land: The American West as Symbol and Myth* (New York: Vintage Books, 1957).

Smith, Paul. *Clint Eastwood: A Cultural Production* (Minneapolis: University of Minnesota Press, 1993).

Stanfield, Peter. *Hollywood, Westerns and the 1930s: The Lost Trail* (Exeter, Devon: University of Exeter Press, 2001).

Stempel, Tom. 'Let's Hear it for Eastwood's "Strong" Women', *Los Angeles Times* Calendar (11 March 1984).

Stevens, Brad. '*Pat Garrett and Billy the Kid*', in Ian Cameron and Douglas Pye (eds), *The Book of Westerns* (New York: Continuum, 1996), pp. 269–76.

Stowell, Peter. *John Ford* (Boston: Twayne, 1986).

Studlar, Gaylyn and Matthew Bernstein (eds). *John Ford Made Westerns: Filming the Legend in the Sound Era* (Bloomington and Indianapolis: Indiana University Press, 2001).

Stutesman, Drake. 'Budd Boetticher Interview', *Framework* vol. 43 no. 1 (Spring 2002), pp. 18–39.

Tompkins, Jane. *West of Everything: The Inner Life of Westerns* (New York: Oxford University Press, 1992).

Turan, Kenneth. 'A Fistful of Memories', *Los Angeles Times* (2 August 1992).

Tuska, Jon. *The American West in Film: Critical Approaches to the Western* (Lincoln: University of Nebraska Press, 1988).

Walker, Janet (ed.). *Westerns: Films through History* (New York: Routledge/American Film Institute, 2001).

Walker, Percy. *The Moviegoer* (New York: Knopf, 1961), p. 7.

Wallington, Mike and Christopher Frayling. 'The Italian Western', *Cinema* (Cambridge) no. 67 (August 1970), pp. 31–8.

Warshow, Robert. *The Immediate Experience* (New York: Anchor/Doubleday, 1962), pp. 96–103.

Waterhouse, Edward. *A Declaration of the State of the Colony and Affaires in Virginia, with a Relation of the Barbarous Massacre, 1622* (Amsterdam: Theatrum Orbis Terrarum, 1970).

Weddle, David. *If They Move ... Kill 'Em* (New York: Grove Press, 1994).

Willemen, Paul. 'Anthony Mann: Looking at the Male', *Framework* nos. 15/16/17 (Summer 1981), p. 16.

Williams, Linda. 'Film Bodies: Gender, Genre and Excess', *Film Quarterly* vol. 44 no. 4 (Summer 1991), pp. 2–13.

Wills, Garry. *John Wayne's America: The Politics of Celebrity* (New York: Touchstone/Simon & Schuster, 1997).

Wollen, Peter. 'Budd Boetticher: A Case Study in Criticism', *New Left Review* no. 32 (July–August 1965), pp. 78–84; as Lee Russell.

——. *Signs and Meaning in the Cinema* (Bloomington and London: Indiana University Press, 1969); rev. edn. 1972.

——. *Singin' in the Rain* (London: BFI, 1992).

Wood, Robin. '*Shall* We Gather at the River?: The Late Films of John Ford', *Film Comment* vol. 7 no. 3 (Autumn 1971), pp. 8–17.

——. 'An Introduction to the American Horror Film', in Bill Nichols (ed.), *Movies and Methods* vol. 2 (Berkeley: University of California Press, 1985), pp. 195–220.

——. 'Drums Along the Mohawk', *CineAction!* (Spring 1987), pp. 58–64.

——. 'Man(n) of the West(ern)', *CineAction!* no. 46, special issue, 'The Western Then and Now' (Summer 1998), pp. 26–33.

Wright, Will. *Six Guns and Society: A Structural Study of The Western* (Berkeley: University of California Press, 1975).

Index

Page numbers in **bold** denote extended/detailed analysis; those in *italics* refer to illustrations

List of Illustrations

Whilst considerable effort has been made to correctly identify the copyright holders, this has not been possible in all cases. We apologise for any apparent negligence and any omissions or corrections brought to our attention will be remedied in any future editions.

The Searchers, C.V. Whitney Pictures Company; *My Darling Clementine*, Twentieth Century-Fox Film Corporation; *Stagecoach*, © Walter Wanger Productions; *Dances with Wolves*, TIG Productions; *Escape from L.A.*, Paramount Pictures; *Open Range*, © Open Range Productions USA Inc.; *Posse*, Working Title Films; *Ride the High Country*, Metro-Goldwyn-Mayer; *The Man Who Shot Liberty Valance*, Paramount Pictures Corporation/John Ford Productions; *She Wore a Yellow Ribbon*, Argosy Pictures Corporation/RKO Radio Pictures; *The Fugitive*, Argosy Pictures Corporation; *3 Godfathers*, Argosy Pictures Corporation; *The Iron Horse*, Fox Film Corporation; *The Horse Soldiers*, Mirisch Company; *Pilgrimage*, Fox Film Corporation; *Drums Along the Mohawk*, Twentieth Century-Fox Film Corporation; *Fort Apache*, Argosy Pictures Corporation/RKO Radio Pictures; *Straight Shooting*, Universal Film Manufacturing Company/Butterfly Pictures; *Wagon Master*, © Argosy Pictures Corporation; *Rio Grande*, © Republic Pictures Corporation; *Sergeant Rutledge*, Warner Bros.; *Two Rode Together*, © Columbia Pictures Corporation/© John Ford Productions/© Shpetner Company; *Cheyenne Autumn*, © Ford-Smith Productions; *7 Women*, © Metro-Goldwyn-Mayer/© John Ford Productions/© Bernard Smith Productions; *Man of the West*, © Ashton Productions; *T-Men*, © Pathé Industries; *Winchester '73*, © Universal Pictures Company; *Devil's Doorway*, Loew's Incorporated/Metro-Goldwyn-Mayer; *The Man from Laramie*, Columbia Pictures Corporation; *The Far Country*, Universal-International; *Ride Lonesome*, © Ranown Pictures Corporation; *The Bullfighter and the Lady*, Republic Pictures Corporation; *The Tall T*, © Producers-Actors Corporation; *Comanche Station*, © Ranown Pictures Corporation; *Seven Men from Now*, Batjac Productions; *The Rise and Fall of Legs Diamond*, United States Pictures; *Major Dundee*, Jerry Bresler Productions/Columbia Pictures Corporation; *The Deadly Companions*, Carousel Films; *The Wild Bunch*, © Warner Bros./© Seven Arts; *The Ballad of Cable Hogue*, Warner Bros.; *Pat Garrett and Billy the Kid*, Metro-Goldwyn-Mayer; *Bring Me the Head of Alfredo Garcia*, Optimus Productions/Estudios Churubusco Azteca, S.A.; *The Good, the Bad and the Ugly*, Produzioni Europee Associati; *Once Upon a Time in the West*, Rafran Cinematografica/San Marco Cinematografica/Euro International Films/Paramount Pictures Corporation; *A Fistful of Dollars*, Jolly Film/Constantin Film AG/Ocean Films; *A Fistful of Dynamite*, Rafran Cinematografica/Euro International Films; *My Name is Nobody*, Rafran Cinematografica/Films Jacques Leitienne/Société Imp. Ex. Ci./Production Alcinter/Rialto Film Preben Philipsen; *The Outlaw Josey Wales*, © Warner Bros.; *Bronco Billy*, Warner Bros./Second Street Films; *Sudden Impact*, Warner Bros.; *High Plains Drifter*, Malpaso Company/Universal Pictures; *Pale Rider*, Malpaso Company/Warner Bros.; *Unforgiven*, © Warner Bros..

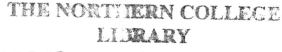